*The*
# PUFFIN BOOK *of*
# TWENTIETH-CENTURY
# CHILDREN'S STORIES

*Also available*

*The*

# PUFFIN BOOK *of*
# TWENTIETH-CENTURY
# CHILDREN'S STORIES

EDITED BY
## Judith Elkin

ILLUSTRATED BY
## Michael Foreman

VIKING

VIKING

Published by the Penguin Group
Penguin Books Ltd, 27 Wrights Lane, London w8 5TZ, England
Penguin Books USA Inc., 375 Hudson Street, New York, New York 10014, USA
Penguin Books Australia Ltd, Ringwood, Victoria, Australia
Penguin Books Canada Ltd, 10 Alcorn Avenue, Toronto, Ontario, Canada M4V 3B2
Penguin Books (NZ) Ltd, 182–190 Wairau Road, Auckland 10, New Zealand

Penguin Books Ltd, Registered Offices: Harmondsworth, Middlesex, England

This collection first published 1991
Published simultaneously in paperback in Puffin Books
1 3 5 7 9 10 8 6 4 2

This collection copyright © Judith Elkin, 1991
Illustrations copyright © Michael Foreman, 1991

The Acknowledgements on pages 521-524 constitute an
extension of this copyright page

Filmset in 14/16 pt Garamond
Printed in England by Clays Ltd, St Ives plc

A CIP catalogue record for this book is available from the British Library

ISBN 0-670-82056-3

# Contents

# CONTENTS

# INTRODUCTION

This has been a wonderful personal excursion through lands and seas and times far beyond anything that one individual may experience. I have revisited beloved and sometimes forgotten territories of my own childhood, faced again joys and fears with my own children and read books which somehow have been missed in my years of perambulations through children's books. What a privilege to have the excuse for such indulgences!

Literature for children is tremendously rich and diverse. Some years ago John Rowe Townsend wrote: 'Children's literature has wild blood in it; its ancestry lies partly in the long ages of storytelling.' Researching for this book, I can only concur. There is strength, power, a sense of tradition, evidence of other worlds and universal truths. Overall, there is a quality of writing which marks out real children's literature: writers who believe in children and have something to say.

My prime aim has been to offer children, broadly between eight and fourteen, a range of extracts from some of the best writing for children of this century. I have deliberately chosen relatively short extracts which I feel are self-sufficient, which do not require lengthy explanation and are meaningful in their own right. Some are funny, some sad, some violent, others puzzling. But I think that in all cases, they carry for me the essential 'spirit' of that individual writer and the essence of the book itself.

I have allowed myself only one extract per writer and chosen the title which for me sums up some particular impact that the writer made, maybe with their first book, perhaps their most recent title. Many of these writers wrote or have written over several decades and to sum up their contribution to children's reading in one extract is impossible.

My overriding concern, however, has been to ensure that the books are accessible to today's child. This is not a book of worthy extracts that today's children will never stomach. These are examples of vital, living writing, as fresh today as when they were first written. The 'wild blood' is here, in imaginative, innovative, stimulating writing, exploring an infinite variety of times, places and worlds.

Within this wealth of writing for children, the final task of selection was inevitably a difficult one. Certain favourites (Paddington Bear, Little Grey Rabbit, Nurse Matilda, Flat Stanley, Worzel Gummidge) excluded themselves by being too young for the overall readership; others (Hester Burton, Farukkh Dhondy) by being largely beyond. Some authors (Angela Brazil, Cynthia Harnett, Elfrida Vipont, Enid Blyton) and certain, even medal-winning titles (*The Swish of the Curtain, We Couldn't Leave Dinah, The Wind on the Moon,* the Doctor Dolittle books) seem now to be dated and somewhat turgid when compared with other writing. There are some excellent writers I would have undoubtedly included, if either space or a suitably succinct extract had been available (Eleanor Farjeon, Barbara Willard, C. Walter Hodges).

I have made no attempt to balance genres of writing,

purely to try and reflect examples of the best, and to show the variety of writing for children. Inevitably, perhaps, fantasy – always a rich area in British children's literature – predominates, but there is also historical, domestic, science fiction and humorous writing here. There is high drama from Rosemary Sutcliff, Henry Treece, Leon Garfield and Richard Adams; humour from *The Sword in the Stone*, *The Third Class Genie* and from Roald Dahl; mystery and foreboding in *Greenwitch*; heightened awareness of the countryside in *The Little Grey Men*, *The Box of Delights*; exploration of miniature worlds in *The Borrowers*, *The Twelve and the Genii*; a reflection of today's world in *A Pair of Jesus-Boots*, *The Runaways*.

British writers dominate, too, because that is a reflection of the undoubted place that British writers have taken in the English-speaking world during this century. But some of the best writing from Australia, New Zealand and the United States is here too.

The final order is by date of publication, offering a journey from 1902 to 1989. Some dates may surprise: 'The Elephant's Child', nearly ninety years old, from 1902; *The Railway Children* from 1906; *Wind in the Willows*, 1908; *Just William*, 1923; *Winnie-the-Pooh*, 1926; *The Hobbit*, 1937.

Finally, I hope that children will be as excited by this collection as I have been, will be stimulated to dip into it, to share it with parents, siblings and friends and be encouraged to read further. Happy reading!

Judith Elkin
January 1991

# RUDYARD KIPLING

## 'THE ELEPHANT'S CHILD'

### FROM *Just So Stories*

In the High and Far-Off Times the Elephant, O Best Beloved, had no trunk. He had only a blackish, bulgy nose, as big as a boot, that he could wriggle about from side to side; but he couldn't pick up things with it. But there was one Elephant – a new Elephant – an Elephant's Child – who was full of 'satiable curtiosity, and that means he asked ever so many questions. *And* he lived in Africa, and he filled all Africa with his 'satiable curtiosities. He asked his tall aunt, the Ostrich, why her tail-feathers grew just so, and his tall aunt the Ostrich spanked him with her hard, hard claw. He asked his tall uncle, the Giraffe, what made his skin spotty, and his tall uncle, the Giraffe, spanked him with his hard, hard hoof. And still he was full of 'satiable curtiosity! He asked his broad aunt, the Hippopotamus, why her eyes were red, and his broad aunt, the Hippopotamus, spanked him with her broad, broad hoof; and he asked his hairy uncle, the Baboon, why melons tasted just so, and his hairy uncle, the Baboon, spanked him with his hairy, hairy paw. And *still* he was full of 'satiable curtiosity! He asked questions about everything that he saw, or heard, or felt, or smelt, or touched, and all his uncles and his aunts spanked him. And still he was full of 'satiable curtiosity!

One fine morning in the middle of the Precession of

the Equinoxes this 'satiable Elephant's Child ask a new fine question that he had never asked before. He asked, 'What does the Crocodile have for dinner?' Then everybody said 'Hush!' in a loud and dretful tone, and they spanked him immediately and directly, without stopping, for a long time.

By and by, when that was finished, he came upon Kolokolo Bird sitting in the middle of a wait-a-bit thornbush, and he said, 'My father has spanked me, and my mother has spanked me; all my aunts and uncles have spanked me for my 'satiable curtiosity; and *still* I want to know what the Crocodile has for dinner!'

Then Kolokolo Bird said, with a mournful cry, 'Go to the banks of the great grey-green greasy Limpopo River, all set about with fever-trees, and find out.'

That very next morning, when there was nothing left of the Equinoxes, because the Precession had preceded according to precedent, this 'satiable Elephant's Child took a hundred pounds of bananas (the little short red kind), and a hundred pounds of sugar-cane (the long purple kind), and seventeen melons (the greeny-crackly kind), and said to all his dear families, 'Goodbye. I am going to the great grey-green, greasy Limpopo River, all set about with fever-trees, to find out what the Crocodile has for dinner.' And they all spanked him once more for luck, though he asked them most politely to stop.

Then he went away, a little warm, but not at all astonished, eating melons, and throwing the rind about, because he could not pick it up.

He went from Graham's Town to Kimberley, and from Kimberley to Khama's Country, and from Khama's Country he went east by north, eating melons all the time, till at last he came to the banks of the great grey-green, greasy Limpopo River, all set about with fever-trees, precisely as Kolokolo Bird had said.

Now you must know and understand, O Best Beloved, that till that very week, and day, and hour, and minute, this 'satiable Elephant's Child had never seen a Crocodile, and did not know what one was like. It was all his 'satiable curtiosity.

The first thing that he found was a Bi-Coloured-Python-Rock-Snake curled round a rock.

''Scuse me,' said the Elephant's Child most politely, 'but have you seen such as thing as a Crocodile in these promiscuous parts?'

'*Have* I seen a Crocodile?' said the Bi-Coloured-Python-Rock-Snake, in a voice of dretful scorn. 'What will you ask me next?'

''Scuse me,' said the Elephant's Child, 'but could you kindly tell me what he has for dinner?'

Then the Bi-Coloured-Python-Rock-Snake uncoiled himself very quickly from the rock, and spanked the Elephant's Child with his scalesome, flailsome tail.

'That is odd,' said the Elephant's Child, 'because my father and my mother, and my uncle and my aunt, not to mention my other aunt, the Hippopotamus, and my other uncle, the Baboon, have all spanked me for my 'satiable curtiosity – and I suppose this is the same thing.'

So he said goodbye very politely to the Bi-Coloured-Python-Rock-Snake, and helped to coil him up on the rock again, and went on, a little warm, but not at all astonished, eating melons, and throwing the rind about, because he could not pick it up, till he trod on what he thought was a log of wood at the very edge of the great grey-green, greasy Limpopo River, all set about with fever-trees.

But it was really the Crocodile, O Best Beloved, and the Crocodile winked one eye – like this!

''Scuse me,' said the Elephant's Child most politely, 'but do you happen to have seen a Crocodile in these promiscuous parts?'

Then the Crocodile winked the other eye, and lifted half his tail out of the mud; and the Elephant's Child stepped back most politely, because he did not wish to be spanked again.

'Come hither, Little One,' said the Crocodile. 'Why do you ask such things?'

''Scuse me,' said the Elephant's Child most politely, 'but my father has spanked me, my mother has spanked me, not to mention my tall aunt, the Ostrich, and my tall uncle, the Giraffe, who can kick ever so hard, as well as my broad aunt, the Hippopotamus, and my hairy uncle, the Baboon, *and* including the Bi-Coloured-Python-Rock-Snake, with the scalesome, flailsome tail, just up the bank, who spanks harder than any of them; and *so*, if it's quite all the same to you, I don't want to be spanked any more.'

'Come hither, Little One,' said the Crocodile, 'for I am the Crocodile,' and he wept crocodile-tears to show it was quite true.

Then the Elephant's Child grew all breathless, and panted, and kneeled down on the bank and said, 'You are the very person I have been looking for all these long days. Will you please tell me what you have for dinner?'

'Come hither, Little One,' said the Crocodile, 'and I'll whisper.'

Then the Elephant's Child put his head down close to the Crocodile's musky, tusky mouth, and the Crocodile caught him by his little nose, which up to that very

week, day, hour, and minute, had been no bigger than a boot, though much more useful.

'I think,' said the Crocodile – and he said it between his teeth, like this – 'I think today I will begin with Elephant's Child!'

At this, O Best Beloved, the Elephant's Child was much annoyed, and he said, speaking through his nose, like this, 'Led go! You are hurtig be!'

Then the Bi-Coloured-Python-Rock-Snake scuffled down from the bank and said, 'My young friend, if you do not now, immediately and instantly, pull as hard as ever you can, it is my opinion that your acquaintance in the large-pattern leather ulster' (and by this he meant the Crocodile) 'will jerk you into yonder limpid stream before you can say Jack Robinson.'

This is the way Bi-Coloured-Python-Rock-Snakes always talk.

Then the Elephant's Child sat back on his little haunches, and pulled, and pulled, and pulled, and his nose began to stretch. And the Crocodile floundered into the water, making it all creamy with great sweeps of his tail, and *he* pulled, and pulled, and pulled.

And the Elephant's Child's nose kept on stretching; and the Elephant's Child spread all his little four legs and pulled, and pulled, and pulled, and his nose kept on stretching; and the Crocodile threshed his tail like an oar, and *he* pulled, and pulled, and pulled, and at each pull the Elephant's Child's nose grew longer and longer – and it hurt him hijjus!

Then the Elephant's Child felt his legs slipping, and he said through his nose, which was now nearly five feet long, 'This is too butch for be!'

Then the Bi-Coloured-Python-Rock-Snake came down

from the bank, and knotted himself in a double-clove-hitch round the Elephant's Child's hind-legs, and said, 'Rash and inexperienced traveller, we will now seriously devote ourselves to a little high tension, because if we do not, it is my impression that yonder self-propelling man-of-war with the armour-plated upper deck' (and by this, O Best Beloved, he meant the Crocodile) 'will permanently vitiate your future career.'

That is the way all Bi-Coloured-Python-Rock-Snakes always talk.

So he pulled, and the Elephant's Child pulled, and the Crocodile pulled; but the Elephant's Child and the Bi-Coloured-Python-Rock-Snake pulled hardest; and at last the Crocodile let go of the Elephant's Child's nose with a plop that you could hear all up and down the Limpopo.

Then the Elephant's Child sat down most hard and sudden; but first he was careful to say 'Thank you' to the Bi-Coloured-Python-Rock-Snake; and next he was kind to his poor pulled nose, and wrapped it all up in cool banana leaves, and hung it in the grey-green, greasy Limpopo to cool.

'What are you doing that for?' said the Bi-Coloured-Python-Rock-Snake.

''Scuse me,' said the Elephant's Child, 'but my nose is badly out of shape, and I am waiting for it to shrink.'

'Then you will have to wait a long time,' said the Bi-Coloured-Python-Rock-Snake. 'Some people do not know what is good for them.'

The Elephant's Child sat there for three days waiting for his nose to shrink. But it never grew any shorter, and, besides, it made him squint. For, O Best Beloved, you will see and understand that the Crocodile had pulled it out into a really truly trunk same as all Elephants have today.

# FRANCES HODGSON BURNETT

Becky stepped aside respectfully to allow the superior servants to pass out first. She could not help casting a longing glance at the box on the table. Something made of blue satin was peeping from between the folds of tissue-paper.

'If you please, Miss Minchin,' said Sara suddenly, 'mayn't Becky stay?'

It was a bold thing to do. Miss Minchin was betrayed into something like a slight jump. Then she put her eyeglass up, and gazed at her show pupil disturbedly.

'Becky!' she exclaimed. 'My dearest Sara!'

Sara advanced a step toward her.

'I want her because I know she will like to see the presents,' she explained. 'She is a little girl too, you know.'

Miss Minchin was scandalized. She glanced from one figure to the other.

'My dear Sara,' she said, 'Becky is the scullery-maid. Scullery-maids – er – are not little girls.'

It really had not occurred to her to think of them in that light. Scullery-maids were machines who carried coal-scuttles, and made fires.

'But Becky is,' said Sara. 'And I know she would enjoy herself. Please let her stay – because it is my birthday.'

Miss Minchin replied with much dignity:

'As you ask it as a birthday favour – she may stay. Rebecca, thank Miss Sara for her great kindness.'

Becky had been backing into the corner, twisting the hem of her apron in delighted suspense. She came forward, bobbing courtesies, but between Sara's eyes and her own there passed a gleam of friendly understanding, while her words tumbled over each other.

'Oh, if you please, miss! I'm that grateful, miss! I did want to see the doll, miss, that I did. Thank you, miss. And thank you, ma'am'– turning and making an alarmed bob to Miss Minchin –'for letting me take the liberty.'

Miss Minchin waved her hand again – this time it was in the direction of the corner near the door.

'Go and stand there,' she commanded. 'Not too near the young ladies.'

Becky went to her place, grinning. She did not care where she was sent, so that she might have the luck of being inside the room, instead of being downstairs in the scullery, while these delights were going on. She did not even mind when Miss Minchin cleared her throat ominously and spoke again.

'Now, young ladies, I have a few words to say to you,' she announced.

'She's going to make a speech,' whispered one of the girls. 'I wish it was over.'

Sara felt rather uncomfortable. As this was her party, it was probable that the speech was about her. It is not agreeable to stand in a schoolroom and have a speech made about you.

'You are aware, young ladies,' the speech began – for it was a speech – 'that dear Sara is eleven years old today.'

'*Dear* Sara!' murmured Lavinia.

'Several of you here have also been eleven years old, but Sara's birthdays are rather different from other little girls' birthdays. When she is older she will be heiress to a large fortune, which it will be her duty to spend in a meritorious manner.'

'The diamond mines,' giggled Jessie, in a whisper.

Sara did not hear her; but as she stood with her green-grey eyes fixed steadily on Miss Minchin, she felt herself growing rather hot. When Miss Minchin talked about money, she felt somehow that she always hated her – and, of course, it was disrespectful to hate grown-up people.

'When her dear papa, Captain Crewe, brought her from India and gave her into my care,' the speech proceeded, 'he said to me, in a jesting way, "I am afraid she will be very rich, Miss Minchin." My reply was, "Her education at my seminary, Captain Crewe, shall be such as will adorn the largest fortune." Sara has become my most accomplished pupil. Her French and her dancing are a credit to the seminary. Her manners – which have caused you to call her Princess Sara – are perfect. Her amiability she exhibits by giving you this afternoon's party. I hope you appreciate her generosity. I wish you to express your appreciation of it by saying aloud all together, "Thank you, Sara!"'

The entire schoolroom rose to its feet as it had done the morning Sara remembered so well.

'Thank you, Sara!' it said, and it must be confessed that Lottie jumped up and down. Sara looked rather shy for a moment. She made a courtesy – and it was a very nice one.

'Thank you,' she said, 'for coming to my party.'

'Very pretty, indeed, Sara,' approved Miss Minchin.

'That is what a real princess does when the populace applauds her. Lavinia' – scathingly – 'the sound you just made was extremely like a snort. If you are jealous of your fellow-pupil, I beg you will express your feelings in some more ladylike manner. Now I will leave you to enjoy yourselves.'

The instant she had swept out of the room the spell her presence always had upon them was broken. The door had scarcely closed before every seat was empty. The little girls jumped or tumbled out of theirs; the older ones wasted no time in deserting theirs. There was a rush toward the boxes. Sara had bent over one of them with a delighted face.

'These are books, I know,' she said.

The little children broke into a rueful murmur, and Ermengarde looked aghast.

'Does your papa send you books for a birthday present?' she exclaimed. 'Why, he's as bad as mine. Don't open them, Sara.'

'I like them,' Sara laughed, but she turned to the biggest box. When she took out the Last Doll it was so magnificent that the children uttered delighted groans of joy, and actually drew back to gaze at it in breathless rapture.

'She is almost as big as Lottie,' some gasped.

Lottie clapped her hands and danced about, giggling.

'She's dressed for the theatre,' said Lavinia. 'Her cloak is lined with ermine.'

'Oh!' cried Ermengarde, darting forward, 'she has an opera-glass in her hand – a blue-and-gold one.'

'Here is her trunk,' said Sara. 'Let us open it and look at her things.'

She sat down upon the floor and turned the key.

The children crowded clamouring around her, as she lifted tray after tray and revealed their contents. Never had the schoolroom been in such an uproar. There were lace collars and silk stockings and handkerchiefs; there was a jewel-case containing a necklace and a tiara which looked quite as if they were made of real diamonds; there was a long sealskin and muff; there were ball dresses and walking dresses and visiting dresses; there were hats and tea-gowns and fans. Even Lavinia and Jessie forgot that they were too elderly to care for dolls, and uttered exclamations of delight and caught up things to look at them.

'Suppose,' Sara said, as she stood by the table, putting a large, black-velvet hat on the impassively smiling owner of all these splendours – 'suppose she understands human talk and feels proud of being admired.'

'You are always supposing things,' said Lavinia, and her air was very superior.

'I know I am,' said Sara undisturbedly. 'I like it. There is nothing so nice as supposing. It's almost like being a fairy. If you suppose anything hard enough it seems as if it were real.'

'It's all very well to suppose things if you have everything,' said Lavinia. 'Could you suppose and pretend if you were a beggar and lived in a garret?'

Sara stopped arranging the Last Doll's ostrich plumes, and looked thoughtful.

'I *believe* I could,' she said. 'If one was a beggar, one would have to suppose and pretend all the time. But it mightn't be easy.'

She often thought afterward how strange it was that just as she had finished saying this – just at that very moment – Miss Amelia came into the room.

'Sara,' she said, 'your papa's solicitor, Mr Barrow, has called to see Miss Minchin, and, as she must talk to him alone and the refreshments are laid in her parlour, you had all better come and have your feast now, so that my sister can have her interview here in the schoolroom.'

Refreshments were not likely to be disdained at any hour, and many pairs of eyes gleamed. Miss Amelia arranged the procession into decorum, and then, with Sara at her side heading it, she led it away, leaving the Last Doll sitting upon a chair with the glories of her wardrobe scattered about her; dresses and coats hung upon chair backs, piles of lace-frilled petticoats lying upon their seats.

Becky, who was not expected to partake of refreshments, had the indiscretion to linger a moment to look at these beauties – it really was an indiscretion.

'Go back to your work, Becky,' Miss Amelia had said; but she had stopped to reverently pick up first a muff and then a coat, and while she stood looking at them adoringly, she heard Miss Minchin upon the threshold, and, being smitten with terror at the thought of being accused of taking liberties, she rashly darted under the table, which hid her by its tablecloth.

Miss Minchin came into the room, accompanied by a sharp-featured, dry little gentleman, who looked rather disturbed. Miss Minchin herself also looked rather disturbed, it must be admitted, and she gazed at the dry little gentleman with an irritated and puzzled expression.

She sat down with a stiff dignity, and waved him to a chair.

'Pray be seated, Mr Barrow,' she said.

Mr Barrow did not sit down at once. His attention seemed attracted by the Last Doll and the things which surrounded her. He settled his eye-glasses and looked at them in nervous disapproval. The Last Doll herself did not seem to mind this in the least. She merely sat upright and returned his gaze indifferently.

'A hundred pounds,' Mr Barrow remarked succinctly. 'All expensive material, and made at a Parisian modiste's. He spent money lavishly enough, that young man.'

Miss Minchin felt offended. This seemed to be a disparagement of her best patron and was a liberty.

Even solicitors had no right to take liberties.

'I beg your pardon, Mr Barrow,' she said stiffly. 'I do not understand.'

'Birthday presents,' said Mr Barrow, in the same critical manner, 'to a child eleven years old! Mad extravagance, I call it.'

Miss Minchin drew herself up still more rigidly.

'Captain Crewe is a man of fortune,' she said. 'The diamond mines alone —'

Mr Barrow wheeled round upon her.

'Diamond mines!' he broke out. 'There are none! Never were!'

Miss Minchin actually got up from her chair.

'What!' she cried. 'What do you mean?'

'At any rate,' answered Mr Barrow quite snappishly, 'it would have been much better if there never had been any.'

'Any diamond mines?' ejaculated Miss Minchin, catching at the back of a chair, and feeling as if a splendid dream was fading away from her.

'Diamond mines spell ruin oftener than they spell wealth,' said Mr Barrow. 'When a man is in the hands of a very dear friend, and is not a business man himself, he had better steer clear of the dear friend's diamonds mines, or gold mines, or any other kind of mines dear friends want his money to put into. The late Captain Crewe –'

Here Miss Minchin stopped him with a gasp.

'The *late* Captain Crewe!' she cried out, 'the *late!* You don't come to tell me that Captain Crewe is –'

'He's dead, ma'am,' Mr Barrow answered with jerky brusqueness. 'Died of jungle fever and business troubles combined. The jungle fever might not have killed him if he had not been driven mad by the business troubles, and the business troubles might not have put an end to him if the jungle fever had not assisted. Captain Crewe is dead!'

Miss Minchin dropped into her chair again. The words he had spoken filled her with alarm.

'What *were* his business troubles?' she said. 'What *were* they?'

'Diamond mines,' answered Mr Barrow, 'and dear friends – and ruin.'

Miss Minchin lost her breath.

'Ruin!' she gasped out.

'Lost every penny. That young man had too much money. The dear friend was mad on the subject of the diamond mine. He put all his own money into it, and all Captain Crewe's. Then the dear friend ran away – Captain Crewe was already stricken with fever when the news came. The shock was too much for him. He died delirious, raving about his little girl – and didn't leave a penny.'

Now Miss Minchin understood, and never had she received such a blow in her life. Her show pupil, her show patron, swept away from the select seminary at one blow. She felt as if she had been outraged and robbed, and that Captain Crewe and Sara and Mr Barrow were equally to blame.

'Do you mean to tell me,' she cried out, 'that he left *nothing*? That Sara will have no fortune? That the child is a beggar? That she is left on my hands a little pauper instead of an heiress?'

Mr Barrow was a shrewd business man, and felt it as well to make his own freedom from responsibility quite clear without any delay.

'She is certainly left a beggar,' he replied. 'And she is certainly left on your hands, ma'am, and she hasn't a relation in the world that we know of.'

# E. NESBIT

FROM *The Railway Children*

'If it wasn't for the railway at the bottom, it would be as though the foot of man had never been there, wouldn't it?'

The sides of the cutting were of grey stone, very roughly hewn. Indeed, the top part of the cutting had been a little natural glen that had been cut deeper to bring it down to the level of the tunnel's mouth. Among the rocks, grass and flowers grew, and seeds dropped by birds in the crannies of the stone had taken root and grown into bushes and trees that overhung the cutting. Near the tunnel was a flight of steps leading down to the line – just wooden bars roughly fixed into the earth – a very steep and narrow way, more like a ladder than a stair.

'We'd better get down,' said Peter; 'I'm sure the cherries would be quite easy to get at from the side of the steps. You remember it was there we picked the cherry blossoms that we put on the rabbit's grave.'

So they went along the fence towards the little swing gate that is at the top of these steps. And they were almost at the gate when Bobbie said:

'Hush. Stop! What's that?'

'That' was a very odd noise indeed – a soft noise, but quite plainly to be heard through the sound of the wind in the branches, and the hum and whirr of the telegraph wires. It was a sort of rustling, whispering sound. As they listened, it stopped and then it began again.

And this time it did not stop, but it grew louder and more rustling and rumbling.

'Look' – cried Peter, suddenly – 'the tree over there!'

The tree he pointed at was one of those that have rough grey leaves and white flowers. The berries, when they come, are bright scarlet, but if you pick them, they disappoint you by turning black before you get them home. And, as Peter pointed, the tree was moving – not just the way trees ought to move when the wind blows through them, but all in one piece, as though it were a live creature and were walking down the side of the cutting.

'It's moving!' cried Bobbie. 'Oh, look! and so are the others. It's like the woods in *Macbeth*.'

'It's magic,' said Phyllis, breathlessly. 'I always knew the railway was enchanted.'

It really did seem a little like magic. For all the trees for about twenty yards of the opposite bank seemed to be slowly walking down towards the railway line, the tree with the grey leaves bringing up the rear like some old shepherd driving a flock of green sheep.

'What is it? Oh, what is it?' said Phyllis; 'it's much too magic for me. I don't like it. Let's go home.'

But Bobbie and Peter clung fast to the rail and watched breathlessly. And Phyllis made no movement towards going home by herself.

The trees moved on and on. Some stones and loose earth fell down and rattled on the railway metals far below.

'It's *all* coming down,' Peter tried to say, but he found there was hardly any voice to say it with. And, indeed, just as he spoke, the great rock, on the top of which the walking trees were, leaned slowly forward. The trees, ceasing to walk, stood still and shivered. Leaning with the rock, they seemed to hesitate a moment, and then rock and trees and grass and bushes, with a rushing sound, slipped right away from the face of the cutting and fell on the line with a blundering crash that could have been heard half a mile off. A cloud of dust rose up.

'Oh,' said Peter, in awestruck tones, 'isn't it exactly like when coals come in? – if there wasn't any roof to the cellar and you could see down.'

'Look what a great mound it's made!' said Bobbie.

'Yes, it's right across the down line,' said Phyllis.

'That'll take some sweeping up,' said Bobbie.

'Yes,' said Peter slowly. He was still leaning on the fence.

'Yes,' he said again, still more slowly.

Then he stood upright.

'The 11.29 down hasn't gone by yet. We must let them know at the station, or there'll be a most frightful accident.'

'Let's run,' said Bobbie, and began.

But Peter cried, 'Come back!' and looked at Mother's watch. He was very prompt and businesslike, and his face looked whiter than they had ever seen it.

'No time,' he said; 'it's ten miles away, and it's past eleven.'

'Couldn't we,' suggested Phyllis, breathlessly, 'couldn't we climb up a telegraph post and do something to the wires?'

'We don't know how,' said Peter.

'They do it in war,' said Phyllis; 'I know I've heard of it.'

'They only *cut* them, silly,' said Peter, 'and that doesn't do any good. And we couldn't cut them even if we got up, and we couldn't get up. If we had anything red, we could go down on the line and wave it.'

'But the train wouldn't see us till it got round the corner, and then it could see the mound just as well as us,' said Phyllis; 'better, because it's much bigger than us.'

'If we only had something red,' Peter repeated, 'we could go round the corner and wave to the train.'

'We might wave, anyway.'

'They'd only think it was just *us*, as usual. We've waved so often before. Anyway, let's get down.'

They got down the steep stairs. Bobbie was pale and shivering. Peter's face looked thinner than usual. Phyllis was red-faced and damp with anxiety.

'Oh, how hot I am!' she said; 'and I thought it was going to be cold; I wish we hadn't put on our – ' she stopped short, and then ended in quite a different tone – 'our flannel petticoats.'

Bobbie turned at the bottom of the stairs.

'Oh, yes,' she cried, '*they're* red! Let's take them off.'

They did, and with the petticoats rolled under their arms, ran along the railway, skirting the newly fallen mound of stones and rock and earth, and bent, crushed, twisted trees. They ran at their best pace. Peter led, but the girls were not far behind. They reached the corner that hid the mound from the straight line of railway that ran half a mile without curve or corner.

'Now,' said Peter, taking hold of the largest flannel petticoat.

'You're not' – Phyllis faltered – 'you're not going to *tear* them?'

'Shut up,' said Peter, with brief sternness.

'Oh, yes,' said Bobbie, 'tear them into little bits if you like. Don't you see, Phil, if we can't stop the train, there'll be a real live accident, with people *killed*. Oh, horrible! Here, Peter, you'll never tear it through the band!'

She took the red flannel petticoat from him and tore it off an inch from the band. Then she tore the other in the same way.

'There!' said Peter, tearing in his turn. He divided each petticoat into three pieces. 'Now, we've got six flags.' He looked at the watch again. 'And we've got seven minutes. We must have flagstaffs.'

The knives given to boys are, for some odd reason, seldom of the kind of steel that keeps sharp. The young saplings had to be broken off. Two came up by the roots. The leaves were stripped from them.

'We must cut holes in the flags, and run the sticks through the holes,' said Peter. And the holes were cut. The knife was sharp enough to cut flannel with. Two of the flags were set up in heaps of loose stones beneath the sleepers of the down line. Then Phyllis and Roberta took each a flag, and stood ready to wave it as soon as the train came in sight.

'I shall have the other two myself,' said Peter, 'because it was my idea to wave something red.'

'They're our petticoats, though,' Phyllis was beginning, but Bobbie interrupted –

'Oh, what does it matter who waves what, if we can only save the train?'

Perhaps Peter had not rightly calculated the number of minutes it would take the 11.29 to get from the station to the place where they were, or perhaps the train was late. Anyway, it seemed a very long time that they waited.

Phyllis grew impatient. 'I expect the watch is wrong, and the train's gone by,' said she.

Peter relaxed the heroic attitude he had chosen to show off his two flags. And Bobbie began to feel sick with suspense.

It seemed to her that they had been standing there for hours and hours, holding those silly little red flannel flags that no one would ever notice. The train wouldn't care. It would go rushing by them and tear round the corner and go crashing into that awful mound. And everyone would be killed. Her hands grew very cold and trembled so that she could hardly hold the flag. And then came the distant rumble and hum of the metals, and a puff of white steam showed far away along the stretch of line.

'Stand firm,' said Peter, 'and wave like mad! When it gets to that big furze bush step back, but go on waving! Don't stand *on* the line, Bobbie!'

The train came rattling along very, very fast,

'They don't see us! They won't see us! It's all no good!' cried Bobbie.

The two little flags on the line swayed as the nearing train shook and loosened the heaps of loose stones that held them up. One of them slowly leaned over and fell on the line. Bobbie jumped forward and caught it up, and waved it; her hands did not tremble now.

It seemed that the train came on as fast as ever. It was very near now.

'Keep off the line, you silly cuckoo!' said Peter, fiercely.

'It's no good,' Bobbie said again.

'Stand back!' cried Peter, suddenly, and he dragged Phyllis back by the arm.

But Bobbie cried, 'Not yet, not yet!' and waved her two flags right over the line. The front of the engine looked black and enormous. Its voice was loud and harsh.

'Oh, stop, stop, stop!' cried Bobbie. No one heard her. At least Peter and Phyllis didn't, for the oncoming rush of the train covered the sound of her voice with a mountain of sound. But afterwards she used to wonder whether the engine itself had not heard her. It seemed almost as though it had – for it slackened swiftly, slackened and stopped, not twenty yards from the place where Bobbie's two flags waved over the line. She saw the great black engine stop dead, but somehow she could not stop waving the flags. And when the driver and the fireman had got off the engine and Peter and Phyllis had gone to meet them and pour out their excited tale of the awful mound just round the corner, Bobbie still waved the flags but more and more feebly and jerkily.

# KENNETH GRAHAME

FROM *The Wind in the Willows*

During luncheon – which was excellent, of course, as everything at Toad Hall always was – the Toad simply let himself go. Disregarding the Rat, he proceeded to play upon the inexperienced Mole as on a harp. Naturally a voluble animal, and always mastered by his imagination, he painted the prospects of the trip and the joys of the open life and the road-side in such glowing colours that the Mole could hardly sit in his chair for excitement. Somehow, it soon seemed taken for granted by all three of them that the trip was a settled thing; and the Rat, though still unconvinced in his mind, allowed his good-nature to over-ride his personal objections. He could not bear to disappoint his two friends, who were already deep in schemes and anticipations, planning out each day's separate occupation for several weeks ahead.

When they were quite ready, the now triumphant Toad led his companions to the paddock and set them to capture the old grey horse, who, without having been consulted, and to his own extreme annoyance, had been told off by Toad for the dustiest job in this dusty expedition. He frankly preferred the paddock, and took a deal of catching. Meantime Toad packed the lockers still tighter with necessaries, and hung nose-bags, nets of onions, bundles of hay, and baskets from the bottom of the cart. At last the horse was caught and harnessed, and they set off, all talking at once, each animal either trudging by the side of the cart or sitting on the shaft, as the humour took him. It was a golden afternoon. The smell of the dust they kicked up was rich and satisfying; out of thick orchards on either side of the road, birds called and whistled to them cheerily; good-natured wayfarers, passing them, gave them 'Good day', or stopped to say nice things about their beautiful cart; and rabbits, sitting at their front doors in the hedgerow, held up their fore-paws, and said, 'O my! O my! O my!'

Late in the evening, tired and happy and miles from home, they drew up on a remote common far from habitations, turned the horse loose to graze, and ate their simple supper sitting on the grass by the side of the cart. Toad talked big about all he was going to do in the days to come, while stars grew fuller and larger all around them, and a yellow moon, appearing suddenly and silently from nowhere in particular, came to keep them company and listen to their talk. At last they turned into their little bunks in the cart; and Toad, kicking out his legs, sleepily said, 'Well, good night, you fellows! This is the real life for a gentleman! Talk about your old river!'

'I *don't* talk about my river,' replied the patient Rat. 'You *know* I don't, Toad. But I *think* about it,' he added pathetically, in a lower tone: 'I think about it – all the time!'

The Mole reached out from under his blanket, felt for the Rat's paw in the darkness, and gave it a squeeze. 'I'll do whatever you like, Ratty,' he whispered. 'Shall we run away tomorrow morning, quite early – *very* early – and go back to our dear old hole on the river?'

'No, no, we'll see it out,' whispered back the Rat. 'Thanks awfully, but I ought to stick by Toad till this trip is ended. It wouldn't be safe for him to be left to himself. It won't take very long. His fads never do. Good night!'

The end was indeed nearer than even the Rat suspected.

After so much open air and excitement the Toad slept very soundly, and no amount of shaking could rouse him out of bed next morning. So the Mole and Rat turned to, quietly and manfully, and while the Rat saw to the horse, and lit a fire, and cleaned last night's cups and platters, and got things ready for breakfast, the Mole trudged off to the nearest village, a long way off, for milk and eggs and various necessaries the Toad had, of course, forgotten to provide. The hard work had all been done, and the two animals were resting, thoroughly exhausted, by the time Toad appeared on the scene, fresh and gay, remarking what a pleasant easy life it was they were all leading now, after the cares and worries and fatigues of housekeeping at home.

They had a pleasant ramble that day over grassy downs and along narrow by-lanes, and camped, as before, on a common, only this time the two guests took care that Toad should do his fair share of work. In consequence, when the time came for starting next morning, Toad was by no means so rapturous about the simplicity of the primitive life, and indeed attempted to resume his place in his bunk, whence he was hauled by force. Their way lay, as before, across country by narrow lanes, and it was not till the afternoon that they came out on the high road, their first high road; and there disaster, fleet and unforeseen, sprang out on them – disaster momentous indeed to their expedition, but simply overwhelming in its effect on the after-career of Toad.

They were strolling along the high road easily, the

Mole by the horse's head, talking to him, since the horse had complained that he was being frightfully left out of it, and nobody considered him in the least; the Toad and the Water Rat walking behind the cart talking together — at least Toad was talking, and Rat was saying at intervals, 'Yes, precisely; and what did *you* say to *him?*– and thinking all the time of something very different, when far behind them they heard a faint warning hum, like the drone of a distant bee. Glancing back, they saw a small cloud of dust, with a dark centre of energy, advancing on them at incredible speed, while from out the dust a faint 'Poop-poop!' wailed like an uneasy animal in pain. Hardly regarding it, they turned to resume their conversation, when in an instant (as it seemed) the peaceful scene was changed, and with a blast of wind and a whirl of sound that made them jump for the nearest ditch, it was on them! The 'poop-poop' rang with a brazen shout in their ears, they had a moment's glimpse of an interior of glittering plate-glass and rich morocco, and the magnificent motor-car, immense, breath-snatching, passionate, with its pilot tense and hugging his wheel, possessed all earth and air for the fraction of a second, flung an enveloping cloud of dust that blinded and enwrapped them utterly, and then dwindled to a speck in the far distance, changed back into a droning bee once more.

The old grey horse, dreaming, as he plodded along, of his quiet paddock, in a new raw situation such as this simply abandoned himself to his natural emotions. Rearing, plunging, backing steadily, in spite of all the Mole's efforts at his head, and the Mole's lively language directed at his better feelings, he drove the cart backwards towards the deep ditch at the side of the road. It wavered an instant — then there was a heartrending crash — and

the canary-coloured cart, their pride and their joy, lay on its side in the ditch, an irredeemable wreck.

The Rat danced up and down in the road, simply transported with passion. 'You villains!' he shouted, shaking both fists, 'you scoundrels, you highwaymen, you – you – road-hogs! – I'll have the law on you! I'll report you! I'll take you through all the Courts!' His homesickness had quite slipped away from him, and for the moment he was the skipper of the canary-coloured vessel driven on a shoal by the reckless jockeying of rival mariners, and he was trying to recollect all the fine and biting things he used to say to masters of steam-launches when their wash, as they drove too near the bank, used to flood his parlour carpet at home.

Toad sat straight down in the middle of the dusty road, his legs stretched out before him, and stared fixedly in the direction of the disappearing motor-car. He breathed short, his face wore a placid, satisfied expression, and at intervals he faintly murmured 'Poop-poop!'

The Mole was busy trying to quiet the horse, which he succeeded in doing after a time. Then he went to look at the cart, on its side in the ditch. It was indeed a sorry sight. Panels and windows smashed, axles hopelessly bent, one wheel off, sardine-tins scattered over the wide world, and the bird in the bird-cage sobbing pitifully and calling to be let out.

The Rat came to help him, but their united efforts were not sufficient to right the cart. 'Hi! Toad!' they cried. 'Come and bear a hand, can't you!'

The Toad never answered a word, or budged from his seat in the road; so they went to see what was the matter with him. They found him in a sort of trance, a happy

smile on his face, his eyes still fixed on the dusty wake of
their destroyer. At intervals he was still heard to murmur
'Poop-poop!'

The Rat shook him by the shoulder. 'Are you coming
to help us, Toad?' he demanded sternly.

'Glorious, stirring sight!' murmured Toad, never offering to move. 'The poetry of motion! The *real* way to
travel! The *only* way to travel! Here today – in next week
tomorrow! Villages skipped, towns and cities jumped –
always somebody else's horizon! O bliss! O poop-poop!
O my! O my!'

'O *stop* being an ass, Toad!' cried the Mole despair-
ingly.

'And to think I never *knew*!' went on the Toad in a
dreamy monotone. 'All those wasted years that lie behind
me, I never knew, never even *dreamt*! But *now* – but now
that I know, now that I fully realize! O what a flowery
track lies spread before me, henceforth! What dust-clouds
shall spring up behind me as I speed on my reckless way!
What carts I shall fling carelessly into the ditch in the
wake of my magnificent onset! Horrid little carts –
common carts – canary-coloured carts!'

# J. M. BARRIE

The men broke into another verse of their song —

> '*Yo ho, the pirate life,*
> *The flag of skull and bones!*
> *A merry hour, a hempen rope —*
> *And hey for Davy Jones!*'

As it ended, Hook called a halt. Like royalty, he sat there surveying the scene, the darkest and cruellest member of all that evil band, yet he had an air of elegance too. His face, long, lean, and ashen pale, was deeply furrowed down the length of his cheeks. His eyebrows were heavy, and beneath them his eyes were a surprising forget-me-not blue, but hard and expressionless as agate — except when he clawed with his hook. Then in each glowed a spot of fire. He wore his hair long on his shoulders, in fat, black corkscrew curls, greasy and set, like so many shiny black candles, slung by their wicks beneath his large, gold-laced hat on which he bore his emblem — the skull and crossbones enamelled in white on black.

Hook had been to a good school — indeed to a famous school — and he still moved with the aristocratic slouch he had learned there. He kept a certain air of civility too, which could be more terrifying than another man's violence. He was most polite when bent on evil, and had been known to apologize most graciously to victims on the high seas before obliging them to walk the plank. His long blue coat, of the style worn in Stuart times, swung elegantly from his broad lean shoulders, his feet were shod in hand-made shoes with silver buckles. The two-way steel hook, spliced in a wooden block, protruded strangely from the lace frills which fell from the large-cuffed sleeve. It was strange that the only thing known to make Hook flinch was the sight of his own blood – but one who had known him in his schooldays swore that Hook *bled yellow*.

The men stopped singing as the raft came to a halt. Starkey spotted Nibs and instantly drew his pistol and took aim – but before he could fire, Hook's claw was in his back and he felt it twisting ominously. His fingers loosened on the trigger, and in terror for his life, he cried out:

'Let go, Capt'n, let go!'

'Put back your pistol,' said Hook, retaining his grasp, but clawing no farther.

'It was one of those plaguy boys,' Starkey pleaded. 'I could have shot him dead, Capt'n.'

'Aye,' drawled Hook, 'and brought Tiger Lily's braves about our ears. Do you want to lose your scalp, Starkey?'

Smee sidled forward with an ingratiating smile, pointing his cutlass with one hand, neatly, and waggling the long fingers of the other.

'You're right, Capt'n, you're right,' he breathed, 'but shall I after him, and tickle him with Johnny Corkscrew here? Johnny's a silent fellow, Capt'n!' He leered towards the tree where Nibs clung shivering to a branch too low for safety.

Hook silenced him with a look. 'It's the whole seven I

want,' he said in a low and deadly voice. 'To the mischief
with them! Scatter, men, and look for them. Search them
out. They must be nigh!'

Smee put his bosun's pipe to his lips and gave the
orders. The men scattered, but he stayed behind. Hook
stepped out of the raft, and seated himself carefully on a
large toadstool.

'All seven,' he repeated '– but their captain, I *must*
have.' His voice rose suddenly to a scream on those
words. Smee glanced over his glasses at him, but without
anxiety. He knew Hook well. 'Yes, Peter Pan!' Hook
snarled. 'Pan – who cut off this hand,' he brandished the
hook. 'I've waited long enough . . . to shake his . . . hand
. . . with THIS!' the snarl rose again to a scream.
'Aaaaaaa-ugh! but I'll tear him when he shakes with
Hook!'

Smee blinked mildly, and pushed his spectacles up his
nose a little way.

'Yet haven't I heard you say, Capt'n, that your hook's
worth a score of hands? For . . . combing the hair, and
other homely purposes?'

'If I were a mother, Smee,' returned Hook feelingly,
'I'd pray to have my children *born* with this . . .' he
shook the hook, 'instead of *that*!' and he lifted his left
hand languidly. 'He flung my arm to a crocodile, Smee,'
he went on in an outraged tone, 'to a crocodile which
just happened to be passing.'

'I had noticed,' Smee observed cautiously, 'that you
have a strange dread of crocodiles, Capt'n.'

'Not of crocodiles,' Hook screamed, 'of ONE crocodile, who liked the taste of me so well, it has followed
me ever since – hoping, Smee, hoping for the rest of
me!' The last words came in a snarling whisper.

'In a way,' Smee said, glancing cunningly at him, 'in a way, it might be a kind of a compliment, wouldn't you say?'

'I want no such compliments,' Hook roared back. 'I want Peter Pan who gave the brute its taste for me. Smee —' his voice dropped, and a quaver came into it, 'it would have had me before this but that by a lucky chance, about the same time, it swallowed a clock which goes on ticking inside it, *tick tock, tick tock*, and before it can reach me I hear the tick and bolt.' He uttered a hollow laugh.

'Some day the clock will run down,' said Smee meditatively, shaking his grizzled head in its red-ringed stocking cap, 'then it'll get you, Capt'n.'

'That's what I'm afraid of!' Hook wailed brokenly. 'That is what *haunts* me, Smee!'

Suddenly something disturbed him, and he spun off the toadstool, exclaiming 'Odds, bobs, hammer, and tongs! I'm burning!'

He felt the seat with his left hand and a crafty look softened his features. 'Smee,' he said, 'this seat's hot, very hot.' With his hook he flung the toadstool over and saw the smoke issuing out of the hole in the ground. More, he heard prattling voices. He nodded silently, as one who understands all.

'It's the boys,' he murmured softly, 'the boys! That's where they live, Smee!'

He listened a little longer, and his face darkened somewhat. 'Pan's from home,' he reported, 'but expected back.'

A wicked smile curled his lips, always so red against the ashen pallor of his cheeks. Smee understood the look. 'Unrip your plan, Capt'n,' he said.

'We'll return to the ship,' said Hook with unholy glee, 'and cook a large rich cake, of jolly thickness, with sugar on the top – *green* sugar, Smee! And we'll leave the cake for them in some good place, like the shores of the lagoon. They are always swimming about there. They'll find the cake and gobble it up. They haven't any mothers to warn them that it's dangerous to eat rich, damp cake, specially when it has *green* sugar on it! They'll eat it – and *die*!'

''Tis the wickedest, prettiest plot I ever heard!' Smee murmured admiringly.

# RICHMAL CROMPTON

FROM *Just William*

It all began with William's aunt, who was in a good temper that morning, and gave him a shilling for posting a letter for her and carrying her parcels from the grocer's.

'Buy some sweets or go to the Pictures,' she said carelessly, as she gave it to him.

William walked slowly down the road, gazing thoughtfully at the coin. After deep calculations, based on the fact that the shilling is the equivalent of two sixpences, he came to the conclusion that both luxuries could be indulged in.

In the matter of sweets, William frankly upheld the superiority of quantity over quality. Moreover, he knew every sweet shop within a two miles radius of his home whose proprietor added an extra sweet after the scale had descended, and he patronized these shops exclusively. With solemn face and eager eye, he always watched the process of weighing, and 'stingy' shops were known and banned by him.

He wandered now to his favourite confectioner and stood outside the window for five minutes, torn between the rival attractions of Gooseberry Eyes and Marble Balls. Both were sold at 4 ounces for 2d. William never purchased more expensive luxuries. At last his frowning brow relaxed and he entered the shop.

'Sixpennoth of Gooseberry Eyes,' he said, with a

slightly self-conscious air. The extent of his purchases rarely exceeded a penny.

'Hello!' said the shopkeeper, in amused surprise.

'Gotter bit of money this mornin',' explained William carelessly, with the air of a Rothschild.

He watched the weighing of the emerald green dainties with silent intensity, saw with satisfaction the extra one added after the scale had fallen, received the precious paper bag, and, putting two sweets into his mouth, walked out of the shop.

Sucking slowly, he walked down the road towards the Picture Palace. William was not in the habit of frequenting Picture Palaces. He had only been there once before in his life.

It was a thrilling programme. First came the story of desperate crooks who, on coming out of any building, glanced cautiously up and down the street in huddled, crouching attitudes, then crept ostentatiously on their way in a manner guaranteed to attract attention and suspicion at any place and time. The plot was involved. They were pursued by police, they leapt on to a moving train and then, for no accountable reason, leapt from that on to a moving motor-car and from that they plunged into a moving river. It was thrilling and William thrilled. Sitting quite motionless, he watched, with wide, fascinated eyes, though his jaws never ceased their rotatory movement and every now and then his hand would go mechanically to the paper bag on his knees and convey a Gooseberry Eye to his mouth.

The next play was a simple country love-story, in which figured a simple country maiden wooed by the squire, who was marked out as the villain by his moustachios.

After many adventures the simple country maiden was won by a simple country son of the soil in picturesque rustic attire, whose emotions were faithfully portrayed by gestures that must have required much gymnastic skill; the villain was finally shown languishing in a prison cell, still indulging in frequent eye-brow play.

Next came another love-story – this time of a noble-hearted couple, consumed with mutual passion and kept apart not only by a series of misunderstandings possible only in a picture play, but also by maidenly pride and reserve on the part of the heroine and manly pride and reserve on the part of the hero that forced them to hide their ardour beneath a cold and haughty exterior. The heroine's brother moved through the story like a good fairy, tender and protective towards his orphan sister and ultimately explained to each the burning passion of the other.

It was moving and touching and William was moved and touched.

The next was a comedy. It began by a solitary work-man engaged upon the re-painting of a door and ended with a miscellaneous crowd of people, all covered with paint, falling downstairs on top of one another. It was amusing. William was riotously and loudly amused.

Lastly came the pathetic story of a drunkard's down-ward path. He began as a wild young man in evening clothes drinking intoxicants and playing cards, he ended as a wild old man in rags still drinking intoxicants and playing cards. He had a small child with a pious and superior expression, who spent her time weeping over him and exhorting him to a better life, till, in a moment of justifiable exasperation, he threw a beer bottle at her head. He then bedewed her bed in Hospital with penitent tears, tore out his hair, flung up his arms towards Heaven, beat his waistcoat, and clasped her to his breast, so that it was not to be wondered at that, after all that excitement, the child had a relapse and with the words 'Goodbye, Father. Do not think of what you have done. I forgive you' passed peacefully away.

William drew a deep breath at the end, and still sucking, arose with the throng and passed out.

Once outside, he glanced cautiously around and slunk down the road in the direction of his home. Then he doubled suddenly and ran down a back street to put his imaginary pursuers off his track. He took a pencil from his pocket and, levelling it at the empty air, fired twice. Two of his pursuers fell dead, the rest came on with redoubled vigour. There was no time to be lost. Running for dear life, he dashed down the next street, leaving in his wake an elderly gentleman nursing his toe and cursing volubly. As he neared his gate, William again drew the pencil from his pocket and, still looking back down the road, and firing as he went, he rushed into his own gateway.

William's father, who had stayed at home that day because of a bad headache and a touch of liver, picked himself up from the middle of a rhododendron bush and seized William by the back of his neck.

'You young ruffian,' he roared, 'what do you mean by charging into me like that?'

William gently disengaged himself.

'I wasn't chargin', Father,' he said, meekly. 'I was only jus' comin' in at the gate, same as other folks. I jus' wasn't looking jus' the way you were coming, but I can't look all ways at once, cause –'

'Be *quiet*!' roared William's father.

Like the rest of the family, he dreaded William's eloquence.

'What's that on your tongue? Put your tongue out.'

William obeyed. The colour of William's tongue would have put to shame Spring's freshest tints.

'How many times am I to tell you,' bellowed William's father, 'that I won't have you going about eating filthy poisons all day between meals?'

'It's not filthy poison,' said William. 'It's jus' a few sweets Aunt Susan gave me 'cause I kin'ly went to the post office for her an' —'

'Be *quiet*! Have you got any more of the foul things?'

'They're not foul things,' said William, doggedly. 'They're good. Jus' have one, an' try. They're jus' a few sweets Aunt Susan kin'ly gave me an' —'

'Be *quiet*! Where are they?'

Slowly and reluctantly William drew forth his bag. His father seized it and flung it far into the bushes. For the next ten minutes William conducted a thorough and systematic search among the bushes and for the rest of the day consumed Gooseberry Eyes and garden soil in fairly equal proportions.

# A. A. MILNE

FROM *Winnie-the-Pooh*

The old grey donkey, Eeyore, stood by himself in a thistly corner of the forest, his front feet well apart, his head on one side, and thought about things. Sometimes he thought sadly to himself, 'Why?' and sometimes he thought, 'Wherefore?' and sometimes he thought 'Inasmuch as which?'– and sometimes he didn't quite know what he *was* thinking about. So when Winnie-the-Pooh came stumping along, Eeyore was very glad to be able to stop thinking for a little, in order to say 'How do you do?' in a gloomy manner to him.

'And how are you?' said Winnie-the-Pooh.

Eeyore shook his head from side to side.

'Not very how,' he said. 'I don't seem to have felt at all how for a long time.'

'Dear, dear,' said Pooh, 'I'm sorry about that. Let's have a look at you.'

So Eeyore stood there, gazing sadly at the ground, and Winnie-the-Pooh walked all round him once.

'Why, what's happened to your tail?' he said in surprise.

'What *has* happened to it?' said Eeyore.

'It isn't there!'

'Are you sure?'

'Well, either a tail *is* there or it isn't there. You can't make a mistake about it, and yours *isn't* there!'

'Then what is?'

'Nothing.'

'Let's have a look,' said Eeyore, and he turned slowly round to the place where his tail had been a little while ago, and then, finding that he couldn't catch it up, he turned round the other way, until he came back to where he was at first, and then he put his head down and looked between his front legs, and at last he said, with a long, sad sigh, 'I believe you're right.'

'Of course I'm right,' said Pooh.

'That Accounts for a Good Deal,' said Eeyore gloomily. 'It Explains Everything. No Wonder.'

'You must have left it somewhere,' said Winnie-the-Pooh.

'Somebody must have taken it,' said Eeyore. 'How Like Them,' he added, after a long silence.

Pooh felt that he ought to say something helpful about it, but didn't quite know what. So he decided to do something helpful instead.

'Eeyore,' he said solemnly, 'I, Winnie-the-Pooh, will find your tail for you.'

'Thank you, Pooh,' answered Eyeore. 'You're a real friend,' said he. 'Not like Some,' he said.

So Winnie-the-Pooh went off to find Eeyore's tail.

It was a fine spring morning in the forest as he started out. Little soft clouds played happily in a blue sky, skipping from time to time in front of the sun as if they had come to put it out, and then sliding away suddenly so that the next might have his turn. Through them and between them, the sun shone bravely; and a copse which had worn its firs all the year round seemed old and dowdy now beside the new green lace which the beeches had put on so prettily. Through copse and spinney marched Bear; down open slopes of gorse and heather, over rocky beds of streams, up steep banks of sandstone into the heather again; and so at last, tired and hungry, to the Hundred Acre Wood. For it was in the Hundred Acre Wood that Owl lived.

'And if anyone knows anything about anything,' said Bear to himself, 'it's Owl who knows something about something,' he said, 'or my name's not Winnie-the-Pooh,' he said. 'Which it is,' he added. 'So there you are.'

Owl lived at The Chestnuts, an old-world residence of great charm, which was grander than anybody else's, or seemed so to Bear, because it had both a knocker *and* a bell-pull. Underneath the knocker there was a notice which said:

PLES RING IF AN RNSER IS REQIRD

Underneath the bell-pull there was a notice which said:

PLEZ CNOKE IF AN RNSR IS NOT REQID

These notices had been written by Christopher Robin, who was the only one in the forest who could spell; for Owl, wise though he was in many ways, able to read and write and spell his own name WOL, yet somehow went all to pieces over delicate words like MEASLES AND BUTTERED TOAST.

Winnie-the-Pooh read the two notices very carefully, first from left to right, and afterwards, in case he had missed some of it, from right to left. Then, to make quite sure, he knocked and pulled the knocker, and he pulled and knocked the bell-rope, and he called out in a very loud voice, 'Owl! I require an answer! It's Bear speaking.' And the door opened, and Owl looked out.

'Hello, Pooh,' he said. 'How's things?'

'Terrible and Sad,' said Pooh, 'because Eeyore, who is

a friend of mine, has lost his tail. And he's Moping about
it. So could you very kindly tell me how to find it for
him?'

'Well,' said Owl, 'the customary procedure in such
cases is as follows.'

'What does Crustimoney Proseedcake mean?' said
Pooh. 'For I am a Bear of Very Little Brain, and long
words Bother me.'

'It means the Thing to Do.'

'As long as it means that, I don't mind,' said Pooh
humbly.

'The thing to do is as follows. First, Issue a Reward,
Then –'

'Just a moment,' said Pooh, holding up his paw. '*What*
do we do to this – what you were saying? You sneezed
just as you were going to tell me.'

'I *didn't* sneeze.'

'Yes, you did, Owl.'

'Excuse me, Pooh, I didn't. You can't sneeze without
knowing it.'

'Well, you can't know it without something having
been sneezed.'

'What I *said* was, "First *Issue* a Reward".'

'You're doing it again,' said Pooh sadly.

'A Reward!' said Owl very loudly. 'We write a notice
to say that we will give a large something to anybody
who finds Eeyore's tail.'

'I see, I see,' said Pooh, nodding his head. 'Talking
about large somethings,' he went on dreamily, 'I generally
have a small something about now – about this time in
the morning,' and he looked wistfully at the cupboard in
the corner of Owl's parlour; 'just a mouthful of con-
densed milk or what-not, with perhaps a lick of honey –'

'Well, then,' said Owl, 'we write out this notice, and we put it up all over the Forest.'

'A lick of honey,' murmured Bear to himself, 'or – or not, as the case may be.' And he gave a deep sigh, and tried very hard to listen to what Owl was saying.

But Owl went on and on, using longer and longer words, until at last he came back to where he started, and he explained that the person to write out this notice was Christopher Robin.

'It was he who wrote the ones on my front door for me. Did you see them, Pooh?'

For some time now Pooh had been saying 'Yes' and 'No' in turn, with his eyes shut, to all that Owl was saying, and having said, 'Yes, yes,' last time, he said, 'No, not at all,' now, without really knowing what Owl was talking about.

'Didn't you see them?' said Owl, a little surprised. 'Come and look at them now.'

So they went outside. And Pooh looked at the knocker and the notice below it, and he looked at the bell-rope and the notice below it, and the more he looked at the bell-rope, the more he felt he had seen something like it, somewhere else, sometime before.

'Handsome bell-rope, isn't it?' said Owl.

Pooh nodded.

'It reminds me of something,' he said, 'but I can't think what. Where did you get it?'

'I just came across it in the Forest. It was hanging over a bush, and I thought at first somebody lived there, so I rang it, and nothing happened, and then I rang it again very loudly, and it came off in my hand, and as nobody seemed to want it, I took it home, and –'

'Owl,' said Pool solemnly, 'you made a mistake. Somebody did want it.'

'Who?'

'Eeyore. My dear friend Eeyore. He was – he was fond of it.'

'Fond of it?'

'Attached to it,' said Winnie-the-Pooh sadly.

So with these words he unhooked it, and carried it back to Eeyore; and when Christopher Robin had nailed it on in its right place again, Eeyore frisked about the forest, waving his tail so happily that Winnie-the-Pooh came over all funny, and had to hurry home for a little snack of something to sustain him. And, wiping his mouth half an hour afterwards, he sang to himself proudly:

> *Who found the Tail?*
> *'I,' said Pooh,*
> *'At a quarter to two*
> *(Only it was quarter*
> *to eleven really),*
> *I found the Tail!'*

# LAURA INGALLS WILDER

FROM *Little House in the Big Woods*

Christmas was coming.

The little log house was almost buried in snow. Great drifts were banked against the walls and windows, and in the morning when Pa opened the door, there was a wall of snow as high as Laura's head. Pa took the shovel and shovelled it away, and then he shovelled a path to the barn, where the horses and cows were snug and warm in their stalls.

The days were clear and bright. Laura and Mary stood on chairs by the window and looked out across the glittering snow at the glittering trees. Snow was piled all along their bare, dark branches, and it sparkled in the sunshine. Icicles hung from the eaves of the house to the snow-banks, great icicles as large at the top as Laura's arm. They were like glass and full of sharp lights.

Pa's breath hung in the air like smoke, when he came along the path from the barn. He breathed it out in clouds and it froze in white frost on his moustache and beard.

When he came in, stamping the snow from his boots, and caught Laura up in a bear's hug against his cold, big coat, his moustache was beaded with little drops of melting frost.

Every night he was busy, working on a large piece of board and two small pieces. He whittled them with his knife, he rubbed them with sandpaper and with the palm

of his hand, until when Laura touched them they felt soft and smooth as silk.

Then with his sharp jack-knife he worked at them, cutting the edges of the large one into little peaks and towers, with a large star curved on the very tallest point. He cut little holes through the wood. He cut the holes in shapes of windows, and little stars, and crescent moons, and circles. All around them he carved tiny leaves, and flowers, and birds.

One of the little boards he shaped in a lovely curve, and around its edges he carved leaves and flowers and stars, and through it he cut crescent moons and curlicues.

Around the edges of the smallest board he carved a tiny flowering vine.

He made the tiniest shavings, cutting very slowly and carefully, making whatever he thought would be pretty.

At last he had the pieces finished and one night he fitted them together. When this was done, the large piece was a beautifully carved back for a smooth little shelf across its middle. The large star was at the very top of it. The curved piece supported the shelf underneath, and it was carved beautifully, too. And the little vine ran around the edge of the shelf.

Pa had made this bracket for a Christmas present for Ma. He hung it carefully against the log wall between the windows, and Ma stood her little china woman on the shelf.

The little china woman had a china bonnet on her head, and china curls hung against her china neck. Her china dress was laced across in front, and she wore a pale pink china apron and little gilt china shoes. She was beautiful, standing on the shelf with flowers and leaves and birds and moons carved all around her, and the large star at the very top.

Ma was busy all day long, cooking good things for Christmas. She baked self-rising bread and rye'n'Injun bread, and Swedish crackers, and a huge pan of baked beans, with salt pork and molasses. She baked vinegar pies and dried-apple pies, and filled a big jar with cookies, and she let Laura and Mary lick the cake spoon.

One morning she boiled molasses and sugar together until they made a thick syrup, and Pa brought in two pans of clean, white snow from outdoors. Laura and Mary each had a pan, and Pa and Ma showed them how to pour the dark syrup in little streams on to the snow.

They made circles, and curlicues, and squiggledy things, and these hardened at once and were candy. Laura and Mary might eat one piece each, but the rest was saved for Christmas Day.

All this was done because Aunt Eliza and Uncle Peter and the cousins, Peter and Alice and Ella, were coming to spend Christmas.

The day before Christmas they came. Laura and Mary heard the gay ringing of sleigh bells, growing louder every moment, and then the big bobsled came out of the woods and drove up to the gate. Aunt Eliza and Uncle Peter and the cousins were in it, all covered up, under blankets and robes and buffalo skins.

They were wrapped up in so many coats and mufflers and veils and shawls that they looked like big, shapeless bundles.

When they all came in, the little house was full and running over. Black Susan ran out and hid in the barn, but Jack leaped in circles through the snow, barking as though he would never stop. Now there were cousins to play with!

As soon as Aunt Eliza unwrapped them, Peter and Alice and Ella and Laura and Mary began to run and shout. At last Aunt Eliza told them to be quiet. Then Alice said:

'I'll tell you what let's do. Let's make pictures.'

Alice said they must go outdoors to do it, and Ma thought it was too cold for Laura to play outdoors. But when she saw how disappointed Laura was, she said she might go, after all, for a little while. She put on Laura's coat and mittens and the warm cape with the hood, and wrapped a muffler around her neck, and let her go.

Laura had never had so much fun. All morning she played outdoors in the snow with Alice and Ella and Peter and Mary, making pictures. The way they did it was this:

Each one by herself climbed up on a stump, and then

all at once, holding their arms out wide, they fell off the stumps into the soft, deep snow. They fell flat on their faces. Then they tried to get up without spoiling the marks they made when they fell. If they did it well, there in the snow were five holes, shaped almost exactly like four little girls and a boy, arms and legs and all. They called these their pictures.

They played so hard all day that when night came they were too excited to sleep. But they must sleep, or Santa Claus would not come. So they hung their stockings by the fireplace, and said their prayers, and went to bed — Alice and Ella and Mary and Laura all in one big bed on the floor.

# P. L. TRAVERS

FROM *Mary Poppins*

'Oh, Uncle Albert – not *again*? It's not your birthday, is it?'

And as she spoke she looked up at the ceiling. Jane and Michael looked up too and to their surprise saw a round, fat, bald man who was hanging in the air without holding on to anything. Indeed, he appeared to be *sitting* on the air, for his legs were crossed and he had just put down the newspaper which he had been reading when they came in.

'My dear,' said Mr Wigg, smiling down at the children, and looking apologetically at Mary Poppins, 'I'm very sorry, but I'm afraid it *is* my birthday.'

'Tch, tch, tch!' said Mary Poppins.

'I only remembered last night and there was no time then to send you a postcard asking you to come another day. Very distressing, isn't it?' he said, looking down at Jane and Michael.

'I can see you're rather surprised,' said Mr Wigg. And, indeed, their mouths were so wide open with astonishment that Mr Wigg, if he had been a little smaller, might almost have fallen into one of them.

'I'd better explain, I think,' Mr Wigg went on calmly. 'You see, it's this way. I'm a cheerful sort of man and very disposed to laughter. You wouldn't believe, either of you, the number of things that strike me as being funny. I can laugh at pretty nearly everything, I can.'

And with that Mr Wigg began to bob up and down, shaking with laughter at the thought of his own cheerfulness.

'Uncle Albert!' said Mary Poppins, and Mr Wigg stopped laughing with a jerk.

'Oh, beg pardon, my dear. Where was I? Oh, yes. Well, the funny thing about me is – all right, Mary, I won't laugh if I can help it! – that whenever my birthday falls on a Friday, well, it's all up with me. Absolutely UP,' said Mr Wigg.

'But why –?' began Jane.

'But how –?' began Michael.

'Well, you see, if I laugh on that particular day I become so filled with Laughing Gas that I simply can't keep on the ground. Even if I smile it happens. The first funny thought, and I'm up like a balloon. And until I can think of something serious I can't get down again.' Mr Wigg began to chuckle at that, but he caught sight of Mary Poppins' face and stopped the chuckle, and continued:

'It's awkward, of course, but not unpleasant. Never happens to either of you, I suppose?'

Jane and Michael shook their heads.

'No, I thought not. It seems to be my own special habit. Once, after I'd been to the Circus the night before, I laughed so much that – would you believe it? – I was up here for a whole twelve hours, and couldn't get down till the last stroke of midnight. Then, of course, I came down with a flop because it was Saturday and not my birthday any more. It's rather odd, isn't it? Not to say funny?

'And now here it is Friday again and my birthday, and you two and Mary P. to visit me. Oh, Lordy, Lordy, don't make me laugh, I beg of you –' But although Jane and Michael had done nothing very amusing, except to stare at him in astonishment, Mr Wigg began to laugh again loudly, and as he laughed he went bouncing and bobbing about in the air, with the newspaper rattling in his hand and his spectacles half on and half off his nose.

He looked so comic, floundering in the air like a great human bubble, clutching at the ceiling sometimes and sometimes at the gas-bracket as he passed it, that Jane and Michael, though they were trying hard to be polite, just couldn't help doing what they did. They laughed. *And* they laughed. They shut their mouths tight to prevent the laughter escaping, but that didn't do any good. And presently they were rolling over and over on the floor, squealing and shrieking with laughter.

'Really!' said Mary Poppins. 'Really, *such* behaviour!'

'I can't help it, I can't help it!' shrieked Michael, as he rolled into the fender. 'It's so terribly funny. Oh, Jane, *isn't* it funny?'

Jane did not reply, for a curious thing was happening to her. As she laughed she felt herself growing lighter and lighter, just as though she were being pumped full of air. It was a curious and delicious feeling and it made her want to laugh all the more. And then suddenly, with a bouncing bound, she felt herself jumping through the air. Michael, to his astonishment, saw her go soaring up through the room. With a little bump her head touched the ceiling and then she went bouncing along it till she reached Mr Wigg.

'*Well!*' said Mr Wigg, looking very surprised indeed. 'Don't tell me it's *your* birthday, too?' Jane shook her head.

'It's not? Then this Laughing Gas must be catching!

Hi – whoa there, look out for the mantelpiece!' This was to Michael, who had suddenly risen from the floor and was swooping through the air, roaring with laughter, and just grazing the china ornaments on the mantelpiece as he passed. He landed with a bounce right on Mr Wigg's knee.

'How do you do,' said Mr Wigg, heartily shaking Michael by the hand. 'I call this really friendly of you – bless my soul, I do! To come up to me since I couldn't come down to you – eh?' And then he and Michael looked at each other and flung back their heads and simply howled with laughter.

'I say,' said Mr Wigg to Jane, as he wiped his eyes. 'You'll be thinking I have the worst manners in the world. You're standing and you ought to be sitting – a nice young lady like you. I'm afraid I can't offer you a chair up here, but I think you'll find the air quite comfortable to sit on. I do.'

Jane tried it and found she could sit down quite comfortably on the air. She took off her hat and laid it down beside her and it hung there in space without any support at all.

'That's right,' said Mr Wigg. Then he turned and looked down at Mary Poppins.

'Well, Mary, we're fixed. And now I can inquire about *you*, my dear. I must say, I am very glad to welcome you and my two young friends here today – why, Mary, you're frowning. I'm afraid you don't approve of – er – all this.'

He waved his hand at Jane and Michael, and said hurriedly:

'I apologize, Mary, my dear. But you know how it is with me. Still, I must say I never thought my two young

friends here would catch it, really I didn't, Mary! I suppose I should have asked them for another day or tried
to think of something sad or something –'

'Well, I must say,' said Mary Poppins primly, 'that I
have never in my life seen such a sight. And at your age,
Uncle –'

'Mary Poppins, Mary Poppins, do come up!' interrupted Michael. 'Think of something funny and you'll
find it's quite easy.'

'Ah, now do, Mary!' said Mr Wigg persuasively.

'We're lonely up here without you!' said Jane, and
held out her arms towards Mary Poppins. '*Do* think of
something funny!'

'Ah, *she* doesn't need to,' said Mr Wigg sighing. 'She
can come up if she wants to, even without laughing –
and she knows it.' And he looked mysteriously and
secretly at Mary Poppins as she stood down there on the
hearth-rug.

'Well,' said Mary Poppins, 'it's all very silly and un-
dignified, but, since you're all up there and don't seem
able to get down, I suppose I'd better come up, too.'

With that, to the surprise of Jane and Michael, she put
her hands down at her sides and without a laugh, without
even the faintest glimmer of a smile, she shot up through
the air and sat down beside Jane.

'How many times, I should like to know,' she said
snappily, 'have I told you to take off your coat when you
come into a hot room?' And she unbuttoned Jane's coat
and laid it neatly on the air beside the hat.

'That's right, Mary, that's right,' said Mr Wigg contentedly, as he leant down and put his spectacles on the
mantelpiece. 'Now we're all comfortable –'

'There's comfort *and* comfort,' sniffed Mary Poppins.

'And we can have tea,' Mr Wigg went on, apparently not noticing her remark. And then a startled look came over his face.

'My goodness!' he said. 'How dreadful! I've just realized – the table's down there and we're up here. What *are* we going to do? We're here and it's there. It's an awful tragedy – awful! But oh, it's terribly comic!' And he hid his face in his handkerchief and laughed loudly into it. Jane and Michael, though they did not want to miss the crumpets and the cakes, couldn't help laughing too, because Mr Wigg's mirth was so infectious.

Mr Wigg dried his eyes.

'There's only one thing for it,' he said. 'We must think of something serious. Something sad, very sad. And then we shall be able to get down. Now – one, two, three! Something *very* sad, mind you!'

They thought and thought, with their chins on their hands.

Michael thought of school, and that one day he would have to go there. But even that seemed funny today and he had to laugh.

Jane thought: 'I shall be grown up in another fourteen years!' But that didn't sound sad at all but quite nice and rather funny. She could not help smiling at the thought of herself grown up, with long skirts and a handbag.

'There was my poor old Aunt Emily,' thought Mr Wigg out loud. 'She was run over by an omnibus. Sad. Very sad. Unbearably sad. Poor Aunt Emily. But they saved her umbrella. That was funny, wasn't it?' And before he knew where he was, he was heaving and trembling and bursting with laughter at the thought of Aunt Emily's umbrella.

'It's no good,' he said, blowing his nose. 'I give it up. And my young friends here seem to be no better at sadness than I am. Mary, can't *you* do something? We want our tea.'

To this day Jane and Michael cannot be sure of what happened then. All they know for certain is that, as soon as Mr Wigg had appealed to Mary Poppins, the table below began to wriggle on its legs. Presently it was swaying dangerously, and then with a rattle of china and with cakes lurching off their plates on to the cloth, the table came soaring through the room, gave one graceful turn, and landed beside them so that Mr Wigg was at its head.

'Good girl!' said Mr Wigg, smiling proudly upon her. 'I knew you'd fix something. Now, will you take the foot of the table and pour out, Mary? And the guests on either side of me. That's the idea,' he said, as Michael ran bobbing through the air and sat down on Mr Wigg's right. Jane was at his left hand. There they were, all together, up in the air and the table between them. Not a single piece of bread-and-butter or a lump of sugar had been left behind.

Mr Wigg smiled contentedly.

'It is usual, I think, to begin with bread-and-butter,' he said to Jane and Michael, 'but as it's my birthday we will begin the wrong way – which I always think is the *right* way – with the Cake!'

And he cut a large slice for everybody.

# GEOFFREY TREASE

FROM *Bows Against the Barons*

'We – want – the Sheriff!' rose the shout again. Dickon had not recognized a face from Sherwood, but he knew that they were all about him, disguised in the dust and rags of pedlars and pilgrims. When the signal was given, bows would appear from nowhere, and the King's men would fall as freely as the King's deer.

Hardly had the last word of that tremendous roar died away than a sudden hush fell on the throng. Like a forest fire, the news sprang from lip to lip. The Sheriff was coming!

Dickon stood on tiptoe and craned his neck.

A double rank of pikemen was advancing slowly through the crowd on the Norman side of the wall. Sullenly the people gave back. Those who were nearest the pikemen were in no hurry to feel the sharp points between their ribs.

'Halt!' barked a voice. The two ranks turned, stepped back, and crossed their pikes, leaving a clear avenue fenced with two lines of steel. Down it rode the Sheriff.

He drew rein at the wall and stared at the bridle-smith on the top of it. Words passed between them, but few could catch what they were.

Suddenly the smith turned and cried to the waiting throng: 'Friends!'

There was a roar of encouragement. When it died away, he went on quickly:

'Neighbours, whoever you are, Normans or Saxons –'

Once more the vast crowd shouted its agreement.

'Our lords and masters will not listen to our demands! So the poor may go hungry while the rich eat themselves sick – and honest men may go to jail for saying so –'

The two nearest pikemen, at a signal from the Sheriff, lunged at him, but he hopped nimbly away. There was a rush of pikemen towards him, and he waited only to utter one last shout before leaping down into safety among the people.

'To the jail, my hearties!'

To the jail!

Suddenly everyone was shouting again as though he were mad. There was a great surge forward, which carried Dickon along with it, as helpless as a twig in a rushing stream. Sticks and other weapons were brandished overhead.

Then the crowd surged back again, and Dickon with them, the breath almost choked out of his body.

I didn't know fighting was like this, he thought ruefully to himself. I can't draw my knife, I can't lift my stick, and I can't even see the enemy. I'm packed as tight as a fish in a barrel.

After a minute or two he was able to scramble on to the wall and see what was happening.

Slowly, fighting step by step, the people were giving back before the remorseless spear-points of the Sheriff's men. Wool jersey and leather apron could not stand against such weapons, and sticks could make no impression on mail coats and steel helmets. Growling like a wounded animal, the crowd walked backwards before that unbroken line.

Part of the square was already cleared, except for a

body here and there, or a wounded man crawling away with shattered collarbone or bleeding limb. The Sheriff rode backwards and forwards behind his men, hounding them on to further efforts.

'Whip them home to their kennels, the puppies!' He twirled his moustaches angrily – and at that moment an egg shattered itself on the nosepiece of his helmet, and spread over most of his face. 'Get the man who threw that!' he screamed. 'I'll have him dancing on air tonight!'

Where was Robin Hood?

Anxious looks were turning every way. He had promised his help, and in a few minutes it would be too late. The crowd would be pushed back into the narrow streets and broken up.

Suddenly a horn rang out. Dickon's heart jumped. He knew that note.

Sixty men leapt on to the wall. They looked like honest country people come to market – one or two, even, wore the skirts and shawls of peasant women – but in every left hand was a six-foot bow, in every right hand a cloth-yard arrow. In a second, every bow was bent, a goose-feather tip drawn to each outlaw's ear.

The crowd had slipped back a little, leaving a clear space in front of the stupefied pikemen. It was safe to shoot.

'Let us pass in peace,' came the high, bell-like voice of Robin Hood. 'Otherwise –'

'Charge!' snarled the Sheriff, urging his horse forward.

'Shoot!' retorted the outlaw.

Sixty shafts gleamed for a moment in the sunshine. They rattled on chain-mail and steel, but some pierced the links and others struck unprotected face and hand

and leg. Several of the men-at-arms crashed forward on
their faces. The whole line wavered, glaring nervously at
the next flight of arrows ready on the string.

This was the bridle-smith's chance. 'To the jail, lads,'
he yelled again, and once more the crowd swept forward.

The pikemen cowered before a second volley of shafts,
and before they knew where they were, they were surrounded. Brawny hands wrenched their pikes from them,
boys tripped them up, and others leapt on their backs
from behind. There was no room to draw their swords.
They were helpless and overpowered.

To the jail! Dickon was well to the fore in the race.
They ran across the empty end of the square like a high
tide. The Sheriff, still partly blinded by his egg, was
pushed aside, his terrified horse rearing and threatening
to bolt. His one concern for the present was to keep in
the saddle.

Hatchets and crowbars were plentiful enough. It was the work of a minute to break down the door of the jail, and of another minute to bring out the prisoners, pale but smiling, into the open air. They were wise enough to make themselves scarce at once.

Not a moment too soon. The cry was raised: 'Horsemen from the Castle! Look out!'

From Friar Lane, the winding, rutted track which led from the market-place to the Castle, came the thunderous drumming of hoofs, the furious rattle of harness and arms.

'All right, lads. We've done what we wanted,' bellowed the bridle-smith. 'Home now. No sense in broken heads for nothing.'

'Back to Sherwood!' sang Robin somewhere near at hand.

Dickon ran with the rest. The horsemen charged in pursuit, lances levelled, long cruel swords swinging. The crowd melted like magic, vanishing into by-streets and alleys, dodging under the archways and the covered sidewalks, anywhere the riders could not follow them. Every now and again a goose-feathered shaft sped from behind a pillar, and a horseman crashed on the cobbles. The outlaws were doing their best to cover the retreat of the townsfolk.

One horseman made for Dickon, his long lance aimed at his heart. Dickon slipped under an overhanging gallery, but it was no use, the lance could reach him there. Out of the corner of his eye he saw a low archway leading into a lane. He ducked as the gleaming point came at him, slipped on the cobbles, and almost threw himself to safety. The man tried to follow, only to bump his head and wheel back, cursing, in search of easier prey.

# JOHN MASEFIELD

## from *A Box of Delights*

Now at last, Kay felt that he was free to look at the Box of Delights. He went up to his bedroom, but even there he was not sure that he could guard himself from being seen. Remembering how those spies had been peering in at the window the night before and how the repulsive Rat had crept about in the secret passages finding out all sorts of things, he locked both doors and hung caps over the keyholes, looked under the beds and finally, as in the past when he had wished to hide from his governess Sylvia Pouncer, he crept under the valance of his dressing-table. No one could possibly see him there.

The Box was of some very hard wood of a very dense grain, covered with shagreen which was black with age and sometimes worn away to show the wood beneath. Both wood and shagreen had been polished until they were as smooth as polished metal. On the side there was a little counter-sunk groove in the midst of which was a knob in the shape of a tiny golden rosebud.

Kay pressed the knob and at once from within the Box there came a crying of birds. As he listened he heard the stockdove brooding, the cuckoo tolling, blackbirds, thrushes and nightingales singing. Then a far-away cock crowed thrice and the Box slowly opened. Inside he saw what he took to be a book, the leaves of which were all chased and worked with multitudinous figures, and the effect that it gave him was that of staring into an opening in a wood. It was lit from within and he saw that the tiny things that were shifting there were the petals of may-blossom from giant hawthorn trees covered with flowers. The hawthorns stood on each side of the entrance to the forest, which was dark from the great trees yet dappled with light. Now, as he looked into it, he saw deer glide with alert ears, then a fox, motionless at his earth, a rabbit moving to new pasture and nibbling at a dandelion and the snouts of the moles breaking the wet earth. All the forest was full of life, all the birds were singing, insects humming, dragonflies darting, butterflies wavering and settling. It was so clear that he could see the flies on the leaves brushing their heads and wings with their legs. 'It's all alive and it's full of summer, there are all the birds singing, there's a linnet, a bullfinch, a robin, and that's a little wren.' Others were singing too: different kinds of tits, the woodpecker drilling, the chiff-chaff repeating his name, the yellowhammer and garden-warbler, and overhead, as the bird went swiftly past, came the sad, laughing cry of the curlew. While he gazed into the heart of summer and listened to the murmur and the singing, he heard another noise like the tinkling of little bells.

'Where did I hear that noise before?' Kay said to himself. He remembered that strange rider who had passed him in the street the day before. That rider, who seemed to have little silver chains dangling from his wrists, had jingled so.

'Oh,' Kay said as he looked, 'there's someone wonderful coming.'

At first he thought the figure was one of those giant red deer, long since extinct, with enormous antlers. Then he saw that it was a great man, antlered at the brow, dressed in deerskin and moving with the silent, slow grace of a stag, yet hung about with little silver chains and bells.

Kay knew at once that this was Herne the Hunter, of whom he had often heard. 'Ha, Kay,' Herne said, 'are you coming into my wild wood?'

'Yes please, sir,' Kay said. Herne stretched out his hand, Kay took it and there he was in the forest between the two hawthorn trees, with the petals of the may-blossom falling on him. All the may-blossoms that fell were talking to him and he was aware of what all the creatures of the forest were saying to each other, what the birds were singing and what it was that the flowers and trees were thinking. And he realized that the forest went on and on for ever and all of it was full of life beyond anything that he had ever imagined, for in the trees, on each leaf and every twig and in every inch of soil there were ants, grubs, worms, little tiny, moving things, incredibly small and yet all thrilling with life.

'Oh dear,' Kay said, 'I shall never know a hundredth part of all the things there are to know.'

'You will, if you stay with me,' Herne the Hunter said. 'Would you like to be a stag with me in the wild wood?'

There was Kay in the green wood, beside a giant stag, so screened with the boughs that they were a part of a dappled pattern of light and shade and the news of the wood came to him in scents upon the wind. They moved off out of the green wood into a rolling grassland where some fox-cubs were playing with a vixen, and presently came down to a pool where moorhens were cocking about in the water, under the fierce eye of a crested grebe. It was lovely, Kay thought, to feel the water cool upon the feet after running, 'and it's lovely too,' he thought, 'to have hard feet and not get sharp bits of twigs into one's soles.' They moved through the water towards some reeds where Kay saw a multitude of wild duck.

'Would you like to be a wild duck, Kay?' Herne asked.

At once, with a great clatter of feathers, the wild duck rose more and more and more, going high up, and, oh joy! Herne and Kay were with them, flying on wings of their own and Kay could just see that his neck was glinting green. There was the pool, blue as a piece of sky below them and the sky above brighter than he had ever seen it. They flew higher and higher in great sweeps and presently they saw the sea like the dark blue on a map.

'Now for the plunge!' Herne cried and instantly they were surging down swiftly and still more swiftly and the pool was rushing up at them and they all went skimming into it with a long, scuttering, rippling splash. And there they all were, paddling together, happy to be in water again.

'How beautiful the water is,' Kay said. Indeed it was beautiful, clear hill-water, with little fish darting this way and that and the weeds waving.

'Would you like to be a fish, Kay?' Herne asked, and instantly Kay was a fish. He and Herne were there in the coolness and dimness, wavering as the water wavered and feeling a cold spring gurgling up just underneath them, tickling their tummies.

While Kay was enjoying the water Herne asked, 'Did you see the Wolves in the wood?'

'No,' Kay said.

'Well, they were there,' Herne said, 'that was why I moved. Did you see the hawks in the air?'

'No,' Kay said.

'Well, they were there,' Herne said, 'and that was why I plunged. And do you see the pike in the weeds?'

'No,' Kay said.

'He is there,' Herne said. 'Look!'

Looking ahead up the stream Kay saw a darkness of weeds wavering in the water and presently a part of the darkness wavered into a shape with eyes that gleamed and hooky teeth that showed. Kay saw that the eyes were fixed upon himself and suddenly the dark shadow leaped swiftly forward with a swirl of water. But Kay and Herne were out of the water. They were trotting happily together over the grass towards the forest, Herne a giant figure with the antlers of the red stag and himself a little figure with budding antlers. And so they trotted together to a great ruined oak tree, so old that all within was hollow, though the great shell still put forth twigs and leaves.

Somehow the figure of Herne became like the oak tree and merged into it till Kay could see nothing but the tree. What had been Herne's antlers were now a few old branches and what had seemed silver chains dangling from Herne's wrists were now the leaves rustling. The oak tree faded and grew smaller till it was a dark point in a sunny glade, and there was Kay standing between the two hawthorn trees which were shedding their blossoms upon him. These too shrank until they were as tiny as the works of a watch and then Kay was himself again under the valance in his room at Seekings, looking at the first page in the Book of Delights contained within the Box.

'No wonder the old man called it a Box of Delights,' Kay said. 'Now I wonder how long I was in that fairyland with Herne the Hunter?' He looked at his watch and found that it was ten minutes to eleven. He had been away only two minutes.

# NOEL STREATFEILD

FROM *Ballet Shoes*

You would have thought that a man who lived for nothing but fossils would have felt there was little left to do when he couldn't go and look for them any more, but Gum wasn't that sort of man.

'I have travelled a lot on land, my dear,' he said to Sylvia, 'but very little by sea. Now I shall really see the world. And maybe I'll be finding something interesting to bring back.'

'There's no need to do that, sir,' Nana broke in firmly. 'The house is full enough as it is. We don't want a lot of carved elephants and that about the place.'

'Carved elephants!' Gum gave Nana a scornful look. 'The world is full of entrancements, woman, any of which I might bring home, and you talk to me of carved elephants!'

But Nana held her ground.

'All right, sir; I'm sure I'm pleased you should see these entrancements, as you call them, but you let them bide. We want nothing more in this house.'

The entrancement that Gum actually brought home was Pauline.

The ship on which he was travelling struck an iceberg, and all the passengers had to take to the boats. In the night one of the boats filled with water and the passengers were thrown into the sea. Gum's boat went to the rescue, but by the time it got there everybody was drowned except a baby who was lying cooing happily on a lifebelt. Gum collected the baby and wrapped her in his coat, and when they were at last rescued by a liner and taken to England, tried to find someone to own her. That was the trouble. Nobody knew for sure whose baby she was; there had been other babies on board, and three were missing. She must go to an orphanage for female orphans, said everybody; but Gum stuck in his toes. Things he found went to the Cromwell Road. He had meant to bring Sylvia back a present. Now, what could be better than this? He fussed and fumed while the adoption papers were made out, then he tucked the baby into the crook of his left arm, took his shabby old hold-all in his right, and rather dot and carry one because of his game leg, walked to the railway station, and went home to London and the Cromwell Road.

Gum, to whom time meant very little indeed, was never able to remember that other people might not be expecting him when he turned up without a word of warning after being away for months. This time he opened his front door, put down his hold-all, and looked round for a suitable place to put the baby. Seeing nowhere but the hall table or the umbrella stand, he called rather angrily for Sylvia.

'Hi, Sylvia! Good gracious me, I keep a pack of women in this house and none of them are about when they are wanted.'

Nana and Sylvia were upstairs marking some new sheets. Nana stopped working, her needle held up as though it were a magic wand which could command silence.

'Hark. Isn't that the Professor's voice?'

Sylvia harked, and in a moment was down the stairs with Nana panting behind.

'Darling Gum, why didn't you let me know you were coming?'

Her uncle kissed her.

'Why should I waste a stamp? Look' – he pushed the baby into her arms – 'I've brought you a present.'

Sylvia pulled the shawl back from the bundle he handed her, and then looked round at Nana, and said in a startled but pleased whisper:

'A baby!'

'A baby!' Nana almost jumped the two last stairs and snatched the child from Sylvia. She turned and faced Gum. 'Really, sir, I don't know what you'll be bringing to the house next. Who do you suppose has time to look after a baby?'

'I thought all woman liked babies,' Gum protested.

'That's as may be.' Nana was pink with rage. 'If Miss Sylvia has any sense she won't take it –'

She broke off, because the baby gave a sudden coo which made her look at it for the first time. Her face changed and seemed to melt, and she began to make noises such as everybody makes to babies. Then suddenly she looked up fiercely at Sylvia.

'Which rooms am I to have for my nurseries?'

Nana coming round like that of course settled the baby's fate. She was given Sylvia's old nurseries at the top of the house, and Nana became her slave, and Sylvia loved doing things for her when she was allowed (which wasn't often) as Nana believed in 'having my nurseries to myself'. Cook and the housemaid considered the baby a figure of romance. 'Might be anybody, even royalty, saved like that from the ravening waves,' Cook would say at the kitchen meals, and the housemaid would sigh and agree with her.

There was some trouble over calling her Pauline. Sylvia chose the name, as she said Saint Paul was rescued from the sea, so it was suitable. Gum, however, wanted to call her after one of his pet fossils, but Nana refused to allow it.

'Babies in my nurseries, sir,' she said firmly, 'never have had outlandish names, and they're not starting now. Miss Sylvia has chosen Pauline, and it's a nice sensible name, and called after a blessed saint, and no other name is going to be used, if you will forgive me speaking plain, sir.'

A year later Gum brought Sylvia a second baby. On his travels this time his leg had given him trouble, and he had been landed and put into hospital. There he had made friends with a Russian, a shabby, depressed fellow who yet somehow conveyed the impression that he hadn't always been shabby and depressed, but had once worn gay uniforms and had swung laughing through the snow in his jingling sleigh amidst rows of bowing peasants. This man had left Russia during the revolution, and he and his wife had tried to train themselves to earn a living. They had not been a success as wage-earners, and the wife became ill and died, leaving a small baby. When the man Boris was going to die too, the nurses in the hospital were most concerned.

'What shall we do?' they said. 'Because there is his little baby in the children's ward.'

'Don't trouble about that,' Gum had answered airily. 'We have one baby at home that I have adopted. We shall have another.'

Sylvia called this baby Petrova, as she had to have a Russian name, and it sounded a bit like Peter, and Nana thought that if one child were called after an apostle the other should be.

Nana did not even talk about not taking the baby this time. There were the nurseries, and there was Pauline.

'Very nice for Pauline to have a companion,' she said. Then she looked at Petrova, who was a dark, sallow baby, very different from the golden-haired, pink-and-white Pauline. 'Let's hope this one has brains, for it's easy to see who's going to be Miss Plain in my nursery.'

Although Nana was quite pleased to welcome Petrova, she spoke firmly to Gum.

'Now, sir, before you go away again, do get it into your head this house is not a crèche. Two babies in the nursery is right and proper, and such as the best homes have a right to expect, but two is enough. Bring one more and I give notice, and then where'd you be, with you and Miss Sylvia knowing no more of babies than you do of hens?'

Perhaps it was fear of what Nana might say, but the last baby Gum did not deliver himself. He sent her round by district messenger in a basket. With her he sent a pair of ballet shoes and a letter. The letter said:

Dear Niece,

Here is yet another Fossil to add to those in my nursery. This is the little daughter of a dancer. The father has just died, and the poor young mother has no time for babies, so I said I would have her. All her mother had to give her child was the little pair of shoes enclosed. I regret not to bring the child myself, but today I ran into a friend with a yacht who is visiting some strange islands. I am joining him, and expect to be away some years. I have arranged for the bank to see after money for you for the next five years, but before then I shall be home.

Your affectionate uncle,

Matthew

PS Her name is Posy. Unfortunate, but true.

The sudden arrival of little Posy caused an upset in the nursery. Nana it was who took in the basket, and when Sylvia got in and went up to see the baby, she found her crumpled and rather pink, lying face downwards on Nana's flannel-aproned knee. Nana was holding an enormous powder puff, and she looked up as Sylvia came in.

'This is too much, this is,' she said severely.

She shook a spray of fuller's earth over the baby.

Sylvia looked humble.

'I quite agree, Nana. But what are we to do? Here she is.'

Nana looked angrily at Posy.

'It isn't right. Here we are with Pauline rising four, and Petrova sixteen months, and down you pop this little fly-by-night. Two's enough, I've always said. I told the Professor so perfectly plain. Who is she? That's another thing I'd like to know.'

'Well her name's Posy, and her mother is a dancer.'

'Posy! With the other two called as nice as can be after the Holy Apostles, that's a foolish sort of name.' Nana gave a snort of disgust, and then, in case the baby should feel hurt, added 'Blessed lamb.'

'Right.' Sylvia turned to the door. 'Now I know how you feel, I'll make other arrangements for her, perhaps an orphanage . . .'

'Orphanage!' Nana's eyes positively blazed. She pulled a tiny vest over Posy's unprotesting little head. 'Who's thinking of orphanages? The Professor's taken her, and here she stays. But no more, and that's my last word.'

'Well, I don't suppose there can be any more for a bit,' Sylvia said hopefully. 'He's gone away for some time, perhaps for five years.'

'Better make it ten,' said Nana, giving Posy a quick

kiss. 'That'll give us a chance.'

About four months later a box arrived at the house in the Cromwell Road, addressed to 'The Little Fossils'. Inside were three necklaces: a turquoise one with 'Pauline' on it; a tiny string of seed pearls marked 'Petrova', and a row of coral for Posy.

'Well,' said Nana, fastening the necklaces round the children's necks. 'I expect that's the last we shall hear of him for some time.'

She was quite right.

# EVE GARNETT

FROM *The Family from One End Street*

The brilliant thought occurred to Lily Rose that it would be an excellent idea and also her 'good deed' for the day (she was a Girl Guide) if she were to finish off the ironing by the time her mother returned. It would be a lovely surprise, and at the same time a way of showing what she could do once she really had a free hand.

The irons were heating on the fire, and Lily Rose, without further hesitation, threw off her hat and coat, rolled up her sleeves, spread out a garment on the ironing blanket and seized one. Forgetting the stand, she put the iron down for a moment on the ironing sheet. Immediately a rich smell of burning blanket filled the room, and Lily Rose was sorry to see a large smouldering hole. She hastily put the iron on the stand and waited patiently for it to cool, testing the heat at intervals by the simple and professional method of spitting on her finger and dabbing it quickly on the iron. After some minutes of this she decided the iron was ready and set to work on a baby's overall. She made quite a good job of this and hung it proudly over a chairback to air, and, encouraged by such success, embarked upon the next garment – a green artificial silk petticoat. Now Lily Rose had heard much talk about the difficulties and dangers of ironing artificial silk, and, although she had never attempted such a thing before, she was not deterred; the great thing, she knew, was not to have too hot an iron. She spread out the petticoat carefully, took what she thought to be the cool iron from the stove and began. She made one long sweep up and down with the iron, and oh! what was happening! The petticoat was shrinking ... shrinking ... shrivelling up ... running away before her eyes! Smaller and smaller it grew, while Lily Rose gazed fascinated and as if rooted to the spot, her eyes and mouth round 'o's' of horror!

At last the shrinking seemed to stop and there it lay, the beautiful green silk petticoat, no bigger than a doll's – too small even for William – had he worn such things!

Poor Lily Rose! The smoking iron-holder in her hand soon told her that she had taken the hot iron from the fire by mistake, and, of course, artificial silk –! Lily Rose put the iron back on the fire, sat down on a pile of airing sheets and wept!

Five minutes later the door opened and in came Mrs Ruggles with William in her arms and Peg hanging on to her skirt. 'Goodness gracious, what a smell of burning!' she cried, 'something's scorching!' and then, catching sight of the tearful Lily Rose: 'What you here so early for – been sent home from school? – In my day we got kept *in* not let *out*.' Then, as Lily Rose made no reply, 'You're not *hurt*?'

But Lily Rose was past speech; she could only point to the table where the remains of the petticoat lay.

'Whatever *is* the matter?' cried Mrs Ruggles. 'Speak, *do*. I can see you've been and burnt my ironing blanket, anyway, and what's this thing?' she added, going up to the table. 'Doll's clothes? *How often have I told you not to touch the irons when I'm out!*'

'It's not doll's clothes,' wept Lily Rose, now very

tearful indeed. 'It's a customer's petticoat; we was all sent home early (sniff) because there was a flood (sniff), and I was trying to help you and do my good deed for the day (sniff) for the Guides (several sniffs).'

Mrs Ruggles was very angry. Although she lost handkerchiefs and *did* shrink woollens occasionally, she was a good and careful worker, and in all her long career as a laundress had certainly never reduced a garment to one-sixth of its original size!

'That petticoat belongs to Mrs Beaseley up at The Laurels in Sycamore Road – one of my best customers, I'd have you know,' she cried. 'Both her children have a clean frock a day each in the summer, and I've given her satisfaction for over three years! It will have to be replaced, and a nice expense *that's* going to be! "Good deed" *in*deed! Well, it don't look like it to me, and I've no patience with these Guides – seems to me Guiding's about the last thing they do. Tomorrow you'll come with me to Mrs Beaseley's and explain as it was you and not your mother, who's a careful, hard-working, reliable laundress, as spoilt her nice petticoat, and she'll have something to say to you, I shouldn't wonder; and you'll get no jam for tea today, and no cake on Sunday neither. Now then, stop that sniffing, put the kettle on and get the tea.'

The next morning Lily Rose and her mother set off to return Mrs Beaseley's laundry.

If only, thought Lily Rose, it hadn't been Saturday! Then she would have been safe at school. But, instead, here she was, helping her mother, still very cross with her, to carry the laundry basket with one hand, and clasping the remains of the green silk petticoat done up in a parcel in the other. And what she felt like inside –

ough! Sick at the very thought of Mrs Beaseley and her house and her fat cook who usually opened the back door to them and made silly remarks. What remarks she'd make today! And Mrs Beaseley herself! Probably she would be going to a party on Sunday and want to wear her beautiful petticoat; perhaps she might even say that Mrs Ruggles must buy her one by this evening, and how awful that would be! Both the twins and Mr Ruggles had had their boots soled this week, and Mr Ruggles's auntie had died and they'd sent a wreath which cost a whole 3s. 6d. – the family funds were very low, she knew. Worse still, perhaps Mrs Beaseley would say Mrs Ruggles needn't wash for her any more after this. And the silly part of it all was that she, Lily Rose, had meant to be so kind and give Mrs Ruggles a surprise. Life was a puzzle, she decided.

At last they reached the house, and Lily Rose, wishing she were dead twice over, knocked at the back door. That fat cook opened it.

'Early today, Mrs Ruggles,' she said. 'Got a helper, I see; come right in and wait a minute, will you?'

Just at that moment Mrs Beaseley herself came into the kitchen. 'Good morning, Mrs Ruggles,' she said, 'you're early today. Is this one of your large family – I don't think I've seen her before? I expect she'd like a glass of lemonade or some cake, wouldn't she?'

'She'd *like* it all right, thank you,' replied Mrs Ruggles, 'but she don't *deserve* it!'

'How's that?' said Mrs Beaseley, turning to Lily Rose, but with such a twinkle in her eye that that young lady felt better at once.

'You tell Mrs Beaseley yourself,' commanded Mrs Ruggles.

'Well, come in and have the cake first, and tell me after,' said Mrs Beaseley. 'Bertha,' she called to the fat cook, 'get a cup of tea for Mrs Ruggles and some cake for the little girl' – she turned to Lily Rose – 'I don't know your name?'

'Please, it's Lily Rose,' said the child shyly – she *hated* telling her name – people so nearly always laughed. But Mrs Beaseley didn't laugh. Surprisingly instead, she said, 'What a pretty name! I don't think anyone with such a nice name could do anything *very* dreadful, do you?' And she smiled so kindly that Lily Rose nearly began to cry again.

'Silly fool I am,' she said to herself, 'she's ever so kind.'

They went into the kitchen, and while Mrs Ruggles drank her tea and Lily Rose ate her cake – she took a good slice for she knew she wasn't going to have any next day at home – Mrs Beaseley asked after Mr Ruggles and the family, and especially the progress of William.

'Grows fine he does,' said Mrs Ruggles, pleased and smiling again at such interest in her family. 'Nurse says he's the best baby at the Welfare Centre – I takes him there once a week to be weighed.'

'You'll have to send him to the baby show in July, Mrs Ruggles,' said Mrs Beaseley.

'Well, *I'd* like to,' said Mrs Ruggles, 'but his father don't hold with them. He gets *Ideas* in his Head, Ruggles does,' she added.

'I'd like to meet your husband, Mrs Ruggles,' laughed Mrs Beaseley. 'I come across so few people with ideas in their heads!'

Lily Rose stared. This was a new way of looking at things. Her own head was always full of ideas – too many it seemed. Yesterday's trouble had been an idea – if only she could explain that to Mrs Beaseley perhaps she wouldn't mind quite so much about her petticoat.

Just then the fat cook returned with the empty laundry basket. 'I'm afraid there's something missing, Mrs Ruggles,' she said. 'There's one green and one pink petticoat on the list, the pink one is here all right – I'm afraid you've forgotten to put in the other.'

Mrs Ruggles looked at Lily Rose, and Lily Rose looked at Mrs Ruggles, while Mrs Beaseley looked inquiringly at them both. 'Please Miss – Madam I mean,' began Lily Rose breathlessly. 'It was an idea (gasp) – I mean I had an idea. I ironed your petticoat to surprise Mum and (gasp), because I'm a Guide and have to do a good deed every day. I didn't mean to spoil it (gasp) – truly I didn't – I used the hot iron by mistake and the stuff ran away soon as I touched it (gasp) – and oh, please, *do* you think you could wear the pink one if you go to a party tomorrow and wait till next week for Mum to get you another (gasp) – because you see Dad and the twins all had their boots soled, and Auntie died (gasp) and we sent a wreath and . . .' thrusting the parcel into Mrs Beaseley's hands, Lily Rose burst into tears.

But when Mrs Beaseley undid the parcel and saw her petticoat *she* burst out laughing. 'I never saw anything so funny!' she cried, 'I should *love* to have seen it running away from the iron – it doesn't matter a bit, Mrs Ruggles. It was a cheap petticoat, and I know artificial silk behaves like that sometimes if the iron is too hot. Cheer up, Lily Rose. Even if your ideas aren't always a success it's a good thing to have them, and I'm sure you meant to do a good deed. I used to be a Guide once,' she added, 'and I've made lots of mistakes over good deeds in my time.

Cheer up now and have some cake and tell me what you're going to do when you leave school?'

There was a long pause. Lily Rose sniffed. 'I want to run a laundry,' she said shyly at last.

# J. R. R. TOLKIEN

FROM *The Hobbit*

There they all sat glum and wet and muttering, while Oin and Gloin went on trying to light the fire, and quarrelling about it. Bilbo was sadly reflecting that adventures are not all pony-rides in May-sunshine, when Balin, who was always their look-out man, said: 'There's a light over there!' There was a hill some way off with trees on it, pretty thick in parts. Out of the dark mass of the trees they could now see a light shining, a reddish comfortable-looking light, as it might be a fire or torches twinkling.

When they had looked at it for some while, they fell to arguing. Some said 'no' and some said 'yes'. Some said they could but go and see, and anything was better than little supper, less breakfast, and wet clothes all the night.

Others said: 'These parts are none too well known, and are too near the mountains. Travellers seldom come this way now. The old maps are no use: things have changed for the worse and the road is unguarded. They have seldom even heard of the king round here, and the less inquisitive you are as you go along, the less trouble you are likely to find.' Some said: 'After all there are fourteen of us.' Others said: 'Where has Gandalf got to?' This remark was repeated by everybody. Then the rain began to pour down worse than ever, and Oin and Gloin began to fight.

That settled it. 'After all we have got a burglar with us,' they said; and so they made off, leading their ponies (with all due and proper caution) in the direction of the light. They came to the hill and were soon in the wood. Up the hill they went; but there was no proper path to be seen, such as might lead to a house or a farm; and do what they could they made a deal of rustling and crackling and creaking (and a good deal of grumbling and dratting), as they went through the trees in the pitch dark.

Suddenly the red light shone out very bright through the tree-trunks not far ahead.

'Now it is the burglar's turn,' they said, meaning Bilbo. 'You must go on and find out all about that light, and what it is for, and if all is perfectly safe and canny,' said Thorin to the hobbit. 'Now scuttle off, and come back quick, if all is well. If not, come back if you can! If you can't, hoot twice like a barn-owl and once like a screech-owl, and we will do what we can.'

Off Bilbo had to go, before he could explain that he could not hoot even once like any kind of owl any more than fly like a bat. But at any rate hobbits can move quietly in woods, absolutely quietly. They take a pride in it, and Bilbo had sniffed more than once at what he called 'all this dwarvish racket', as they went along, though I don't suppose you or I would have noticed anything at all on a windy night, not if the whole cavalcade had passed two feet off. As for Bilbo walking primly towards the red light, I don't suppose even a weasel would have stirred a whisker at it. So, naturally, he got right up to the fire – for fire it was – without disturbing anyone. And this is what he saw.

Three very large persons sitting round a very large

fire of beech-logs. They were toasting mutton on long spits of wood, and licking the gravy off their fingers. There was a fine toothsome smell. Also there was a barrel of good drink at hand, and they were drinking out of jugs. But they were trolls. Obviously trolls. Even Bilbo, in spite of his sheltered life, could see that: from the great heavy faces of them, and their size, and the shape of their legs, not to mention their language, which was not drawing-room fashion at all, at all.

'Mutton yesterday, mutton today, and blimey, if it don't look like mutton again tomorrer,' said one of the trolls.

'Never a blinking bit of manflesh have we had for long enough,' said a second. 'What the 'ell William was a-thinkin' of to bring us into these parts at all, beats me — and the drink runnin' short, what's more,' he said jogging the elbow of William, who was taking a pull at his jug.

William choked. 'Shut yer mouth!' he said as soon as he could. 'Yer can't expect folk to stop here for ever just to be et by you and Bert. You've et a village and a half between yer, since we come down from the mountains. How much more d'yer want? And time's been up our way, when yer'd have said "thank yer Bill" for a nice bit o' fat valley mutton like what this is.' He took a big bite off a sheep's leg he was toasting, and wiped his lips on his sleeve.

Yes, I am afraid trolls do behave like that, even those with only one head each. After hearing all this Bilbo ought to have done something at once. Either he should have gone back quietly and warned his friends that there were three fair-sized trolls at hand in a nasty mood, quite likely to try toasted dwarf, or even pony, for a change; or else he should have done a bit of good quick burgling.

A really first-class and legendary burglar would at this
point have picked the trolls' pockets – it is nearly always
worthwhile, if you can manage it – pinched the very
mutton off the spits, purloined the beer, and walked off
without their noticing him. Others more practical but
with less professional pride would perhaps have stuck a
dagger into each of them before they observed it. Then
the night could have been spent cheerily.

Bilbo knew it. He had read of a good many things he
had never seen or done. He was very much alarmed, as
well as disgusted; he wished himself a hundred miles
away, and yet – and yet somehow he could not go
straight back to Thorin and Company empty-handed. So
he stood and hesitated in the shadows. Of the various
burglarious proceedings he had heard of, picking the
trolls' pockets seemed the least difficult, so at last he
crept behind a tree just behind William.

Bert and Tom went off to the barrel. William was
having another drink. Then Bilbo plucked up courage
and put his little hand in William's enormous pocket.
There was a purse in it, as big as a bag to Bilbo. 'Ha!'
thought he warming to his new work as he lifted it
carefully out, 'this is a beginning!'

It was! Trolls' purses are the mischief, and this was no
exception. ''Ere, 'oo are you?' it squeaked, as it left the
pocket; and William turned round at once and grabbed
Bilbo by the neck, before he could duck behind the tree.

'Blimey, Bert, look what I've copped!' said William.

'What is it?' said the others coming up.

'Lumme, if I knows! What are yer?'

'Bilbo Baggins, a bur–a hobbit,' said poor Bilbo, shaking all over, and wondering how to make owl-noises
before they throttled him.

'A burrahobbit?' said they a bit startled. Trolls are slow in the uptake, and mighty suspicious about anything new to them.

'What's a burrahobbit got to do with my pocket, anyways?' said William.

'And can ye cook 'em?' said Tom.

'Yer can try,' said Bert, picking up a skewer.

'He wouldn't make above a mouthful,' said William, who had already had a fine supper, 'not when he was skinned and boned.'

'P'raps there are more like him round about, and we might make a pie,' said Bert. 'Here you, are there any more of your sort a-sneakin' in these here woods, yer nasty little rabbit,' said he looking at the hobbit's furry feet; and he picked him up by the toes and shook him.

'Yes, lots,' said Bilbo, before he remembered not to give his friends away. 'No none at all, not one,' he said immediately afterwards.

'What d'yer mean?' said Bert, holding him right way up, by the hair this time.

'What I say,' said Bilbo gasping. 'And please don't cook me, kind sirs! I am a good cook myself, and cook better than I cook, if you see what I mean. I'll cook beautifully for you, a perfectly beautiful breakfast for you, if only you won't have me for supper.'

'Poor little blighter,' said William. He had already had as much supper as he could hold; also he had had lots of beer. 'Poor little blighter! Let him go!'

'Not till he says what he means by *lots* and *none at all*,' said Bert. 'I don't want to have me throat cut in me sleep! Hold his toes in the fire, till he talks!'

'I won't have it,' said William. 'I caught him anyway.'

'You're a fat fool, William,' said Bert, 'as I've said afore this evening.'

'And you're a lout!'

'And I won't take that from you, Bill Huggins,' says Bert, and puts his fist in William's eye.

Then there was a gorgeous row. Bilbo had just enough wits left, when Bert dropped him on the ground, to scramble out of the way of their feet, before they were fighting like dogs, and calling one another all sorts of perfectly true and applicable names in very loud voices. Soon they were locked in one another's arms, and rolling nearly into the fire kicking and thumping, while Tom whacked at them both with a branch to bring them to their senses – and that of course only made them madder than ever.

That would have been the time for Bilbo to have left.

But his poor little feet had been very squashed in Bert's big paw, and he had no breath in his body, and his head was going round; so there he lay for a while panting, just outside the circle of firelight.

Right in the middle of the fight up came Balin. The dwarves had heard noises from a distance, and after waiting for some time for Bilbo to come back, or to hoot like an owl, they started off one by one to creep towards the light as quietly as they could. No sooner did Tom see Balin come into the light than he gave an awful howl. Trolls simply detest the very sight of dwarves (uncooked). Bert and Bill stopped fighting immediately, and 'a sack, Tom, quick!' they said. Before Balin, who was wondering where in all this commotion Bilbo was, knew what was happening, a sack was over his head, and he was down.

'There's more to come yet,' said Tom, 'or I'm mighty mistook. Lots and none at all, it is,' said he. 'No burrahob-bits, but lots of these here dwarves. That's about the shape of it!'

'I reckon you're right,' said Bert, 'and we'd best get out of the light.'

And so they did. With sacks in their hands, that they used for carrying off mutton and other plunder, they waited in the shadows. As each dwarf came up and looked at the fire, and the spilled jugs, and the gnawed mutton, in surprise, pop! went a nasty smelly sack over his head, and he was down. Soon Dwalin lay by Balin, and Fili and Kili together, and Dori and Nori and Ori all in a heap, and Oin and Gloin and Bifur and Bofur and Bombur piled uncomfortably near the fire.

'That'll teach 'em,' said Tom; for Bifur and Bombur had given a lot of trouble, and fought like mad, as dwarves will when cornered.

Thorin came last – and he was not caught unawares. He came expecting mischief, and didn't need to see his friends' legs sticking out of sacks to tell him that things were not all well. He stood outside in the shadows some way off, and said: 'What's all this trouble? Who has been knocking my people about?'

'It's trolls!' said Bilbo from behind a tree. They had forgotten all about him. 'They're hiding in the bushes with sacks,' said he.

'O! are they?' said Thorin, and he jumped forward to the fire, before they could leap on him. He caught up a big branch all on fire at one end; and Bert got that end in his eye before he could step aside. That put him out of the battle for a bit. Bilbo did his best. He caught hold of Tom's leg – as well as he could, it was thick as a young tree-trunk – but he was sent spinning up into the top of some bushes, when Tom kicked the sparks up in Thorin's face.

Tom got the branch in his teeth for that, and lost one of the front ones. It made him howl, I can tell you. But just at that moment William came up behind and popped a sack right over Thorin's head and down to his toes. And so the fight ended. A nice pickle they were all in now: all neatly tied up in sacks, with three angry trolls (and two with burns and bashes to remember) sitting by them, arguing whether they should roast them slowly, or mince them fine and boil them, or just sit on them one by one and squash them into jelly; and Bilbo up in a bush, with his clothes and his skin torn, not daring to move for fear they should hear him.

It was just then that Gandalf came back. But no one saw him. The trolls had just decided to roast the dwarves now and eat them later – that was Bert's idea, and after a lot of argument they had all agreed to it.

'No good roasting 'em now, it'd take all night,' said a voice. Bert thought it was William's.

'Don't start the argument all over again, Bill,' he said, 'or it *will* take all night.'

'Who's a-arguing?' said William, who thought it was Bert that had spoken.

'You are,' said Bert.

'You're a liar,' said William; and so the argument began all over again. In the end they decided to mince them fine and boil them. So they got a great black pot, and they took out their knives.

'No good boiling 'em! We ain't got no water, and it's a long way to the well and all,' said a voice. Bert and William thought it was Tom's.

'Shut up!' said they, 'or we'll never have done. And yer can fetch the water yerself, if ye say any more.'

'Shut up yerself!' said Tom, who thought it was William's voice. 'Who's arguing but you, I'd like to know.'

'You're a booby,' said William.

'Booby yerself!' said Tom.

And so the argument began all over again, and went on hotter than ever, until at last they decided to sit on the sacks one by one and squash them, and boil them next time.

'Who shall we sit on first?' said the voice.

'Better sit on the last fellow first,' said Bert, whose eye had been damaged by Thorin. He thought Tom was talking.

'Don't talk to yerself!' said Tom. 'But if you wants to sit on the last one, sit on him. Which is he?'

'The one with the yellow stockings,' said Bert.

'Nonsense, the one with the grey stockings,' said a voice like William's.

'I made sure it was yellow,' said Bert.

'Yellow it was,' said William.

'Then what did yer say it was grey for?' said Bert.

'I never did. Tom said it.'

'That I never did!' said Tom. 'It was you.'

'Two to one, so shut yer mouth!' said Bert.

'Who are you a-talkin' to?' said William.

'Now stop it!' said Tom and Bert together. 'The night's gettin' on, and dawn comes early. Let's get on with it!'

'Dawn take you all, and be stone to you!' said a voice that sounded like William's. But it wasn't. For just at that moment the light came over the hill, and there was a mighty twitter in the branches. William never spoke for he stood turned to stone as he stooped; and Bert and Tom were stuck like rocks as they looked at him. And there they stand to this day, all alone, unless the birds perch on them; for trolls, as you probably know, must be underground before dawn, or they go back to the stuff of the mountains they are made of, and never move again. That is what had happened to Bert and Tom and William.

'Excellent!' said Gandalf, as he stepped from behind a tree, and helped Bilbo to climb down out of a thorn-bush. Then Bilbo understood. It was the wizard's voice that had kept the trolls bickering and quarrelling, until the light came and made an end of them.

# T. H. WHITE

FROM *The Sword in the Stone*

'Excuse me, sir,' said the Wart, 'but can you tell me the way to Sir Ector's castle, if you don't mind?'

The aged gentleman put down his bucket and looked at the Wart.

'Your name would be Wart,' he said.

'Yes, sir, please, sir,' said the Wart.

'My name,' said the aged gentleman, 'is Merlyn.'

'How do you do?' said the Wart.

'How do you do?' said Merlyn. 'It is clement weather, is it not?'

'It is,' said the Wart, 'for the time of the year.'

When these formalities had been concluded, the Wart had leisure to examine his new acquaintance more closely. The aged gentleman was staring at him with a kind of unwinking and benevolent curiosity which made him feel that it would not be at all rude to stare back, no ruder than it would be to stare at one of his guardian's cows who happened to be ruminating his personality as she leaned her head over a gate.

Merlyn had a long white beard and long white moustache which hung down on either side of it, and close inspection shewed that he was far from clean. It was not that he had dirty finger-nails or anything like that, but some large bird seemed to have been nesting in his hair. The Wart was familiar with the nests of spar-hawk and Gos, those crazy conglomerations of sticks and oddments which had been taken over from squirrels and crows, and he knew how the twigs and the tree foot were splashed with white mutes, old bones, muddy feathers and castings. This was the impression which he gathered from Merlyn. The old gentleman was streaked with droppings over his shoulders, among the stars and triangles of his gown, and a large spider was slowly lowering itself from the tip of his hat, as he gazed and slowly blinked at the little boy in front of him. He had a faintly worried expression, as though he were trying to remember some name which began with Chol but which was pronounced in quite a different way, possibly Menzies or was it Dalziel? His mild blue eyes very big and round under the tarantula spectacles, gradually filmed and clouded over as he gazed at the boy and then he turned his head away with a resigned expression, as though it was all too much for him after all.

'Do you like peaches?' asked the old gentleman.

'Very much indeed,' answered the Wart, and his mouth began to water so that it was full of sweet, soft liquid.

'It is only July, you know,' said the old man reprovingly, and walked off in the direction of the cottage without looking round.

The Wart followed after him, since this was the simplest thing to do, and offered to carry the bucket (which seemed to please the old gentleman, who gave it to him) and waited while he counted his keys, and muttered and mislaid them and dropped them in the grass. Finally, when they had got their way into the black and white cottage with as much trouble as if they were burglaring it, he climbed up the ladder after his host and found himself in the upstairs room.

It was the most marvellous room that the Wart had ever been in.

There was a real corkindrill hanging from the rafters, very lifelike and horrible with glass eyes and scaly tail stretched out behind it. When its master came into the room it winked one eye in salutation, although it was stuffed. There were hundreds of thousands of brown books in leather bindings, some chained to the book- shelves and others propped up against each other as if they had had too much spirits to drink and did not really trust themselves. These gave out a smell of must and solid brownness which was most secure. Then there were stuffed birds, popinjays, and maggot-pies and kingfishers, and peacocks with all their feathers but two, and tiny birds like beetles, and a reputed phoenix which smelt of incense and cinnamon. It could not have been a real phoenix, because there is only one of these at a time. Over the mantelpiece there was a fox's mask, with GRAF- TON. BUCKINGHAM TO DAVENTRY, 2 HRS 20 MINS writ- ten under it, and also a forty-pound salmon with AWE, 43 MIN., BULLDOG written under it, and a very life-like basilisk with CROWHURST OTTER HOUNDS in Roman print. There were several boars' tusks and the claws of tigers and libbards mounted in symmetrical patterns, and a big head of Ovis Poli, six live grass snakes in a kind of aquarium, some nests of the solitary wasp nicely set up in a glass cylinder, an ordinary beehive whose inhabitants went in and out of the window unmolested, two young hedgehogs in cotton wool, a pair of badgers which im- mediately began to cry Yik-Yik-Yik-Yik in loud voices as soon as the magician appeared, twenty boxes which contained stick caterpillars and sixths of the puss-moth, and even an oleander that was worth two and six, all feeding on the appropriate leaves, a guncase with all sorts of weapons which would not be invented for half a

thousand years, a rob-box ditto, a lovely chest of drawers full of salmon flies which had been tied by Merlyn himself, another chest whose drawers were labelled Mandragora, Mandrake, Old Man's Beard, etc., a bunch of turkey feathers and goose-quills for making pens, an astrolabe, twelve pairs of boots, a dozen purse-nets, three dozen rabbit wires, twelve cork-screws, an ant's nest between two glass plates, ink-bottles of every possible colour from red to violet, darning-needles, a gold medal for being the best scholar at Eton, four or five recorders, a nest of field mice all alive-o, two skulls, plenty of cut glass, Venetian glass, Bristol glass and a bottle of Mastic varnish, some satsuma china and some cloisonné, the fourteenth edition of the *Encyclopaedia Britannica* (marred as it was by the sensationalism of the popular plates), two paint-boxes (one oil, one water-colour), three globes of the known geographical world, a few fossils, the stuffed head of a camel-leopard, six pismires, some glass retorts with cauldrons, Bunsen burners, etc., and the complete set of cigarette cards depicting wild fowl by Peter Scott.

Merlyn took off his pointed hat when he came into this extraordinary chamber, because it was too high for the roof, and immediately there was a little scamper in one of the dark corners and a flap of soft wings, and a young tawny owl was sitting on the black skull-cap which protected the top of his head.

'Oh, what a lovely owl!' cried the Wart.

But when he went up to it and held out his hand, the owl grew half as tall again, stood up as stiff as a poker, closed its eyes so that there was only the smallest slit to peep through, as one is in the habit of doing when told to shut one's eyes at hide-and-seek, and said in a doubtful voice:

'There is no owl.'

Then it shut its eyes entirely and looked the other way.

'It's only a boy,' said Merlyn.

'There is no boy,' said the owl hopefully, without turning round.

The Wart was so startled by finding that the owl could talk that he forgot his manners and came closer still. At this the owl became so nervous that it made a mess on Merlyn's head — the whole room was quite white with droppings — and flew off to perch on the farthest tip of the corkindrill's tail, out of reach.

'We see so little company,' explained Merlyn, wiping his head with half a worn-out pair of pyjama tops which he kept for that purpose, 'that Archimedes is a little shy of strangers. Come, Archimedes, I want you to meet a friend of mine called Wart.'

Here he held out his hand to the owl, who came waddling like a goose along the corkindrill's back — he waddled with this rolling gait so as to keep his tail from being damaged — and hopped down on to Merlyn's finger with every sign of reluctance.

'Hold out your finger,' said Merlyn, 'and put it behind his legs. No, lift it up under his train.'

When the Wart had done this Merlyn moved the owl gently backwards, so that the Wart's finger pressed against its legs from behind, and it either had to step back on the finger or get pushed off its balance altogether. It stepped back. The Wart stood there delighted, while the furry little feet held tight on to his finger and the sharp claws prickled his skin.

'Say how d'you do properly,' said Merlyn.

'I won't,' said Archimedes, looking the other way and holding very tight.

'Oh, he *is* lovely,' said the Wart again. 'Have you had him very long?'

'Archimedes has stayed with me since he was quite small, indeed since he had a tiny head like a chicken's.'

'I wish he would talk to me,' said the Wart.

'Perhaps if you were to give him this mouse here, politely, he might learn to know you better.'

Merlyn took the dead mouse out of his skull-cap – 'I always keep them there,' he explained, 'and worms too, for fishing. I find it most convenient' – and handed it to the Wart, who held it out rather gingerly towards Archimedes. The nutty little curved beak looked as if it were capable of doing damage, but Archimedes looked closely at the mouse, blinked at the Wart, moved nearer

on the finger, closed his eyes and leaned forward. He stood there with closed eyes and an expression of rapture on his face, as if he were saying grace, and then, with the absurdest little sideways nibble, took the morsel so gently that he would not have broken a soap bubble. He remained leaning forward with closed eyes, with the mouse suspended from his beak, as if he were not sure what to do with it. Then he lifted his right foot – he was right-handed – and took hold of the mouse. He held it up like a boy holding a stick of rock or a constable with his truncheon, looked at it, nibbled its tail. He turned it round so that it was head first, for the Wart had offered it the wrong way round, and gave one gulp. He looked round at the company with the tail hanging out of the corner of his mouth – as much as to say, 'I wish you would not all stare at me so' – turned his head away, politely swallowed the tail, scratched his sailor's beard with his left toe, and began to ruffle out his feathers.

'Let him alone,' said Merlyn, 'now. For perhaps he does not want to be friends with you until he knows what you are like. With owls, it is never easy-come and easy-go.'

'Perhaps he will sit on my shoulder,' said the Wart, and with that he instinctively lowered his hand, so that the owl, who liked to be as high as possible, ran up the slope and stood shyly beside his ear.

'Now breakfast,' said Merlyn.

The Wart saw that the most perfect breakfast was laid out neatly for two, on the table before the window. There were peaches. There were also melons, strawberries and cream, rusks, brown trout piping hot, grilled perch which were much nicer, chicken devilled enough to burn one's mouth out, kidneys and mushrooms on toast, fricassee, curry, and a choice of boiling coffee or best chocolate made with cream in large cups.

'Have some mustard,' said Merlyn, when they had got to the kidneys.

The mustard-pot got up and walked over to his plate on thin silver legs that waddled like the owl's. Then it uncurled its handles and one handle lifted its lid with exaggerated courtesy while the other helped him to a generous spoonful.

'Oh, I love the mustard-pot!' cried the Wart. 'Where ever did you get it?'

At this the pot beamed all over its face and began to strut a bit; but Merlyn rapped it on the head with a teaspoon, so that it sat down and shut up at once.

'It's not a bad pot,' he said grudgingly. 'Only it is inclined to give itself airs.'

# B.B.

When the gnomes awakened on the following evening they found a change in the weather. They had slept during the day in a willow root close to a deep brown pool, bored out by the floods of many winters. Hunger demanded immediate appeasement, and they began at once to put their fishing lines together.

Gone was the golden weather which had so far favoured their trip; instead the sky was overcast and gloomy, and a strong wind was whipping the trees and bushes, turning the pale undersides of the leaves uppermost. Curious swirls and V-shaped eddy-marks creased the pool by the willow; the reeds bent and bent again before the rude breath of the stormy wind, their sharp tips cutting the water.

On all sides stretched the lush meadows; the gnomes could see the waves of wind passing over the mowing grass so that the surface was undulating exactly like the surface of the sea, the rollers following one behind another, a sea of grass instead of water. Though the evening was not cold, the gnomes were glad of their skin coats.

In a very short time they had caught some thumping perch, and they fished until they had broken all their hooks. They were not used to these heavy game fish. Seven fat fellows lay on the root of the willow when they at last wound in their lines, and you may depend upon it, it was not long before those fish were neatly cut up and grilled over a fire. They ate themselves cross-eyed and for some time were quite incapable of movement.

'It's almost like an autumn night,' remarked Baldmoney at length, as he lit his pipe with an ember from the fire; 'we're going to have rain before dawn, that's why the fish are biting.'

Sneezewort was homesick and also very full of perch, so he did not answer. He watched the wind ripples passing over the mowing grass and the spots of yellow foam spinning slowly round the pool; a little higher upstream there was a big clot of it caught against a submerged reed.

He was thinking how cosy the oak root would be on a night like this, and how the glow of the fire used to light up the rugged interior of the tree. How was the owl family getting on, and Dodder, and Watervole? Perhaps after all they had made a mistake to come on this trip; a lot might have happened to Cloudberry in all those months which had passed since he went away. And truth to say, there was something a little sinister in this gloomy evening, and the chasing ripples and sighing wind seemed heavy with foreboding.

The next instant his heart gave a bump, and all these sentimental thoughts had gone in the instinct of self-preservation. For downstream, threading its way close to the water, was the lithe brown form of one of their most dreaded enemies, Stoat! He was puzzling on their scent. Unknown to them he had followed them for a long way along the Folly bank, now the scent was getting stale and he was almost on the point of giving up.

With a lightning-like movement both gnomes were on their feet, for both had seen their dreaded enemy almost at the same instant. There was no chance of climbing up inside the willow, for the barrel of the tree was not hollow. They must make a break for it while there was time. To be cornered inside the root would be disastrous.

Each had the presence of mind to grab his stick and bundle. They slipped out of the tree, keeping it between them and their pursuer, and made their way as fast as they could up the stream. Not far distant it took a wide bend to the left and the bank was clothed with thick bushes, but stoats can climb bushes with agility.

Their safest chance lay in a tree up which they could climb. Unfortunately, as you may have noticed, few trees have branches very low to the ground which would have given them a start, and, anyway, there was not a tree in sight save some elms across the meadow. The gnomes might have made a dash for these, but if the stoat was really hot on their trail, he could overtake them. When in a hurry the little devil in brown can move like lightning.

One point was in their favour, they had a good start, and stoats do not as a rule hunt by sight until they are very near their quarry.

The gnomes ran as fast as they could up the shingle; now and again they glanced over their shoulders. Stoat had gone inside the willow stump and was smelling around. Perhaps he would find the heads and bones of the perch which might delay him, but it was a forlorn hope. Such things happened at the Oak Pool, but they were never far from the old tree, and when chased could simply run inside and bar the door.

For the next ten minutes they ran as fast as their short legs could carry them. Baldmoney led, but after a while

began to get a little puffed. Sneezewort, in better training and lighter build, began to make the running.

They reached the bend and the next moment their pursuer was hidden from view; perhaps he would give up the chase and content himself with exploring the willow root. Both gnomes were now puffing and blowing; their little anxious faces, always red at the best of times, were deep crimson and beads of sweat rolled off them. The heavy bundles hampered them in their flight, but they contained all they possessed and would not be abandoned unless things became very hot indeed.

'I can't see him,' gasped Sneezewort, looking back.

'Don't stop running,' puffed Baldmoney, 'he's very likely still on our trail.'

Round the bend there was a fallen log which lay almost across the stream. The water gurgled and swilled round the end of it, deep and swift, but it was jumpable. They scurried across the log and landed safely on the far bank, though Baldmoney, tired and spent, wet his right leg to the knee. They found themselves in a dense sedge-bed. The ground was miry and black, but they plunged in among the reeds.

A startled water-vole plopped into the stream and a reed-bunting flew up, excitedly flirting his white-edged tail and looking about on all sides at the shaking reeds.

Had you or I been standing on the bank we should have thought a rat or mouse was rustling through the water plants, for the gnomes were quite hidden, only the sedges quivered. At last, the reeds thinned and in their place a forest of sturdy dock plants, with stout and hairy stems, raised their broad umbrellas overhead. It was fine cover, but no cover in the world avails a gnome or rabbit when a stoat is once on the hunting trail, so they pushed on.

Then the docks thinned and they could see the light once more and the brown Folly open to the sky, crinkling in a thousand catspaws over a wide shallow, and beyond, a deep pool. They crossed the shallows to their original bank hoping that the stoat would lose the scent in the running water. They were now utterly spent and must find some sort of hiding-place. Leaning over the pool was a willow branch, its main stem half awash, and the slender rods grew straight up in a thick pallisade. Right at the end the gnomes caught sight of a moorhen's nest; it might have been one of the many 'rest' nests that the cock bird builds as rafts for his babies when they are hatched. You will nearly always find two moorhens' nests belonging to the same pair of birds.

They would have liked to have gone farther, but both were blown, and this was the only possible cover in sight. They crept out along the half-submerged branch, squeezing in between the willow wands until they reached the nest, and into it they tumbled, one on top of the other.

The nest, which contained three handsome eggs (quite cold, for the hen had not begun to sit), was substantially built, but very damp. They made themselves as small as possible, squeezing in between the eggs and taking care not to break them, and lay peeping fearfully down the stream.

Below them the brown water slid and hissed, strings of bubbles showed far down under the surface and the gnomes could see shoals of little silver minnows, a whole school of them, passing like a cloud.

'Is he following us?' whispered Baldmoney when he had got his breath. 'I can't see a sign of anything.'

Sneezewort did not reply. He was breathing so fast

and his heart was a-hammering so quickly he could hardly see.

Downstream they could just discern the log where they had crossed to the far bank; beyond that, the bend and the steep sandy bank hid everything. There was nothing to be seen save an old rook flying across the rim of the meadow. He came oaring his way along and alighted on the shingle at the shallows where, after a quick look round on all sides, he began to hunt for mussels. Rooks and crows love freshwater mussels.

He waddled about in the shallow water and along the edge of the reed bed, turning over some old empty shells which he found lying about.

A large spot of rain came plop! into the pool, then another and another. They rattled on the leaves like bullets, the falling drops making little tents in the water. As the minutes passed the heavy breathing of the gnomes quietened and they began to feel secure. The rain, lashed by the wind, increased in violence and the gnomes began to shiver.

Up by the reed bed the rook had at last found a mussel and he flew away with it over the fields. The vista downstream showed no sign of life.

'I think he's given up,' whispered Baldmoney; 'he hasn't come any farther than the willow.'

Sneezewort, knowing the ways of stoats, was not so sure. It all depended whether the stoat was hungry.

As the gnomes lay in the bottom of the nest with their chins on the rim of it, it occurred to them what a fine meal the eggs would make. A big black water-boatman came up from the depths of the pool and lay on the surface with his oars outspread. And close to the nest a whole crowd of tiny silver beetles were weaving about on the surface of the water; they moved and glistened like minute racing cars.

Then the gnomes saw Stoat. He was puzzling up the bank, quartering the ground like a hound. He went along the log and stopped, for it was a big jump for him, and he did not like the look of it. At other times it might have been interesting to watch the little hunter at work, but it was no fun when the quarry was yourself, and Baldmoney and Sneezewort trembled with apprehension. Stoat ran back along the log and began coming up the bank on the other side. Then the gnomes realized that they had made a mistake — that they should not have recrossed the brook. Had they remained in the reed bed they would have been safe. But Stoat now had nothing to guide him. He came along slowly with frequent pauses, showing his yellowish-white chest as he sat up in the grass. When he ran, his body was arched in a hump, the black-tipped tail held high. Nearer and nearer he came, and the poor little gnomes crouched lower in the nest.

Stoat was now not more than thirty paces from their tree, and the next moment was at the shallows where they had crossed. He must have struck their scent then, for he came on at the hunting run with his muzzle fairly low.

Neither gnome spoke, but each loosened his knife in its leather sheath in a meaning sort of way, as though he meant to sell his life dearly.

Stoat reached the log; the watching gnomes could now see every detail of the cruel flat head, the sharp muzzle and the primrose-yellow chest. They could see the whiskers, like needles, and the working nose. He reared himself up on his hind legs with his front paws on the end of the willow branch, and the next moment was looking in their direction with cruel little button eyes. Then he began to come along the tree, threading the willow wands with lithe purpose.

Baldmoney and Sneezewort waited until he was almost at the nest before acting. Perhaps they were hypnotized by the deadly little beast. Had they been rabbits they would have simply sat back and squealed. But not so the gnomes. As Stoat came almost within springing distance they dived over the edge of the nest like young moorhens, one on one side, and one on the other, down into the brown water, taking their bundles with them.

Stoat chittered with rage, displaying a sudden row of ivory needles. A foot away was the unhappy Sneezewort's head, drifting downstream with the current, and a little to the left, Baldmoney's, both swimming as gracefully as frogs.

For a second Stoat was inclined to follow, for stoats swim with ease. And then he saw the three smooth eggs lying in the cup of the nest. In a moment the gnomes were forgotten, here was a far greater delicacy, EGGS!

Stoats love a nice fresh egg; every year thousands of birds lose their precious clutches to the little brown robber. He climbs the blackthorn to get to the nest of blackbird and thrush, finch and blackcap, and not only eggs fall to him but baby birds as well.

In a second or two he was breaking open the moorhen's eggs, greedily sucking the contents, and then, when he had eaten them all, he curled round in the nest and went fast asleep like a full-fed dog.

# C. S. LEWIS

'BUT what *are* you?' said the Queen again. 'Are you a great overgrown dwarf that has cut off his beard?'

'No, your Majesty,' said Edmund, 'I never had a beard, I'm a boy.'

'A boy!' said she. 'Do you mean you are a Son of Adam?'

Edmund stood still, saying nothing. He was too confused by this time to understand what the question meant.

'I see you are an idiot, whatever else you may be,' said the Queen. 'Answer me, once and for all, or I shall lose my patience. Are you human?'

'Yes, your Majesty,' said Edmund.

'And how, pray, did you come to enter my dominions?'

'Please, your Majesty, I came in through a wardrobe.'

'A wardrobe? What do you mean?'

'I – I opened a door and just found myself here, your Majesty,' said Edmund.

'Ha!' said the Queen, speaking more to herself than to him. 'A door. A door from the world of men! I have heard of such things. This may wreck all. But he is only one, and he is easily dealt with.' As she spoke these words she rose from her seat and looked Edmund full in the face, her eyes flaming; at the same moment she raised her wand. Edmund felt sure that she was going to do something dreadful but he seemed unable to move. Then, just as he gave himself up for lost, she appeared to change her mind.

'My poor child,' she said in quite a different voice, 'how cold you look! Come and sit with me here on the sledge and I will put my mantle round you and we will talk.'

Edmund did not like this arrangement at all but he dared not disobey; he stepped on to the sledge and sat at her feet, and she put a fold of her fur mantle round him and tucked it well in.

'Perhaps something hot to drink?' said the Queen. 'Should you like that?'

'Yes please, your Majesty,' said Edmund, whose teeth were chattering.

The Queen took from somewhere among her wrappings a very small bottle which looked as if it were made of copper. Then, holding out her arm, she let one drop fall from it on the snow beside the sledge. Edmund saw the drop for a second in mid-air, shining like a diamond. But the moment it touched the snow there was a hissing sound and there stood a jewelled cup full of something that steamed. The dwarf immediately took this and handed it to Edmund with a bow and a smile; not a very nice smile. Edmund felt much better as he began to sip the hot drink. It was something he had never tasted before, very sweet and foamy and creamy, and it warmed him right down to his toes.

'It is dull, Son of Adam, to drink without eating,' said the Queen presently. 'What would you like best to eat?'

'Turkish Delight, please, your Majesty,' said Edmund.

The Queen let another drop fall from her bottle on to the snow, and instantly there appeared a round box, tied with green silk ribbon, which, when opened, turned out to contain several pounds of the best Turkish Delight. Each piece was sweet and light to the very centre and Edmund had never tasted anything more delicious. He was quite warm now, and very comfortable.

While he was eating the Queen kept asking him questions. At first Edmund tried to remember that it is rude to speak with one's mouth full, but soon he forgot about this and thought only of trying to shovel down as much Turkish Delight as he could, and the more he ate the more he wanted to eat, and he never asked himself why the Queen should be so inquisitive. She got him to tell her that he had one brother and two sisters, and that one of his sisters had already been in Narnia and had met a Faun there, and that no one except himself and his brother and his sisters knew anything about Narnia. She seemed especially interested in the fact that there were four of them, and kept on coming back to it. 'You are sure there are just four of you?' she asked. 'Two Sons of Adam and two Daughters of Eve, neither more nor less?' and Edmund, with his mouth full of Turkish Delight, kept on saying, 'Yes, I told you that before,' and forgetting to call her 'Your Majesty', but she didn't seem to mind now.

At last the Turkish Delight was all finished and Edmund was looking very hard at the empty box and wishing that she would ask him whether he would like some more. Probably the Queen knew quite well what he was thinking; for she knew, though Edmund did not, that this was enchanted Turkish Delight and that anyone who had once tasted it would want more and more of it, and would even, if they were allowed, go on eating it till they killed themselves. But she did not offer him any more. Instead, she said to him,

'Son of Adam, I should so much like to see your brother and your two sisters. Will you bring them to see me?'

'I'll try,' said Edmund, still looking at the empty box.

'Because, if you did come again – bringing them with you of course – I'd be able to give you some more Turkish Delight. I can't do it now, the magic will only work once. In my own house it would be another matter.'

'Why can't we go to your house now?' said Edmund. When he had first got on to the sledge he had been afraid that she might drive away with him to some unknown place from which he would not be able to get back; but he had forgotten about that fear now.

'It is a lovely place, my house,' said the Queen. 'I am sure you would like it. There are whole rooms full of Turkish Delight, and what's more, I have no children of my own. I want a nice boy whom I could bring up as a Prince and who would be King of Narnia when I am gone. While he was Prince he would wear a gold crown and eat Turkish Delight all day long; and you are much the cleverest and handsomest young man I've ever met, I think I would like to make you the Prince – some day, when you bring the others to visit me.'

'Why not now?' said Edmund. His face had become very red and his mouth and fingers were sticky. He did not look either clever or handsome, whatever the Queen might say.

'Oh, but if I took you there now,' said she, 'I shouldn't see your brother and your sisters. I very much want to know your charming relations. You are to be the Prince and – later on – the King; that is understood. But you must have courtiers and nobles. I will make your brother a Duke and your sisters Duchesses.'

'There's nothing special about *them*,' said Edmund, 'and, anyway, I could always bring them some other time.'

'Ah, but once you were in my house,' said the Queen, 'you might forget all about them. You would be enjoying yourself so much that you wouldn't want the bother of going to fetch them. No. You must go back to your own country now and come to me another day, *with them*, you understand. It is no good coming without them.'

'But I don't even know the way back to my own country,' pleaded Edmund. 'That's easy,' answered the Queen. 'Do you see that lamp?' She pointed with her wand and Edmund turned and saw the same lamp-post under which Lucy had met the Faun. 'Straight on, beyond that, is the way to the World of Men. And now look the other way' – here she pointed in the opposite direction –'and tell me if you can see two little hills rising above the trees.'

'I think I can,' said Edmund.

'Well, my house is between those two hills. So next time you come you have only to find the lamp-post and look for those two hills and walk through the wood till you reach my house. But remember – you must bring the others with you. I might have to be very angry with you if you came alone.'

'I'll do my best,' said Edmund.

'And, by the way,' said the Queen, 'you needn't tell them about me. It would be fun to keep it a secret between us two, wouldn't it? Make it a surprise for them. Just bring them along to the two hills – a clever boy like you will easily think of some excuse for doing that – and when you come to my house you could just say "Let's see who lives here" or something like that. I

am sure that would be best. If your sister has met one of
the Fauns, she may have heard strange stories about me
– nasty stories that might make her afraid to come to me.
Fauns will say anything, you know, and now –'

'Please, please,' said Edmund suddenly, 'please
couldn't I have just one piece of Turkish Delight to eat
on the way home?'

'No, no,' said the Queen with a laugh, 'you must wait
till next time.' While she spoke, she signalled to the
dwarf to drive on, but as the sledge swept away out of
sight, the Queen waved to Edmund, calling out, 'Next
time! Next time! Don't forget. Come soon.'

Edmund was still staring after the sledge when he heard
someone calling his own name, and looking round he saw
Lucy coming towards him from another part of the wood.

'Oh, Edmund!' she cried. 'So you've got in too! Isn't
it wonderful and now –'

'All right,' said Edmund, 'I see you were right and it is a magic wardrobe after all. I'll say I'm sorry if you like. But where on earth have you been all this time? I've been looking for you everywhere.'

'If I'd known you had got in I'd have waited for you,' said Lucy, who was too happy and excited to notice how snappishly Edmund spoke or how flushed and strange his face was. 'I've been having lunch with dear Mr Tumnus, the Faun, and he's very well and the White Witch has done nothing to him for letting me go, so he thinks she can't have found out and perhaps everything is going to be all right after all.'

'The White Witch?' said Edmund; 'who's she?'

'She is a perfectly terrible person,' said Lucy. 'She calls herself the Queen of Narnia though she has no right to be queen at all, and all the Fauns and Dryads and Naiads and Dwarfs and Animals – at least all the good ones – simply hate her. And she can turn people into stone and do all kinds of horrible things. And she has made a magic so that it is always winter in Narnia – always winter, but it never gets to Christmas. And she drives about on a sledge, drawn by reindeer, with her wand in her hand and a crown on her head.'

Edmund was already feeling uncomfortable from having eaten too many sweets, and when he heard that the Lady he had made friends with was a dangerous witch he felt even more uncomfortable. But he still wanted to taste that Turkish Delight again more than he wanted anything else.

'Who told you all that stuff about the White Witch?' he asked.

'Mr Tumnus, the Faun,' said Lucy.

'You can't always believe what Fauns say,' said

Edmund, trying to sound as if he knew far more about them than Lucy.

'Who said so?' asked Lucy.

'Everyone knows it,' said Edmund; 'ask anybody you like. But it's pretty poor sport standing here in the snow. Let's go home.'

'Yes, let's,' said Lucy. 'Oh, Edmund, I *am* glad you've got in too. The others will have to believe in Narnia now that both of us have been there. What fun it will be!'

But Edmund secretly thought that it would not be as good fun for him as for her. He would have to admit that Lucy had been right, before all the others, and he felt sure the others would all be on the side of the Fauns and the animals; but he was already more than half on the side of the Witch. He did not know what he would say, or how he would keep his secret once they were all talking about Narnia.

By this time they had walked a good way. Then suddenly they felt coats around them instead of branches and next moment they were both standing outside the wardrobe in the empty room.

'I say,' said Lucy, 'you do look awful, Edmund. Don't you feel well?'

'I'm all right,' said Edmund, but this was not true. He was feeling very sick.

'Come on then,' said Lucy, 'let's find the others. What a lot we shall have to tell them! And what wonderful adventures we shall have now that we're all in it together.'

# MARY NORTON

Arrietty watched him move away from the step and then she looked about her. Oh, glory! Oh, joy! Oh, freedom! The sunlight, the grasses, the soft, moving air and half-way up the bank, where it curved round the corner, a flowering cherry-tree! Below it on the path lay a stain of pinkish petals and, at the tree's foot, pale as butter, a nest of primroses.

Arrietty threw a cautious glance towards the front doorstep and then, light and dancey, in her soft red shoes, she ran towards the petals. They were curved like shells and rocked as she touched them. She gathered several up and laid them one inside the other . . . up and up . . . like a card castle. And then she spilled them. Pod came again to the top of the step and looked along the path. 'Don't you go far,' he said after a moment. Seeing his lips move, she smiled back at him: she was too far already to hear the words.

A greenish beetle, shining in the sunlight, came towards her across the stones. She laid her fingers lightly on its shell and it stood still, waiting and watchful, and when she moved her hand the beetle went swiftly on. An ant came hurrying in a busy zigzag. She danced in front of it to tease it and put out her foot. It stared at her, nonplussed, waving its antennae; then pettishly, as though put out, it swerved away. Two birds came down, quarrelling shrilly, into the grass below the tree. One

flew away but Arrietty could see the other among the
moving grass stems above her on the slope. Cautiously
she moved towards the bank and climbed a little nervously
in amongst the green blades. As she parted them gently
with her bare hands, drops of water plopped on her skirt
as she felt the red shoes become damp. But on she went,
pulling herself up now and again by rooty stems into this
jungle of moss and wood-violet and creeping leaves of
clover. The sharp-seeming grass blades, waist high, were
tender to the touch and sprang back lightly behind her as
she passed. When at last she reached the foot of the tree,
the bird took fright and flew away and she sat down
suddenly on a gnarled leaf of primrose. The air was filled
with scent. 'But nothing will play with you,' she thought
and saw the cracks and furrows on the primrose leaves
held crystal beads of dew. If she pressed the leaf these
rolled like marbles. The bank was warm, almost too
warm here within the shelter of the tall grass, and the
sandy earth smelled dry. Standing up, she picked a
primrose. The pink stalk felt tender and living in her
hands and was covered with silvery hairs, and when she
held the flower, like a parasol, between her eyes and the
sky, she saw the sun's pale light through the veined
petals. On a piece of bark she found a wood-louse and
she struck it lightly with her swaying flower. It curled
immediately and became a ball, bumping softly away
downhill in amongst the grass roots. But she knew about
wood-lice. There were plenty of them at home under the
floor. Homily always scolded her if she played with them
because, she said, they smelled of old knives. She lay
back among the stalks of the primroses and they made a
coolness between her and the sun, and then, sighing, she
turned her head and looked sideways up the bank among

the grass stems. Startled, she caught her breath. Something had moved above her on the bank. Something had
glittered. Arrietty stared.

It was an eye. Or it looked like an eye. Clear and bright
like the colour of the sky. An eye like her own but
enormous. A glaring eye. Breathless with fear, she sat
up. And the eye blinked. A great fringe of lashes came
curving down and flew up again out of sight. Cautiously,
Arrietty moved her legs: she would slide noiselessly in
among the grass stems and slither away down the bank.

'Don't move!' said a voice, and the voice, like the eye,
was enormous but, somehow, hushed – and hoarse like a
surge of wind through the grating on a stormy night in
March.

Arrietty froze. 'So this is it,' she thought, 'the worst
and most terrible thing of all: I have been "seen"! Whatever happened to Eggletina will now, almost certainly,
happen to me!'

There was a pause and Arrietty, her heart pounding in
her ears, heard the breath again drawn swiftly into the
vast lungs. 'Or,' said the voice, whispering still, 'I shall
hit you with my ash stick.'

Suddenly Arrietty became calm. 'Why?' she asked.
How strange her own voice sounded! Crystal thin and
harebell clear, it tinkled on the air.

'In case,' came the surprised whisper at last, 'you ran
towards me, quickly, through the grass . . . in case,' it
went on, trembling a little, 'you scrabbled at me with
your nasty little hands.'

Arrietty stared at the eye; she held herself quite still.
'Why?' she asked again, and again the word tinkled – icy
cold it sounded this time, and needle sharp.

'Things do,' said the voice. 'I've seen them. In India.'

Arrietty thought of her *Gazetteer of the World.* 'You're not in India now,' she pointed out.

'Did you come out of the house?'

'Yes,' said Arrietty.

'From whereabouts in the house?'

Arrietty stared at the eye. 'I'm not going to tell you,' she said at last bravely.

'Then I'll hit you with my ash stick!'

'All right,' said Arrietty, 'hit me!'

'I'll pick you up and break you in half!'

Arrietty stood up. 'All right,' she said and took two paces forward.

There was a sharp gasp and an earthquake in the

grass: he spun away from her and sat up, a great mountain in a green jersey. He had fair, straight hair and golden eyelashes. 'Stay where you are!' he cried.

Arrietty stared up at him. So this was 'the boy'! Breathless, she felt, and light with fear. 'I guessed you were about nine,' she gasped after a moment.

He flushed. 'Well, you're wrong, I'm ten.' He looked down at her, breathing deeply. 'How old are you?'

'Fourteen,' said Arrietty. 'Next June,' she added, watching him.

There was silence while Arrietty waited, trembling a little. 'Can you read?' the boy said at last.

'Of course,' said Arrietty. 'Can't you?'

'No,' he stammered. 'I mean – yes. I mean I've just come from India.'

'What's that got to do with it?' said Arrietty.

'Well, if you're born in India, you're bilingual. And if you're bilingual, you can't read. Not so well.'

Arrietty stared up at him: what a monster, she thought, dark against the sky.

'Do you grow out of it?' she asked.

He moved a little and she felt the cold flick of his shadow.

'Oh yes,' he said, 'it wears off. My sisters were bilingual; now they aren't a bit. They could read any of those books upstairs in the schoolroom.'

'So could I,' said Arrietty quickly, 'if someone could hold them, and turn the pages. I'm not a bit bilingual. I can read anything.'

'Could you read out loud?'

'Of course,' said Arrietty.

'Would you wait here while I run upstairs and get a book now?'

'Well,' said Arrietty; she was longing to show off; then a startled look came into her eyes. 'Oh —' she faltered.

'What's the matter?' The boy was standing up now. He towered above her.

'How many doors are there in this house?' She squinted up at him against the bright sunlight. He dropped on one knee.

'Doors?' he said. 'Outside doors?'

'Yes.'

'Well, there's the front door, the back door, the gun-room door, the kitchen door, the scullery door ... and the french windows in the drawing room.'

'Well, you see,' said Arrietty, 'my father's in the hall, by the front door, working. He ... he wouldn't want to be disturbed.'

'Working?' said the boy. 'What at?'

'Getting material,' said Arrietty, 'for a scrubbing-brush.'

'Then I'll go in the side door'; he began to move away but turned suddenly and came back to her. He stood a moment, as though embarrassed, and then he said: 'Can you fly?'

'No,' said Arrietty, surprised; 'can you?'

His face became even redder. 'Of course not,' he said angrily; 'I'm not a fairy!'

'Well, nor am I,' said Arrietty, 'nor is anybody. I don't believe in them.'

He looked at her strangely. 'You don't believe in them?'

'No,' said Arrietty; 'do you?'

'Of course not!'

Really, she thought, he is a very angry kind of boy.

'My mother believes in them,' she said, trying to appease him. 'She thinks she saw one once. It was when she was a girl and lived with her parents behind the sand pile in the potting-shed.'

He squatted down on his heels and she felt his breath on her face: 'What was it like?' he asked.

'About the size of a glow-worm with wings like a butterfly. And it had a tiny little face, she said, all alight and moving like sparks and tiny moving hands. Its face was changing all the time, she said, smiling and sort of shimmering. It seemed to be talking, she said, very quickly – but you couldn't hear a word . . .'

'Oh,' said the boy, interested. After a moment he asked: 'Where did it go?'

'It just went,' said Arrietty. 'When my mother saw it, it seemed to be caught in a cobweb. It was dark at the time. About five o'clock on a winter's evening. After tea.'

'Oh,' he said again and picked up two petals of cherry-blossom which he folded like a sandwich and ate slowly. 'Supposing,' he said, staring past her at the wall of the house, 'you saw a little man, about as tall as a pencil, with a blue patch in his trousers, half-way up a window curtain, carrying a doll's tea-cup – would you say it was a fairy?'

'No,' said Arrietty, 'I'd say it was my father.'

'Oh,' said the boy, thinking this out, 'does you father have a blue patch on his trousers?'

'Not on his best trousers. He does on his borrowing ones.'

'Oh,' said the boy again. He seemed to find it a safe sound, as lawyers do. 'Are there many people like you?'

'No,' said Arrietty. 'None. We're all different.'

'I mean as small as you?'

Arrietty laughed. 'Oh, don't be silly!' she said. 'Surely you don't think there are many people in the world your size?'

# E. B. WHITE

FROM *Charlotte's Web*

One evening, a few days after the writing had
appeared in Charlotte's web, the spider called a
meeting of all the animals in the barn cellar.

'I shall begin by calling the roll. Wilbur?'

'Here!' said the pig.

'Gander?'

'Here, here, here!' said the gander.

'You sound like three ganders,' muttered Charlotte.
'Why can't you just say "here"? Why do you have to
repeat everything?'

'It's my idio-idio-idiosyncrasy,' replied the gander.

'Goose?' said Charlotte.

'Here, here, here!' said the goose. Charlotte glared at
her.

'Goslings, one through seven?'

'Bee-bee-bee!' 'Bee-bee-bee!' 'Bee-bee-bee!' 'Bee-bee-
bee!' 'Bee-bee-bee!' 'Bee-bee-bee!' 'Bee-bee-bee!' said the
goslings.

'This is getting to be quite a meeting,' said Charlotte.
'Anybody would think we had three ganders, three geese,
and twenty-one goslings. Sheep?'

'He-aa-aa!' answered the sheep all together.

'Lambs?'

'He-aa-aa!' answered the lambs all together.

'Templeton?'

No answer.

'Templeton?'

No answer.

'Well, we are all here except the rat,' said Charlotte. 'I guess we can proceed without him. Now, all of you must have noticed what's been going on around here the last few days. The message I wrote in my web, praising Wilbur, has been received. The Zuckermans have fallen for it, and so has everybody else. Zuckerman thinks Wilbur is an unusual pig, and therefore he won't want to kill him and eat him. I dare say my trick will work and Wilbur's life can be saved.'

'Hurray!' cried everybody.

'Thank you very much,' said Charlotte. 'Now I called this meeting in order to get suggestions. I need new ideas for the web. People are already getting sick of reading the words "SOME PIG!" If anybody can think of another message, or remark, I'll be glad to weave it into the web. Any suggestions for a new slogan?'

'How about "Pig Supreme"?' asked one of the lambs.

'No good,' said Charlotte. 'It sounds like a rich dessert.'

'How about "Terrific, terrific, terrific"?' asked the goose.

'Cut that down to one "terrific" and it will do very nicely,' said Charlotte. 'I think "terrific" might impress Zuckerman.'

'But Charlotte,' said Wilbur, 'I'm *not* terrific.'

'That doesn't make a particle of difference,' replied Charlotte. 'Not a particle. People believe almost anything they see in print. Does anybody here know how to spell "terrific"?'

'I think,' said the gander, 'it's tee double ee double rr double rr double eye double ff double eye double see see see see see.'

'What kind of acrobat do you think I am?' said Charlotte in disgust. 'I would have to have St Vitus's Dance to weave a word like that into my web.'

'Sorry, sorry, sorry,' said the gander.

Then the oldest sheep spoke up. 'I agree that there should be something new written in the web if Wilbur's life is to be saved. And if Charlotte needs help in finding words, I think she can get it from our friend Templeton. The rat visits the dump regularly and has access to old magazines. He can tear out bits of advertisements and bring them up here to the barn cellar, so that Charlotte can have something to copy.'

'Good idea,' said Charlotte. 'But I'm not sure Templeton will be willing to help. You know how he is – always looking out for himself, never thinking of the other fellow.'

'I bet I can get him to help,' said the old sheep. 'I'll appeal to his baser instincts, of which he has plenty. Here he comes now. Everybody keep quiet while I put the matter up to him!'

The rat entered the barn the way he always did – creeping along close to the wall.

'What's up?' he asked, seeing the animals assembled.

'We're holding a directors' meeting,' replied the old sheep.

'Well, break it up!' said Templeton. 'Meetings bore me.' And the rat began to climb a rope that hung against the wall.

'Look,' said the old sheep, 'next time you go to the dump, Templeton, bring back a clipping from a magazine. Charlotte needs new ideas so she can write messages in her web and save Wilbur's life.'

'Let him die,' said the rat. 'I should worry.'

'You'll worry all right when next winter comes,' said the sheep. 'You'll worry all right on a zero morning next January when Wilbur is dead and nobody comes down here with a nice pail of warm slops to pour into the trough. Wilbur's left-over food is your chief source of supply, Templeton. *You* know that. Wilbur's food is your food; therefore Wilbur's destiny and your destiny are closely linked. If Wilbur is killed and his trough stands empty day after day, you'll grow so thin we can look right through your stomach and see objects on the other side.'

Templeton's whiskers quivered.

'Maybe you're right,' he said gruffly. 'I'm making a trip to the dump tomorrow afternoon. I'll bring back a magazine clipping if I can find one.'

'Thanks,' said Charlotte. 'The meeting is now adjourned. I have a busy evening ahead of me. I've got to tear my web apart and write TERRIFIC.'

Wilbur blushed. 'But I'm *not* terrific, Charlotte. I'm just about average for a pig.'

'You're terrific as far as *I'm* concerned,' replied Charlotte, sweetly, 'and that's what counts. You're my best friend, and *I* think you're sensational. Now stop arguing and go and get some sleep!'

# LUCY M. BOSTON

FROM *The Children of Green Knowe*

When he woke Mrs Oldknow was standing by his bed smiling at him.

'It's time to get up. Look, the floods have all gone in the night. Come and see.' She opened the window to lean out. 'Tolly! Quick! Quick!'

Under the high window all the lawns were emerald green. Beyond them the river flowed obediently in its own course, and beyond that again were miles of green meadow. Right in front of the window where the last pool was draining away from a hollow in the grass, a large silvery thing was twisting and jumping violently in the sun.

'It's a great big fish.'

'It's one of Toby's carp from the moat. Silly thing – it got left behind when the water went away. Run, Tolly, put on your coat and your wellingtons and throw it back into the moat.'

Tolly ran as fast as he could, slithering down the steep winding stairs in his socks and pulling on his wellingtons by the front door. He reached the fish before anyone else, but it was nearly as big as himself, and flapped so wildly when he picked it up that he was afraid and let it fall again. Then it gasped horribly and lay still, and now he was afraid to touch it in case it was dying. Just then Boggis arrived with a wheelbarrow.

'Quick, quick, Mr Boggis! It's Toby's fish. It's dying! It's Toby's! Mr Boggis, quick!'

Boggis came without any hurry and bent his bright red face down to look.

'Ay, it's one of Master Toby's sure enough. What a size it have grown to! Must be hundreds of years old.'

He put the fish in his barrow and led Tolly to the moat, which was a ring of deep water all round the garden. There he tipped the barrow up and the fish plopped in and disappeared. They stood and looked at the place where it had fallen.

'Was it still alive?' asked Tolly. As he spoke, a fish face was poked above the surface, then there was a swirl of water, a flip of a tail, and it was gone.

'Sure enough it was!' said Boggis.

'It was a very ugly fish,' said Toseland.

'T'aint no beauty. No more will you be when you're a hundred years old! Master Toby used to feed it with bread.'

'It came when he called it,' added Mrs Oldknow, joining them. 'Its name is Neptune. Toby used to tell Linnet that it understood Latin. He always talked to it in Latin. She was very much impressed.'

'What did he say to it?'

'He said "*Veni Neptune. Panem dabo tibi et vermes*".'

'I don't know any Latin.'

'Neither did Linnet. It means "Come Neptune. I will give you bread and worms". In the garden you will find a platform over a pool where he fed them.'

They fed the birds together. Tolly wanted his hands to be buttered again, but was told that that was only for the introduction ceremony, not for every day.

'Do the birds understand Latin?'

'No, not Latin. Music. Alexander used to play the flute to them. They used to sing when he played, but all different tunes. Only the thrushes learnt his tune and the starlings who never sang it properly – they only made fun of it.'

'What tune did the thrushes sing?'

' "Greensleeves", for one.'

'Oh Granny, I know "Greensleeves". I do really. At school we had it on the wireless. I wish I had a flute.'

'Perhaps you'll get one for Christmas. That's quite soon, you know. Now finish your breakfast and then you can explore the garden.'

The garden had looked very desolate when the water was over it, but now even the trees looked different and every path seemed to lead just where it was most exciting to go. First he went round the east corner of the house that he had not yet seen. Broken stones stuck out all up the wall, as if there had once been a building there that had been pulled down. In fact there was still a high garden wall with arched slits in it that must once have been windows. Ferns and shrubs and ivy were growing out of the cracks between the stones and there was a lovely smell in the air. Quite suddenly he became aware of something so big that at first he had not seen it.

Against the side of the house, immensely tall and half covered with festoons of Old Man's Beard, was a stone figure. The first thing that attracted his attention to it was, close to the ground, some stone fishes swimming in what looked like stone water, as though the flood had left something behind. Then he saw that behind the fishes were two huge bare stone feet that seemed to be paddling with stone ripples round the ankles; above them, legs and folds of clothing. High above that, so that he had to step back to look up at it, among the twining strings of the creeper he saw the head of a giant

stone man, carrying a child on his shoulders.

Tolly was astonished. He looked and looked at it and could not go away. He played round its feet for a long time, collecting coloured pebbles out of the gravel, and stones that were like different things, such as a peg-top, an egg, a calf's face, a hammer-head; and a real marble. Every now and then he would look up to see the statue again. Its surface was worn soft by rain and frost and wind, not shiny and hard like monuments in churches. It looked friendly and nearly alive. Tolly loved it.

At last curiosity led him away to see where the other paths would lead him. There were many big trees and wild places where there were only little paths like rabbit runs. As he went along the birds went with him. They whistled and chirped on every side and always flew out of the bushes just before he arrived there, to perch on others just ahead. He followed a track round the edge of the moat, shuffling his feet in the dead leaves and pine-needles and stooping under low branches. Here, in a little clearing between two huge trees he found his next great surprise.

Standing on the grass with its ears pricked up as if it had just heard him was a deer that was a bush. It was like Toby's deer in the picture, but cut out of live evergreen with brown bush-stalk legs growing out of the ground. Toseland stroked it; its neck felt soft. It seemed so much alive that it was queer that of course it couldn't have eyes. How wild it looks without eyes, he thought. How magic! It took his breath away. And then he saw, sitting under a big beech tree, a green yew squirrel with a high tail. That seemed to be listening too. Other living things beside the birds were rustling in the bushes, and he heard other calls, more like children than birds. Tolly ran, hoping to catch them. He found nothing but a live rabbit that bolted in long hops and shot down a hole. He ran on down the little path, past a yew peacock — that was comparatively ordinary. Further on there was a green hare sitting very erect by the water's edge; then the path suddenly turned and left the water, going by a bank of trees and dense undergrowth and brambles where it would be almost impossible to walk. It came out between a yew cock and hen, on to a large lawn.

Tolly wanted to get back to the water again, and by-and-by he found a flight of steps which led down towards it. Here the moat formed a deep pool overshadowed by trees, though now it was winter and the branches were bare except for the birds that had followed him and perched there. The water was brown with a blue gloss relfected on it from the sky, like a starling's back. The steps ended in a wooden platform. As Tolly stood and looked into the water he thought he saw, deep down, a great, shadowy fish swimming slowly. This, then, was Toby's platform.

Tolly tried to remember the Latin, but he knew it was

hopeless. He would only make silly noises and the fish would know it was wrong. Just then something fell in the water. He couldn't see what it was because it sank and wobbled as it went down, but the old carp rose slowly to meet it and opened his mouth to suck it in. Then he sank again out of sight. What can that have been, thought Toseland. Perhaps a greedy blackbird took more breakfast that it could eat and threw its last crust away. And yet I don't believe that. It couldn't have tut-tutted and called so much if its mouth was full.

He began to retrace his steps and now in the wood path he was sure there were others beside himself. Of couse, he thought suddenly. It's hide-and-seek! 'Coo-ee!' he called. 'The Green Deer is den!' He ran as fast as he could till he stopped, out of breath, with his arms round the Green Deer's neck. Then he heard unmistakable breathless laughter quite close to him and felt something on his head. He put his hand up and found a twig. It was not something that could have fallen off any of the trees round him. It was cut out of a reddish bush and made a perfect T.

When he got back to the house he turned for another look at the stone man. Mrs Oldknow was there with some garden scissors cutting branches off the shrubs, which he now noticed with a little disappointment were covered with the peculiar flowers he had first seen in the entrance hall.

'When I first came,' he said, 'I thought those were magic flowers in the hall.'

'So you were afraid I was a witch?'

'Yes, before I saw you.'

'Well, this flower is called Witchhazel. And this is Winter Sweet, and this is Daphne. She was turned into a bush, you know.' Mrs Oldknow, who saw everything, was looking at the twig T in his hand. 'You found the Green Deer? And somebody's been teasing you, I see. When I was little I used to find a twig L in my lap. You see, my Christian name is Linnet.'

'Did they play hide-and-seek with you?'

'Yes.'

Toseland was looking at the stone man. 'Who is he?'

'He is our own St Christopher, and these ruins are where his chapel stood until some stupid wretch pulled it down. There is always a St Christopher by an old ford, and the ford across this river was at the end of the garden. You know the story? He carried the infant Jesus across in a storm, thinking it would be easy, but half-way across he began to feel the child as heavy as the sorrow of the whole world. Linnet loved St Christopher quite specially. She always liked to play here. I planted what you thought were magic flowers for winter incense. This if my favourite part of the garden too. Now, tell me where you've been this morning?'

'I've seen the Green Deer and all the other green things.'

'*All?* Which have you seen?'

'The deer and the squirrel and the peacock and the hare and the cock and the hen.'

Mrs Oldknow seemed relieved. 'And what else?'

'And I found Toby's steps by the water. And I saw the fish again. And *they* played hide-and-seek.'

Tolly was glad that Mrs Oldknow seemed not at all surprised by the hide-and-seek. He was not quite sure whether she thought that he and she were playing a game together pretending that there were other children, or whether she thought, as he did, that the children were really there.

# ROSEMARY SUTCLIFF

FROM *The Eagle of the Ninth*

It was full daylight before the next attack came. Somewhere, a war-horn brayed, and before the wild note
died, the tribesmen broke for cover, yelling like fiends
out of Tartarus as they swarmed up through the bracken;
heading for the gates this time, with tree-trunks to serve
as rams, with firebrands that gilded the falling mizzle
and flashed on the blade of sword and heron-tufted war
spear. On they stormed, heedless of the Roman arrows
that thinned their ranks as they came. Marcus, standing
in the shooting turret beside the Praetorian gate, saw a
figure in their van, a wild figure in streaming robes that
marked him out of the half-naked warriors who charged
behind him. Sparks flew from the firebrand that he
whirled aloft, and in its light the horns of the young
moon, rising from his forehead, seemed to shine with a
fitful radiance of its own. Marcus said quietly to the
archer beside him, 'Shoot me that maniac.'

The man nocked another arrow to his bow, bent and
loosed in one swift movement. The Gaulish Auxiliaries
were fine bowmen, as fine as the British; but the arrow
sped out only to pass through the wild hair of the leaping
fanatic. There was no time to loose again. The attack
was thundering on the gates, pouring in over the dead in
the ditch with a mad courage that took no heed of losses.
In the gate towers the archers stood loosing steadily into
the heart of the press below them. The acrid reek of

smoke and smitch drifted across the fort from the Dexter Gate, which the tribesmen had attempted to fire. There was a constant two-way traffic of reserves and armament going up to the ramparts and wounded coming back from them. No time to carry away the dead; one toppled them from the rampart walk that they might not hamper the feet of the living, and left them, though they had been one's best friend, to be dealt with at a fitter season.

The second attack drew off at last, leaving their dead lying twisted among the trampled fern. Once more there was breathing space for the desperate garrison. The morning dragged on; the British archers crouched behind the dark masses of uprooted blackthorn that they had set up under cover of the first assault, and loosed an arrow at any movement on the ramparts; the next rush might come at any moment. The garrison had lost upward of fourscore men, killed or wounded: two days would bring them reinforcements from Durinum, if only the mizzle which obscured the visibility would clear, just for a little while, long enough for them to send up the smoke signal, and for it to be received.

But the mizzle showed no signs of lifting, when Marcus went up to the flat signal-roof of the Praetorium. It blew in his face, soft and chill-smelling, and faintly salt on his lips. Faint grey swathes of it drifted across the nearer hills, and those beyond were no more than a spreading stain that blurred into nothingness.

'It is no use, sir,' said the auxiliary who squatted against the parapet, keeping the great charcoal brazier glowing.

Marcus shook his head. Had it been like this when the Ninth Legion ceased to be? he wondered. Had his father and all those others watched, as he was watching now, for the far hills to clear so that a signal might go through? Suddenly he found that he was praying, praying as he had never prayed before, flinging his appeal for help up through the grey to the clear skies that were beyond. 'Great God Mithras, Slayer of the Bull, Lord of the Ages, let the mists part and thy glory shine through! Draw back the mists and grant us clear air for a space, that we go not down into the darkness. O God of the Legions, hear the cry of thy sons. Send down thy light upon us, even upon us, thy sons of the Fourth Gaulish Cohort of the Second Legion.'

He turned to the auxiliary, who knew only that the Commander had stood beside him in silence for a few moments, with his head tipped back as though he was looking for something in the soft and weeping sky. 'All we can do is wait,' he said. 'Be ready to start your smother at any moment.' And swinging on his heel, he rounded the great pile of fresh grass and fern that lay ready near the brazier, and went clattering down the narrow stairway.

Centurion Fulvius was waiting for him at the foot with some urgent question that must be settled, and it was some while before he snatched another glance over the ramparts; but when he did, it seemed to him that he could see a little farther than before. He touched Drusillus, who was beside him, on the shoulder. 'Is it my imagining, or are the hills growing clearer?'

Drusillus was silent a moment, his grim face turned towards the east. Then he nodded. 'If it is your imagining, it is also mine.' Their eyes met quickly, with hope that they dared not put into any more words; then they went each about their separate affairs.

But soon others of the garrison were pointing,

straining their eyes eastward in painful hope. Little by little the light grew: the mizzle was lifting, lifting . . . and ridge behind wild ridge of hills coming into sight.

High on the Praetorium roof a column of black smoke sprang upward, billowed sideways and spread into a drooping veil that trailed across the northern rampart, making the men there cough and splutter; then rose again, straight and dark and urgent, into the upper air. In the pause that followed, eyes and hearts were strained with a sickening intensity toward those distant hills. A long, long pause it seemed; and then a shout went up from the watchers, as, a day's march to the east, a faint dark thread of smoke rose into the air.

The call for help had gone through. In two days, three at the most, relief would be here; and the uprush of confidence touched every man of the garrison.

Barely an hour later, word came back to Marcus from the northern rampart that the missing patrol had been sighted on the track that led to the Sinister Gate. He was in the Praetorium when the word reached him, and he covered the distance to the gate as if his heels were winged; he waved up the Cavalry waiting beside their saddled horses, and found Centurion Drusillus once again by his side.

'The tribesmen have broken cover, sir,' said the centurion.

Marcus nodded. 'I must have half a Century of the reserves. We can spare no more. A trumpeter with them and every available man on the gate, in case they try a rush when it opens.'

The centurion gave the order, and turned back to him. 'Better let me take them, sir.'

Marcus had already unclasped the fibula at the shoulder

of his cloak, and flung off the heavy folds that might hamper him. 'We went into that before. You can lend me your shield, though.'

The other slipped it from his shoulder without a word, and Marcus took it and swung round on the half Century who were already falling in abreast of the gate. 'Get ready to form testudo,' he ordered. 'And you can leave room for me. This tortoise is not going into action with its head stuck out!'

It was a poor joke, but a laugh ran through the desperate little band, and as he stepped into his place in the column head, Marcus knew that they were with him in every sense of the word; he could take those lads through the fires of Tophet if need be.

The great bars were drawn, and men stood ready to swing wide the heavy valves; and behind and on every side he had a confused impression of grim ranks massed to hold the gate, and draw them in again if ever they won back to it.

'Open up!' he ordered; and as the valves began to swing outward on their iron-shod posts, 'Form testudo.' His arm went up as he spoke, and through the whole column behind him he felt the movement echoed, heard the light kiss and click of metal on metal, as every man linked shield with his neighbour, to form the shield-roof which gave the formation its name. 'Now!'

The gates were wide; and like a strange many-legged beast, a gigantic woodlouse rather than a tortoise, the testudo was out across the causeway and heading straight downhill, its small, valiant cavalry wings spread on either side. The gates closed behind it, and from rampart and gate-tower anxious eyes watched it go. It had all been done so quickly that at the foot of the slope battle had only just joined, as the tribesmen hurled themselves yelling on the swiftly formed Roman square.

The testudo was not a fighting formation; but for rushing a position, for a break through, it had no equal. Also it had a strange and terrifying aspect that could be very useful. Its sudden appearance now, swinging down upon them with the whole weight of the hill behind it, struck a brief confusion into the swarming tribesmen. Only for a moment their wild ranks wavered and lost purpose; but in that moment the hard-pressed patrol saw it too, and with a hoarse shout came charging to join their comrades.

Down swept Marcus and his half Century, down and forward into the raging battle-mass of the enemy. They were slowed almost to a standstill, but never quite halted; once they were broken, but re-formed. A mailed wedge cleaving into the wild ranks of the tribesmen, until the moment came when the tortoise could serve them no longer; and above the turmoil Marcus shouted to the trumpeter beside him: 'Sound me "Break testudo".'

The clear notes of the trumpet rang through the uproar. The men lowered their shields, springing sideways to gain fighting space; and a flight of pilums hurtled into the swaying horde of tribesmen, spreading death and confusion wherever the iron heads struck. Then it was 'Out swords', and the charge driven home with a shout of 'Caesar! Caesar!' Behind them the valiant handful of cavalry were struggling to keep clear the line of retreat; in front, the patrol came grimly battling up to join them. But between them was still a living rampart of yelling, battle-frenzied warriors, amongst whom Marcus glimpsed again that figure with the horned moon on its forehead. He laughed, and sprang against them, his men storming behind him.

Patrol and relief force joined, and became one.

Instantly they began to fall back, forming as they did so a roughly diamond formation that faced outward on all sides and was as difficult to hold as a wet pebble pressed between the fingers. The tribesmen thrust in on them from every side, but slowly, steadily, their short blades like a hedge of living, leaping steel, the cavalry breaking the way for them in wild rushes, they were drawing back towards the fortress gate – those that were left of them.

Back, and back. And suddenly the press was thinning, and Marcus, on the flank, snatched one glance over his shoulder, and saw the gate-towers very near, the swarming ranks of the defenders ready to draw them in. And in that instant there came a warning yelp of trumpets and a swelling thunder of hooves and wheels, as round the curve of the hill towards them, out of cover of the woodshore, swept a curved column of chariots.

Small wonder that the press had thinned.

The great battle-wains had long been forbidden to the tribes, and these were light chariots such as the one Marcus had driven two days ago, each carrying only a spearman beside the driver; but one horrified glance, as they hurtled nearer behind their thundering teams, was enough to show the wicked, whirling scythe-blades on the war-hubs of the wheels.

Close formation – now that their pilums were spent – was useless in the face of such a charge; again the trumpets yelped an order, and the ranks broke and scattered, running for the gateway, not in any hope of reaching it before the chariots were upon them, but straining heart and soul to gain the advantage of the high ground.

To Marcus, running with the rest, it seemed suddenly that there was no weight in his body, none at all. He was filled through and through with a piercing awareness of life and the sweetness of life held in his hollowed hand, to be tossed away like the shining balls that the children played with in the gardens of Rome. At the last instant, when the charge was almost upon them, he swerved aside from his men, out and back on his tracks, and flinging aside his sword, stood tensed to spring, full in the path of the oncoming chariots. In the breath of time that remained, his brain felt very cold and clear, and he seemed to have space to do quite a lot of thinking. If he sprang for the heads of the leading team, the odds were that he would merely be flung down and driven over without any check to the wild gallop. His best chance was to go for the charioteer. If he could bring him down, the whole team would be flung into confusion, and on that steep scarp the chariots coming behind would have difficulty in clearing the wreck. It was a slim chance, but if it came off it would gain for his men those few extra moments that might mean life or death. For himself, it was death. He was quite clear about that.

They were right upon him, a thunder of hooves that seemed to fill the universe; black manes streaming against the sky; the team that he had called his brothers, only two days ago. He hurled his shield clanging among them, and side-stepped, looking up into the grey face of Cradoc, the charioteer. For one splinter of time their eyes met in something that was almost a salute, a parting salute between two who might have been friends; then Marcus leapt in under the spearman's descending thrust, upward and sideways across the chariot bow. His weight crashed on to the reins, whose ends, after the British fashion, were wrapped about the charioteer's waist, throwing the team into instant chaos; his arms were round Cradoc, and they went half down together. His ears were full of the sound of rending timber and the hideous scream of a horse. Then sky and earth changed places, and with his hold still unbroken, he was flung down under the trampling hooves, under the scythe-bladed wheels and the collapsing welter of the overset chariot; and the jagged darkness closed over him.

# WILLIAM MAYNE

FROM *A Swarm in May*

The Cathedral clock struck four. The swarm still floated high. Soon it would be beyond the Precincts, beyond the city wall, and over the town ditch, and find itself not thirty but eighty feet in the air. But what could be done? The swarm was too far away to be sprayed with water and made cool. Perhaps an expert beekeeper would have flung the hat into the air, scooped the swarm up in it, and brought it home. What was the other thing? Make a noise. There were only shouting and singing he could do alone. If he had brought the tin tray he could have made a great deal of noise comfortably. But now he had only his voice.

He began 'Men of Harlech', looking at the bees all the time. They began to hover, then they came down a little way; and then flew on faster than before. Owen walked faster, and gave them an Easter hymn with loud joyful alleluias. The bees slowed down, and came lower. 'Lead us, Heavenly Father, lead us' brought them down to ten feet, and turned them a little to the south, where they might go into Canon Fredley's garden. Owen gave them something loud: a Vaughan Williams *Te Deum* in G, which is often sung with half a dozen trumpets to help the organ. Out here, on the grass, with no brass and no organ and only solo treble the *Te Deum* sounded like a Zulu war song; but it brought the bees to eye level: they cruised at walking speed until they flew into the corner of the cricket net, on the inside; and there, though they could have flown through the mesh, they stayed.

Owen stopped at 'we therefore pray Thee, help Thy servants', which is a quiet phrase; put the hat down, and sprayed the bees with water.

Although they had landed there was almost as much noise as before, something like the buzzing of one of the Cathedral windows when Dr Sunderland played deep notes. But the bees were all in one place now, like a huge wicket-keeping glove blown there by a gale.

The spray of water brought them together more compactly. They began to make themselves into little down-hanging castle walls, on the net and on the corner post; and they would suddenly bring the walls apart, and hang them somewhere else, or lose them among the other bees.

Owen gave them 'Flocks in pastures green abiding' and then 'Up, up my heart with gladness'; both sung very quick and quiet and to the bees alone. Every now and then he gave them a spoonful of water; and they gradually started to be a single castle built of bees, hanging from the top cord of the net.

Owen dared not leave them. He looked round. There was still no one to be seen anywhere.

How could the bees be put in a hat and carried back to the hive? If he gave a gentle shake to the net post, and held the hat underneath them, they might go in. But would they stay? Would they go in?

He began to do it. He felt the post. It had been securely guyed, and it was immovable; he lifted it, and it came up two inches, enough to lift the spike from the ground. But the guy ropes were outside the net, and stretched to the top of the post; so the nearer they came to the net the more they were out of reach. Owen sang 'John Brown's Body', and 'To Thee O Lord our hearts we raise'; got out his penknife, cut two threads of the net, and reached through to the guy rope; his face was no more than a foot from the swarm; and he suddenly saw that the mass of bees was hollow; a tube of bees reaching up, looking inside like a mitten; a mitten of bees. One guy rope broke and the net sagged. The post was loose now.

Owen turned round; and out from his pocket came threepence and a handkerchief and the Prior's key, all tangled in the chain; and they fell on the grass. Owen picked them up with his left hand, so he was unable to put them back in his pocket – there was only one in his cassock. The right hand was holding the post. He changed tunes to 'There's a hole in my bucket', and changed hands on the post, to bring the right hand where it could break through and cut the second guy rope. The other one had to control a pocketful of things as well as the post; but he managed it.

When the guy was cut the post began to lean inwards, and the net to droop against his shoulders. He put away the knife and let the post down lower. The bees began to hang at a different angle. He juggled the handkerchief over his right hand, picked up the hat, and held it by the rim. 'They don't sting when they're swarming,' he thought, sang 'In His hand are all the corners of the earth', and worked out what he had to do. His right hand held all his clutter now: he had changed things from hand to hand as he went, the key and threepence, and the handkerchief over his wrist, and the hat itself. The syringe was on the ground at his feet; the bees were on the post; and the post was under his left hand. He

held the hat under the bees. He shook the post sharply. The net on either side billowed out like a wave. The bees rippled and shook, and suddenly they were in the hat falling like a great blob of jam.

They were heavier than he had expected. His hand went down with the weight, until he bent his elbow and brought it up again. But by that time the bees had collected themselves and boiled over, and left the hat empty; and they were suddenly hanging from his unprepared hand, and then the weight was not directly on his hand but on something in his hand; and the thing they clung to was the white globe on the Prior's key.

He had the chain and the key in his hand, and all the weight of the bees was on them. They hung there quietly, but still with an internal buzzing and movement. And what kept them was the white globe. From the globe came that curious smell; but now it stayed, and hung round the bees.

Owen slid the chain down between his fingers, and held the key across the palm of his hand. The weight of the swarm pulled the metal into his skin, so he wrapped the handkerchief round it. With a little contortion and ingenuity he sprayed some water on the swarm, as a safeguard. Then, putting the empty hat on his head, carrying the swarm with his right hand and the syringe with his left, he began to walk back to Dr Sunderland's house.

The people who saw him thought that the choirboys of the Cathedral wore a quaint uniform; but no one thought he had ten pounds-worth of bees hanging from his right hand.

# HENRY TREECE

FROM *Viking's Dawn*

Then suddenly Harald was awake again. The fire had gone out completely now, but the hall was full of movement. Then there was the flash of flint on iron and a torch flamed out. Harald saw that the vikings were on their feet, their weapons drawn. There was a great shout in his ear. Aun yelled, 'Out steel, we are betrayed.' Then the hall was full of leaping shapes and swords rose and fell, vicious in the dim light.

Harald found himself between Aun and Gnorre. Horic was somewhere behind them, grunting as he struck out. A Pict, wearing feathers in his helmet, came at them. Harald saw the mad light in his eyes as the man thrust out with a long leaf-bladed sword. The weapon seemed to flash before the boy's very eyes, then the man screamed and tumbled forward with the impetus of his rush, almost knocking Harald's feet from under him. Aun bent and swung up his axe again. Gnorre said, 'Don't fall, lad, or it will be your end. Keep your feet and we may win to the door.'

They began a slow rhythmic movement across the hall. They passed Björn, who stood over the bodies of Hasting and Ivar. He was beset on every side, but spared a word as he swung his axe. 'Do not stay, Aun Doorback,' he said. 'If Odin wills it, I shall come down to the ship again. If not, then he means me to travel with these two vikings home.'

Harald saw that Hasting and Ivar had not survived their wounds, gained earlier in the sea-fight. Then he saw Thorkell at the far end of the hall, surrounded by their dark-skinned enemies. Feinn, with whom he had taken the blood-oath that night, pressed close at him, taunting him. 'So this is what men mean when they say: "Trust a viper before a viking!" I had not thought you would so soon forget your friend's promise.'

Thorkell swept his long blade about the circle that tried to close on him. 'It is you, Feinn, who are the breaker of vows. I have done nothing worse than trying to get a night's sleep since I last saw you.'

Feinn and his followers laughed in derision, and lunged in at the golden-haired leader.

Gnorre looked round and said, 'I do not see Ragnar, or any of those who follow him rather than Thorkell. Come, Aun, we must spare a blow for Thorkell before we go!'

The four of them pressed forward to where their leader fought. He was a fine sight, even though outnumbered. His hair was disarranged, and his shirt of mail pulled on carelessly. Even the strappings of his hide breeches dangled behind him as he shuffled now in this direction, now in that, to meet and slash at a foeman. Yet, for all that, he looked a hero, even the son of Thor himself, thought Harald.

Aun yelled, 'Up Thorkell! Up the *Nameless*!' Gnorre joined him in the cry, but Horic and Harald were silent. Yet all pushed on, and now, with the men beside him, even Harald felt a strange desire for battle. It seemed to him that now they were fighting with good cause, and not merely to win treasure. They were fighting a treacherous enemy, for their very lives, and to save their leader, to whom they had pledged themselves.

They took the Picts by surprise. Some of them turned at Aun's first shout and put up sword or small buckler as defence. But two at least of them were too late, Peacegiver rose and fell, rose and fell. Horic's rough sword thrust to left and to right. Then a bundled dark shape launched itself at Harald. He heard Gnorre's shout of warning, but it came too late. The man was on him, stabbing furiously with a short dagger. Harald felt the blade sear his shoulder, and then, in a great anger, he shortened his spear, and using it like a sword, struck with all his force at the man who attacked him. He felt the jar of the blow along his arm and then the man seemed to run on past him, sideways, dragging the spear from his grasp.

Gnorre said, 'Your first blood! Hail viking! Thorkell shall give you another weapon now.'

Harald's heart swelled, for he saw Thorkell's eyes glance at him and a grim smile come across his leader's face. Thorkell had seen him fight his first battle. Then a great wave of nausea swept over the boy, and he wished that the Pict had never run at him.

The next thing he knew he was standing next to Thorkell, and they were all pushing their terrible way to the open door, through which Harald saw the stars shining out of a deep blue-black sky.

Behind them, still clustered in the hall, were their enemy. Feinn was leaning against the wall, his hand over his chest, the dark blood ebbing between his white fingers, a vicious grin on his swarthy face.

Harald heard him gasp, 'Thorkell Traitor, though you leave me so, my gods will follow you. Their arm is long.'

Thorkell's face twisted in a smile of sadness. It was as

though he wished to go to Feinn. Then with a shrug he remembered where he was and they turned to go through the door into the night.

Yet, even as they turned, a dark shape lying in the doorway moved. A man raised himself on his elbow and flung the short axe he had clenched in his hand. The blow was meant for Thorkell, but Gnorre saw the axe as it flew through the air and stepped towards it, keeping it from the leader. Harald heard the haft thud on Gnorre's temples, and stepped across to catch him as he fell. Aun gave a great roar of anger and struck down towards the floor. The man lay still.

Gnorre was unconscious and the blood flowed down his face. Aun took him on to his broad back and carried him. Horic and Thorkell paused for a moment in the doorway. They called Björn, but he would not come. He still stood over the bodies of his comrades, singing quietly to himself, a terrible rhythm of death, like the song that oarsmen sing when they battle against a contrary tide.

'Up–ay–aa! Up–ay–aa!'

His sword struck again and again. His eyes were glazed. He did not know where he was, it seemed.

Thorkell whispered, 'Odin holds out his hands for Björn. He will never come away now.'

Then he called out softly, 'Farewell, viking. We must go down to the ship your hands built. May they build even better ships where you are going.'

Harald felt the hot tears running down his cheeks. He saw that Thorkell was crying too. As they turned, Björn snatched up a pine torch and was swinging it round him as he shambled towards the ring of men who waited, like hungry wolves, for his great strength to fail.

When they were half-way down the hill that gave on to the beach, they looked back at the sudden glow in the sky behind them.

'Björn has made himself a funeral pyre,' said Aun. 'Now if Feinn lives, he must build himself another hall!'

Then they saw the *Nameless*. She was already afloat and ready to move away. Thorkell shouted, and down below them Ragnar answered, 'Hurry, Thorkell,' he said. 'We had given you up for lost. The tide pulls us away. Hurry!'

They struggled over the rough shingle and on into the water, breast-high before they reached the longship. Rough hands dragged them aboard. Harald saw Gnorre's eyes flicker, and he heard him whisper something to Aun, who bent over him like a mother over her child.

Horic whispered, 'Gnorre's wound is not deep, lad. Sleep happily.'

Then Harald fell his length on the hard wet boards, exhausted in body and in mind. He did not hear the gulls crying or the wind slapping against the great mainsail. He did not hear Thorkell's harsh words to Ragnar, or Ragnar's ironic laughter. Nor did he hear Ragnar say, 'You are a fool, Thorkell. I and my band raided their treasure house while you slept. We have brought enough away to make us all rich men. And that is the thanks I get!'

Thorkell said, 'You traitorous dolt! I had taken a blood-oath with Feinn.'

Ragnar pulled at his black beard and said, 'The oath bound you, not me, my friend!'

Harald did not see Thorkell strike the Dane full across the face then, for all men to watch. The boy was deep in sleep.

# PHILIPPA PEARCE

FROM *Tom's Midnight Garden*

Up he went – up and up, and burst at last from the
dim interior into an openness of blue and fiery
gold. The sun was the gold, in a blue sky. All round him
was a spreading, tufted surface of evergreen. He was on
a level with all the yew-tree tops round the lawn; nearly
on a level with the top of the tall south wall.

Tom was on a level, too, with the upper windows of
the house, just across the lawn from him. His attention
was caught by a movement inside one of the rooms: it
came, he saw, from the same maid he had once seen in
the hall. She was dusting a bedroom, and came now to
the window to raise the sash and shake her duster outside.
She looked casually across to the yew-trees as she did so,
and Tom tried waving to her. It was like waving to the
He in blindman's-buff.

The maid went back into the depths of the room, to
her dusting. She left the window open behind her, and
Tom cound now see more. There was someone else in
the room besides the maid – someone who stood against
the far wall, facing the window. The maid evidently
spoke to her companion occasionally as she worked, for
Tom could hear the faint coming and going of voices.
He could not see the other figure at all clearly, except
that it was motionless, and there was the whiteness and
shape of a face that was always turned in his direction.
That steadfastness of direction embarrassed Tom. Very

gradually he began to draw his head downwards, and then suddenly ducked it below tree-level altogether.

Tom saw more people later, in the garden itself. He stalked them warily, and yet – remembering his invisibility to the house-maid – with a certain confidence too.

He was pretty sure that the garden was used more often than he knew. He often had the feeling of people having just gone – and an uncomfortable feeling, out of which he tried to reason himself, again and again, of someone who had *not* gone: someone who, unobserved, observed him. It was a relief really to see people, even when they ignored his presence: the maid, the gardener, and a severe-looking woman in a long dress of rustling purple silk, face to face with whom Tom once came unexpectedly, on a corner. She cut him dead.

Visibility . . . invisibility . . . If he were invisible to the people of the garden, he was not completely so at least to some of the other creatures. How truly they saw him he could not say; but birds cocked their heads at him, and flew away when he approached.

And had he any bodily weight in this garden, or had he not? At first, Tom thought not. When he climbed the yew-tree he had been startled to feel that no bough swung beneath him, and not a twig broke. Later – and this was a great disappointment to him – he found that he could not, by the ordinary grasping and pushing of his hand, open any of the doors in the garden, to go through them. He could not push open the door of the greenhouse or of the little heating-house behind it, or the door in the south wall by the sundial.

The doors shut against Tom were a check upon his curiosity, until he saw a simple way out: he would get through the doorways that interested him by following at the heels of the gardener. He regularly visited the greenhouse, the heating-house, and used the south wall door.

Tom concentrated upon getting through the south wall door. That entry promised to be the easiest, because the gardener went through so often, with his tools. There must be a tool-shed somewhere through there.

The gardener usually went through so quickly and shut the door so smartly behind him, that there was not time for anyone else to slip through as well. However, he would be slower with a wheelbarrow. Tom judged; and he waited patiently for that opportunity. Yet even then the man somehow only made a long arm to open the door ahead of the wheelbarrow, wheeled it very swiftly through, caught the door-edge with the toe of his boot as he passed and slammed the door in Tom's face.

Tom glared at the door that once more was his barrier. Once more, without hope, he raised his hand to the latch and pressed it. As usual, he could not move it: his fingers seemed to have no substance. Then, in anger, he pressed with all imaginable might: he knitted his brows, and brought all his will to bear upon the latch, until he felt that something had to happen. It did: his fingers began to go through the latch, as though the latch, and not his fingers, now, were without substance. His fingers went through the ironwork of the latch altogether, and his hand fell back into place by his side.

Tom stared down at that ever-memorable right hand. He felt it tenderly with his left, to see if it were bruised or broken: it was quite unhurt – quite as before. Then he looked at the latch: it looked as real as any latch he had ever seen anywhere.

Then the idea came to Tom that the door might be no more solid than the latch, if he really tried it.

Deliberately he set his side against the door, shoulder, hip and heel, and pressed. At first, nothing gave, either of himself or the door. Yet he continued the pressure, with still greater force and greater determination; and gradually he became aware of a strange sensation, that at first he thought was a numbness all down his side — but no, it was not that.

'I'm going through,' Tom gasped, and was seized with alarm and delight.

On the other side of the wall, the gardener had emptied his barrow-load of weeds and was sitting on the handle of his barrow, in front of a potting-shed, eating his midday dinner. If he had been able to see Tom at all he would have seen a most curious sight: a very thin slice of a boy, from shoulder to foot, coming through a perfectly solid wooden door. At first the body came through evenly from top to bottom; then, the upper part seemed to stop, and the bottom part came through in its entirety, legs first. Then one arm came through, then another. Finally, everything was through except the head.

The truth was that Tom was now a little lacking courage. The passing through the door of so much of his body had not been without enormous effort and peculiar, if indescribable, sensations. 'I'm just resting a minute,' said Tom's head, on the garden side of the door; yet he knew that he was really delaying because he was nervous. His stomach, for instance, had felt most uncomfortable as it passed through the door; what would the experience be like for his head — his eyes, his ears?

On the other hand — and the new idea was even worse than the old — supposing that, like a locomotive-engine

losing steam-pressure, he lost his present force of body and will-power in this delay? Then, he would be unable to move either forwards or backwards. He would be caught here by the neck, perhaps for ever. And just supposing someone came along, on the far side of the wall, who by some evil chance *could* see him – supposing a whole company came: they would see an entirely defenceless stern sticking out – an invitation to ridicule and attack.

With a convulsive effort, eyes closed, lips sealed, Tom dragged his head through the door, and stood, dizzy, dazed, but whole, on the far side of it.

# PAULINE CLARKE

FROM *The Twelve and the Genii*

The sherry was certainly putting heart into the Twelves. The more they sucked the more noisy they became, and some began to shake their fists as if they meant battle. Max swooped down his finger and thumb, silently took the glass away and returned it to the cupboard. They looked for it for a little, but soon gave up and began to explore again. As they were so very brave and gay at the moment, he decided to risk picking one up. He chose the tall leader, whom somebody had called the Duke. The Duke looked a little amazed at feeling himself clutched and flying through the air, but he did not stiffen, he felt wriggly and lively like the lizard. Max put him down on the open piano and said softly:

'If your Grace likes to march along here it will be as good as a band.' His Grace stepped on to a slippery white key, which gradually let him down and thundered out a deep note. Feeling himself going down, he held out his arms to keep his balance and strode quickly on from note to note up the scale, filling the drawing-room with a tinkle of music.

This seemed to excite the rest even more. Butter Crashey had led a small party towards the french window, where they were looking out to the garden with their hands against the glass. The person called Monkey had climbed up a pile of books waiting to be put away, had

reached the swinging curtain cord, and was now swarming up it like a sailor. After him went the two who were
called Crackey and Tracky, as if the cords were the rig-
ging of a ship. As they climbed, the cord swung.

Meanwhile, poor Bravey, overcome first by Brutus
and then by the sherry, had stumbled as far as the white
fur rug by the fireplace and was marching bravely over it
like a man over a snowdrift, sinking up to his knees and
often falling flat upon his face. As he scrambled up he
was still saying, 'Give us good cheer, eat, drink, dance
and be merry,' though the voice was certainly a little
thick.

Max kept his eye on them all in turn, for he did not
want to lose any. The Duke had reached the top of the
scale, and was now skating back, making an exciting trill
as he skimmed lightly over the notes.

Max decided that he was hungry and saw that it was
tea-time. First, shutting the soldiers carefully into the
drawing-room, he went out to the kitchen, took Brutus
from the window-sill, and gave him his milk outside the
back door. Then he fetched the cake and the buns and the
loaf, the butter and jam, a large mug of milk and everything else he needed, and put them on to the kitchen table.

Now, he went back to the drawing-room. He did not
want to pick everyone up without any warning, in case it
frightened them and spoilt their fun. Added to this, the
most interesting part of the affair was to see what they
could arrange on their own.

He went over to Butter Crashey, who, with his few
followers, was now watching the antics of Monkey,
Crackey and Tracky on the curtain cord. The cord was
swinging wildly. Monkey wanted to slide down, Tracky
wanted to get to the top, and Crackey was caught like a

pig in the middle. Monkey kicked him from above, Tracky butted him from below. The patriarch's men were standing at the bottom of the cord, urging on their favourites, and the noise was like a weasel fight.

The patriarch himself was trying to stop the quarrel and calm the fighters, by holding his arms up, clapping slowly and saying:

'Hush! Halt! Have done!' Max lifted up Crashey, as he still said 'halt', and whispered: 'I want you all to come into the kitchen. How can we collect everyone?'

The patriarch looked at him a moment with his mouth open and then replied, 'Without doubt, the Duke must blow his trumpet. This is what he always did, when he was a humble trumpeter, and the Twelves obeyed. Tell him to do this, and see what follows.'

'But he hasn't got a trumpet,' Max said.

'No, he has become too grand since he was Duke,' said the patriarch.

'What is he duke of?' said Max.

'He is Arthur Wellesley, Duke of Wellington,' said Butter Crashey, solemnly, 'which honour came to him after the famous battle of Waterloo. But perhaps you do not know about Waterloo?'

'I know all about Waterloo,' Max said. 'I'll tell him to tootle without a trumpet.'

Still carrying Crashey, he went over to the piano.

'The patriarch commands your Grace to collect the Twelves,' explained Max.

The Duke stopped dead on middle C, and lifted his empty hands in despair. However, the tootle he produced from his own small throat was bold, piercing and commanding (it reminded Max of a bird's whistle) and before he had finished Max saw the soldiers gathering.

He put the patriarch on the carpet, lifted down the Duke of Wellington, and helped Bravey out of his jungle. Tracky slid down the curtain cord, followed quickly by the others, and soon the whole band was marshalled behind the Duke and marching towards the kitchen.

Max lifted them gingerly one by one on to the kitchen table, and was pleased to see that they did not seem to mind. Then he sat down to enjoy his tea and watch what they would do at the same time.

They marched all round the kitchen table as if to make sure where they were. Then they came nearer to Max's end, and walked round the bread board, pointing up at the loaf as if it were a hillock. They showed great interest in the butter, too, all the more when Max cut a piece off and carried it to his own plate.

Then they gathered round his plate, sat in a circle, and watched each mouthful he took.

'Like Brutus,' Max said. 'I bet you're hungry.'

He gave each man a large crumb of bread, followed by a smaller crumb of cake, and they ate with relish.

'Tell me about your famous expedition to carve out your kingdom amongst the Ashanti,' Max said. 'I know it is ignorant of me not to have heard of it,' he added, 'but I am only eight.'

'Crackey is only five,' remarked a grave-looking soldier whom Max had not noticed much before, 'and *he* has heard of it.'

'Of course he's heard of it if he went on it,' argued Max, rather rudely. And the whole lot threw back their heads and laughed at the grave soldier, who looked sourer than ever. The jaunty one even pointed and jeered.

'You are answered, Gravey,' said the Duke.

'Why is he called Gravey?' asked Max. 'Did he fall in the gravy, or is it to rhyme with Bravey?'

'Both,' said several soldiers, thoughtlessly.

'Neither,' said Butter Crashey. 'He is grave and melancholy, so his name is naturally Gravey.'

'I say, Gravey,' began Max, seeing the poor fellow scowling and drawing his brows together. 'I am sorry I answered you back. Please tell me about the expedition.'

The soldiers began to twitter, and those next to the patriarch nudged him with their elbows.

The patriarch swallowed his last crumb of cake, cleared his throat, and began to speak.

'We set out in a ship called the *Invincible*,' he said. 'I was the captain, Cheeky was the surgeon, and the most stout-hearted man in the ship. The rest were trumpeters and sailors, and those fellows you saw climbing the rope were middies. After many adventures, including storms, and battles with enemies, we reached Africa, fought the Ashanti, and began to build our first town —'

At this minute there was a loud engine noise in the yard, the doors of the motor-car slammed, footsteps ran towards the house, voices yelled and called, and the back door, which Max had carefully closed to keep Brutus out, was flung open with a whoop by Jane.

The effect of all this noise was horrifying. The Twelves scattered in all directions. Several ran to the edge of the table and fell hurtling to the ground. The lively one bumped against the bread board and went flat on his face at the foot of bread hill, lying as if he were stunned. Some simply swooned where they were and slumped as if dead. The patriarch stumbled over the butter dish, fell head first, and was caught by his head and fists in the soft mound.

'Here he is, here he is!' shrieked Jane.

Max, scarlet in the face with rage and fright, dived under the table to rescue the fallen. There was no time to be polite or gentle. He seized them up, counting as he went. One had crawled towards the stove, and Jane's foot was nearly on him.

'Look OUT,' yelled Max.

'All right,' she said crossly. 'What is it? What's the matter?'

'Eight, nine,' muttered Max, standing up, his hair over his eyes. 'Ten,' he said, seizing the greasy Butter Crashey, 'eleven,' he added, tenderly rescuing the little soldier on the bread board.

'Eleven,' said Max, worried.

'Eleven what? What are you doing? Oh, those dirty old soldiers.'

'Shut up,' said Max.

'Don't be so cross, Maxy dear, here we all are. What is it?'

'You're back much earlier than you said,' Max scowled.

'We didn't say,' said Mr Morley. 'Let's have some tea.'

'Yes, come on. Move up, Max, and we'll lay it properly,' said his mother, dumping her parcels.

'Our little man seems upset,' remarked Philip. 'I'm ravening,' he said, taking a bun.

'I've had my tea,' Max said with dignity, clutching his soldiers to his chest, 'and there's one of the Twelves missing, so please don't tread on him. *Please*. He's here somewhere.'

'The twelves?' Mrs Morley said, putting the kettle on. 'What is the twelves?'

'The soldiers. The old soldiers.'

'Oh well, find it, and rescue it, darling.'

'I don't know where he's gone.'

'You've put him down somewhere, he hasn't *gone*.'

'He *has* gone,' said Max, stubbornly. And he turned and went out of the kitchen and tramped slowly up the stairs.

He could feel what had happened. They were all stiff and wooden in his hands, they were frozen. He laid them into their box and their faces were blurred and old again.

'Oh, do come back soon, don't freeze for ever, please, please don't. I want to hear about the expedition,' Max whispered.

# CLIVE KING

### FROM *Stig of the Dump*

Far below was the bottom of the pit. The dump. Barney could see strange bits of wreckage among the moss and elder bushes and nettles. Was that the steering wheel of a ship? The tail of an aeroplane? At least there was a real bicycle. Barney felt sure he could make it go if only he could get at it. They didn't let him have a bicycle.

Barney wished he was at the bottom of the pit.

And the ground gave way.

Barney felt his head going down and his feet going up. There was a rattle of falling earth beneath him. Then he was falling, still clutching the clump of grass that was falling with him.

'This is what it's like when the ground gives way,' thought Barney. Then he seemed to turn a complete somersault in the air, bumped into a ledge of chalk halfway down, crashed through some creepers and ivy and branches, and landed on a bank of moss.

His thoughts did those funny things they do when you bump your head and you suddenly find yourself thinking about what you had for dinner last Tuesday, all mixed up with seven times six. Barney lay with his eyes shut, waiting for his thoughts to stop being mixed up. Then he opened them.

He was lying in a kind of shelter. Looking up he could see a roof, or part of a roof, made of elder branches, a very rotten old carpet, and rusty old sheets of iron. There was a big hole, through which he must have fallen. He could see the white walls of the cliff, the trees and creepers at the top, and the sky with clouds passing over it.

Barney decided he wasn't dead. He didn't even seem to be very much hurt. He turned his head and looked around him. It was dark in this den after looking at the white chalk, and he couldn't see what sort of a place it was. It seemed to be partly a cave dug into the chalk, partly a shelter built out over the mouth of the cave. There was a cool, damp smell. Woodlice and earwigs dropped from the roof where he had broken through it.

But what had happened to his legs? He couldn't sit up when he tried to. His legs wouldn't move. Perhaps I've broken them, Barney thought. What shall I do then? He looked at his legs to see if they were all right, and found they were all tangled up with creeper from the face of the cliff. Who tied me up? thought Barney. He kicked his legs to try to get them free, but it was no use, there were yards of creeper trailing down from the cliff. I suppose I got tangled up when I fell, he thought. Expect I would have broken my neck if I hadn't.

He lay quiet and looked around the cave again. Now that his eyes were used to it he could see further into the dark part of the cave.

There was somebody there!

Or Something!

Something, or Somebody, had a lot of shaggy black hair and two bright black eyes that were looking very hard at Barney.

'Hullo!' said Barney.

Something said nothing.

'I fell down the cliff,' said Barney.

Somebody grunted.

'My name's Barney.'

Somebody-Something made a noise that sounded like 'Stig'.

'D'you think you could help me undo my feet, Mr Stig?' asked Barney politely. 'I've got a pocket-knife,' he added, remembering that he had in his pocket a knife he'd found among the wood-shavings on the floor of Grandfather's workshop. It was quite a good knife except that one blade had come off and the other one was broken in half and rather blunt.

'Good thing I put it in my pocket,' he thought. He wriggled so he could reach the knife, and managed to open the rusty half-blade. He tried to reach the creepers round his legs, but found it was difficult to cut creepers with a blunt knife when your feet are tied above your head.

The Thing sitting in the corner seemed to be interested. It got up and moved towards Barney into the light. Barney was glad to see it was Somebody after all. 'Funny way to dress though,' he thought, 'rabbit skins round the middle and no shoes or socks.'

'Oh puff!' said Barney. 'I can't reach my feet. You do it, Stig!'

He handed the knife to Stig.

Stig turned it over and felt it with his strong hairy hands, and tested the edge with a thumb. Then instead of trying to cut the creepers he squatted down on the ground and picked up a broken stone.

He's going to sharpen the knife, thought Barney.

But no, it seemed more as if he was sharpening the

stone. Using the hard knife to chip with, Stig was care-fully flaking tiny splinters off the edge of the flint, until he had a thin sharp blade. Then he sprang up, and with two or three slashes cut through the creeper that tied Barney's feet.

Barney sat up. 'Golly!' he said. 'You *are* clever! I bet my Grandad couldn't do that, and he's *very* good at making things.'

Stig grinned. Then he went to the back of the cave and hid the broken knife under a pile of rubbish.

'My knife!' protested Barney. But Stig took no notice. Barney got up and went into the dark part of the cave.

He'd never seen anything like the collection of bits and pieces, odds and ends, bric-à-brac and old brock, that this Stig creature had lying about his den. There were stones and bones, fossils and bottles, skins and tins, stacks of sticks and hanks of string. There were motor-car tyres and hats from old scarecrows, nuts and bolts and bobbles from brass bedsteads. There was a coal scuttle full of dead electric light bulbs and a basin with rusty screws and nails in it. There was a pile of bracken and newspapers that looked as if it were used for a bed. The place looked as if it had never been given a tidy-up.

'I wish I lived here,' said Barney.

Stig seemed to understand that Barney was approving of his home and his face lit up. He took on the air of a householder showing a visitor round his property, and began pointing out some of the things he seemed par-ticularly proud of.

First, the plumbing. Where the water dripped through a crack in the roof of the cave he had wedged the mud-guard of a bicycle. The water ran along this, through the tube of a vacuum-cleaner, and into a big can with writing on it. By the side of this was a plastic football carefully cut in half, and Stig dipped up some water and offered it to Barney. Barney had swallowed a mouthful before he made out the writing on the can: it said WEEDKILLER. However, the water only tasted of rust and rubber.

It was dark in the back of the cave. Stig went to the front where the ashes of a fire were smoking faintly, blew on them, picked up a book that lay beside his bed, tore out a page and rolled it up, lit it at the fire, and carried it to a lamp set in a niche in the wall. As it flared up Barney could see it was in fact an old teapot, filled with some kind of oil, and with a bootlace hanging out of it for a wick.

In the light of the lamp Stig went to the very back of the cave and began to thump the wall and point, and explain something in his strange grunting language. Barney did not understand a word but he recognized the tone of voice – like when grown-ups go about about: 'I'm thinking of tearing this down, and building on here, and having this done up . . .' Stig had been digging into the wall, enlarging his cave. There was a bit of an old bed he had been using as a pick, and a baby's bath full of loose chalk to be carried away.

Barney made the interested sort of noises you are supposed to make when people tell you they are going to put up plastic wallpaper with pictures of mousetraps on it, but Stig reached up to a bunch of turnips hanging from a poker stuck in the wall. He handed Barney a turnip, took one for himself, and began to eat it. Barney sat down on a bundle of old magazines done up with string and munched the turnip. The turnip at least was fresh, and it tasted better to him than the cream of spinach he'd hidden under his spoon at dinner-time.

Barney looked at Stig. Funny person to find living next door to you, he thought. Stig did not seem much bigger than himself, but he looked very strong and his hands looked cleverer than his face. But how old was he? Ten? Twenty? A hundred? A thousand?

'You been here long?' asked Barney.

Stig grinned again. 'Long,' he said. 'Long, long, long.' But it sounded more like an echo, or a parrot copying somebody, than an answer to his question.

'I'm staying at my Grandmother's house,' said Barney. Stig just looked at him. 'Oh well,' thought Barney, 'if he's not interested in talking I don't mind.' He stood up.

'I better go now,' he said. 'Thank you for having me. Can I have my knife back, please?'

Stig still looked blank.

'Knife,' said Barney, and made cutting movements with his hand. Stig picked up the sharp worked flint from the floor of the cave and gave it to Barney.

'Oo, can I have that!' exclaimed Barney. 'Thank you!'

He looked at the stone, hard and shiny, almost like a diamond and much more useful. Then he put it in his pocket, said goodbye again, and went out of the low door of the shelter.

It was getting late in the autumn evening, and it was already dark and gloomy in the pit. Barney knew there was a way out right at the other end of the pit, and by going a long way round he could get back to the house. There were rustlings in dry leaves and muffled sounds from the middle of bramble patches, but somehow Barney found he didn't mind. He felt the hard stone in his pocket and thought of Stig in his den under the cliff. You weren't likely to find anything stranger than Stig wherever you looked. And, well, Stig was his friend.

# IVAN SOUTHALL

FROM *Ash Road*

Wallace was half-awake, half-asleep. He had been asleep for a while, but had become partly aware of his surroundings again, of the wind and the heat. He was wet with perspiration. Graham had been right about sleeping-bags and ovens. Wallace felt that he was being cooked, and his right hip was bruised and sore. He had dug a little hole for his hip, but he must have turned away from it. The trouble was, he couldn't completely wake up. He was in a sort of limbo of acute discomfort but was too hazy in the head to do anything about it.

When at last he managed to open his eyes he became aware of a faint glow. He thought he could smell methylated spirits. He even thought he could see Graham.

'Is that you?' he said.

'Yes,' said Graham.

'What are you doin'?'

'Making coffee.'

Wallace sat up, panting. He felt giddy. 'What are you makin' coffee for?'

'I'm thirsty. Do you want a cup?'

'What's the time?'

'Twenty past one.'

'Yeh. I'll have a cup.'

Wallace peeled his sleeping-bag down to the waist, and felt better. 'Twenty past one!'

'About that.'

'Harry's sleepin' all right.'

'Trust Harry,' said Graham. 'He could sleep any-where.'

Wallace thought he had heard something like that before, but couldn't remember when. 'Funny in the bush at night, isn't it? Awful dark.'

'Noisy, too. I heard a tree fall down. Not far away either. Woke me up.'

'It's the wind.'

'Guess so.'

'Stinkin' hot, isn't it?'

'You can say that again. But this water's awful slow coming to the boil.'

'The wind, I suppose.'

'It's taken two lots of metho already,' said Graham.

'Have you got the lid on?'

'Can't see when it boils if you've got the lid on.'

'Put the lid on, I reckon, or it'll never boil.'

'Don't know where the lid is, do you?'

'*Feel* for it. It's there somewhere. Use your torch.'

'The battery's flat. Blooming thing. Must have been a crook battery. Hardly used it at all. *Now* look what I've done! There's the metho bottle knocked for six.'

'You dope,' cried Wallace. 'Pick it up quick. Or we'll lose it all.'

'The cork's in it.' Graham groped for it, feeling a bit of a fool, and said, 'Crumbs.'

'Now what?'

'The cork's *not* in it, that's what. It must have come out.'

'How could it come out? Honest to goodness –'

'It's *burning*,' howled Graham.

A blue flame snaked from the little heater up through

the rocks towards the bottle in the boy's hand; or at least that was how it seemed to happen. It happened so swiftly it may have deceived the eye. Instinctively, to protect himself, Graham threw the bottle away. There was a shower of fire from its neck, as from the nozzle of a hose.

'Oh my gosh,' yelled Wallace and tore off his sleeping-bag. 'Harry!' he screamed. 'Wake up, Harry!'

They tried to stamp on the fire, but their feet were bare and they couldn't find their shoes. They tried to smother it with their sleeping-bags, but *it* seemed to be everywhere. Harry couldn't even escape from his bag; he couldn't find the zip fastener, and for a few awful moments in his confusion between sleep and wakefulness he thought he was in his bed at home and the house had burst into flames around him. He couldn't come to grips with the situation; he knew only dismay and the wildest kind of alarm. Graham and Wallace, panicking, were throwing themselves from place to place, almost sobbing, beating futilely at a widening arc of fire. Every desperate blow they made seemed to fan the fire, to scatter it farther, to feed it.

'Put it out,' shouted Graham. 'Put it out.'

It wasn't dark any longer. It was a flickering world of tree trunks and twisted boughs, of scrub and saplings and stones, of shouts and wind and smoke and frantic fear. It was so quick. It was terrible.

'Put it out,' cried Graham, and Harry fought out of his sleeping-bag, knowing somehow that they'd never get it out by beating at it, that they'd have to get water up from the creek. But all they had was a four-pint billy-can.

The fire was getting away from them in all directions,

crackling through the scrub down-wind, burning fiercely back into the wind. Even the ground was burning; grass, roots, and fallen leaves were burning, humus was burning. There were flames on the trees, bark was burning, foliage was flaring, flaring like a whip-crack; and the heat was savage and searing and awful to breathe.

'We can't, we can't,' cried Wallace. 'What are we going to do?'

They beat at it and beat at it and beat at it.

'Oh gee,' sobbed Graham. He was crying, and he hadn't cried since he was twelve years old. 'What have I done? *We've got to get it out!*'

Harry was scrambling around wildly, bundling all their things together. It was not that he was more level-headed than the others; it was just that he could see the end more clearly, the hopelessness of it, the absolute certainty of it, the imminent danger of encirclement, the possibility that they might be burnt alive. He could see all this because he hadn't been in it at the start. He wasn't responsible; he hadn't done it; and now that he was wide awake he could see it more clearly. He screamed at them: 'Grab your stuff and run for it.' But they didn't hear him or didn't want to hear him. They were blackened, their feet were cut, event their hair was singed. They beat and beat, and fire was leaping into the tree tops, and there were no black shadows left, only bright light, red light, yellow light, light that was hard and cruel and terrifying, and there was a rushing sound, a roaring sound, explosions, and smoke, smoke like a hot red fog.

'No,' cried Graham. 'No, no, no.' His arms dropped to his sides and he shook with sobs and Wallace dragged him away. 'Oh, Wally,' he sobbed. 'What have I done?'

'We've got to get out of here,' shouted Harry. 'Grab the things and run.'

'Our shoes?' cried Wallace. 'Where are they?'

'I don't know. I don't know.'

'We've got to find our shoes.'

'They'll kill us,' sobbed Graham. 'They'll kill us. It's a terrible thing, an awful thing to have done.'

'Where'd we put our shoes?' Wallace was running around in circles, blindly. He didn't really know what he was doing. Everything had happened so quickly, so suddenly.

'For Pete's sake run!' shouted Harry.

Something in his voice seemed to get through to Wallace and Graham, and they ran, the three of them, like frightened rabbits. They ran this way and that, hugging their packs and their scorched sleeping-bags, blundering into the scrub, even into the trunks of trees. Fire and confusion seemed to be all around them. The fire's rays darted through the bush; it was like an endless chain with a will of its own, encircling and entangling them, or like a wall that leapt out of the earth to block every fresh run they made for safety. Even the creek couldn't help them. They didn't know where it was. There might as well not have been a creek at all.

'This way,' shouted Harry. 'A track.'

They stumbled back down the track towards Tinley; at least they thought it was towards Tinley, they didn't really know. Perhaps they were running to save their lives, running simply from fear, running away from what they had done.

When they thought they were safe they hid in the bush close to a partly constructed house. They could hear sirens wailing; lights were coming on here and there; the headlamps of cars were beaming and sweeping around curves in the track. They could hear shouts on the wind, they heard a woman cry hysterically, they heard Graham sobbing.

Over all was a red glow.

# JOHN CHRISTOPHER

FROM *The White Mountains*

In the afternoon we found a clump of horse-radish, and pulled the roots up and ate them. The taste was bitter and fiery, but it was food. We had left the valley, starting a climb up long but fairly moderate slopes of rough scrubland, and the Tripod was out of view again. But not out of mind. The feeling of hopelessness, of being caught in a trap which in due course must close, continually strengthened. I had followed the fox-hunts on foot back at Wherton, but I would have had no stomach for them after this. Even the sun, which beat down more warmly than ever out of a clear sky, could not cheer me. When, with its rays slanting low from the west, Beanpole called a halt, I dropped on to the grass empty and exhausted. The other two, after resting a while, stirred themselves and began foraging, but I did not move. I lay on my back, eyes closed against the light, hands clasped under the back of my neck. I still did not move when they came back, arguing about whether one could eat snakes – Henry had seen one but failed to kill it – and whether, anyway, they were hungry enough to eat it raw since there was no kindling for a fire. I kept my eyes shut when Henry, in quite a different, sharper voice, said:

'What's that?'

It would not, I was sure, be anything that mattered. Beanpole said something, in a lower voice, which I did not catch. They were whispering together. I kept my closed eyes on the sun, which would soon be gone behind the hills. They whispered again. Then Beanpole said:

'Will.'

'Yes.'

'Your shirt is torn, under the arm.'

I said: 'I know. I ripped it on a thorn bush coming up from the river.'

'Look at me, Will.' I opened my eyes, and saw him standing over me, looking down. There was a strange look on his face. 'What is it you have, under your arm?'

I got into a sitting position. 'Under my arm? What are you talking about?'

'You do not know?' I had put my right hand under my left arm. 'No, the other one.'

I used my left arm this time, feeling into my arm-pit. I touched something whose texture was not the texture of flesh, but smoother and harder – something like a small metal button, on whose surface my finger-tips traced faint corrugations, a kind of mesh. I craned my head round, trying to look at it, but could not. It seemed to melt into my skin, with no clear division between them. I looked up, and saw the other two watching me.

'What is it?'

'It is the metal of the Caps,' Beanpole said. 'It grows into the skin, as the Caps do.'

'The Tripod . . .' I said. 'When it caught me, outside the castle, do you think . . .?'

I did not need to finish the sentence. Their faces showed me what they thought. I said wildly:

'You don't think I've been guiding it – that I'm under its control?'

Henry said: 'It's been following since a few days after

you caught up with us. We can't throw it off, can we? Have you got a better way of accounting for it?'

I stared at him. The mystery of the Tripod's ability to find us, time after time, and the mystery of the small metal button, somehow welded to my body – they could not be separated, they must belong together. And yet my mind was my own: I was no traitor. I had the same certainty of that as I had of my very existence. But how could I prove it? There was no way I could see.

Henry turned to Beanpole. 'What are we going to do with him?'

Beanpole said: 'We must think carefully, before we do anything.'

'We haven't got time for that. We know he's one of them. He's been sending messages to it with his mind. He's probably sent one saying he's been found out. It may be coming after us right now.'

'Will told us of the Tripod,' Beanpole said. 'That it caught him, and released him again – that he was unconscious and could remember nothing. If his mind had been a servant of the Tripods, would he have said those things? And would he not have taken care, when his shirt was torn, rather than lie so that we could see it? Moreover, it is very small, not like the Caps, and not near the brain.'

'But it is tracking us through him!'

'Yes, I believe so. The compass – it points to the north, because there must be much iron there. If you bring other iron near, it will point to that. One cannot see or feel the thing that makes it do this. The Tripod caught him, going away from the castle, when everyone there was asleep. He was un-Capped, but it did not Cap him. Maybe it was curious about what he would do, where he was going. And put this thing on him which it could follow, like a needle on a compass.'

It made sense: I was sure what he said was true. I could feel the button under my arm with every small movement I made – not hurting, but I knew it was there. Why had I not felt it before? The same thought must have occurred to Henry.

'But he must have known about it,' he said. 'A thing like that.'

'Perhaps not. Do you have in your country . . . people who make show . . . with animals, those who swing through the air from bars, strong men, and such?'

'Circuses,' Henry said. 'I saw one once.'

'One that came to my town had a man who did strange things. He told people to sleep, and to obey his commands, and they did as he ordered, even doing things which made them look foolish. Sometimes the commands lasted for a time. A sailor with a crippled hip walked with no limp for a week – afterwards, the pain and the limp returned.'

'I can feel it now,' I said.

'We have shown it to you,' Beanpole said. 'It may be that breaks the command.'

Henry said impatiently: 'None of this alters the facts. The Tripod can trace him through that thing, and can pick us up along with him.'

I saw his point. I said: 'There's only one thing to do.'

'What is that?' Beanpole asked.

'If we separate, and I go a different way from you – it can follow me still, but you will be all right.'

'A different way to the White Mountains? But you will still lead it there. Most likely, that is what it wishes.'

I shook my head. 'I won't go there. I'll double back.'

'And be caught again. And Capped?'

I remembered the moment of being plucked from Aristide's back, the ground shrinking beneath me. I hoped I was not going white with the fear I felt. I said:

'It will have to catch me first.'

'It will catch you,' Beanpole said. 'You have no chance of escaping.'

I said, trying not to think of what it entailed:

'I can lead it away, at least.'

There was a silence. It was, as I had said, the only thing to do, and they were bound to agree with it. There was no need, really, for them to say anything. I got to my feet, turning away from their faces. Beanpole said:

'Wait.'

'For what?'

'I said that we must think. I have been thinking. This thing under your arm – it is small, and though it is fastened to the skin I do not think it goes far beneath.'

He paused. Henry said: 'Well?'

Beanpole looked at me. 'It is clear of the big vein. But it will hurt if we cut it out.'

I had not seen what he was driving at, and hope, when I did, made me dizzy.

'Do you think you can?'

'We can try.'

I began stripping off my shirt. 'Let's not waste time then!'

Beanpole was not to be hurried. He made me lie down, with my arm up, and explored the button and the skin around it with his fingers. I wanted him to get on with it, but I was in his hands, and realized there was no point in showing impatience. At last, he said:

'Yes, it will hurt. I will do it as quickly as I can, but you will need something to bite on. And, Henry – you must hold his arm out, so that he cannot draw it back.'

He gave me the leather strap of his pack to hold between my teeth; I felt the sour harsh taste of it on my tongue. The knife was one he had picked up in the great-city. It had a good edge, having been protected by grease and he had spent some time sharpening it since then. It could not be too sharp for my liking. At a word from Beanpole, Henry took my arm, and stretched it out and back behind me. I was lying on my left hip, my face towards the ground. An ant scurried along and disappeared between blades of grass. Then there was the weight of Beanpole squatting over me, his left hand feeling again at the flesh under my arm, outlining the shape of the button. I was making a trial bite at the leather when he made the first cut, and my whole body jerked and I very nearly pulled my hand free from Henry's grasp. The pain was excruciating.

It was followed by another slash, and another. I tried to concentrate on the leather strap, through which my teeth seemed to be almost meeting. I was sweating so much that I felt drops rolling down the side of my face, and I saw one splash in the dust. I wanted to cry to him to stop, to let me have a rest from the pain, and was on the point of spitting the strap out to be able to speak when a new jab made me bite it again, and the side of my tongue with it. There was the hot salty taste of blood in my mouth, and tears in my eyes. Then, from a great distance, I heard him say: 'You can let go now,' and my hand and arm were free. The pain was furious still, but mild compared with what it had been a little earlier. Beanpole got up from me, and I started to drag myself to my feet. I had to move my arm to do so, and felt sick with what it did to me.

'As I thought,' Beanpole said, 'it is on the surface only. Observe.'

I got rid of the gag, and looked at what he was holding in his hand. It was silvery grey, about half an inch in diameter, thicker in the centre and tapering towards the edge. It was solid, but gave the impression of hundreds of tiny wires just below the surface. Attached to it were the bloody scraps of my flesh which Beanpole had cut away.

Beanpole poked the button with his finger.

'It is curious,' he said. 'I would like to study this. It is a pity we must leave it.'

His gaze was one of dispassionate interest. Henry, who was also looking, had a greenish tinge to his face. Staring at the gobbets of flesh adhering, nausea rose in me again, and this time I had to turn away to be sick. When I recovered, Beanpole was still staring at the button.

Gasping, I said: 'Throw it away, and let's get going. The further we are from here, the better.'

# ROALD DAHL

## FROM *Charlie and the Chocolate Factory*

During the next two weeks, the weather turned very cold. First came the snow. It began very suddenly one morning just as Charlie Bucket was getting dressed for school. Standing by the window, he saw the huge flakes drifting slowly down out of an icy sky that was the colour of steel.

By evening, it lay four feet deep around the tiny house, and Mr Bucket had to dig a path from the front door to the road.

After the snow, there came a freezing gale that blew for days and days without stopping. And oh, how bitter cold it was! Everything that Charlie touched seemed to be made of ice, and each time he stepped outside the door, the wind was like a knife on his cheek.

Inside the house little jets of freezing air came rushing in through the sides of the windows and under the doors, and there was no place to go to escape them. The four old ones lay silent and huddled in their bed, trying to keep the cold out of their bones. The excitement over the Golden Tickets had long since been forgotten. Nobody in the family gave a thought now to anything except the two vital problems of trying to keep warm and trying to get enough to eat.

There is something about very cold weather that gives one an enormous appetite. Most of us find ourselves beginning to crave rich steaming stews and hot apple

pies and all kinds of delicious warming dishes; and because we are all a great deal luckier than we realize, we
usually get what we want – or near enough. But Charlie
Bucket never got what he wanted because the family
couldn't afford it, and as the cold weather went on and
on, he became ravenously and desperately hungry. Both
bars of chocolate, the birthday one and the one Grandpa
Joe had bought, had long since been nibbled away, and
all he got now were those thin, cabbagy meals three
times a day.

Then all at once, the meals became even thinner.

The reason for this was that the toothpaste factory,
the place where Mr Bucket worked, suddenly went bust
and had to close down. Quickly, Mr Bucket tried to get
another job. But he had no luck. In the end, the only
way in which he managed to earn a few pennies was by
shovelling snow in the streets. But it wasn't enough to
buy even a quarter of the food that seven people needed.
The situation became desperate. Breakfast was a single
slice of bread for each person now, and lunch was maybe
half a boiled potato.

Slowly but surely, everybody in the house began to
starve.

And every day, little Charlie Bucket, trudging through
the snow on his way to school, would have to pass Mr
Willy Wonka's giant chocolate factory. And every day,
as he came near to it, he would lift his small pointed
nose high in the air and sniff the wonderful sweet smell
of melting chocolate. Sometimes, he would stand motionless outside the gates for several minutes on end, taking
deep swallowing breaths as though he were trying to *eat*
the smell itself.

'That child,' said Grandpa Joe, poking his head up

from under the blanket one icy morning, 'that child has *got* to have more food. It doesn't matter about us. We're too old to bother with. But a *growing boy*! He can't go on like this! He's beginning to look like a skeleton!'

'What can one *do*?' murmured Grandma Josephine miserably. 'He refuses to take any of ours. I hear his mother tried to slip her own piece of bread on to his plate at breakfast this morning, but he wouldn't touch it. He made her take it back.'

'He's a fine little fellow,' said Grandpa George. 'He deserves better than this.'

The cruel weather went on and on.

And every day, Charlie Bucket grew thinner and thinner. His face became frighteningly white and pinched. The skin was drawn so tightly over the cheeks that you could see the shapes of the bones underneath. It seemed doubtful whether he could go on much longer like this without becoming dangerously ill.

And now, very calmly, with that curious wisdom that seems to come so often to small children in times of hardship, he began to make little changes here and there in some of the things that he did, so as to save his strength. In the mornings, he left the house ten minutes earlier so that he could walk slowly to school, without ever having to run. He sat quietly in the classroom during break, resting himself, while the others rushed outdoors and threw snowballs and wrestled in the snow. Everything he did now, he did slowly and carefully, to prevent exhaustion.

Then one afternoon, walking back home with the icy wind in his face (and incidentally feeling hungrier than he had ever felt before), his eye was caught suddenly by something silvery lying in the gutter, in the snow. Charlie stepped off the kerb and bent down to examine it. Part of it was buried under the snow, but he saw at once what it was.

*It was a half-crown piece!*

Quickly he looked around him.

Had somebody just dropped it?

No – that was impossible because of the way part of it was buried.

Several people went hurrying past him on the pavement, their chins sunk deep in the collars of their coats, their feet crunching in the snow. None of them was searching for any money; none of them was taking the slightest notice of the small boy crouching in the gutter.

Then was it *his*, this half-crown?

Could he *have* it?

Carefully, Charlie pulled it out from under the snow. It was damp and dirty, but otherwise perfect.

*A WHOLE half-crown!*

He held it tightly between his shivering fingers, gazing down at it. It meant one thing to him at that moment, only *one* thing. It meant FOOD.

Automatically, Charlie turned and began moving towards the nearest shop. It was only ten paces away . . . it was a newspaper and stationery shop, the kind that sells almost everything, including sweets and cigars . . . and what he would *do*, he whispered quickly to himself . . . he would buy one luscious bar of chocolate and eat it *all* up, every bit of it, right then and there . . . and the rest of the money he would take straight back home and give to his mother.

Charlie entered the shop and laid the damp half-crown on the counter.

'One Wonka's Whipple-Scrumptious Fudgemallow De-light,' he said, remembering how much he had loved the one he had on his birthday.

The man behind the counter looked fat and well fed. He had big lips and fat cheeks and a very fat neck. The fat around his neck bulged out all around the top of his collar like a rubber ring. He turned and reached behind him for the chocolate bar, then he turned back again and handed it to Charlie. Charlie grabbed it and quickly tore off the wrapper and took an enormous bite. Then he took another . . . and another . . . and oh, the joy of being able to cram large pieces of something sweet and solid into one's mouth! The sheer blissful joy of being able to fill one's mouth with rich solid food!

'You look like you wanted that one, sonny,' the shop-keeper said pleasantly.

Charlie nodded, his mouth bulging with chocolate.

The shopkeeper put Charlie's change on the counter. 'Take it easy,' he said. 'It'll give you a tummy-ache if you swallow it like that without chewing.'

Charlie went on wolfing the chocolate. He couldn't stop. And in less than half a minute, the whole thing had disappeared down his throat. He was quite out of breath, but he felt marvellously, extraordinarily happy. He reached out a hand to take the change. Then he paused. His eyes were just above the level of the counter. They were staring at the little silver coins lying there. The coins were all sixpences. There were four of them alto-gether. Surely it wouldn't matter if he spent just one more . . .

'I think,' he said quietly, 'I think . . . I'll have just one more of those chocolate bars. The same kind as before, please.'

'Why not?' the fat shopkeeper said, reaching behind him again and taking another Whipple-Scrumptious Fudgemallow Delight from the shelf. He laid it on the counter.

Charlie picked it up and tore off the wrapper . . . and *suddenly* . . . from underneath the wrapper . . . there came a brilliant flash of gold.

Charlie's heart stood still.

'It's a Golden Ticket!' screamed the shopkeeper, leaping about a foot in the air. 'You've got a Golden Ticket! You've found the last Golden Ticket! Hey, would you believe it! Come and look at this, everybody! The kid's found Wonka's last Golden Ticket! There it is! It's right there in his hands!'

# LEON GARFIELD

## FROM *Smith*

He was called Smith and was twelve years old. Which, in itself, was a marvel; for it seemed as if the smallpox, the consumption, brain-fever, gaol-fever and even the hangman's rope had given him a wide berth for fear of catching something. Or else they weren't quick enough.

Smith had a turn of speed that was remarkable, and a neatness in nipping down an alley or vanishing in a court that had to be seen to be believed. Not that it was often seen, for Smith was rather a sooty spirit of the violent and ramshackle Town, and inhabited the tumbledown mazes about fat St Paul's like the subtle air itself. A rat was like a snail beside Smith, and the most his thousand victims ever got of him was the powerful whiff of his passing and a cold draught in their dexterously emptied pockets.

Only the sanctimonious birds that perched on the church's dome ever saw Smith's progress entire, and as their beady eyes followed him, they chattered savagely, '*Pick*-pocket! *Pick*-pocket! Jug him! Jug-jug-jug him!' as if they'd been appointed by the Town to save it from such as Smith.

His favourite spot was Ludgate Hill, where the world's coaches, chairs and curricles were met and locked, from morning to night, in a horrible, blasphemous confusion. And here, in one or other of the ancient doorways, he leaned and grinned while the shouting and cursing and scraping and raging went endlessly, hopelessly on – till, sooner or later, something prosperous would come his way.

At about half past ten of a cold December morning an old gentleman got furiously out of his carriage, in which he'd been trapped for an hour, shook his red fist at his helpless coachman and the roaring but motionless world, and began to stump up Ludgate Hill.

'*Pick*-pocket! *Pick*-pocket!' shrieked the cathedral birds in a fury.

A country gentleman – judging by his complexion, his clean, old-fashioned coat and his broad-legged, lumbering walk which bumped out his pockets in a manner most provoking.

Smith twitched his nose and nipped neatly along like a shadow . . .

The old man's pace was variable: sometimes it was brisk for his years, then he'd slow down, hesitate, look about him – as if the Town had changed much since last he'd visited and he was now no longer confident of his way. He took one turning, then another; stopped, scratched the crisp edge of his wig, then eyed the sallow, seedy city gentry as if to ask the way, till he spied another turn, nodded, briskly took it – and came straight back into Ludgate Hill . . .

A dingy fellow creaked out of the doorway, like he was hinged on it, and made to accost the old man: but did not. He'd glimpsed Smith. Looks had been exchanged, shoulders shrugged – and the old villain gave way to the young one.

On went the old gentleman, confident now in his bearings, deeper and deeper into the musty, tottering forest of the Town where Smith hunted fastest and best.

Now a sharpish wind sprang up, and the cathedral birds eyed the leaden sky (which looked too thick and heavy to admit them), screeched, and flew to the lower eminence of Old Bailey. Here, they set up a terrific commotion with their legal brethren, till both Church and Law became absorbed in watching the progress of Smith.

'*Pick*-pocket! *Pick*-pocket! Jug-jug-jug him!'

The old gentleman was very deep in Smith's country now, and paused many a time to peer down the shambling lanes and alleys. Then he'd shake his head vaguely and touch at his coat pocket – as if a queer, deep sense had warned him of a pair of sharp eyes fairly cutting into the cloth like scissors. At last he saw something familiar – some landmark he'd remembered – Godliman Street. Yes: he was in Godliman Street . . .

As suddenly as it had sprung up, the wind died – and the cathedral birds flew back to their dome.

'*Pick*-pocket! *Pick*-pocket!'

The old gentleman began to stump very particularly down Godliman Street, eyeing the old, crumbly houses that were lived in by God knew how many quiet, mysterious souls. And, as he went, he seemed to have two shadows – his own and another, a thin cautious shadow that was not so much seen as sensed . . .

This was the deepest heart of Smith's forest, hidden even from the cathedral birds. Here, the houses reared and clustered as if to shut out the sky, and so promoted the growth of the flat, pale and unhealthy moon-faces of the clerks and scriveners, glimpsed in their dark caves through dusty windows, silent and intent.

Now came a slit between two such properties, a quiet way roofed over at first floor level: Curtis Alley, leading to Curtis Court.

Framed by the darkness of its alley, Curtis Court presented a grey and peaceful brightness – a neglected clearing in the forest of the Town, where nothing grew, and all save one of the enclosed houses had had their eyes put out with bricks (on account of the tax).

As the old gentleman's steps echoed in the alley, a solitary, dusty raven flew up out of the court with a bitter croak.

Suddenly, the old gentleman gave an involuntary shudder, as if someone – something – had swiftly passed him by and made a draught.

'Someone's walked over me grave!' he muttered, shook his head and entered Curtis Court.

'Beg pardon, sir! Beg pardon –'

Out of a doorway on the left of the court came Smith. Which was the first time the old man had ever laid eyes on him; though all the way from Ludgate Hill there'd never been more than two yards between them.

He stopped, flustered, about six paces from the end of the alley. Which way was the damned urchin going? This way? That way? Angrily he shifted, and Smith, with a quaint clumsiness, brushed against him, and – it was done! In an instant! Smith had emptied the old gentleman's pocket of –

He halted. His eyes glittered sharply. Footsteps in the alley! It would be blocked! He changed direction as briefly as a speck in the wind – and vanished back into his doorway. But so quickly that, seconds after he'd disappeared, the old gentleman was still staggering and bewildered.

Out of the alley came two men in brown. Curious fellows of a very particular aspect – which Smith knew well. Uneasily, he scowled – and wished he might vanish through the crumbling bricks.

The old gentleman had recovered himself. He stared round angrily – till courtesy got the better of him.

'Good day to ye, gentlemen!' he said, with an apologetic smile.

The newcomers glanced quickly across the court towards the house that had kept one window, and grinned.

'And good day to *you*!'

They moved very neat, and with no communication. They were proficient in their trade. The taller came at the old man from the front; the other took on his back – and slid a knife into it.

The old gentleman's face was fatefully towards a certain dark doorway. He seemed to peer very anxiously round the heavy shoulder of the man who was holding him – as if for a better view. His eyes flickered with pain at the knife's quick prick. Then he looked surprised – amazed, even – as he felt the cold blade slip into his warm heart.

'Oh! Oh! Oh my –' he murmured, gave a long sigh – and died.

His last sight on this earth had been of a small, wild and despairing face whose flooded eyes shone out of the shadows with all the dread and pity they were capable of.

(Smith was only twelve and, hangings apart, had seen no more than three men murdered in all his life.)

They say that murdered men's eyes keep the image of their last sight for – for how long? Do they take it, hereafter, up to the Seat of Judgement? Smith shivered. He'd no wish for his face to be shown in any place of judgement – in this world or the next!

In a terror as violent as his dislike, he watched the two men in brown. They were dragging the luckless old gentleman towards the darkness of the alley. (Why hadn't he stayed in the country where he'd belonged? What business had he to come stumping – so stupid and defenceless – into Smith's secret forest?)

Now Smith could hear the quick fumbling sounds of searching; methodical gentry. Still no commotion. Oh, they knew what they were at! But the sounds grew harsh and hasty. Even irritable. Muttered one, 'God rot the old fool! He ain't got it!'

Came a new sound. A very queer one. A tapping, limping, scraping sound – as of a lame man's footsteps on the cobbles. Then a soft, gentlemanly voice.

'Well?'

'Nothing – nothing, yer honour!'

'Liars! Fools! Look again!'

Again the sounds of searching – accompanied by strained, indrawn breath.

'Told you so. Nothing.'

A groan: a very dreadful affair.

'Again! Again! It *must* be there!'

'Well it ain't, yer honour! And if we stays much longer, we'll be on our way to join 'im . . . on the end of a rope! Come – let's be off.'

'Again! Search once more!'

'With respect – do it yerself, sir.'

'No!'

'Then we're off! Quick! Quick! There's someone coming –'

There was a scuffling and scraping, then the alley and court were momentarily quiet. A shadow crossed the broken, moss-piped paving. It was the raven, making ready to return.

But Smith did not move yet. Voices and clustering

footsteps could be heard coming from the far side of the alley. The pale-faced clerks and scriveners and thin-necked attorneys had caught the scent of spilt blood. They'd come out of their rooms and chambers to congregate solemnly and stare.

(But no one came out from the houses within the court; not even from the house with the single window.)

Now the crowd had grown and oozed into the court itself. The raven flapped sourly up to a gable and croaked with a sardonic air; Smith had invisibly joined the outskirts of the crowd, muttering away with the best of them; then he was through, like a needle through shoddy, to Godliman Street and beyond.

As he went, a door opened in the court, and someone came quietly out . . .

A quarter mile off, on the other side of St Paul's, Smith stopped running. He sat on some steps and fumbled in his ragged, ancient coat. What had he got this time? Something valuable. Something that had been worth the old gentleman's life.

He fished it out. A document. *A document?* Smith stood up, swore, spat and cursed. For, though he was quicker than a rat, sharper than a stoat, foxier than a fox, though he knew the Town's corners and alleys and courts and byways better than he knew his own heart, and though he could vanish into the thick air in the twinkling of an eye, he lacked one necessary quality for the circumstances in hand. He could not read. Not so much as a word!

# RUSSELL HOBAN

FROM *The Mouse and His Child*

The sky was beginning to pale, and the air was sharp with morning as Ralphie and the mouse and his child came through the woods along a path to the Meadow Mutual Hoard and Trust Company, an earthen bank beside a stream. There were many tracks in the snow, and following these, they went through the entrance between the roots of a great sycamore tree.

The interior of the bank was chill and dim and hushed; the acorn-cup tallow lamps did little more than cast their own shadows and catch the glint of frost and mica on the earth walls. In the half-light a drowsy chipmunk teller looked up from the sunflower seeds he was counting as the rat walked in with the mouse and his child. The father pushed the son up to the rock behind which the chipmunk sat, then stood treading the ground until his spring unwound. The chipmunk looked at the paper bag they carried, then at Ralphie, and he felt for the alarm twig with his foot.

'Um yes,' he said. 'May I help you?'

Ralphie squinted cautiously into the shadows around him, saw no guards, and at once forgot everything Manny Rat had told him. 'All right,' he said, snarling and showing his teeth, 'this is a stick-up. Take me to the vault.'

'Um yes, sir!' said the chipmunk, stepping hard on the alarm twig as he spoke. The twig passed through a hole in the dirt wall behind him, and its other end vibrated against the snout of the badger guard who was dozing behind the stone that was the door of the vault. The badger woke up and smiled.

'This way, please,' said the chipmunk. Ralphie wound up the mouse father, and they went through a short tunnel to where the stone blocked the opening of the vault. 'Here is the vault,' said the chipmunk.

'Well, open it up,' said Ralphie.

'Um certainly,' said the chipmunk. He moved the stone and stepped out of the way as Ralphie rushed into the waiting jaws of the badger, who ate him up.

'Them city fellows ain't much at robbing banks,' chuckled the badger when he had finished, 'but they're good eating. Young fellows nowadays, they don't know how to pull a job. All they know is hurry, hurry, hurry.' He picked his teeth with a sliver of bone. 'What about them other two?' he asked the chipmunk.

The chipmunk looked back through the tunnel and out past the entrance of the bank. The mouse and his child, spun about by the violence of Ralphie's rush into the vault, had stumbled out of the Meadow Mutual Hoard and Trust company into the blue dawn, leaving their paper bag behind them. The chipmunk watched them walk down the path until they bumped into a rock and fell over. He shook his head. 'Whatever they are, they're harmless,' he said. 'Let them go.'

The mouse and his child lay in the snow where they had fallen, rattling with tinny, squeaking laughter. 'Skreep, skreep, skreep!' laughed the father. 'The frog was right – Ralphie *did* go on a long journey.'

'Skreek, skreek!' laughed the child. 'There was good eating too, for the badger! Skreek!'

'Seven o'clock!' called the clock on the steeple of the

church across the meadow as it struck the hour.

'Listen!' said the father as he heard it. 'It's time for silence. Skreep!' And he began laughing all over again.

'If it's time for silence, how is it that we're still talking, Papa?' giggled the child.

'You've already broken one of the clockwork rules by crying on the job,' said the father, 'so we might as well break the other one too, and have done with it.'

'But I've often tried to speak after dawn,' said the child, 'and I never could till now. I wonder how it happened?'

'Perhaps your laughter freed you from the ancient clockwork laws,' said a deep voice, and the bullfrog fortune-teller hopped out from behind a tree. In the daylight he seemed smaller than he had at night, and much of his mystery was gone. He was not a young frog; the glove he wore was shabby. In the cold light of morning he could be clearly seen for what he was: an old, eccentric traveller, neither respectable nor reliable, hung with odd parcels, tricked out with a swinging coin, and plying his trade where chance might take him. He set the mouse and his child on their feet and considered them thoughtfully. 'I have never heard a toy laugh before,' he said.

'Did you see what happened?' said the father, and he told the frog about the attempted bank robbery.

'A rash youth, Ralphie,' said Frog. 'He had no patience, poor boy! For once I read the future truly, and it came with fearful swiftness. But are you not curious about my presence here?'

'Why are you here?' asked the child.

'Because I followed you,' said Frog. 'Something draws me to you, and in the seeds I saw your fate and mine bound inextricably together. I said nothing at the time – I was afraid. There were dark and fearful things in that

design, and unknown perils that can only be revealed by time.' He shook his head, and the coin swung like a pendulum from the string around his neck.

'Are you still afraid?' asked the father.

'Utterly,' said Frog. 'Do you choose to go ahead?'

'There is no going back,' said the father; 'we cannot dance in circles any more. Will you be our friend, and travel with us?'

'Be my uncle,' said the child. 'Be my Uncle Frog.'

'Ah!' said Frog. 'I had better make no promises; I am at best an infirm vessel. Do not expect too much. I will be your friend and uncle for as long as our destined roads may lie together; more than that I cannot say.' He gestured towards the snowy meadow that sparkled in the sunlight beyond the trees ahead, and pointed back along the shadowy pathway they had taken to the bank. 'Which shall it be?' he said. 'Towards the town, or out into the open country?'

'Maybe we could look for the elephant and the seal and the doll's house that used to be in the store with us,' said the child. 'Couldn't we, Papa?'

'What in the world for?' said the father.

'So we can have a family and be cosy,' answered the child.

'To begin with,' said the father, 'I cannot imagine myself being cosy with that elephant. But, putting that aside for the moment, the whole idea of such a quest is impossible. Despite what she said, she and the doll's house were very likely for sale just as we and the seal were, and by now they might be anywhere at all. It would be hopeless to attempt to find any of them.'

'She sang me a lullaby,' said the child.

'Really,' said the father, 'this is absurd.'

'I want the elephant to be my mama and I want the

seal to be my sister and I want to live in the beautiful house,' the child insisted.

'What is all this talk of elephants and seals?' asked Frog.

'It's nonsense,' said the father, 'and yet it's not the child's fault. Our motor is in me. He fills the empty space inside himself with foolish dreams that cannot possibly come true.'

'Not so very foolish, perhaps,' said Frog. 'This seal, was she made of tin, and black and shiny? Did she have a small platform on her nose that revolved while a sparrow performed acrobatic tricks on it?'

'No,' said the father. 'She had a red and yellow ball on her nose.'

'She could have lost the ball,' said the child. 'Maybe she does have a platform on her nose now. Where is the seal you saw?' he asked Frog.

'I don't know where she is now,' said Frog. 'But two years ago she was with a travelling theatrical troupe that comes to the pine woods every year.'

'If Uncle Frog could take us there, maybe we could find the seal,' said the mouse child to his father, 'and then we could all look for the elephant together.'

'Finding the elephant would be as pointless as looking for her,' said the father. 'But since I cannot convince you of that, we might just as well travel to the pine woods as anywhere else. At any rate we shall see something of the world.'

'Very well,' said Frog. 'On to the pine woods.'

'EXTRA!' screamed a raucous voice above them as a bluejay flashed by in the sunlight. 'RAT SLAIN IN BANK HOLD-UP ATTEMPT. WIND-UPS FLEE WITH GETAWAY FROG. LATE SCORES: WOODMICE LEAD MEADOW TEAM IN ACORN BOWLING. VOLES IDLE.'

# E. L. KONIGSBURG

FROM *From the Mixed-up Files*
*of Mrs Basil E. Frankweiler*

Jamie entered the men's room. He had arrived, as was
his custom, shortly before the first bell rang, the bell
that warned everyone that the museum would close
in five minutes. He waited; the bell rang. He got into a
booth. First bell, second bell, it was routine just as board-
ing the school bus had once been routine. After the first
day, they had learned that the staff worked from nine
a.m. until five p.m., a work schedule just like their
father's. Routine, routine. The wait from nine when the
staff came until ten when the public came seemed long.
Claudia and Jamie had decided that the washrooms were
good for the shorter evening wait when the help left at
the same time as the visitors, but the washrooms were
less satisfactory for the long morning wait . . . especially
after Jamie's close call that first morning. So time from
eight forty-five until some safe time after ten in the
mornings was spent under various beds. They always
checked for dust under the bed first. And for once Claudia's fussiness was not the reason. Reason was the reason.
A dustless floor meant that it had been cleaned very
recently, and they stood less chance of being caught by a
mop.

Jamie stood on the toilet seat waiting. He leaned his
head against the wall of the booth and braced himself for
what would happen next. The guard would come in and

make a quick check of his station. Jamie still felt a ping during that short inspection; that was the only part that still wasn't quite routine, and that's why he braced himself. Then the lights would be turned out. Jamie would wait twelve minutes (lag-time, Claudia called it) and emerge from hiding.

Except.

Except the guard didn't come, and Jamie couldn't relax until after he felt that final ping. And the lights stayed on, stayed on. Jamie checked his watch ten times within five minutes; he shook his arm and held the watch up to his ear. It was ticking slower than his heart and much more softly. What was wrong? They had caught Claudia! Now they would look for him! He'd pretend he didn't speak English. He wouldn't answer any questions.

Then he heard the door open. Footsteps. More foot-

steps than usual. What was happening? The hardest part was that every corpuscle of Jamie's nine-year-old self was throbbing with readiness to run, and he had to bind up all that energy into a quiet lump. It was like trying to wrap a loose peck of potatoes into a neat four-cornered package. But he managed to freeze. He heard the voices of two men talking over the sound of water running in the sink.

'I guess they expect even more people tomorrow.'

'Yeah. Sundays are always jammed up anyway.'

'It'll be easier to move the people in and out of the Great Hall.'

'Yeah. Two feet of marble. What do you figure it weighs?'

'I dunno. Whatever it weighs, it has to be handled delicate. Like it was a real angel.'

'C'mon. They probably have the new pedestal ready. We can start.'

'Do you think they'll have as many people as they had for the Mona Lisa?'

'Naw! The Mona Lisa was here for a short time only. Besides it was the real McCoy.'

'I think this one's . . .'

The men left, turning off the lights as they did so. Jamie heard the door close before he melted. Legs first. He sat down on the seat as he allowed the familiar darkness as well as new realization to fill him.

They were moving Angel. Did Claudia know? They wouldn't have women moving the statue. There would be no one in the ladies' room washing up. Who would give her the information? He would. By mental telepathy. He would think a message to Claudia. He folded his hands across his forehead and concentrated. 'Stay put,

Claudia, stay put. Stay put. Stay put. Claudia, stay put.'
He thought that Claudia would not approve of the gram-
mar in his mental telegram; she would want him to think
*stay in place*. But he didn't want to weaken his message by
varying it one bit. He continued thinking STAY PUT.

He must have thought STAY PUT exactly hard
enough, for Claudia did just that. They never knew
exactly why she did, but she did. Perhaps she sensed
some sounds that told her that the museum was not yet
empty. Maybe she was just too tired from running around
in Central Park. Maybe they were not meant to get
caught. Maybe they were meant to make the discovery
they made.

They waited for miles and miles of time before they
came out of hiding. At last they met in their bedroom.
Claudia was sorting the laundry when Jamie got there.
In the dark, mostly by feel. Although there is no real
difference between boys' stretch socks and girls', neither
ever considered wearing the other's. Children who have
always had separate bedrooms don't.

Claudia turned when she heard Jamie come up and
said, 'They moved the statue.'

'How did you know? Did you get my message?'

'Message? I saw the statue on my way here. They have
a dim light on it. I guess so that the night guard won't
trip over it.'

Jamie replied, 'We're lucky we didn't get caught.'

Claudia never thought very hard about the plus-luck
she had; she concentrated on the minus-luck. 'But they
held us up terribly. I planned on our taking baths tonight.
I really can't stand one night more without a bath.'

'I don't mind,' Jamie said.

'Come along, Sir James. To our bath. Bring your

most elegant pyjamas. The ones embroidered in gold with silver tassels will do.'

'Where, dear Lady Claudia, dost thou expect to bathe?'

'In the fountain, Sir James. In the fountain.'

Jamie extended his arm, which was draped with his striped flannel pyjamas, and said, 'Lady Claudia, I knew that sooner or later you would get me to that restaurant.'

Lady Claudia and Sir James quietly walked to the entrance of the restaurant. They easily climbed under the velvet rope that meant that the restaurant was closed to the public. Of course they were not the public. They shed their clothes and waded into the fountain. Claudia had taken powdered soap from the restroom. She had ground it out into a paper towel that morning. Even though it was freezing cold, she enjoyed her bath. Jamie, too, enjoyed his bath. For a different reason.

When he got into the pool, he found bumps on the bottom; smooth bumps. When he reached down to feel one, he found that it moved! He could even pick it up. He felt its cool roundness and splashed his way over to Claudia. 'Income, Claudia, income!' he whispered.

Claudia understood immediately and began to scoop up bumps she had felt on the bottom of the fountain. The bumps were pennies and nickels people had pitched into the fountain to make a wish. At least four people had thrown in dimes and one had tossed in a quarter.

# TED HUGHES

FROM *The Iron Man*

The Iron Man came to the top of the cliff.

How far had he walked? Nobody knows. Where had he come from? Nobody knows. How was he made? Nobody knows.

Taller than a house, the Iron Man stood at the top of the cliff, on the very brink, in the darkness.

The wind sang through his iron fingers. His great iron head, shaped like a dustbin but as big as a bedroom, slowly turned to the right, slowly turned to the left. His iron ears turned, this way, that way. He was hearing the sea. His eyes, like headlamps, glowed white, then red, then infra-red, searching the sea. Never before had the Iron Man seen the sea.

He swayed in the strong wind that pressed against his back. He swayed forward, on the brink of the high cliff.

And his right foot, his enormous iron right foot, lifted – up, out, into space, and the Iron Man stepped forward, off the cliff, into nothingness.

CRRRAAAASSSSSSH!

Down the cliff the Iron Man came toppling, head over heels.

CRASH!

CRASH!

CRASH!

From rock to rock, snag to snag, tumbling slowly. And as he crashed and crashed and crashed

His iron legs fell off.

His iron arms broke off, and the hands broke off the arms.

His great iron ears fell off and his eyes fell out.

His great iron head fell off.

All the separate pieces tumbled, scattered, crashing, bumping, clanging, down on to the rocky beach far below.

A few rocks tumbled with him.

Then

Silence.

Only the sound of the sea, chewing away at the edge of the rocky beach, where the bits and pieces of the Iron Man lay scattered far and wide, silent and unmoving.

Only one of the iron hands, lying beside an old, sand-logged washed-up seaman's boot, waved its fingers for a minute, like a crab on its back. Then it lay still.

While the stars went on wheeling through the sky and the wind went on tugging at the grass on the cliff-top and the sea went on boiling and booming.

Nobody knew the Iron Man had fallen.

Night passed.

Just before dawn, as the darkness grew blue and the shapes of the rocks separated from each other, two sea-gulls flew crying over the rocks. They landed on a patch of sand. They had two chicks in a nest on the cliff. Now they were searching for food.

One of the seagulls flew up – Aaaaaark! He had seen something. He glided low over the sharp rocks. He landed and picked something up. Something shiny, round and hard. It was one of the Iron Man's eyes. He brought it back to his mate. They both looked at this strange thing. And the eye looked at them. It rolled from side to side looking first at one gull, then at the other. The gulls, peering at it, thought it was a strange kind of clam, peeping at them from its shell.

Then the other gull flew up, wheeled around and landed and picked something up. Some awkward, heavy thing. The gull flew low and slowly, dragging the heavy thing. Finally, the gull dropped it beside the eye. This new thing had five legs. It moved. The gulls thought it was a strange kind of crab. They thought they had found a strange crab and a strange clam. They did not know they had found the Iron Man's eye and the Iron Man's right hand.

But as soon as the eye and the hand got together the eye looked at the hand. Its light glowed blue. The hand stood up on three fingers and its thumb, and craned its forefinger like a long nose. It felt around. It touched the eye. Gleefully it picked up the eye, and tucked it under its middle finger. The eye peered out, between the forefinger and thumb. Now the hand could see.

It looked around. Then it darted and jabbed one of the gulls with its stiffly held finger, then darted at the other and jabbed him. The two gulls flew up into the wind with a frightened cry.

Slowly then the hand crept over the stones, searching. It ran forward suddenly, grabbed something and tugged. But the thing was stuck between two rocks. The thing was one of the Iron Man's arms. At last the hand left the arm and went scuttling hither and thither among the rocks, till it stopped, and touched something gently. This thing was the other hand. This new hand stood up and hooked its finger round the little finger of the hand with the eye, and let itself be led. Now the two hands, the seeing one leading the blind one, walking on their

fingertips, went back together to the arm, and together they tugged it free. The hand with the eye fastened itself on to the wrist of the arm. The arm stood up and walked on its hand. The other hand clung on behind as before, and this strange trio went searching.

An eye! There it was, blinking at them speechlessly beside a black and white pebble. The seeing hand fitted the eye to the blind hand and now both hands could see. They went running among the rocks. Soon they found a leg. They jumped on top of the leg and the leg went hopping over the rocks with the arm swinging from the hand that clung to the top of the leg. The other hand clung on top of that hand. The two hands, with their eyes, guided the leg, twisting it this way and that, as a rider guides a horse.

Soon they found another leg and the other arm. Now each hand, with an eye under its palm and an arm dangling from its wrist, rode on a leg separately about the beach. Hop, hop, hop, they went, peering among the rocks. One found an ear and at the same moment the other found the giant torso. Then the busy hands fitted the legs to the torso, then they fitted the arms, each fitting the other, and the torso stood up with legs and arms but no head. It walked about the beach, holding its eyes up in its hands, searching for its lost head. At last, there was the head – eyeless, earless, nested in a heap of red seaweed. Now in no time the Iron Man had fitted his head back, and his eyes were in place, and everything in place except for one ear. He strode about the beach searching for his lost ear, as the sun rose over the sea and the day came.

The two gulls sat on their ledge, high on the cliff. They watched the immense man striding to and fro over the rocks below. Between them, on the nesting ledge, lay a great iron ear. The gulls could not eat it. The baby gulls could not eat it. There it lay on the high ledge.

Far below, the Iron Man searched.

At last he stopped, and looked at the sea. Was he thinking the sea had stolen his ear? Perhaps he was thinking the sea had come up, while he lay scattered, and had gone down again with his ear.

He walked towards the sea. He walked into the breakers, and there he stood for a while, the breakers bursting around his knees. Then he walked in deeper, deeper, deeper.

The gulls took off and glided down low over the great iron head that was now moving slowly out through the swell. The eyes blazed red, level with the wavetops, till a big wave covered them and foam spouted over the top of the head. The head still moved out under water. The eyes and the top of the head appeared for a moment in a hollow of the swell. Now the eyes were green. Then the sea covered them and the head.

The gulls circled low over the line of bubbles that went on moving slowly out into the deep sea.

# HELEN CRESSWELL

from *The Night-Watchmen*

As he drew nearer he could see that a kind of hoop-shaped canvas hut had been erected in his absence. It sat snugly under the middle arch on the narrow strip of green, and Henry could see Josh and Caleb nearby busy with their unpacking.

Caleb pounced on the carrier bag the minute Henry set it down and swiftly checked off the items, examining each with care if not actual suspicion. He even opened the bag of tomatoes and felt them, one by one. Henry was glad he had remembered to ask for firm ones. He would not have liked to see Caleb confronted by a pound of squashy tomatoes.

'That's all right, then,' said Caleb, satisfied at last. 'Any change?'

Henry handed it over and Caleb counted it and handed it to Josh saying, 'Yours, Josh. I'll get the stove lit.'

He disappeared into the hut. Henry, left alone with Josh, decided to ask some of the questions he had thought of during the past hour.

'What are you going to do with the hole now that you've dug it?' he began.

Josh looked up from his sorting. Henry noticed that the boxes seemed to contain paper, mostly.

'Oh, the hole's done with now it's dug,' he said. 'It's just a bit of background, as you might say. It'll just stop there till it gets filled in again.'

'And when will that be?' asked Henry.

'When we flits,' explained Josh. 'When we've finished.'

'Will it be very long?' persisted Henry.

'Can't say. But I liked the way this town ticked, or we shouldn't have gone to the trouble to dig a hole in the first place. We should've stuck it out for a few nights in the park.'

Henry considered this. Light began to dawn.

'You mean you've dug a *hole* so that you can put up the *hut*!' he cried. The whole amazing pattern was beginning to fall into shape.

Josh lowered his voice.

'You see, if we was to go putting up huts all over the place, there'd be questions asked. There'd be police and Authority on us before we'd so much as got the stove lit. But a hut with a *hole*, ah, that's a different matter!'

Henry, delighted, could see that it was.

'It blends in with the background natural, d'ye see,' Josh went on. 'Just dig a hole and put up a red flag and you could camp till doomsday and not a question asked. Worked it out a few years back, we did, the summer Caleb got pneumonia park-sleeping.'

'It's marvellous!' cried Henry. 'Absolutely marvellous!'

'It's beating 'em at their own game,' said Josh, 'that's the way we look at it. Dozens of holes we've dug, the long and broad of England, and not so much as the bat of an eyelid. You could dig one outside the Houses of Parliament, if you'd a mind to, and as long as nobody fell in it there'd be no questions asked. That's what you got to watch. If anyone was to fall in you'd have the Authorities on you and the game *would* be up.'

Henry saw his opening.

'What game?' he asked. 'What do you do?'

'Do?' said Josh. 'I wouldn't rightly say that we do anything. It's more a matter of what we *are* than what we *do*.'

'What are you, then?' pressed Henry desperately.

Josh hesitated. Then:

'Night-watchmen,' he said at last. 'That's what we are. Night-watchmen.'

Henry stared at him.

'Among other things,' added Josh.

As Henry opened his mouth Caleb's thin face poked from the hut.

'*He's* not stopping, is he?' he said. 'There ain't enough herbs for three.'

Henry, startled, looked at his watch.

'Dinner!' he cried. 'I'm late! Back this afternoon!'

He had gone only a few yards when he heard Josh. He turned.

'Supper!' called Josh. 'Come to supper! Seven sharp!'

Henry nodded. Somehow he would manage it.

'Seven!' he called back. 'Thank you!'

All the way home he was so preoccupied with inventing a convincing reason for his lateness that he did not have time to wonder what Josh had meant by that last mysterious statement, just before Caleb had interrupted them. Which was just as well. Henry had had about as much mystery as he could stand, for the time being.

# SYLVIA SHERRY

FROM *A Pair of Jesus-Boots*

Unable to settle, he went quietly out of the room, leaving his mother asleep. The cold and darkness of the Square revived his spirits, and he went round calling on the gang to come to the hideout. They could play cards and he could show them the transistor.

'Where'd yer get it, Rocky?' asked Billy.

'I did a job.'

'Yer mean yer nicked it?'

'I'm not admitting ter nothing.'

Billy played a card in silence, but little Chan said, 'It is a bad thing to steal what belongs to somebody else.'

'Ah go on!' said the Nabber. 'Who knows about it?'

'*We* all know,' said little Chan. 'My father says it is a sin to steal. You begin with a penny, and you end up with a thousand pounds.'

Rocky glared at him. 'That's the whole idea – honestly! Some people! Yer mean yer haven't seen *that* yet? Anyway, yer came in on the first break-in, didn't you?'

'Yer know Chick and Spadge's been sent away? Chick's mam came home crying from the court.'

The boys reflected on this. Rocky knew all about the scenes that followed on a boy's being sent away. He'd seen it happen a lot with Joey.

'I would be careful, Rocky,' said Billy. 'I wouldn't flash it around – the transistor, I mean . . .'

'I can watch out fer meself, thanks! 'Ere, that's my

trick, and yer owe me threepence, Beady!'

But when the gang went, he still felt restless. And he didn't want to leave the transistor in the hideout either. It was his now – or half his. When Joey came home, he would tell him where he could sell it, then he'd split the money with the Nabber. But till then, he would use it.

To take his mind off it, he wandered off towards the pub in Joseph Terrace. Now that Chick and Spadge had gone, the territory was free to the Cats, and he hoped he might see the wingy. He liked chatting to the wingy because he didn't treat him like a kid.

As he walked, he switched on the transistor and held it to his ear.

Under the light above the door of the pub, Mr Oliver was talking to another man. As Rocky approached, they separated and Mr Oliver came down the steps towards him. For once he seemed sober.

'Hello, Rocky! How's tricks?'

'All right, Mr Oliver.'

They stood together at the corner, watching the sparse night life of Joseph Terrace.

'Good match this afternoon, Rocky. Did yer hear Everton beat Chelsea?'

'I heard it, Mr Oliver – on the transistor.'

'Yer did? Coming up in the world, aren't yer? Where'd yer get that from?'

'It was – do yer want to hear it?'

'Go on then – only don't wake the neighbours . . .'

Engrossed in finding a programme, Rocky didn't notice Constable McMahon approaching on his beat until the policeman had stopped beside them. Then he switched the radio off, but he knew the constable had seen it.

'Hello, Davey. How's life?' asked McMahon.

'Not so bad. How's yerself? Not a fit night for a dog ter be out, is it?'

'It is not. And that lad looks frozen through. It's Rocky O'Rourke, isn't it? That wouldn't be a transistor you've got there, would it?'

'What if it is?'

'Yours, is it?'

Rocky nodded. Suddenly his mouth was too dry for him to speak.

'Mind if I have a look?'

Reluctantly, Rocky handed it over and stood waiting for the questions to start. Constable McMahon examined it closely, then stood with it in his hands.

'All right. Just checking up, yer know. There was transistors taken from the Buildings that time, but not one of this make.'

'Oh, Rocky's not a thief, aren't yer not, Rocky? He's a footballer.'

'So long as he keeps to it. Where d'you get it?' He handed it back, and Rocky clutched it thankfully.

'Me mam. She had a win on the bingo.'

'She'd have done better to have bought yer some warm clothes – an' a pair of shoes,' said the policeman.

'Me shoes is all right,' muttered Rocky defiantly. The thing he had against Mr Oliver was his friendship with the police – calling them Mac, and Sarge, and Fred.

'They're all right, Rocky,' he would say. 'They're just doin' a job. Now somebody has to keep the rules, haven't they? Stands ter reason, doesn't it?'

But Rocky couldn't be persuaded to that point of view. They'd taken Joey away. That was enough.

'Sure it was yer mam gave it to yer?' repeated the constable.

Rocky went cold. He was still suspicious, the scuffer.

'I said so, didn't I? Think I'm telling lies? It's always the same. Like me mam says, it doesn't pay ter tell the truth – you'll not be believed . . .'

Something in Rocky's voice woke the wingy up to the fact that there was trouble somewhere and, not understanding but wanting to support Rocky, he said, 'That's right, Mac, that's right. It was his mother. She told me herself.'

'She did?' The constable sounded surprised, and looked steadily at Mr Oliver.

'Aye.' The wingy looked away. 'She did.'

'All right, Davey. I'll believe yer,' said Constable McMahon, meaningly. 'And I won't forget . . .'

He paced off down the Terrace.

Rocky and the wingy watched him go, past the pub, past the shops due for demolition, past the off-licence and round the corner. A fine rain was drizzling down now, and grey, misty clouds lay heavily over the city. Opposite them, the archway into the Buildings was dark, and light after light came on in the flats above.

'So, Rocky,' said the wingy, who suddenly seemed very sober, 'he was right, was he? Old Mac seems to know yer better than me.'

'What d'yer mean . . .?'

'I mean, Rocky, yer nicked that radio set, didn't yer?'

'Honest, Mr Oliver, honest . . .' Rocky began to protest.

'Come off it, lad, I wasn't born yesterday . . .' Mr Oliver turned and began walking away. Rocky stood in the doorway of the pub, still clutching the radio, but with a feeling of loneliness and depression. Mr Oliver was giving him up.

But suddenly, the wingy turned and came striding back, his right hand gesticulating fiercely at Rocky.

'I'm telling yer, lad . . . just you listen ter me! It's not the lorry-skipping, like, or the hanging around Lime Street Station picking up coppers . . .'

Rocky was amazed. 'How d'yer know I goes . . .'

'Look, lad, I did the same meself when I was a kid. It's kids' stuff. Well it is, isn't it? I mean, yer don't find grown men doing it, do yer?'

'Well, no, leastways I haven't seen em,' Rocky conceded reluctantly.

'Not likely to neither! But all right – we'll ferget *that*. Yer'll grow out of it. And when yer comes to me and says, "Mr Oliver, I've given up the lorry-skipping. It's a mug's game," I'll say to you, "Rocky, wack, shake hands.

Yer a man!'' That's what I'll say. But *this* – *this* sort of business!'

With another wave of disgust the wingy turned and stalked away again, only to return once more, still gesticulating.

'Yer know where it ends? I mean, apart from the rights and wrongs on it. Yer know where it gets yer? In the clink!'

'No it doesn't – no it . . .'

'Doesn't it? What about yer kid brother? What about Chick and Spadge?'

'They was . . .'

'Fools – idiots!' His voice dropped. 'Listen, Rocky. You learn sense, lad, and I'll do more'n shake yer hand. I'll . . . I'll . . .' Ideas failed him, and he came up with the only thing he could think of, 'I'll buy yer a pint!'

'But I don't . . . Me mam wouldn't let me . . .'

'And just think, Rocky. I don't suppose yer pinched that off anybody as could afford ter lose it, did yer? Yer got it off somebody who's missing it right now and hasn't the money to replace it! Ah shurrup, Rocky! Wake up ter yerself!'

The wingy swung round and was off, charging away through the night towards the Buildings. Rocky, left by himself, was trembling, suddenly cold and miserable and indignant all at once.

'Who does he think he is?' he asked himself, and then yelled, 'Who d'yer think yer are? Me granny?'

He began to run home, skirting round the Buildings, and not wanting to see the wingy again. It was *his* transistor. No matter what he said. It was his and he was keeping it.

But in the Square, he hesitated. A whole jumble of

thoughts and feelings confused him. McMahon had seen him with it. The wingy thought nothing of him for taking it, and maybe the old woman there was missing it . . .

Rocky turned disconsolately towards the old woman's house.

# PETER DICKINSON

The loft stank. Five windows gave real light. Dawn was coming fast. Sleeping children littered the mouldy hay in attitudes horribly like those of the two dead robbers on the grass outside the barn. But three were already woken to the nightmare day, and wailing. Nicky put her finger to her lips. The wailing stopped, but the wailers shrank from her as though she'd been a poisonous spider. More of them were stirring now – older ones.

'It's quite all right,' said Nicky. 'We've come to help you.'

The words came out all strange and awkward. Nicky wasn't used to being hated and feared.

'Go away!' said a red-headed girl, about her own age.

More children were moving. A six-year-old boy sat suddenly bolt up, as though someone had pinched him; he stared at Nicky for five seconds and began to screech. Some of them were standing now, but still cowering away from her. A babble like a playground rose – this was wrong, awful, dangerous. Everything depended on keeping the children quiet until the attack on the house had started.

'Shut up!' shouted Nicky, and stamped her foot. There was a moment's silence, then the noise began to bubble up again, then it hushed. Ajeet walked past Nicky as though she wasn't there, right to the end of the stinking loft, turned, settled cross-legged on to a bale and held the whole room still with her dark, beautiful eyes. Just as the silence was beginning to crumble, she spoke.

'Be quiet, please,' she said in a clear voice. 'I am going to tell you a story. Will you all sit down please?'

Every child settled . . .

'There was a tiger once which had no soul,' said Ajeet. 'All day and all night it raged through the forest, seeking a soul which it could make its own. Now, in those forests there lived a woodman, and he had two sons . . .'

Her hands were moving already. The jungle grew at her fingertips, and through it the tiger stalked and roared, and the woodman's sons adventured. Nicky saw a child which had slept through the din wake slowly, sit up and start listening, as though this were how every morning of its life began. Terrified of breaking the spell, Nicky tiptoed to a window.

She could see the house clearly now; white and square, very big, with a low slate roof ending in a brim like a Chinese peasant's hat. Here a cheerful stockbroker had lived six months before; along these paths his children had larked or mooned as the mood took them; an old gardener had mown the big lawns smooth enough for croquet. And now they were all gone, and the lawns were lank, and murder crept across them. Any minute now . . .

A crash of glass, and a cry, and then a wild yelling. A naked white man was running across the lawn with a Sikh after him. The naked man ran faster and disappeared among trees, and the Sikh stopped and trotted back to the house. A cracked bell began a raucous clank – the alarm signal – but stopped before it had rung a dozen times. One, two, three, four men jumped from an upstair window and ran to the largest of the outbuildings. From another window a figure flew, tumbling as he fell; when he hit the grass he lay still, and a second later Nicky heard the crash of the big pane through which he had been thrown. In the twanging silence that followed Nicky studied the geography of the buildings and tried to plan for disaster. Suppose a sortie of robbers rushed from the house, would there be time to get the children down the stairs? The robbers had chosen the barn for their hostages because it was set nearly a hundred yards from the other buildings, and they could fire it without endangering themselves. Supposing the four men now cowering in the large outbuilding – just as far away across the paddock-like turf, but more to the left – plucked up their courage for revenge . . . A hoarse yell wavered across the grass, rising to a sharp scream, cut short.

Nicky looked over her shoulder to see how the children were taking these desperate noises. Should they leave now, and risk meeting a party of escaping robbers, or a returning patrol? No. Ajeet still held them enthralled: the woodman's second son was exchanging riddles with the tiger that had no soul. The tiger had already possessed the soul of the elder son, but needed a second man's soul to make up a whole tiger's soul. Nicky crossed the room and looked down the steep stair. Gopal had finished soaking the straw and was standing, watchful but relaxed, behind one doorpost. He had closed the other leaf. Nicky was on the point of going down to ask what he thought about moving the children when his stance tensed. She darted back to her window.

A man had led a huge horse from the outbuilding door. A strange figure moved beyond the animal and two other men came behind. The horse stopped. The two men went to the strange figure, bent out of sight and heaved.

The knight erupted into his saddle. He still looked strange, because his armour was so clumsy, but now he looked terrifying too – a giant toy which someone has put together from left-over bits of puppets and dolls, and then brought to gawky life. He put out his hand and a man passed him up his spear; a little crimson flag fluttered below the point. Now the man passed him a big timber axe and the knight hooked it into his belt, then turned and said something to the men. Two of them went back into the stables, but the third put a trumpet to his lips and blew a long, shivering note. The knight kicked his heels against the horse's ribs and the big animal started a slow trot over the lawn, towards the barn. Nicky heard the second leaf of the door creak shut, and the bar fall into place. The third man had followed the other two into the stables.

Beyond the knight a dark figure appeared from a downstairs window and stood for a moment, round as a bubble, against the whitewashed wall. Then Uncle Chacha was trotting across the grass, unhurriedly, as though he were slightly late for an appointment. Nicky could see the knight's face now, for the gawky helmet hung back over his shoulders and clanked dully as he bounced in his saddle. His hair was tight gold curls, his cheeks smooth; his nose was a ruin – broken in some old fight and mended all lopsided; below it his handsome mouth grinned cheerfully. As he came he fitted the lance into a holder, so that it stood up like a mast behind his thigh. Now he could wield his axe, two-handed.

Nicky looked round the room for something to throw, though none of the windows was near enough over the door; she might unsettle the horse for a minute, perhaps. But there seemed to be nothing in the loft except hay and children. She craned back out of the stench into the murderous sweet air.

The knight had ranged his horse alongside the door, and already the big axe was swung up over his shoulder for a blow. His armour had gaps between the separate pieces, to allow his limbs to move freely; really it was only pieces of boiler and drainpipe held together with straps.

He looked up to Nicky's window; his green mad eyes caught and held hers; then he laughed, as Mr Tom had said, like a lover, and swung the axe. The blade crunched through the half-rotted planking and he wrenched it free and hefted it for another blow. Nicky didn't dare look to where Uncle Chacha came trotting over the sward: his best hope – his only hope – was to catch the knight unawares and thrust through one of the joints of his armour. Instead she looked towards the stable.

The three men were out of the door again, two of them carrying another brazier and the third an armful of weapons. The carriers put the brazier down and one of them pointed at Uncle Chacha. The third man dropped the weapons, lifted the trumpet and blew, just as the axe crashed in again. One fierce note floated across the green.

The knight heard it, looked over his shoulder, saw the pointing arm, saw his attacker, and kicked the big horse round. As it turned he hooked the axe back on to his belt and lifted the lance out of its holder on the return movement. The pennon dipped. The brazier party stood still to watch the fun. The knight's boots drubbed mercilessly at the horse's ribs, so that horse and man rushed

on Uncle Chacha like a landslide. Uncle Chacha glanced once over his shoulder to see whether danger threatened from behind, then waited for the charge, his curved grey blade held low in his right hand. Nicky tried to look away again, but the dread of the sight held her transfixed.

Uncle Chacha just stood and waited for the lance-point. He was a round, easy, still target. Only when the bitter tip was a second away did he begin to move, to his left, out from the path of the horse.

Nicky gulped. He had dodged too soon. The point had followed him round.

But with a single flowing twist, long after he had seemed committed to his leftward dodge, he was rolling and falling to the right, in towards the battering hooves, the way the knight could not expect him to go; and then, as the spear-point spiked uselessly past, he was still falling but rolling out, with his sword whistling up behind his back in a long, wristy slash.

The stroke did not seem to have hit anything, but by the time the knight was turning his horse for a fresh charge Uncle Chacha was on his feet and picking up something from the grass – a stick with a red rag near the end. Three foot of severed spear. He felt the point, turned for a moment to wave a cheerful hand to Nicky, threw his small round shield to one side and waited for the knight in the same pose as before – except that now the pennoned point hung parallel to the sword, his left hand grasping the cut shaft.

The three men by the stables had put the brazier down and were sharing out the weapons. One of them shouted to the knight and he called back, then came again more cautiously.

His boots drubbed and the horse bore in. The knight seemed to have an incredible advantage, fighting down at the small round man from that moving tower of muscle, and protected too by all his armour. And his axe – though he had to hold it one-handed, rather far up the shaft, as he needed his other hand for the reins – was so heavy that even held like that any blow from it would surely cleave turban and skull. The knight seemed to think so, for he was grinning as he came.

Uncle Chacha balanced to meet the charge. Nicky thought she knew what he would do. He would wait again until his enemy was almost on him, feint one way to commit the axe to a blow that side, then dodge round the other side of the horse and either pull the knight from his saddle, or wound or kill the horse so that he could fight the knight level. He would have to be quick, though: the other three men would soon be dangerously near.

But this time he didn't wait. When the horse was six feet away from him he made a long skip to his right, so that the knight had to turn the horse in to him, one-handed. As the big animal came awkwardly round Uncle Chacha moved again, leaping forward with a shrill, gargling shout. The knight's axe came up, ready for him, but the fat man leaped direct for the charging horse, sweeping the pennoned spear sideways and up in front of its nose at the very moment that the wolf-cry of his shout cut short in a snapping bark. The terrified horse, bred and trained to pull brewer's drays through orderly streets, shied sideways from the onslaught, and half-reared in a swirling spasm that gave the knight far too much to do to allow him to smite at his attacker. Uncle Chacha struck with his sword and the knight had to drop the reins and raise his iron arm to parry the whistling blade; even before the steel clanged into the drainpipe, the knight's own spearpoint was lancing up into the armpit which the raised arm had exposed.

He was still grinning as he toppled.

# JOAN LINGARD

FROM *The Twelfth Day of July*

For a moment there was silence. They could hear the hum of the city traffic in the distance, but they were only concerned with what was going to happen here, in this street. This is what they had been waiting for all week: to stand face-to-face, on either side of the road. One or two shivered, either with fear or the thrill of expectation. But none moved away. It was as if a magnet held them there irresistibly.

The moment of quiet passed. Now the voices were raised, soft and taunting to begin with.

'Dirty Micks!'

'Filthy ould Prods!'

Tempers flared. The voices grew louder.

'Kick the Pope!'

'To hell with King Billy!'

No one knew who threw the first stone. One seemed to come from each side simultaneously.

It was as if a whistle had been blown. Suddenly, children appeared from every direction; they came swarming out of side streets, yelling, cheering, booing. Their hands scoured the ground for any ammunition they could find, large stones, small ones, pieces of wood, half-bricks. They advanced on to the road. The gap between the two sides narrowed.

Sadie was in the front line. Her face glowed, and her heart thudded with excitement. She felt as though a fever possessed her. And then for a second she paused, a yell trapped at the back of her throat. She had seen Brede's face. Brede stood behind the Catholics, not shouting, or throwing, just standing.

At that moment a brick flew high over the heads of the crowd. Sadie saw Brede duck. But she was too late; the brick caught her full on the side of the head.

Brede went down and disappeared amongst the swirling bodies of the Catholics.

'Brede!' roared Sadie.

Brede was hurt. Brede . . . why Brede? Inside Sadie felt cold. There was no fever now, no excitement, only a desperate need to get across and find out what had happened to the fallen girl. With another roar Sadie surged forward.

'Come back, Sadie,' someone yelled behind her. 'They'll murder you.'

Sadie fought through the lines, hauling children out of her way. She felt hands trying to grasp her, but the strength in her body was so great they could not stop her. She reached the group gathered round Brede's body.

A boy caught hold of her roughly.

'Leave her be,' said Kevin McCoy quietly, looking up from where he knelt beside his sister.

Sadie knelt beside him.

'Is she bad?'

'Think so.'

Brede lay still, her arms sprawled at her sides, her eyes closed. There was blood on her head.

The sound of a police siren screamed further along the road. Children flew to right and left, dropping their ammunition as they ran. By the time the police car arrived

the street was almost empty. Only four children remained.

Tommy crossed the road to join Sadie and Kevin. He squatted beside them, staring down at Brede.

'Stupid,' he said. 'Stupid, stupid, stupid!'

The car doors slammed; two policemen got out and came towards them.

'Now then, what's been going on?'

'We'll need an ambulance,' said Kevin.

An ambulance was summoned, and arrived within minutes with its blue light flashing. The other three children stood back to allow the men to lift Brede on to a stretcher. They covered her with a blanket and carried her into the ambulance.

Sadie, Tommy and Kevin went into the back of the police car. They swept through the late-night streets behind the ambulance, watching its flashing light, listening to its wail. The sound made Sadie shudder.

At the hospital the lights were bright and blinding. Brede was taken away; doors closed behind her.

The waiting-room was warm, but Sadie could not stop shivering. Keven took a bar of chocolate from his pocket and broke it into three pieces. They ate in silence, sitting side by side on a bench.

After a few minutes a police officer appeared to take down their statements. He shook his head.

'Why can't you keep to your own sides of the road?'

'Will she die?' Sadie burst out, unable to control the question any longer.

'We don't know yet.'

The door opened, and in came Mr McCoy looking white and shaken. He began to shout when he saw Kevin.

'I can't trust you kids an inch. I knew you'd end up in trouble. And there's your ma in Tyrone . . .'

'Come on,' said the police officer to Sadie and Tommy. 'I'll get someone to take you home.'

'Can't we wait and see how she is?' asked Tommy.

'Your parents will be worrying about you. Don't you think you've caused enough trouble for one night? But I'll see if there's any news before you go.'

Sadie looked back at Kevin. 'I hope she'll be all right.'

Kevin nodded.

They left him with his father. As soon as the door closed they heard Mr McCoy starting to shout again. They waited in the corridor whilst the policeman went to inquire.

'If I got my hands on the one that did it!' said Tommy.

'Does it matter?' said Sadie wearily.

'You mean it could just as easily have been me?'

'Aye. Or me.'

The policeman returned.

'They're going to perform an emergency operation,' he said. 'They're getting her ready for the theatre now.'

The twelfth of July. The Protestants were astir early, polishing their shoes, laying out their clothes, their sashes and their bowler hats. Mr Jackson brushed his and laid it on the hall table. Mrs Jackson hurried over to Mrs Mullet's to cook ham and eggs and brought them back sizzling in the frying pan.

'Time you were up,' she called up the stairs. 'Linda's up and dressed.'

She dished out the breakfast and still there was no movement overhead. She climbed the stairs and pushed open Sadie's door.

'Breakfast's out. If you don't come now it'll be cold.'

'Not hungry.' Sadie's voice came from beneath the bed-clothes.

'Suit yourself. Your father'll eat the extra. Tommy, are you wanting your breakfast?' she called through to him.

'No.'

'It's no wonder the two of you aren't hungry after that carry-on last night. A right disgrace it was! If you're not careful you'll end up being late.'

Whilst Mr and Mrs Jackson ate their breakfast they discussed again the happenings of the night before. When Sadie and Tommy had returned home in the small hours of the morning they had had to give a full acount of what had taken place. At the end of it they had been told they would be allowed to walk in the parade, even though they did not deserve to. 'So as not to let the Lodge down,' Mr Jackson had impressed upon them. 'Other-wise you'd have had it!'

'Of course,' said Mrs Jackson as she mopped up the egg yolk with a piece of bread, 'it was that other lot. They're always wanting to cause trouble on the "Twelfth".'

Mr Jackson nodded. He took another piece of toast. He needed a good breakfast under his belt before he set out on the long walk to the 'field'. Mrs Jackson would take a picnic and join them there for the speeches.

She went to the foot of the stairs again. 'Get up or you'll miss the procession altogether.'

She took her basin of dishes across to the Mullets. Mrs Mullet was dressing Linda's hair, teasing it into ringlets and tying it up with ribbons.

'I believe your two were in hot water last night,' said Mrs Mullet, speaking awkwardly through a mouthful of hairpins. She took them out. 'I just heard when I went to the shop for rolls.'

Mrs Jackson unpacked the dirty dishes and put them into the sink. 'There were more than my two in hot water,' she said and looked round at Linda, who looked back with wide, innocent eyes. 'But the rest run off to save their skins.'

'Your Sadie's a one, though, you can't deny it.' Mrs Mullet tweaked one of Linda's ringlets to make it more like a corkscrew. 'You can always count on her being there when anything's going on.'

'She's not a coward. I will say that for her.' Mrs Jackson turned to her washing up, regretting bitterly that she had to take advantage of Mrs Mullet's hospitality.

'Is she ready?' asked Linda. 'Will I go over for her?'

'No, not yet. I'll send her to call for you when she's dressed.'

Mrs Jackson returned home with the clean dishes. Sadie and Tommy were still in bed. She climbed the stairs again.

'This is the last time I'm telling you. If you're late now it'll be your own faults.'

Sadie was lying with her eyes open, her arms above her head on the pillow.

'Ma,' she said, 'I'm not going.'

'Not going?' Mrs Jackson laid her hand on her throat. 'Do you mean you're not going to walk?' She was almost spluttering. 'Are you all right? Are you sick, or what?'

'I just don't feel like going.'

'Don't talk daft! You've been practising for weeks and you've got your costume. Think of all the money I spent on it!'

Mrs Jackson looked at the purple velvet outfit hanging in front of the wardrobe. Sadie looked too and sighed.

'I know. I'm sorry.'

'Sorry! Tommy, come and talk sense into your sister's head.'

Tommy came into Sadie's room in his pyjamas, his feet bare. 'I'm not going either.'

Mrs Jackson sat down on the end of Sadie's bed. 'You're joking. You're having me on.'

'I know it's a shock, ma,' said Sadie, 'but we can't help it.'

Mrs Jackson went downstairs and Mr Jackson came up.

'What's all this nonsense I'm hearing? You'll have to go. You can't disappoint your mother. She's been looking forward to seeing you walk for weeks.'

'I'm sorry,' said Tommy, 'but we've made up our minds.'

'What about all the money we've spent on you?'

'We'll pay it back out of our pocket money,' said Sadie.

'I don't know what's happened to you kids.' Mr Jackson scratched his head. 'Well, I'm getting ready or I'll be late. And I've never been late for the walk in my life.' He left them.

The doorbell rang and the front door opened.

'Are you ready, Sadie?' Linda called out.

'I'm not going,' Sadie called back.

'Not going?'

'I don't think she's feeling too well,' said Mrs Jackson.

'She'll be awfully disappointed . . .' Linda's voice died away.

When Mr and Mrs Jackson were dressed and ready to go out they came into Sadie's room.

'You're letting us down badly, you realize that, don't you?' said Mr Jackson.

'I never thought you'd do a thing like this to us,' said Mrs Jackson.

And then they went out.

Sadie and Tommy sat side by side on the bed listening. The street was busy with feet going up and down. The men would be assembling at their lodges, the bands gathering with their pipes and flutes and drums, the drum majorettes high-stepping and twirling their batons. And then they heard the music beginning: the drums tapping soft, then loud, the tootle of the flutes, the deeper notes of the pipes. Tommy's foot tapped.

'It's a pity,' he said.

'For Brede, too,' said Sadie.

'Aye.'

# GILLIAN AVERY

FROM *A Likely Lad*

The Town Hall was huge. It reared upwards with complicated roof tops, and spread outwards with thousands of windows, filling the whole of one side of Albert Square. Mr Overs' mind, however, was not on the Town Hall yet. He was pointing out the statue of Cobden.

'There you are, Willy, the Apostle of Free Trade; Manchester's tribute to one of her great men. Mark it well, Willy, and remember the date that you first saw it.'

But Willy, staring obediently at the begrimed figure on its plinth, could only think how uncomfortable it must be to have pigeon droppings all over you like that. He followed his father into the Town Hall. His father was taking off his hat as if it was chapel, so Willy took off his too, and stood gazing about him in awe. Immense marble floors with pictures in them spread in front of him; the people who were scurrying over it seemed like midgets in comparison and their voices just a murmur in the vastness of the place. There was a staircase grander than anything he could have imagined, two sets of stairs coming down facing each other, and where they met, becoming one staircase. He felt his father was expecting some sort of response from him.

'It's like a palace, Father,' he said weakly.

'It's a palace of palaces, Willy. There's not many as could boast a place like this, I can tell you. Do you know how many cubic feet of stone went into it? 480,000. And 16,500,000 bricks. Just think of it, Willy! And how many masons would you say was working on it? Think, Willy.'

'A million?' hazarded Willy feverishly.

'Seven hundred,' said his father severely. 'A hundred more than ever worked on the Houses of Parliament in London. What do you think of that now?'

But Willy could only think that the numbers didn't sound anywhere near as big as they ought to be. 'It's very big,' he said feebly after a long pause. 'I like the floor and the stairs. Thank you for bringing me, Father.'

'But you haven't seen what I brought you here for. What I told you about last Sunday. You come over here.'

Beckoning Willy on he led him to the wall on one side of the door through which they had just come. It was lined with niches which held the busts of rather fleshy men with whiskers.

'Is one of them Cobden, Father?' ventured Willy, faintly. 'Or Cobbett or Smiles?' he said wildly, sensing that his first guess was hopelessly wrong.

'None of them,' said his father with irritation. 'No, Willy, what I brought you to see were *those*!' Holding Willy's shoulder he pointed with a trembling finger to a group of empty niches beyond. But here Willy's powers of improvisation, such as they were, completely left him. He looked blankly at the niches, and then blankly up at his father's face.

'There's one there reserved for *you*, Willy boy. Nobody knows yet which one it is, but one day, I'll come in, an old, old man, and I'll point to one of those niches that Manchester keeps for her most famous men, for those who have served her with glory, and I'll say that's my

Willy! And they'll say, Sir William Overs − (you'll be
knighted by then, Willy) − you know him? And I'll say,
know him? Why, he's my son!'

On his way home Mr Overs enlarged on his plans for
Willy's future. He frequently blew his nose, much moved
by his words. Willy was to raise himself into a position
of great importance in the Northern Star, and from there
he was to step into public service, Councillor he would
be, Alderman, Lord Mayor, and finish up by having
streets and hospitals and schools called after him, and his
bust in the Town Hall. He went on about this at dinner-
time when they got back.

 'Can't you do all these things if you've got a shop,
Father?' asked George towards the end of the meal,
shovelling up his treacle pudding.

''Course you can,' said Mr Overs stoutly. 'Manchester's glory is her trade, and there's plenty who's risen from humble beginnings here.'

'Then why don't you have a try, Father?' George demanded, lovingly licking every vestige of treacle off his spoon and contemplating it between licks.

'Because it's too late for me. I did my bit in putting enough behind me to buy my shop – and I can tell you there weren't many boys of my sort who would have managed to earn an honest living, let alone put enough by to have his own business. But you boys are different, I've taken care to give you a good start, and I only hope I'll live to see you make use of it.'

Willy had always been given to daydreams, and now he had an entirely new theme for them – Sir William Overs, in velvet robes and gold chain, advancing with stately dignity down the splendid staircase in the Town Hall, towards expectant crowds waiting on the marble floor below. It buoyed him up for several weeks, and even carried him through the ordeal of the October first Sunday at Trafford. No need for him to feel ill at ease now as he usually did in Cromwell Villas. He could sit serenely gazing at his plate, thinking that the time would soon be coming when the whole Sowter family would be enviously discussing his banquets at the Town Hall.

# RICHARD ADAMS

FROM *Watership Down*

Hazel turned his head and looked down the course of the brook. Far away, between the two copses, he could see the cherry tree where two days before he had sat with Blackberry and Fiver in the sunrise. He remembered how Bigwig had chased Hawkbit through the long grass, forgetting the quarrel of the previous night in the joy of their arrival. He could see Hawkbit running towards him now and two or three of the others – Silver, Dandelion and Pipkin. Dandelion, well in front, dashed up to the gap and checked, twitching and staring.

'What is it, Hazel? What's happened? Fiver said –'

'Bigwig's in a wire. Let him alone till Blackberry tells us. Stop the others crowding round.'

Dandelion turned and raced back as Pipkin came up.

'Is Cowslip coming?' said Hazel. 'Perhaps *he* knows –'

'He wouldn't come,' replied Pipkin. 'He told Fiver to stop talking about it.'

'Told him *what*?' asked Hazel incredulously. But at that moment Blackberry spoke and Hazel was beside him in a flash.

'This is it,' said Blackberry. 'The wire's on a peg and the peg's in the ground – there, look. We've got to dig it out. Come on – dig beside it.'

Hazel dug once more, his fore-paws throwing up the soft, wet soil and slipping against the hard sides of the peg. Dimly, he was aware of the others waiting near by.

After a time he was forced to stop, panting. Silver took his place, and was followed by Buckthorn. The nasty, smooth, clean, man-smelling peg was laid bare to the length of a rabbit's ear, but still it did not come loose. Bigwig had not moved. He lay across the wire, torn and bloody, with closed eyes. Buckthorn drew his head and paws out of the hole and rubbed the mud off his face.

'The peg's narrower down there,' he said. 'It tapers. I think it could be bitten through, but I can't get my teeth to it.'

'Send Pipkin in,' said Blackberry. 'He's smaller.'

Pipkin plunged into the hole. They could hear the wood splintering under his teeth – a sound like a mouse in a shed wainscot at midnight. He came out with his nose bleeding.

'The splinters prick you and it's hard to breathe, but the peg's nearly through.'

'Fiver go in,' said Hazel.

Fiver was not long in the hole. He, too, came out bleeding.

'It's broken in two. It's free.'

Blackberry pressed his nose against Bigwig's head. As he nuzzled him gently the head rolled sideways and back again.

'Bigwig,' said Blackberry in his ear, 'the peg's out.'

There was no response. Bigwig lay still as before. A great fly settled on one of his ears. Blackberry thrust at it angrily and it flew up, buzzing, into the sunshine.

'I think he's gone,' said Blackberry. 'I can't feel his breathing.'

Hazel crouched down by Blackberry and laid his nostrils close to Bigwig's, but a light breeze was blowing and he could not tell whether there was breath or not.

The legs were loose, the belly flaccid and limp. He tried to think of what little he had heard of snares. A strong rabbit could break his neck in a snare. Or had the point of the sharp wire pierced the wind-pipe?

'Bigwig,' he whispered, 'we've got you out. You're free.'

Bigwig did not stir. Suddenly it came to Hazel that if Bigwig was dead — and what else could hold *him* silent in the mud? — then he himself must get the others away before the dreadful loss could drain their courage and break their spirit — as it would if they stayed by the body. Besides, the man would come soon. Perhaps he was already coming, with his gun, to take poor Bigwig away. They must go; and he must do his best to see that all of them — even he himself — put what had happened out of mind, for ever.

'My heart has joined the Thousand, for my friend stopped running today,' he said to Blackberry, quoting a rabbit proverb.

'If only it were not Bigwig,' said Blackberry. 'What shall we do without him?'

'The others are waiting,' said Hazel. 'We have to stay alive. There has to be something for them to think about. Help me, or it will be more than I can do.'

He turned away from the body and looked for Fiver amont the rabbits behind him. But Fiver was nowhere to be seen and Hazel was afraid to ask for him, in case to do so should seem like weakness and a need for comfort.

'Pipkin,' he snapped, 'why don't you clean up your face and stop the bleeding? The smell of blood attracts elil. You know that, don't you?'

'Yes, Hazel. I'm sorry. Will Bigwig —'

'And another thing,' said Hazel desperately. 'What

was it you were telling me about Cowslip? Did you say he told Fiver to be quiet?'

'Yes, Hazel. Fiver came into the warren and told us about the snare, and that poor Bigwig –'

'Yes, all right. And then Cowslip –?'

'Cowslip and Strawberry and the others pretended not to hear. It was ridiculous, because Fiver was calling out to everybody. And then as we were running out Silver said to Cowslip, "Surely you're coming?" And Cowslip simply turned his back. So then Fiver went up and spoke to him very quietly, but I heard what Cowslip answered. He said, "Hills of Inlé, it's all one to me where you go. You hold your tongue." And then he struck at Fiver and scratched his ear.'

'I'll kill him,' gasped a low, chilling voice behind them. They all leapt round. Bigwig had raised his head and was supporting himself on his fore-paws alone. His body was twisted and his hind-parts and back legs still lay along the ground. His eyes were open, but his face was such a fearful mask of blood, foam, vomit and earth that he looked more like some demon-creature than a rabbit. The immediate sight of him, which should have filled them with relief and joy, brought only terror. They cringed away and none said a word.

'I'll kill him,' repeated Bigwig, spluttering through his fouled whiskers and clotted fur. 'Help me, rot you! Can't anyone get this stinking wire off me?' He struggled, dragging his hind-legs. Then he fell again and crawled forward, trailing the wire through the grass with the broken peg snickering behind it.

'Let him alone!' cried Hazel, for now they were all pressing forward to help him. 'Do you want to kill him? Let him rest! Let him breathe!'

'No, not rest,' panted Bigwig. 'I'm all right.' As he spoke he fell again and immediately struggled up on his fore-paws as before. 'It's my back legs. Won't move. That Cowslip! I'll kill him!'

'Why do we let them stay in that warren?' cried Silver. 'What sort of rabbits are they? They left Bigwig to die. You all heard Cowslip in the burrow. They're cowards. Let's drive them out – kill them! Take the warren and live there ourselves!'

'Yes! Yes!' they all answered. 'Come on! Back to the warren! Down with Cowslip! Down with Silverweed! Kill them!'

'O *embleer Frith!*' cried a squealing voice in the long grass.

At this shocking impiety, the tumult died away. They looked about them, wondering who could have spoken. There was silence. Then, from between two great tussocks of hair-grass came Fiver, his eyes blazing with a frantic urgency. He growled and gibbered at them like a witch-hare and those nearest to him fell back in fear. Even Hazel could not have said a word for his life. They realized that he was speaking.

'The warren? You're going to the warren? You fools! That warren's nothing but a death-hole! The whole place is one foul elil's larder! It's snared – everywhere, every day! That explains everything: everything that's happened since we came here.'

He sat still and his words seemed to come crawling up the sunlight, over the grass.

'Listen, Dandelion. You're fond of stories, aren't you? I'll tell you one – yes, one for El-ahrairah to cry at. Once there was a fine warren on the edge of a wood, overlooking the meadows of a farm. It was big, full of rabbits.

Then one day the white blindness came and the rabbits fell sick and died. But a few survived, as they always do. The warren became almost empty. One day the farmer thought, "I could increase those rabbits: make them part of my farm – their meat, their skins. Why should I bother to keep rabbits in hutches? They'll do very well where they are." He began to shoot all elil – lendri, homba, stoat, owl. He put out food for the rabbits, but not too near the warren. For his purpose they had to become accustomed to going about in the fields and the wood. And then he snared them – not too many: as many as he wanted and not as many as would frighten them all away or destroy the warren. They grew big and strong and healthy, for he saw to it that they had all of the best, particularly in winter, and nothing to fear – except the running knot in the hedge-gap and the wood-path. So they lived as he wanted them to live and all the time there were a few who disappeared. The rabbits became strange in many ways, different from other rabbits. They knew well enough what was happening. But even to themselves they pretended that all was well, for the food was good, they were protected, they had nothing to fear but the one fear; and that struck here and there, never enough at a time to drive them away. They forgot the ways of wild rabbits. They forgot El-ahrairah, for what use had they for tricks and cunning, living in the enemy's warren and paying his price? They found out other marvellous arts to take the place of tricks and old stories. They danced in ceremonious greeting. They sang songs like the birds and made shapes on the walls; and though these could help them not at all, yet they passed the time and enabled them to tell themselves that they were splendid fellows, the very flower of Rabbitry, cleverer than magpies. They had no Chief Rabbit – no, how could they? – for a Chief Rabbit must be El-ahrairah to his warren and keep them from death: and here there was no death but one, and what Chief Rabbit could have an answer to that? Instead, Frith sent them strange singers, beautiful and sick like oak-apples, like robins' pin-cushions on the wild rose. And since they could not bear the truth, these singers, who might in some other place have been wise, were squeezed under the terrible weight of the warren's secret until they gulped out fine folly – about dignity and acquiescence, and anything else that could make believe that the rabbit loved the shining wire. But one strict rule they had; oh yes, the strictest. No one must ever ask where another rabbit was and anyone who asked, "Where?" – except in a song or a poem – must be silenced. To say "Where?" was bad enough, but to speak openly of the wires – that was intolerable. For that they would scratch and kill.'

He stopped. No one moved. Then, in the silence, Bigwig lurched to his feet, swayed a moment, tottered a few steps towards Fiver and fell again. Fiver paid him no heed but looked from one to another among the rabbits. Then he began speaking again.

'And then *we* came, over the heather in the night. Wild rabbits, making scrapes across the valley. The warren rabbits didn't show themselves at once. They needed to think what was best to be done. But they hit on it quite soon. To bring us into the warren and tell us nothing. Don't you see? The farmer only sets so many snares at a time and if one rabbit dies, the others will live that much longer. You suggested that Hazel should tell them our adventures, Blackberry, but it didn't go down well, did it? Who wants to hear about brave deeds when he's ashamed of his own, and who likes an open, honest tale from someone he's deceiving? Do you want me to go on? I tell you, every single thing that's happened fits like a bee in a foxglove. And kill them, you say, and help ourselves to the great burrow? We shall help ourselves to a roof of bones, hung with shining wires! Help ourselves to misery and death!'

Fiver sank down into the grass. Bigwig, still trailing his horrible, smooth peg, staggered up to him and touched his nose with his own.

'I'm still alive, Fiver,' he said. 'So are all of us. You've bitten through a bigger peg than this one I'm dragging. Tell us what to do.'

'Do?' replied Fiver. 'Why, go – now. I told Cowslip we were going before I left the burrow.'

'Where?' said Bigwig. But it was Hazel who answered.

'To the hills,' he said.

# JUDY BLUME

FROM *Tales of a Fourth Grade Nothing*

I will never forget Friday, May tenth. It's the most important day of my life. It didn't start out that way. It started out ordinary. I went to school. I ate my lunch. I had gym. And then I walked home from school with Jimmy Fargo. We planned to meet at our special rock in the park as soon as we changed our clothes.

In the elevator I told Henry I was glad summer was coming. Henry said he was too. When I got out at my floor I walked down the hall and opened the door to my apartment. I took off my jacket and hung it in the closet. I put my books on the hall table next to my mother's purse. I went straight to my room to change my clothes and check Dribble.

The first thing I noticed was my chain latch. It was unhooked. My bedroom door was open. And there was a chair smack in the middle of my doorway. I nearly tumbled over it. I ran to my dresser to check Dribble. He wasn't there! His bowl with the rocks and water was there – but Dribble was gone.

I got really scared. I thought, *Maybe he died while I was at school and I didn't know about it.* So I rushed into the kitchen and hollered, 'Mom . . . where's Dribble?' My mother was baking something. My brother sat on the kitchen floor, banging pots and pans together. 'Be quiet!' I yelled at Fudge. 'I can't hear anything with all that noise.'

'What did you say, Peter?' my mother asked me.

'I said I can't find Dribble. Where is he?'

'You mean he's not in his bowl?' my mother asked.

I shook my head.

'Oh dear!' my mother said. 'I hope he's not crawling around somewhere. You know I don't like the way he smells. I'm going to have a look in the bedrooms. You check in here, Peter.'

My mother hurried off. I looked at my brother. He was smiling. 'Fudge, do you know where Dribble is?' I asked calmly.

Fudge kept smiling.

'Did you take him? Did you, Fudge?' I asked not so calmly.

Fudge giggled and covered his mouth with his hands.

I yelled. 'Where is he? What did you do with my turtle?'

No answer from Fudge. He banged his pots and pans together again. I yanked the pots out of his hand. I tried to speak softly. 'Now tell me where Dribble is. Just tell me where my turtle is. I won't be mad if you tell me. Come on, Fudge . . . please.'

Fudge looked up at me. 'In tummy,' he said.

'What do you mean, in tummy?' I asked, narrowing my eyes.

'Dribble in tummy!' he repeated.

'What tummy?' I shouted at my brother.

'This one,' Fudge said, rubbing his stomach. 'Dribble in this tummy! Right here!'

I decided to go along with his game. 'OK. How did he get in there, Fudge?' I asked.

Fudge stood up. He jumped up and down, and sang out, 'I ATE HIM . . . ATE HIM . . . ATE HIM!' Then he ran out of the room.

My mother came back into the kitchen. 'Well, I just can't find him anywhere,' she said. 'I looked in all the dresser drawers and the bathroom cabinets and the shower and the bath and . . .'

'Mom,' I said, shaking my head. 'How could you?'

'How could I what, Peter?' Mom asked.

'How could you let him do it?'

'Let who do what, Peter?' Mom asked.

'LET FUDGE EAT DRIBBLE!' I screamed.

My mother started to mix whatever she was baking. 'Don't be silly, Peter,' she said. 'Dribble is a turtle.'

'HE ATE DRIBBLE!' I insisted.

'*Peter Warren Hatcher!* STOP SAYING THAT!' Mom hollered.

'Well, ask him. Go ahead and ask him,' I told her.

Fudge was standing in the kitchen doorway with a big grin on his face. My mother picked him up and patted his head. 'Fudgie,' she said to him, 'tell Mommy where brother's turtle is.'

'In tummy,' Fudge said.

'What tummy?' Mom asked.

'MINE!' Fudge laughed.

My mother put Fudge down on the kitchen counter where he couldn't get away from her. 'Oh, you're fooling Mommy . . . right?'

'No fool!' Fudge said.

My mother turned very pale. 'You really ate your brother's turtle?'

Big smile from Fudge.

'YOU MEAN THAT YOU PUT HIM IN YOUR MOUTH AND CHEWED HIM UP . . . LIKE THIS?' Mom made believe she was chewing.

'No,' Fudge said.

A smile of relief crossed my mother's face. 'Of course you didn't. It's just a joke.' She put Fudge down on the floor and gave me a *look*.

Fudge babbled. 'No chew. No chew. Gulp ... gulp ... all gone turtle. Down Fudge's tummy.'

Me and my mother stared at Fudge.

'You didn't!' Mom said.

'Did so!' Fudge said.

'No!' Mom shouted.

'Yes!' Fudge shouted back.

'Yes?' Mom asked weakly, holding on to a chair with both hands.

'Yes!' Fudge beamed.

My mother moaned and picked up my brother. 'Oh no! My angel! My precious little baby! OH ... NO ...'

My mother didn't stop to think about my turtle. She didn't even give Dribble a thought. She didn't even stop to wonder how my turtle liked being swallowed by my brother. She ran to the phone with Fudge tucked under one arm. I followed. Mom dialled the operator and cried, 'Oh help! This is an emergency. My baby ate a turtle ... STOP THAT LAUGHING,' my mother told the operator. 'Send an ambulance right away; 25 West 68th Street.'

Mom hung up. She didn't look too well. Tears were running down her face. She put Fudge down on the floor. I couldn't understand why she was so upset. Fudge seemed just fine.

'Help me, Peter,' Mom begged. 'Get me blankets.'

I ran into my brother's room. I grabbed two blankets from Fudge's bed. He was following me around with that silly grin on his face. I felt like giving him a pinch. How could he stand there looking so happy when he had my turtle inside him?

I delivered the blankets to my mother. She wrapped
Fudge up in them and ran to the front door. I followed
and grabbed her purse from the hall table. I figured
she'd be glad I thought of that.

Out in the hall I pressed the elevator buzzer. We had
to wait a few minutes. Mom paced up and down in front
of the elevator. Fudge was cradled in her arms. He sucked
his fingers and made that slurping noise I like. But all I
could think of was Dribble.

# BETSY BYARS

FROM *The Eighteenth Emergency*

'You ever been hit before, Mouse? I mean, hard?'

Mouse sighed. The conversation had now passed beyond the question of whether Hammerman would attack. It was now a matter of whether he, Mouse Fawley, could survive the attack. He said thickly, remembering, 'Four times.'

'Four times in one fight? I mean, you stood up for four hits, Mouse?' There was grudging admiration in his voice.

Mouse shook his head. 'Four hits – four fights.'

'You went right down each time? I mean POW and you went down, POW and you went down, POW and you went –'

'Yes!'

'Where did you take these hits?' Ezzie asked, straightening suddenly. Ezzie had never taken a single direct blow in his life because he was a good dodger. Sometimes his mother chased him through the apartment, striking at him while he dodged and ducked, crying, 'Look out, Mom, look out now! You're going to hit me!'

He asked again, 'Where were you hit?'

Mouse said, 'In the stomach.'

'All four times?'

'Yeah.' Mouse suddenly thought of his stomach as having a big red circular target on it with HIT HERE printed in the centre.

'Who hit you?'

'Two boys in Cincinnati when I was on vacation, and a boy named Mickey Swearinger, and somebody else I don't remember.' He lowered his head because he remembered the fourth person all right, but he didn't want to tell Ezzie about it. If he had added the name of Viola Angotti to the list of those who had hit him in the stomach, Ezzie's face would have screwed up with laughter. 'Viola Angotti hit you? No fooling, Viola Angotti?' It was the sort of thing Ezzie could carry on about for hours. 'Viola Angotti. *The* Viola Angotti?'

And Mouse would have had to keep sitting there saying over and over, 'Yes, Viola Angotti hit me in the stomach. Yes, *the* Viola Angotti.' And then he would have to tell Ezzie all about it, every detail, how one recess long ago the boys had decided to put some girls in the school trash cans.

It had been one of those suggestions that stuns everyone with its rightness. Someone had said, 'Hey, let's put those girls over there in the trash cans!' and the plan won immediate acceptance. Nothing could have been more appropriate. The trash cans were big and had just been emptied, and in an instant the boys were off chasing the girls and yelling at the tops of their lungs.

It had been wonderful at first, Mouse remembered. Primitive blood had raced through his body. The desire to capture had driven him like a wild man through the school yard, up the sidewalk, everywhere. He understood what had driven the cave man and the barbarian, because this same passion was driving him. Putting the girls in the trash cans was the most important challenge of his life. His long screaming charge ended with him red-faced, gasping for breath – and Viola Angotti pinned against the garbage cans.

His moment of triumph was short. It lasted about two seconds. Then it began to dim as he realized, first, that it *was* Viola Angotti, and, second, that he was not going to be able to get her into the garbage can without a great deal of help.

He cried, 'Hey, you guys, come on. I've got one,' but behind him the school yard was silent. Where was everybody? he had wondered uneasily. As it turned out, the principal had caught the other boys, and they were all being marched back in the front door of the school, but Mouse didn't know this.

He called again, 'Come on, you guys, get the lid off this garbage can, will you?'

And then, when he said that, Viola Angotti had taken two steps forward. She said, 'Nobody's putting *me* in no garbage can.' He could still remember how she had looked standing there. She had recently taken the part of the Statue of Liberty in a class play, and somehow she seemed taller and stronger at this moment than when she had been in costume.

He cried, 'Hey, you guys!' It was a plea. 'Where are you?'

And then Viola Angotti had taken one more step, and with a faint sigh she had socked him in the stomach so hard that he had doubled over and lost his lunch. He hadn't known it was possible to be hit like that outside a boxing ring. It was the hardest blow he had ever taken. Viola Angotti could be heavyweight champion of the world.

As she walked past his crumpled body she said again, 'Nobody's putting me in no garbage can.' It had sounded like one of the world's basic truths. The sun will rise. The tides will flow. Nobody's putting Viola Angotti in no garbage can.

# MARJORIE DARKE

FROM *Ride the Iron Horse*

'D idn't I say there 'ud be trouble?'

Ezra came into the cottage, slamming the door behind him. He took off the sacking cape that was soggy with rain and hung it on the peg behind the door.

John had been staring through the rain-washed window-panes at the trees straining under the force of the gale. With his father's return the tension of the storm moved inside the cottage.

Ezra pulled off his sodden boots and put them down in the hearth near the smoking fire, which sizzled and spat as raindrops fell down the chimney on to the hot logs. There was a pleasant smell of rabbit stew coming from the big iron pot hanging from the hook. Hannah lifted it down and hung the kettle in its place. Then she filled a bowl with meat and gravy. Ezra sniffed and frowned, but said nothing, accepting it without another word.

John felt some of his fears subside. At least his father was not going to raise hell about his poaching activities.

'Whatever's up?' Hannah asked. She had taken the precaution of keeping her questions until her husband had swallowed a few mouthfuls of food.

Ezra shook his head. 'Squire's mad!' He made the pronouncement in a voice of doom. 'He'm besotted with them new-fangled machines. It's all round the village ever since Tom Wardle saw the gentlemen from London measuring up the land. He says Mr Corley told him Squire's like a man possessed. Won't see no obstacles. A permanent way is to run straight through the Bumble, Tom says. The ground to be cut into, though how that's to be I don't know. I do know it ent right. Everyone knows about the bones lying below and it's not right to disturb the dead. Mark my words, no good'll come of it.' He dipped a lump of bread in the gravy, chewed it, then added: 'What do we want with a permanent way? Terrible things they be. If Squire builds one here it'll be worse than them threshing machines.'

Excitement and fear tingled through John's body. A permanent way . . . the railway! It was really coming. Tom Wardle had seen Mr Hartlipp too! Tom's eyes were as sharp as his ears, missing neither traces of poachers on his game preserves, nor strangers measuring up the land. John had a healthy respect for the gamekeeper's powers of observation and for his persuasive tongue. If there were any secrets to be prised out, Tom Wardle would manage it.

Hannah wiped her hands on her apron and sat down. 'How can it harm us?' She rocked a little, her face lined and anxious.

Ezra swallowed his bread. 'They'll dig up our fields and take the grazing, and the dangers with sparks from them engine furnaces is terrible. Hayricks go up in flames . . . I don't doubt that the growing corn could burn an' all.'

John risked saying: 'Perhaps it won't be that bad.'

'Course it will and probably a sight worse. Fearsome great things them engines, Josh Perry says. Old man Garbitt that lives alongside Josh, was shaking fit to fall to pieces at the very idea of them monsters. Said it would bring disaster on us all and he'm right. You don't need a memory as long as his'n to remember what happened afore.' Ezra wiped his bowl clean with bread, put it on the table and stretched out his feet to the embers. 'Fire's low,' he grumbled.

'I've to watch the firewood. There's little enough.' Hannah got up and reached for the kettle. 'Shall I fill your mug now? 'Tis herb tea . . . all I could manage, but it's hot.'

Ezra grunted and took the steaming mug.

'You, John?' She looked at him.

He shook his head, feelings churning inside him like a mill-race. What did his dad mean? No railway had been built before in this part of the country. There must be good things to come out of having one. It couldn't be all disaster.

'Folk'll be able to see a bit of the world,' he said.

'And what good is that to us,' Ezra answered. 'You wants to think a bit more about life as it is and do a mite less dreaming. Me and your Mam have lived through anxious times. We know what it's about.'

And you think I don't, John thought. The troubled days of his infancy were some of the unresolved pieces of information that he carried around. The bad times were still mentioned in the village, but everyone avoided detailed explanation.

He risked a tentative question: 'What happened then, Dad?'

'Nothing you need concern yourself with.'

'How can you say that! I lives here, don't I?' The words jumped out before he could stop them.

Ezra looked up and John read warning signals in his expression.

'Haven't I told you afore not to pester me with them

questions? There's no good comes from rubbing old sores. Enough folk are ready to do that without you joining in.'

'Don't get on to him, Ezra. 'Tis natural for him to be curious. After all he's well nigh a man.'

John warmed to his mother. Encouraged by her support he tried a different tack: 'Them engines, Dad . . . did Josh tell you what they looked like?'

'Great iron monsters, he said. Course he ent seen them himself but Farmer Woolacombe told him. They makes a noise like thunder and hisses steam enough to frighten a body to death. Just imagine what the farm stock'll do when one of them comes racing through the fields! They'll bolt for sure. Everyone says the cows dry up. Why folk have to spend their lives chasing summat different is past understanding. What's wrong with the way we lives and works the land now? Us workers'll be thrown on the scrap heap.'

John could not believe that the railway would put everyone out of work and said as much.

'That ent all,' Ezra said fiercely. 'Tom says Squire's bent on having one of them threshing machines and that to be worked by steam if you please. Where'll it end? Feelings are running high and that Joby Cooper's been seen talking with folk, and he's a troublemaker.'

John could scarcely believe his luck. A threshing machine as well; a steam driven one! He felt giddy with conflicting emotions of which joy was the greatest. He glanced at his parents. Neither of them had noticed his brimming delight. How could they be so unobservant? He shivered with excitement which turned to apprehension at the thought of Joby Cooper. He was blacksmith at Ram Green. A huge oak of a man with a temper

that matched his great body. He was famed for bare knuckle fighting. No one had been known to beat him. If he was against the machines then there was bound to be a fight. John felt sick at the thought of facing Joby, but whatever the cost he had to side with Squire. Perhaps the changes would slide in smoothly? But he knew this to be as much of a dream as his father's idea of holding them back.

'Pour me another mug of tea,' said Ezra.

Hannah took the kettle, wiping her watering eyes with the back of her hand. Ezra made an impatient noise with his tongue.

'Give over snivelling! Tears won't mend matters.'

She sniffed but said nothing. John felt exasperated with her and annoyed by his father's touchiness. Why did he always have to work off his moods on her? And why didn't she ever stand up for herself?

Ezra spat into the fire. The storm was gathering strength and the wind buffeted the cottage.

'Reckon there's summat in the notion all this is just punishment for the wicked things that go on in the village.' As if to underline Ezra's statement, there was a loud crash.

Hannah started up and ran to the window, craning over John's shoulder.

'What is it?'

'Reckon that elm has blown down at the back of Wilf Newbold's cottage,' John said. He was thinking of the lesson he was to have had tonight. Miserably he decided Miss Frances would never come out in such weather. The heavens had opened and great sheets of water ran over the window-panes. Hannah gave his shoulder a sympathetic squeeze. For a brief moment he thought she must understand his disappointment. He stared hard into the darkening sky to hide his feelings. The wind howled through the trees and drew whining music round the chimney stacks while the rain drummed harder and harder. Daylight was fading fast and there was no fire-light to brighten the room. Hannah sighed and went to the table, collecting crockery into a bowl.

'I'll leave these till morning,' she said. 'I'm plum out of water and in any case fire's too low to boil the kettle.' She looked at John. 'Best get to bed, lad. There's nothing to stay up for.'

Did she guess? It was not possible. No one knew about his visit to Ted Rollins' hut. But there was no denying the sympathy in her voice. Reluctantly he came away from the window, still tantalized by unanswered questions. Ezra was slumped in his chair and did not reply when John wished him goodnight. This display of sur-liness sparked off a burst of irritation. His lips tightened into a hard line as he stared down at the bent figure and with a little twist of amazement, he realized that his father was an old man. The thought kindled a kind of desperate courage. He was tired of being excluded. The events of the past must have a bearing on the present. He could only decide if it were true that the village was under threat of disaster, in the light of shared experience.

'I've got to know about the troubles, Dad.'

Ezra shot him a look of displeasure. 'You'm like the rest of the youngsters . . . got no respect for your elders.'

'It ent nothing to do with respect!' John was trying hard to contain his exasperation. 'All I wants is to have some part in what goes on. You talked of a Captain Swing the night Squire died.'

He might have uttered some awful blasphemy, the

way his father reacted.

'You won't be told, will you? Them machines coming is fair punishment all right . . . and that elm falling is an omen!'

'That were only a tree blown down in the gale,' John retorted, without weighing the consequences.

'John!' Hannah's reproach came like lightning and Ezra's growl of anger was a rumble of thunder.

'I'll not have you cheeking me! You ent of age yet. Get to bed or you'll not be able to sit down for a week.'

Obstinacy hardened, covering the chattering fear of childhood. 'I'll not go, Dad. I ent a babby now. I've a right to speak my mind.'

The battle of wills suddenly changed into a storm greater than the one outside. Already made insecure by the fear of losing work, Ezra saw John's attitude as an attack on his position as head of the family. He half rose in his chair.

'Talk of your rights would you? I'll show you what they are!'

Before John could duck, he fetched him a blow across the ear that made his head ring.

'Ezra don't . . . don't! You drove our Joe away . . . I can't bear for it to happen all over again.' Hannah was crying, tears spilling down her worn cheeks and so much dismay in her face that John forgot his own pain and fury at the sight of her distress. She got out of her chair and went to put a restraining hand on Ezra's arm but was roughly shoved away.

'You too,' he bellowed. 'Siding with that no good son of yourn.' His hands were already unbuckling the broad leather belt which he wore round his waist. Hannah choked over her tears, but John did not wait to taste the searing pain of cutting leather which he knew well enough. He could have stood it for himself, but could not bear to see the dreadful distress brought to Hannah's face. He ran up the ladder and threw himself face down on the bed.

For a long time he remained in the same position torn by anger, shame, frustration and a new sensation he could not name but which tantalized him like a scent that tickles the memory but eludes capture. The division between him and his parents was wider than ever. It had opened when he first saw the mill-wheel. Without being told he had known that to try and share his feelings about it would be useless. They would only laugh and tell him not to talk nonsense. All this was long before Joe had revolted against Ezra's tyranny. On that awful night when the row broke, the crack became a yawning pit. Joe and Ezra fought, there in the downstairs room, with Hannah screaming and he and Polly crouching against the wall upstairs, clinging to one another for comfort. He did not see the outcome. It was more than he dare do to peep through the trap door, but sudden silence fell, as it had fallen now, and Joe had left the cottage, going to sleep with Wilf Newbold until the morning. Then he had taken his bundle and left for America, though whether he had ever got there no one knew.

He turned over on the bed. That was it . . . he no longer felt afraid! He was afraid of the strap but not of the man who wielded it. He held a key to greater understanding of the world than his father possessed. Knowledge was to be his power, not physical force and he sensed that his was the greater weapon. The direction of his thoughts brought back the longing to learn. It was like toothache nagging him. He was so ignorant! Driving under the eaves, the rain hammered on the window and the wind still roared round the walls of the cottage. But gradually the storm lessened.

His parents were in bed; he could tell from the creaks as first one and then the other turned on the lumpy mattress. Neither spoke and he assumed from the snores that they were asleep. He did not know that his mother was lying wide-eyed, listening to every sound, knowing when the casement rattled, understanding the scuffles as he heaved himself through the narrow opening and, grabbing what handhold he could to break his fall, dropped on to the soaking ground. He did not know she knew about his nocturnal escapades until many months had passed.

# PENELOPE LIVELY

FROM *The Ghost of Thomas Kempe*

It was tacked to the wooden frame of the notice-board
with a rusty nail. Almost before James had read it he
knew what was coming. The writing was larger this
time, and the letters rather more carefully formed. It was
obviously intended to be a notice, or, more precisely, an
advertisement. It said:

> For the discoverie of goodes loste by the crystalle or
> by booke and key or with the sieve & sheeres seeke
> me at my dwellynge which lyes at the extremetie of
> East Ende Lane. I have muche skille also in such artes
> as alchemie, astronomie etc. & in physicke & in the
> seekynge out of wytches & other eville persons. My
> apprentice, who dwells at the same howse, will bring
> me messages.

It was signed, rather flamboyantly, with much swirl and
flourish:

> Thos. Kempe Esq. Sorcerer.

'There!' said James, with a mixture of triumph and
despair. 'There! Now do you believe me?'

Simon took his glasses off, scrubbed round them with
his fingers and read the notice for a second time. 'Well,'
he said cautiously.

'Well what?'

'Somebody could have put it there.'

'Such as who?'

'I don't know.'

'Such as me, perhaps?' said James in a freezing voice.

'No. Not you. You've been with me all morning. You know something?'

James didn't answer.

'If anyone sees it,' Simon went on amiably, 'they might sort of connect it with you. Because it mentions your house.'

James' anger gave way to alarm. 'What shall I do?'

Simon glanced up and down the street. There was no one in sight. The police-station windows stared blankly down at them.

'Take it off. Quickly.'

James hesitated. Then he darted forward, tweaked the notice from the nail and began to walk quickly away down the road, stuffing it in his pocket. Simon caught him up.

'Let's have another look.'

Pulling the notice out again, James saw with indignation that his own red biro had been used once more, and a page from his exercise book. He tore it into very small pieces and put it in a litter basket by the bus stop.

'Whoever he is, this person,' said Simon, 'he's got some pretty funny ideas, hasn't he? Jiggery-pokery with sieves and whatnot to find out who stole things. He'd make a pretty rotten policeman. And leaves for medicines and all that. It wouldn't work – not now there's penicillin and things.'

'He just wants things done like they were in his time,' said James. 'With him doing them. And me helping.'

'Oh,' said Simon. 'I see.' He sounded very polite. Too polite.

James said, 'You don't believe he's a ghost, do you?'

'I didn't say I didn't.'

'But you don't.'

'I kind of half do and half don't,' said Simon with great honesty. 'I do when I'm with you but I think if I was by myself I wouldn't.'

They walked on for a few minutes in silence. Then Simon said, 'What are you going to do? I mean, whatever it is or whoever it is he keeps getting you into trouble.'

'I know. And I'm getting fed up with it. What *can* I do?'

'If he is – what you think,' said Simon, 'there's one thing you could try.'

'What?'

'Ask him to stop it.'

James stared. 'Talk back to him?'

'That's it. Worth trying anyway.'

'Yes. I s'pose it might be.' Somehow that had not occurred to him. But, when you stopped and thought about it, there was no reason why this should be a one way conversation. If he was here, this Thos. Kempe, Sorcerer, making a right nuisance of himself, then the best thing might well be to talk straight back at him. Maybe that was all that was needed. Just explain quietly and firmly that this sort of thing really wouldn't do, and he'd see reason and go away. Back where he came from, wherever that might be.

Feeling rather more hopeful about the future James parted from Simon at his gate and went home for lunch.

A feeling of dissatisfaction hovered around the house. Mrs Harrison was suffering one of her attacks of hay-fever, which made her red-eyed and irritable. Mr Harrison had fallen over a bucket of water standing in the porch, and was resignedly mopping up the mess as James arrived. He followed James into the kitchen, carrying bucket and cloth, which he dumped down by the sink.

'I don't want to interfere with the housekeeping arrangements,' he said, 'but I must point out that the best place for a full bucket of water is not the centre of the front porch.'

'Not guilty,' said his wife, sneezing violently. 'Must have been a child. And don't talk to me about water. I think I'm about to melt as it is.' She began peeling potatoes, with vicious stabs.

'I've only just come in, haven't I?' said James.

'Good gracious!' said Mr Harrison. 'You don't imagine I'd ever suspect it might have been you, do you?' James gave him a suspicious look and went out into the garden to make sure Helen hadn't been interfering with his hole. He found that Tim had located a tributary to the original rat-hole in the drain, and had spent a happy morning digging up a clump of irises. James hastily re-planted them: Tim never seemed to understand that he was only living with them on sufferance as it was and might one day go too far. Mr Harrison had several times said darkly, 'That dog will have to go.'

James patted him kindly. 'You didn't know they weren't weeds, did you?' he said. 'Like you couldn't know Dad still wanted that pair of slippers. Lucky thing I found where you'd buried them, eh?' Tim dropped his head slightly, and bared his teeth in a kind of pink grin, which was the nearest he came to a gesture of affection. He wasn't one of those dogs who climb all over you. He had dignity.

'Come here, sir,' said James sternly. He saw himself and Tim, suddenly, as an intrepid team of criminal-trackers: Harrison of the Yard and his famous trained

Rumanian Trufflehound, the Burglar's Scourge. He began to slink along the side of the house with a ferocious scowl on his face, towing a reluctant Tim by the collar. On the other side of that drainpipe lurked the notorious Monte Carlo Diamond Gang, armed to the teeth . . .

'Lunch!' shouted Mrs Harrison from the scullery window. Tim shook himself free and bolted for the back door.

After lunch the pewter clouds that had been slowly massing above the village all morning opened up into determined, continuous rain. Mrs Harrison said she felt as though she was being drowned from without as well as within, and went to bed with a book. Mr Harrison went to sleep in an armchair. Helen went to see a friend.

James remembered he had some homework to do. He climbed up to his bedroom, closed the door, and sat down at his table. Tim padded round the room once or twice, jumped up on the bed, swirled the covers around several times until he achieved a satisfactory position, and went to sleep. Outside, the rain drummed on the roof and poured in oily rivers down the window.

James opened his project book, looked at his notes, and began to write. It was a project about ancient Greece, and he was enjoying it. He looked things up, and wrote, and stuck some pictures in, and thought about Alexander the Great, and drew a picture of a vase with blokes having a battle on it, and forgot about everything except what he was doing. Around him, the room rustled occasionally: a piece of paper floated to the floor, and a pen rolled across the table. Tim twitched in his sleep.

All of a sudden something nudged James' foot. It was a sheet from his exercise book. He picked it up and read:

I am glad to see thee at thy studies, though I lyke not thy bookes. Where is thy Latin? & where are thy volumes of Astrologie? But to our businesse . . . I have putt out the water for people to knowe wee are seeking thieves: it will doe for a crystalle. Thy father's baldnesse could be stayed by bathing with an ointment made from the leaves of Yarrow (a herb of Venus) but there is no cure for thy mother's ailmente of the eyes for it is caused by wytcherie. Nothing will suffice save to seeke out the wytch & bring her to justice. This muste wee doe with all haste.

James swung round in his chair. Then he got up and searched the room, even looking under the bed. There was nothing to be seen, and nothing moved.

He read the note again. The reference to his father's baldness he found particularly annoying. That was cheek, that was. In fact, he thought, he's a proper busybody, that's what he is.

And then he remembered Simon's suggestion. All right then, let's have a go. Let's try talking to him.

He cleared his throat, feeling distinctly foolish at ad-dressing the empty room, even though there was no one to hear, and said 'Er – Mr Kempe.'

Silence. Tim uncurled himself and looked up, yawn-ing.

James took a deep breath and said firmly. 'I'm afraid I can't do the things you want me to do because people don't go in much for sorcery nowadays. I don't think they'd really be very interested. You see we don't use those kind of medicines now because we've got penicillin and that and we've got policemen for finding out if anyone's pinched things and catching thieves and my

mother gets hay-fever every year and it really isn't anything to do with witchcraft it's because she's allergic
to . . .'

There was a loud crash behind him. He whirled round.
One of his clay pots had fallen on to the floor and
smashed. Even as he looked, a second one raised itself
from the shelf, flew across the room, narrowly missing
his right ear, and dashed itself against the opposite wall.
Tim leapt from the bed and rushed about the room,
barking furiously.

'Hey! Stop that!' shouted James.

A gust of wind swept wildly round the room, lifting
all the papers on the table and whirling them about the
floor. The ink-bottle scuttered to the edge of the table
and hung there till James grabbed hold of it with one
hand while with the other he made ineffectual dabs at the
flying pages from his project book.

'Here! Lay off! Cut it out!'

The door opened and banged itself shut again, twice.

The windows rattled as though assaulted by a sudden thunderstorm. The calendar above the bed reared up, twitched itself from the hook, and flapped to the floor. A glass of water on the bedside table tipped over and broke making a large puddle on the mat. Downstairs, James could hear the sitting-room door open, and his father's footsteps across the hall.

'Please!' he squeaked breathlessly, using one hand to steady the chair, which was bucking about like a ship in a storm, while with the other he warded off Volume 1 of *A Child's Encyclopaedia* which had risen from the bookshelf and hurled itself at his head.

'Please! Don't! Look, perhaps I could . . .'

Mrs Harrison's bedroom door opened and her voice could be heard saying something loud and not very friendly on the landing. Mr Harrison was coming up the stairs.

The bedcover whisked off the bed, whirled round once or twice, and sank to the floor, engulfing a frantic Tim in its folds.

'All right!' shouted James. 'All right! I'll do it. Anything. If you stop.'

The room subsided. Tim struggled out from under the bedcover and dived for the shelter of the bed. The door opened and Mr Harrison came in. James stood amid the wreckage of his room and waited for the storm to break.

# JOAN AIKEN

FROM *Tales of Arabel's Raven*

Every Thursday Mr Jones drove the local fishmonger, Mr Finney, over to Colchester to buy oysters at five in the morning. So, early next day, up he got, off he went. Made himself a cup of tea, finished the milk in the jug, never looked in the fridge.

An hour after he had gone Mrs Jones got up and put on the kettle. Finding the milk jug empty she went yawning to the fridge and pulled the door open, not noticing that it had been prevented from shutting properly by the handle of a burnt feather-duster which had fallen against the hinge. But she noticed what was inside the fridge all right. She let out a shriek that brought Arabel running downstairs.

Arabel was little and fair with grey eyes. She was wearing a white nightdress that made her look like a lampshade with two feet sticking out from the bottom. One of the feet had a blue sock on.

'What's the matter, Ma?' she said.

'There's a great awful *bird* in the fridge!' sobbed Mrs Jones. 'And it's eaten all the cheese and a blackcurrant tart and five pints of milk and a bowl of dripping and a pound of sausages. All that's left is the lettuce.'

'Then we'll have lettuce for breakfast,' said Arabel.

But Mrs Jones said she didn't fancy lettuce that had spent the night in the fridge with a great awful bird. 'And how are we going to get it out of there?'

'The lettuce?'

'The *bird*!' said Mrs Jones, switching off the kettle and pouring hot water into a pot without any tea in it.

Arabel opened the fridge door, which had swung shut. There sat the bird, among the empty milk bottles, but he was a lot bigger than they were. There was a certain amount of wreckage around him – torn foil, and cheese wrappings, and milk splashes, and bits of pastry, and crumbs of dripping, and rejected lettuce leaves. It was like Rumbury Waste after a picnic Sunday.

Arabel looked at the raven, and he looked back at her.

'His name's Mortimer,' she said.

'No it's not, no it's not!' cried Mrs Jones, taking a loaf from the bread bin and absent-mindedly running the tap over it. 'We said you could have a hamster when you were five, or a puppy or a kitten when you were six, and of course call it what you wish, oh my *stars*, look at that creature's toe-nails, if nails they can be called, but not a bird like that, a great hairy awful thing eating us out of house and home, as big as a fire extinguisher and all black –' But Arabel was looking at the raven and he was looking back at her. 'His name's Mortimer,' she said. And she put both arms round the raven, not an easy thing to do, all jammed in among the milk bottles as he was, and lifted him out.

'He's very heavy,' she said, and set him down on the kitchen floor.

'So I should think, considering he's got a pound of sausages, a bowl of dripping, five pints of milk, half a pound of New Zealand cheddar, and a blackcurrant tart inside him,' said Mrs Jones. 'I'll open the window. Perhaps he'll fly out.'

She opened the window. But Mortimer did not fly

out. He was busy examining everything in the kitchen very thoroughly. He tapped the table legs with his beak – they were metal, and clinked. Then he took everything out of the waste bin – a pound of peanut shells, two empty tins, and some jam tart cases. He particularly liked the jam tart cases, which he pushed under the lino. Then he walked over to the fireplace – it was an old-fashioned kitchen – and began chipping out the mortar from between the bricks.

Mrs Jones had been gazing at the raven as if she were under a spell, but when he began on the fireplace, she said, '*Don't* let him do that.'

'Mortimer,' said Arabel, 'we'd like you not to do that, please.'

Mortimer turned his head right round on its black feathery neck and gave Arabel a thoughtful, considering look. Then he made his first remark, which was a deep, hoarse, rasping croak.

# BERNARD ASHLEY

Keith's father led the boys out of the ground through the scattered peanut shells and the gathering piles of paper. Although they waited a full five minutes before moving, the exits were still bottle-necks when they got there, and Keith and Donovan had to link arms so as not to lose one another. There was a buzz of excited sound. Most of the crowd around them were talking about the unexpected win. None of them had really given City East much chance. A few transistors held above the bobbing heads gave out the news of other cup ties, and when the knowledge of who else was through began to spread amongst the crowd, they started to speculate about the draw for the next round.

'Arsenal's through. A penalty. How about Arsenal?'

'Or Leeds. I'd like to see Leeds down here . . .'

Keith didn't feel much like talking. There wasn't much he could say which wouldn't sound like crowing to poor old Donovan. It took the edge off it really, seeing him so disappointed.

Mr Chapman went before them, his tall tanned figure a landmark for the boys. He heard the comments of the people around him; on the face of it he had every reason to be as happy as they; but underneath he was thinking about Mr Croft. He was sorry for Mr Croft. The man was clearly cut-up about the boy not saying anything that afternoon. At one stage he had obviously thought

the boy would, and at the end, when everyone was shouting 'Shoot!', Mr Croft had been on the top line for
Donovan to say it too. But when he hadn't, the look on
Mr Croft's face had been unforgettable. Like a father at
the birth of a stillborn baby. On the other hand, the
more Mr Chapman thought about it, the more he realized
that no one had promised that Donovan would speak
today. It had only ever been a chance. They'd all thought
the circumstances were right, and they'd all worked themselves up thinking it was bound to happen, when it
hadn't been bound to happen at all. 'Things don't work
just because we want them to,' he thought, and it was
silly to be disappointed when they didn't.

He edged his way past a hot-dog stand, the warm
smell of the fried onions making him feel hungry. He
supposed they'd better ask Mr Croft back to tea. It was
the least they could do.

A few metres behind Mr Chapman, Donovan followed
the blue and white scarf which was back round Keith's
neck. His eyes concentrated on the bobbles of knitted
wool, the blue wisps hanging off, the light and shade in
the white squares. He drew in a deep sad breath. During
the last week, since the trouble with Fluff and Keith's
kindness, he had begun to see more of what was around
him. He had begun to feel more as if he was part of what
was going on, as if he mattered again. He felt important
to someone. That terrible hurt in the pit of his stomach
wasn't there all the time now. It only came and went. It
came when he thought about his mother, when he saw
her face, felt her hands, smelt her soft sweet smell; it
came then and he was cut-up inside with longing. But it
went as well. It didn't come quite so often, and it went.
It went when he did things with Keith, when Keith

wanted him to be around, when Keith talked to him and said good things. Then Donovan began to feel alive again, a part of the world.

He had begun to emerge into the outside again like a patient from a hospital; he had begun to make a recovery, but for a while he would be convalescent.

Part of that pain had gone. But now he felt a different pain: the pervading hurt of failure. He had been with his father, Keith had been there, he had seen his Park Lane team play. He had felt good: warm, content, and happy, as if the nightmare had ended and he had woken up to find the sun in all the dark corners. He had had a pleasurable feeling of belonging where he was. It was just like the old days. Then, in the game, Henderson had dithered with the ball – he did that sometimes – and everyone else had shouted 'Shoot!' at the tops of their voices. Donovan had wanted to shout 'Shoot!' with the rest, pleased to do so. He had opened his mouth and shouted. Or he had thought he shouted. But in fact he had only shouted as in a dream, the harder he had tried, the farther he had slipped from success, and the words ringing clearly in his head had been only silence to the others.

Donovan knew his failure well. It had a poisonous taste. For the first time for weeks he had wanted to communicate, and the sound he needed to do it with had refused to come.

Head down on his chest again, he followed Keith out through the big gates. They crossed the road in a wave of people, the cars forced to halt like woodlice caught in a stream of ants. Mr Chapman led them into the doorway of a closed shop, and there they waited for the crowd to thin, Keith and his father on their toes looking for Mr Croft.

It must have been ten minutes before any of them saw him. In his search for tea and tablets he had had to go deep into the hollow grandstand to a general-purposes bar where a large crowd of celebrating men were making the most of the afternoon licence. He queued for a long time, but he got what he had gone for at long last, and when he came out again he made straight for the nearest exit from the ground. It turned out to be fifty metres or so farther down the road than the gate the others had used.

Mr Chapman saw him first, looking this way and that, puzzled at the roadside. The crowd had thinned by now, but there were enough people standing about to bewilder Mr Croft momentarily.

'There he is,' said Mr Chapman. 'Down there on the other side . . .'

'Hey! Mr Croft!' shouted Keith. But he was too far away from the man to be heard.

Mr Croft looked about him, seeming to get more and more agitated. Then he made to walk farther down the road to the next gate. He had completely lost his bearings, as he sometimes did when the cinema turned the last house out by a side door. Instead of going towards the group he was seeking, he was about to walk off in the opposite direction.

'Run and get him, Keith,' said Mr Chapman, 'or we'll lose him and we'll be here all night . . .'

Immediately, Keith darted out after Mr Croft. He ran straight into the road which had just recently been a pedestrian thoroughfare, his eyes fixed on the disappearing Mr Croft.

The car bearing down on him was first seen by Donovan, before Mr Chapman even. It was coming fast down the one-way street on the near side, the driver laughing with the man beside him, his attention lost in the enjoyment of a joke. Donovan saw it all like a flash photograph – with Keith in the foreground in the path of the car.

Without a second's conscious thought, Donovan yelled:

'Keith! Car! Look out!'

Keith heard the cry and turned instinctively back to the safety of the pavement. Hearing the roar of an engine, he threw himself forward, tripping over the kerb, and with a nasty hard crack to the head he landed on the flat slab.

The car driver, jerked back to his senses by the fright of almost running down the boy, hooted his horn in anger and drove on his way with a curse. But he eased his foot off the throttle. He had missed the boy by no more than a few centimetres.

Keith's father picked him up, lifting him under the armpits and dragging him into the shop doorway like the victim of an urban explosion. The boy looked stunned. His face was deathly white and his eyes rolled. Mr Chapman took away the scarf from around his neck and tried to sit him up. Keith rubbed his head where it hurt. Gradually, a hazy idea of where he was came back to him. He was in the street, on the pavement, leaning up against a wall. His dad was there, and some other people. A lot of them were talking, but amongst the blurred colours and the muzzy voices he felt sure he could hear the heaving sobbing wail of a boy crying, a throaty full-blooded cry which seemed almost to take pleasure in the sound it created.

In all the noise Keith could hear a familiar voice, a man's, very close, soft and gentle, talking in a calm and

comforting way. Was it speaking to him, or to someone else? He couldn't quite be sure. But he seemed to be saying something . . . something like . . .

'There, boy, let it out. Let it all come out. Cry all you like. For your daddy, boy. Everything's going to be all right. Just you see, boy. All right. Just you see . . . just you see, boy . . .'

Then Keith lost consciousness again, and he floated off into the darkness for a while. The next thing he knew he was being piggy-backed along Transport Avenue by his father, with Mr Croft propping him up at the back and Donovan holding on to a dangling hand. He looked down at the other boy and smiled. Donovan smiled back. It had all seemed like a dream.

'All right, Don?' he said, weakly.

Donovan nodded. They walked on a few more paces.

'Yes,' he said. 'Yes, Keith . . .'

# SUSAN COOPER

FROM *Greenwitch*

Under the sunset sky the sea was glass-smooth. Long
slow rollers from the Atlantic, rippling like muscles
beneath the skin, made the only sign of the great invisible
strength of the ocean in all the tranquil evening. Quietly
the fishing-boats moved out, a broad fishtail wake
spreading behind each one; their engines chugged softly
through the still air. Jane stood at the end of Kemare
Head, on the crest of a granite outfall that tumbled its
rocks two hundred feet to the sea, and she watched them
go. Toy boats, they seemed from there: the scatter of a
fishing fleet that every week, every month, every year
for endless years had been going out after the pilchard or
the mackerel before dusk, and staying at the chase until
dawn. Every year there were fewer of them, but still
every year they went.

The sun dropped at the horizon, a fat glowing ball
spreading yellow light over all the smooth sea, and the
last boat crept out of Trewissick harbour, its engine
thumping like a muffled heart-beat in Jane's ears. As the
last spreading lines of the boat's wake washed against the
harbour wall, in a final swift rush the great sun dropped
below the horizon, and the light of the April evening
began very slowly to die. A small wind sprang up. Jane
shivered, and pulled her jacket around her; there was
suddenly a coldness in the darkening air.

As if in answer to the beginning breeze, a light starred

up suddenly across Trewissick Bay, on the headland opposite Kemare Head. At the same time there was a sudden
warmth behind Jane's back. She swung round, and saw
dark figures against tall flames, where a light had been
set to the towering pile of driftwood and branches that
had lain waiting to become a bonfire for this one night.
Mrs Penhallow had told her that the two beacons would
burn until the fishing-boats came back, flames leaping all
through the night until the dawn.

Mrs Penhallow: now there was a mystery. Jane
thought again of the moment that afternoon when she
had been alone in the living-room, flipping through a
magazine, waiting for Simon. She had heard a nervous
clearing of the throat, and there in the kitchen doorway
Mrs Penhallow was standing, round and rosy and un-
usually fidgety.

'Ef you fancy comin' to the makin' tonight, m'dear,
you'm welcome,' she said abruptly.

Jane blinked at her. 'The making?'

'The makin' of the Greenwitch.' The lilt of Mrs Penhallow's Cornish accent seemed more marked than usual. 'It
do take all the night, 'tes a long business, and no outsiders allowed near, generally. But if you feel you'd like
. . . you being the only female close to the Perfessor, and
all . . .' She waved a hand as if to catch words. 'The
women did agree it's all right, and I'd be happy to take
'ee.'

'Thank you very much,' said Jane, puzzled but pleased.
'Er . . . can Mrs Stanton come too?'

'No,' Mrs Penhallow said sharply. She added more
gently, as Jane's eyebrows went up, 'She'm a furriner,
you see. Tisn't fitting.'

Up on the headland, gazing at the fire, Jane remembered the flat finality of the words. She had accepted the pronouncement and, without even trying to explain the situation to Fran Stanton, had come out after supper to the headland with Mrs Penhallow.

Yet still she had been given no idea of what was to happen. Nobody had told her what the thing called the Greenwitch would be like, or how it would be made, or what would happen to it. She knew only that the business would occupy the whole night, and end when the fishermen came home. Jane shivered again. Night was falling, and she was not overfond of the nights of Cornwall; they held too much of the unknown.

Black shadows ran over the rocks around her, dancing and disappearing as the flames leapt. Instinctively seeking company, Jane moved forward into the circle of bright light around the bonfire; yet this too was unnerving, for now the other figures moved to and fro at the edge of the darkness, out of sight, and she felt suddenly vulnerable. She hesitated, frightened by the tension in the air.

'Come, m'dear,' said Mrs Penhallow's soft voice, beside her. 'Come by here.' There was a hint of urgency in her tone. Hastily she took Jane by the arm and led her aside. 'Time for the makin',' she said. 'You want to keep out of the way, if you can.'

Then she was gone again, leaving Jane alone near a group of women busying themselves with something not yet visible. Jane found a rock and sat down, warmed by the fire; she watched. Scores of women were there, of all ages: the younger ones in jeans and sweaters, the rest in sturdy dark skirts, long as overcoats, and high heavy boots. Jane could see a big pile of stones, each the size of a man's head, and a far higher pile of green branches – hawthorn, she thought – too leafy to be intended for the fire. But she did not understand the purpose of either of these.

Then one tall woman moved out before the rest, and held one arm high in the air. She called out something Jane could not understand, and at once the women set to working, in a curiously ordered way in small groups. Some would take up a branch, strip it of leaves and twigs, and test it for flexibility; others then would take the branch, and in some swift practised way weave it together with others into what began very slowly to emerge as a kind of frame.

After a while the frame began to show signs of becoming a great cylinder. The cleaning and bending and tying went on for a long time. Jane shifted restlessly. The leaves on some of the branches seemed to be of a different shape from the hawthorn. She was not close enough to see what they might be, and she did not intend to move. She felt she would only be safe here, half-invisible on her rock, unnoticed, watching from a little way off.

At her side suddenly she found the tall woman who had seemed the others' leader. Bright eyes looked down at her out of a thin face, framed by a scarf tied under the chin. 'Jane Drew, it is,' the woman said, with a Cornish accent that sounded oddly hard. 'One of those who found the grail.'

Jane jumped. The thought of the grail was never fully out of her mind, but she had not linked it with this strange ceremony here. The woman, however, did not mention it again.

'Watch for the Greenwitch,' she said conversationally. It was like a greeting.

The sky was almost black now, with only a faint rim of the glow of daylight. The lights of the two bonfires burned brightly on the headlands. Jane said hastily, clutching at this companionship against the lonely dark, 'What are they doing with those branches?'

'Hazel for the framework,' the woman said. 'Rowan for the head. Then the body is of hawthorn boughs, and hawthorn blossoms. With the stones within, for the sinking. And those who are crossed, or barren, or who would make any wish, must touch the Greenwitch then before she be put to cliff.'

'Oh,' Jane said.

'Watch for the Greenwitch,' said the woman pleasantly again, and moved away. Over her shoulder she said, 'You may make a wish too, if you like. I will call you, at the right time.'

Jane was left wondering and nervous. The women were busier now, working steadily, singing in a strange kind of wordless humming; the cylinder shape grew more distinct, closer-woven, and they carried the stones and put them inside. The head began to take shape: a huge head, long, squarish, without features. When the framework was done, they began weaving into it green branches starred with white blossoms. Jane could smell the heavy sweetness of the hawthorn. Somehow it reminded her of the sea.

Hours went by. Sometimes Jane dozed, curled beside her rock; whenever she woke, the framework seemed to look exactly as it had before. The work of weaving seemed endless. Mrs Penhallow came twice with hot tea from a flask. She said anxiously, 'Now if you do feel you've had enough, m'dear, you just say so. Easy to take you along home.'

'No,' Jane said, staring at the great leafy image with

its court of steady workers. She did not like the Green-witch; it frightened her. There was something menacing in its broad squat shape. Yet it was hypnotic too; she could scarcely take her eyes off it. *It*. She had always thought of witches as being female, but she could feel no *she* quality in the Greenwitch. It was unclassifiable, like a rock or a tree.

The bonfire still burned, fed carefully with wood, its warmth was very welcome in the chill night. Jane moved away to stretch her stiff legs, and saw inland a faint greyness beginning to lighten the sky. Morning would be coming soon. A misty morning: fine drops of moisture were flicking at her face already. Against the lightening sky she could see Trewissick's standing stones, five of them, ancient skyward-pointing fingers half-way along Kemare Head. She thought: that's what Greenwitch is like. It reminds me of the standing stones.

When she turned back again towards the sea, the Green-witch was finished. The women had drawn away from the great figure; they sat by the fire, eating sandwiches, and laughing, and drinking tea. As Jane looked at the huge image that they had made, out of leaves and branches, she could not understand their lightness. For she knew suddenly, out there in the cold dawn, that this silent image somehow held within it more power than she had ever sensed before in any creature or thing. Thunder and storms and earthquakes were there, and all the force of the earth and sea. It was outside Time, boundless, ageless, beyond any line drawn between good and evil. Jane stared at it, horrified, and from its sightless head the Greenwitch stared back. It would not move, or seem to come alive, she knew that. Her horror came not from fear, but from the awareness she suddenly felt from the image of an appalling, endless loneliness. Great power

was held only in great isolation. Looking at the Greenwitch, she felt a terrible awe, and a kind of pity as well.

But the awe, from her amazement at so inconceivable
a force, was stronger than anything else.

'You feel it, then.' The leader of the women was
beside her again; the hard, flat words were not a question.
'A few women do. Or girls. Very few. None of those
there, not one.' She gestured contemptuously at the cheerful group beyond. 'But one who has held the grail in her
hands may feel many things . . . Come. Make your wish.'

'Oh no.' Jane shrank back instinctively.

In the same moment a cluster of four young women
broke away from the crowd and ran to the broad, shadowy leaf-image. They were shaking with giggles, calling
to one another; one, larger and noisier than the rest,
rushed up and clasped the hawthorn sides that stretched
far above her head.

'Send us all rich husbands, Greenwitch, pray thi'!' she shouted.

'Or else send her young Jim Tregoney!' bellowed another. Shrieking with laughter, they all ran back to the group.

'See there!' said the woman. 'No harm comes to the foolish, which is most of them. And therefore none to those with understanding. Will you come?'

She walked over to the big silent figure, laid a hand on it, and said something that Jane could not hear.

Nervously Jane followed. As she came close to the Greenwitch she felt again the unimaginable force it seemed to represent, but again the great loneliness too. Melancholy seemed to hover about it like a mist. She put out her hand to grasp a hawthorn bough, and paused. 'Oh dear,' she said impulsively, 'I wish you could be happy.'

She thought, as she said it: how babyish, when you could have wished for anything, even getting the grail back . . . even if it's all a lot of rubbish, you could at least have tried . . . But the hard-eyed Cornishwoman was looking at her with an odd surprised kind of approval.

'A perilous wish!' she said. 'For where one may be made happy by harmless things, another may find happiness only in hurting. But good may come of it.'

Jane could think of nothing to say. She felt suddenly extremely silly.

Then she thought she heard a muffled throbbing sound out at sea; she swung round. The woman too was looking outward, at a grey streak of horizon where none had been before. Out on the dark sea, lights were flickering, white and red and green. The first fishermen were coming home.

# NINA BAWDEN

FROM *The Peppermint Pig*

A week passed – and something much worse did happen to Theo than being teased by Noah Bugg. Aunt Sarah knitted him a pink woollen vest and he had to wear it to school.

It was made of thick, soft wool and knitted in a pretty, lacy pattern. Mother said, ' Sarah must have sat up till all hours, it is good of her. She says she'll have another one ready time this one needs to be washed.' She saw Theo's sickly grin and added in a coaxing voice, 'Your Aunt Sarah is worried about you getting a chill, this bitter cold weather.'

'I'd rather get a chill than wear that,' Theo said. 'It's a girl's vest. I'd rather die.'

He meant it: he felt really desperate. Mocking laughter filled his dreams; tormenting boys danced round him, gimlet-eyed. *We can see what you're wearing, Baby Theo Greengrass!* He prayed for a miracle – for the house to burn down and the hateful vest with it while they were all safely out – but his prayers were not answered. The first day of school, the humiliating garment was laid out on the chair at the end of his bed. He put it on and came down to breakfast wishing the earth would open and swallow him.

Poll tried to comfort him. 'No one will see the vest under your clothes. No one will know.'

'I'll know!' He pushed the porridge round his plate, the tears springing.

Mother looked at him helplessly. She said, 'Sarah's so good to us, Theo. I can't tell her you wouldn't wear it.'

'All right, all *right*. I'm wearing the beastly thing, aren't I?' Tears fell into his uneaten porridge and Poll began to cry too, in sympathy.

Mother said, 'Oh, you two!' She got up from the table, went to the scullery and began to throw dirty pots into sink, making more noise than seemed necessary. George, off to school early, hitched his satchel up on his shoulder and said, 'For Heaven's sake, Theo, can't you see you're upsetting her? Don't be so childish.'

'I *am* a child,' Theo said, sullenly hiccuping, but George had already gone. He went out the front door, calling back, 'Mother, the milkman's here.'

She came out of the scullery, drying her hands and muttering under her breath. She forgot to pick up the blue and white jug from the table and when she reached the door, she called Poll to bring it.

The milkman was saying, '. . . so the old sow farrowed early. D'you want a peppermint pig, Mrs Greengrass?'

Poll looked at him, thinking of sweets, but there was a real pig poking its snout out of the milkman's coat pocket. It was the tiniest pig she had ever seen. She touched its hard little head and said, 'What's a peppermint pig?'

'Not worth much,' Mother said. 'Only a token. Like a peppercorn rent. Almost nothing.'

'Runt of the litter,' the milkman added. 'Too small for the sow to raise. He'd only get trampled in the rush.'

Mother took the pig from him and held it firmly while it kicked and squealed piercingly. She tipped it to look at its stomach and said, 'Well, he seems strong enough. And even runts grow.'

The milkman took the jug from Poll and went to his cart to ladle milk out of his churn.

'Oh,' Poll said. 'Oh, *Mother*.' She stroked the small, wriggling body. Stroked one way, its skin felt silky to touch; the other way, stiff little hairs prickled her fingers. He was a pale apricot colour all over.

The milkman came back. Mother said, 'Will you take a shilling?' and he nodded and grinned. Poll took the milk to the kitchen and flew upstairs for her mother's purse. 'Theo,' she shouted, 'look what we've got!'

An old pint beer mug stood on the dresser. Mother laughed suddenly and popped the pig in it. He made such a fearsome noise that they put their hands over their ears. Poll picked him out and said, 'Whatever made you do that?'

'I just thought he would fit, and he did!'

Poll put him down and he scampered desperately round the kitchen, dainty feet skittering on slippery lino. He shot into the scullery and went to ground in the little hole under the copper.

Mother said, 'Leave him now, poor little fellow, he's scared to death. He'll settle down while you're at school.'

Poll groaned tragically. 'Must we go? Oh, I can't bear it, I can't bear to leave him.'

'He'll be here when you come home dinner time,' Mother said.

Poll counted the hours. Not just that day, but the next and the next, the thought of the baby pig, waiting at home, distracted her attention so she had no time left to be naughty: by the end of the first week, she had not once been rapped over the knuckles or stood in the corner. She made a best friend called Annie Dowsett who was older than she was and who told her how babies were born. 'The butcher comes and cuts you up the stomach with his carving knife,' Annie said. 'But don't tell your mother I told you.' Poll didn't really believe this, because if it were true, women would never have more than one baby, but it was an interesting idea all the same and she began to feel she quite liked this new school. She even liked her teacher, Miss Armstrong, who had a long, mild, sheep's face, and was proud that her Aunt was Headmistress with her name on a brass plate on the outside of the building. Everyone was a little scared of Aunt Sarah but not of Aunt Harriet who was called, Miss Harry to her face and Old Harry behind her back, who romped in the playground with the little ones until her wispy hair came down under her hat, and always brought potatoes to school to bake in the stove for the children who lived too far away to go home for their dinner.

Even Theo was happier because of the pig. The excitement of its arrival carried him through the first day, and although after that the horrible shame of the pink, girlish vest hidden under his clothes still haunted him sleeping and walking, especially when he caught Noah Bugg's rolling, gooseberry eye in the classroom, he managed to live with it. No one, he told himself, was likely to fall upon him and tear his clothes off, and even if he was sometimes tormented because of his size, he was used to that, and it was a comfort to run home and pick up the pig and whisper in his floppy ear, 'Peppermint pig, peppermint pig, I'm a peppermint *boy*, so there's two of us, runts in this family.'

Mother called the pig Johnnie, saying (rather oddly the children thought) that he reminded her of her grandfather, and it wasn't long before he answered to his name, grunting and running whenever they called him. At night, he slept in the copper hole on a straw bed; during the day he trotted busily round behind Mother or sat on the hearth rug staring thoughtfully into the fire.

Lily said, 'You can't keep a pig indoors, Mother!'

'Oh, we had all sorts of animals in the house when I was young,' Mother said. 'Jackdaws, hedgehogs, newly hatched chicks. I remember times you couldn't get near our fire.'

'But not *pigs*,' Lily said.

'I can't see why not. You'd keep a dog and a pig has more brains than a dog let me tell you. If you mean pigs are dirty, that's just a matter of giving a pig a bad name to my mind. Why, our Johnnie was house-trained in a matter of days and with a good deal less trouble than *you* gave me, my girl!'

Poll giggled and Lily went pink.

Mother said, 'Give a pig a chance to keep clean and he'll take it, which is more than you can say of some humans. You tell me now, does Johnnie smell?'

If he did, it was only of a mixture of bran and sweet milk which was all he ate to begin with, although as he grew older, Mother boiled up small potatoes and added scraps from the table. She said there was no waste in a house with a pig and when the summer came they would go round the hedgerows and collect dandelions and sow thistle so he would have plenty of fresh food and grow strong and healthy. 'What he eats is important,' she said. 'Pigs are a poor person's investment.'

# ROBERT LEESON

FROM *The Third Class Genie*

Baffled and bewildered, Alec held the can in his hands. Was he dreaming? Was Alec Bowden truly the master of Abu Salem, Genie Third Class, approximately 975 years old? Or was Alec Bowden off his trolley? Had the strain of the day been too much? There were his plimsolls with a big hole burnt in them by helpful old Grandad. There was his project on the Crusades, all soaked in eau-de-Canal. The disasters were real enough. But what about the triumph?

He held up the can to the light; it gleamed. He held it to his nose; it smelt beery. He held it to his ears and heard a distinct snoring sound. That could mean only one thing. Abu was sleeping off that enormous meal. Was it mackerel and rice pudding, or pheasants and sherbet? Still the memory was clear. His mouth watered.

He rubbed the can briskly and held it up again. The snoring had stopped. He rubbed it again. No sign. Inspiration struck him. Bending his mouth close to the can opening, he said firmly, 'Salaam Aleikum, O Abu Salem.'

The familiar voice repeated sleepily, 'Peace to you, Keef Haalak? How are you?'

'I am well, apart from about two thousand problems,' said Alec.

'Aieee, I feared as much. No peace for the genie. Speak, O Alec. What is thy will?'

'My first will is a new pair of plimsolls.'

'Plimsolls? What are plimsolls?'

'Slippers.'

In a flash the scorched plimsolls had vanished from Alec's feet, and were instantly replaced by the most elegant pair of pink and gold, plush, satin slippers with curled toes.

'You Great Arabian Nit,' said Alec, 'you'll have me drummed out of the Third Year!'

'Are the slippers not to your liking?' Abu sounded a little offended.

'They're lovely, they're gorgeous, but they're not me,' said Alec. 'I want rubber-soled gym shoes.'

'What is rubber?'

'Good grief,' said Alec. Then he thought. What is rubber? How do you make it? How do you explain it to a 975-year-old genie, who hasn't had the benefits of Western civilization? All he could remember was a description of plantation life in the geography book. He told Abu. Immediately in front of him there was a tall smooth-trunked tree, standing in the middle of the room, with white liquid seeping from a cut in the bark and flowing down on to the bedroom floor. Alec bent down and poked the liquor which seemed to be setting like a jelly. Now, what to do? For the life of him, he couldn't remember the next stage in rubber-making.

Did you fry it, or hang it out of the window, or beat it? He wished he'd listened properly in geography or chemistry.

'Ah well, Abu,' he said, 'let's have my old plimsolls back. I'll have to buy a new pair.'

'Thy will is my command,' said Abu, as though he'd worked miracles.

'Now, you see my project book over there on the bed. I want it cleaned up.'

For a second the project book vanished, or seemed to. Then it reappeared. But what had the raving genie done now? The front of the book and the first ten pages, which had been stained with canal mud, had been cleaned up. They'd been wiped clean, completely. There was nothing on them.

'Put it back, Abu, put it back,' he yelled.

There was silence for a second.

'Come on, genie-us,' demanded Alec, 'make with the project.'

From the front room Alec's mother knocked on the ceiling.

'A bit less noise up there, our Alec.'

Alec groaned. Then Abu said hesitantly,

'I fear I cannot put back what you wrote. For I cannot know what it might have been.'

Alec stared. That hadn't occurred to him. It wasn't Abu who was daft; it was he. He'd just have to be more careful what he asked. Abu had warned him about all the disasters that had happened to his previous masters.

'It was a story of the Crusades,' he said.

'Crusades?'

'When King Richard and the other knights went out to the Holy Land to drive out the Saracens and fought Saladin.'

'Aha, Sultan Salah ad-Din Yusuf, Lord of Ishshaan, mighty hammer of the faithless. Who does not know that great story?'

'Do you? It took me an awful time to look it up in the school library. If I have to do all that again . . .'

'Fear not, Alec. Take up thy pen. I shall tell, you shall

write and the empty pages shall be full once more with great truth. Let us begin with the mighty victory for the true faith at the battle of Hattin . . .'

Alec rushed to his desk, got out his fountain pen, and began to write, while Abu tirelessly told of sieges, battles, storms of arrows, flash of scimitar and sword, thunder of hooves, and burning sand and sun. There was still much to tell, when Alec had filled up the blank space in his project book. But his mother knocked on the ceiling again which was the signal for him to get ready for bed. Outside it was dark now and Alec was tired, but he felt happy again. His project was rescued. True, his plimsolls were still in a disastrous state, but surely with Abu's aid he could put that right.

Now that he had Abu Salem, genie of the light brown ale on his side, nothing was too much. From now on, triumphs would hammer disasters ten nil every day. Thanks to Abu. Good Old Abu.

'Well, Abu, I'm off to bed, if you'd like to climb back into your can. I'll leave the lid up slightly to give you some fresh air. It must smell like a brewery in there. Cheerio for now.'

'Ma'asalaama,' murmured Abu.

Alec undressed, wandered out to the bathroom to brush his teeth, but at the top of the stairs, he stopped. He could hear his mother and father talking in the kitchen where they were having a cup of cocoa.

'I don't know, Connie love. I doesn't matter how you switch around those bedrooms, we haven't really got room.'

'Well, I'm fed up with it, Harold. For one reason or another we've never had enough room.'

'We could get a four-bedroomed house if we moved to Moorside.'

'The only way you'll get me to Moorside is to carry me in a coffin. Miles from anywhere, freezing cold in winter . . .'

'All right, all right, Connie. Anyway, let's get to bed. Is our Kim in yet?'

'Not her, still, she's got the backdoor key.'

Alec heard them move their chairs down in the kitchen and shot quickly back into his own bedroom. He switched off the light and looked out of the window. The railway arch loomed up against the skyline; the Tank, hidden in the dark shadows of the arch, could not be seen. But Alec knew it was here. He had his hideout, and his new friend Abu. Ginger Wallace, Mr Cartwright and all infidels would bite the dust from now on. Flash Bowden, Scourge of the Cosmos, Defender of the Faith, Keeper of the Kan, was on the war-path.

He tucked the can carefully under his pillow and went to sleep.

# ROBERT WESTALL

FROM *The Machine Gunners*

The next Wednesday evening started quite well. Mr McGill was on the two-till-ten shift, so there were only Chas and his mum for tea. But Cousin Gordon called, on leave again, bright in brass and airforce blue. He was carrying his rifle, because he had to be ready to Defend Britain Against Invasion at any time, and because Aunt Rose said she wouldn't have the great greasy murderous thing round *her* house while he was out.

He was just letting Chas play with it (with clips of dummy bullets) when the siren went.

'Get down the shelter, you two, while I put this sausage and chips on to plates. This is one meal Hitler's not spoiling.'

It was nearly as good as a picnic, scrambling down into the Anderson with knives and forks, teapot and plate of dried bread. Chas sat by the shelter door to eat his tea, staring at the garden path.

'If I was that beetle out there, I might be wiped out at any moment by a piece of shrapnel. But in here, I'm safe.' It had all the pleasure of standing dry in a doorway, watching the rain make everything else wet. He thought of the steel and earth above him, and felt deliciously safe eating his chips. He nodded at Cousin Gordon's rifle.

'Pity you didn't bring home something bigger. Then you and me could have had a go at the bombers when they come.'

'No need,' said Cousin Gordon, who liked playing the expert. 'You can shoot down a bomber with a rifle. We're trained for it. You have to aim a hand's breadth in front of them, to allow for their speed.'

'But bombers fly too high!'

'Don't you believe it. Most bombers fly at five thousand feet, which is a mile. This thing can kill at a mile.' He stroked his rifle.

'Can the . . . German guns fire that far?'

'Yeah, far further. Their Schmeissers can go right through the trunk of a tree.'

'What's a Schmeisser?'

'Machine gun.'

Chas finished his chips thoughtfully, impaling five on his fork at once and then ramming the lot into his mouth.'

'How often have I got to tell you?' said Mrs McGill. '*Cut* them before you put them into your mouth.

Around ten, the all-clear went. Nothing had happened but two showers of rain, and long before the end, you could hear people standing chatting by their shelter doors.

'What a waste of time,' said Mrs McGill. 'I could have done the ironing. Goodnight, Gordon. Tell your mother I'll call on Friday.'

'Goodnight. I'd better get back while it's quiet.'

They heard his boots click away, and sat waiting for another clink of boots up the path, and the clicking of a pushed bicycle. Dad.

'Hello, love,' Mrs McGill kissed her grimy husband on the cheek. Chas had never seen his father come through the back door without his mother kissing him on the cheek. It must taste awfully sooty and oily. How much soot and oil she must have swallowed since she married him!

'Here's your supper, nice and hot.'

Mr McGill washed his hands but not his face. That came after eating. First things first. He didn't take his grimy boots off, either. Mrs McGill always put a copy of the *Daily Express* under his chair to save the carpet.

'Nice having the raid over early for once. I could do with a good night's sleep in me own bed.'

'Don't count your chickens. There's still a yellow alert on.'

'But the all-clear went!'

'That's the end of the red alert. The buggers are still hanging about somewhere. I think I'd better get me uniform on.' Mr McGill, foreman at the gasworks, knew such things.

'But your tea will be spoiled.'

'Put it back in the oven.'

Mrs McGill sniffed and picked up the *Daily Express* off the floor. Work-boots might never be cleaned, but ARP boots were always spotless and shining. Mr McGill, immaculate now, beret under shoulder strap, sat down again to eat.

Next moment, the lights went out. Then the cracks round the drawn black-out curtains lit up with successive streaks of light. Mr McGill's plate went crash on the floor.

'Oh those lovely sausages!' screamed his wife.

'Get down, hinny. Turn your face from the window. It's one of those sneak raiders.'

But it wasn't. Chas, lying face-down under the sofa heard the sound of many engines.

'Run for it!' They ran down the front passage and

pulled open the front door. It was like day outside, there were so many parachute-flares falling. You could have seen a pin on the crazy-paving path to the shelter.

'The insurance policies!' screamed his mother, trying to turn back. His father stopped her bodily, and for a moment his parents wrestled like drunks in the front passage.

'Run, for God's sake,' panted his father.

The moment Chas set foot on the path outside, the bombs began to scream down. Chas thought his legs had stopped working for good; the black hole of the shelter door seemed to get further away instead of nearer. They said you never hear the bomb that hit you, but how could they know? Only the dead knew that, like the girl who had worked in the greengrocer's. Chas saw the top half of her body, still obscenely weighing out potatoes . . .

Then he threw himself through the shelter door. He caught his knee on a corner of the bunk, and it was agony. Then his mother landed on top of him, knocking him flat, and he heard Dad's boots running, as he had never heard them before. Then a crack like thunder, and another and another and another and another. Great thunder-boots walking steadily towards them. The next would certainly crush them.

But the next never came; only the sound of bricks falling, like coalmen tipping coal into the cellar and glass breaking and breaking . . .

His father drew down the heavy tarpaulin over the shelter door, and his mother lit the little oil-lamp with her third trembling match. Then she lit the candle under a plant-pot that kept the shelter warm.

'Did you shut the front door love?' she said to his father. 'I'm frightened someone'll nip in and steal those

THE MACHINE GUNNERS 341

insurance policies. And where's Mrs Spalding and Colin?'

*Chug, chug, chug, chug.*

'The buggers is coming again!' shouted Mr McGill. 'Where's the guns, where's the fighters?'

Above the chugging came a kind of rhythmic panting-screeching; and a kind of dragging-hopping, like a kangaroo in its death-throes. It was even more frightening than the chugging, and it came right up to the shelter door. A body fell through. It was Mrs Spalding.

'Is she dead?' said Mrs McGill.

'No, but she's got her knickers round her ankles,' said Mr McGill.

'Aah had tey hop aal the way,' gasped Mrs Spalding. 'I was on the outside lav and I couldn't finish. The buggers blew the lav door off, and they've hit the Rex Cinema as well. Is there a spot of brandy?'

'Aah pulled the chain, Mam. It flushed all right.' It was Colin, with a self-satisfied smirk on his face.

'You'll get the Victoria Cross for that,' said Chas with a wild giggle.

'Shut up, Charles. Have you got no feelings?' Mum turned to Mrs Spalding who had crawled on to her bunk and was busy pulling up her knickers. 'I'm sorry, love. We got down the shelter so quick I left the brandy and the case behind. I'm worried about the insurance, too. Jack didn't shut the front door. Go back and get them, Jack!'

But the bombs had begun whining down again. Every time he heard one, Chas stared hard at the shelter wall. Mr McGill had painted it white, and set tiny bits of cork in the wet paint to absorb condensation. Chas would start to count inside his head. When the counting reached twenty, he would either be dead, or he would see little bits of cork fall off the shelter wall with the shock-wave, and know he had survived ... till the next whistling started. It was a silly pointless game, with no real magic in it, but it stopped you wanting to scream ...

# ALAN GARNER

FROM *The Stone Book*

Mary stood at the gate and looked up. High clouds moving made the steeple topple towards her.

'Father!'

She could hear his hammer, tac, tac, as he combed the stone.

The golden spark was a weathercock. It had been put up that week, and under its spike was the top platform. Father's head showed over the edge of the platform.

'Below!' His voice sounded nearer than he looked.

'I've brought your baggin!' Mary shouted.

'Fetch it, then!'

'All the way?'

'Must I come down when I'm working?'

'But what about the Governor?' said Mary.

'He's gone! I'm the Governor of this gang! There's only me stayed to finish! Have you the tea?'

'Yes!'

'Plenty of sugar?'

'Yes!'

'I can't spit for shouting! Come up!'

Mary hitched her frock and put the knot of the baggin cloth between her teeth and climbed the ladder.

The ladders were spiked and roped, but the beginning of the steeple was square, a straight drop, and the ladders clattered on the side. She didn't like that.

'Keep fast hold of that tea!' she heard Father call, but

she didn't lift her head, and she didn't look down.

Up she went. It felt worse than a rock because it was so straight and it had been made. Father had made parts of it. She knew the pattern of his combing hammer on the sandstone.

Up she went.

'Watch when you change to the spire!' Father's voice sounded no nearer.

At the spire, the pitch of the ladders was against the stone, and Mary had to step sideways to change. The ladders were firmer, but she began to feel a breeze. She heard an engine get up steam on the railway. The baggin cloth kept her mouth wet, but it felt dry.

The spire narrowed. There were sides to it. She saw the shallow corners begin. Up and up. Tac, tac, tac, tac, above her head. The spire narrowed. Now she couldn't stop the blue sky from showing at the sides. Then land. Far away.

Mary felt her hands close on the rungs, and her wrists go stiff.

Tac, tac, tac, tac. She climbed to the hammer. The spire was thin. Father was not working, but giving her a rhythm. The sky was now inside the ladder. The ladder was broader than the spire.

Father's hand took the baggin cloth out of Mary's mouth, and his other hand steadied her as she came up through the platform.

The platform was made of good planks, and Father had lashed them, but it moved. Mary didn't like the gaps between. She put her arms around the spire.

'That was a bonny climb,' said Father.

'I do hope the next baby's a lad,' said Mary.

'Have some tea,' said Father.

She drank from the bottle. The cold sweet drink stopped her trembling.

'Don't look yet,' said Father. 'And when you do, look away first, not near. How's Mother?'

'Resting. She could only do five hours at the picking today, it got that hot.'

'That's why I've stayed,' said Father. 'They want us to finish for Sunday, and there's one more dab of capping to do. There may be a sixpence for it.'

'Doesn't it fear you up here?' said Mary.

'Now why should it?' said Father. 'Glaze Hill's higher.'

'But you can't fall off Glaze Hill,' said Mary. 'Not all at once.'

'There's nothing here to hurt you,' said Father. 'There's stone, and wood and rope, and sky, same as at home. It's the same ground.'

'It's further,' said Mary.

'But it'll never hurt. And I'll go down with you. Down's harder.'

'I hope the next one's a lad,' said Mary, 'I'm fed up with being a lad – Father! See at the view! Isn't it!'

Mary stood and looked out from the spire.

'And the church,' she said. 'It's so far away.' She knelt and squinted between the planks. 'The roof's as far as the ground. We're flying.'

Father watched her; his combing hammer swung from his arm.

'There's not many who'll be able to say they've been to the top of Saint Philip's.'

'But I'm not at the top,' said Mary.

The steeple cap was a swelling to take the socket for the spike of the golden cockerel. Mary could touch the spike. Above her the smooth belly raced the clouds.

'You're not frit?'

'Not now,' said Mary. 'It's grand.'

Father picked her up. 'You're really not frit? Nobody's been that high. It was reared from the platform.'

'Not if you help me,' said Mary.

'Right,' said Father. 'He could do with a testing. Let's see if he runs true.'

Father lifted Mary in his arms, thick with work from wrist to elbow. For a moment again the steeple wasn't safe on the earth when she felt the slippery gold of the weathercock bulging over her, but she kicked her leg across its back, and held the neck.

'Get your balance,' said Father.

'I've got it,' said Mary.

The swelling sides were like a donkey, and behind her the tail was stiff and high. Father's head was at her feet, and he could reach her.

'I'm set,' she said.

Father's face was bright and his beard danced. He took off his cap and swept it in a circle and gave the cry of the summer fields.

'Who-whoop! Wo-whoop! Wo-o-o-o!'

Mary laughed. The wind blew on the spire and made the weathercock seem alive. The feathers of its tail were a marvel.

Father twisted the spike with his hands against the wind, and the spike moved in its greased socket, shaking a bit, juddering, but firm. To Mary the weathercock was waking. The world turned. Her bonnet fell off and hung by its ribbon, and the wind filled her hair.

'Faster! Faster!' she shouted. 'I'm not frit!' She banged her heels on the golden sides, and the weathercock boomed.

'Who-whoop! Wo-whoop! Wo-o-o-o!' cried Father.
The high note of his voice crossed parishes and town-
ships. Her hair and her bonnet flew, and she felt no
spire, but only the brilliant gold of the bird spinning the
air.

# GENE KEMP

FROM *The Turbulent Term of Tyke Tiler*

*'Dem bones, dem bones gonna roll around . . .'*

*'What's the fastest thing in the water?'*
*'A motor pike.'*

'You've got bones on the brain. That's because you're a bonehead, I suppose . . .'

'But I tell you it's a real skellinton, Tyke. I tell you where I seen it. Down in the leat. I went there yesterday when you was out. Come on. Come and look. I bet it's somebody what's bin murdered.'

'I got into enough trouble over that marrow bone . . .'

But Danny had set off along the road as if he was warming up for the fifteen hundred metres. He belted down the bank, where the old city walls stand, that drops down to the river and the leats, the oldest part of the city, Sir says. I soon caught up with him, Crumble at my heels, her ears ruffling out in the wind.

'Which leat are the bones in?'

There are two, Cricklepit and Walter, that cut off from the river below the weir. The leats and the river make an island that's mostly a deserted place. Danny panted:

'By the bridge. Near the warehouses.'

'They weren't there last week.'

'The rain and high water brung 'em out.'

We ran on, past the old, broken water-wheel, hidden in the trees and bushes, where the kingfisher flies sometimes. I've seen him quite a lot lately. I threw a broken brick into the water sluicing through an iron grid. The brown colour had gone but it was still high. Everywhere was quiet. No one comes round here much. Everything's either being knocked down or rotting away; it's a place for secrets and adventures.

Perhaps this was an adventure. Perhaps the bones were the skeleton of a murdered man, or valuable prehistoric remains. We ran through the square where my Gran used to live before it was demolished and on to a little sandstone bridge. Beside it was a wall and a railing and a long drop to the leat. We climbed over and inspected the filthy water.

'There. There it is.'

Danny pointed at what looked like a huge set of teeth decorated with floating strands of green slime. Other bones were scattered around. Crumble made eeking noises on the other side of the wall, so I lifted her over.

'It's lovely, Tyke.'

'It's a sheep, you nutter. It's like that one Martin Kneeshaw brought off the moor and went round showing off.'

'No it's not. It's a man, I tell you. Somebody murdered that man and chucked his body in here and he mouldered and mouldered away till he was that skellinton.'

'It's a sheep . . .'

He took no notice.

'We'll be on telly. Danny Price and Tyke Tiler found a murdered skellinton. Do you think there'll be a reward?' Crumble ran up and down the muddy bank, taking great interest in the bones as well. I didn't think she would leap off the bank, though, as it was a long way down to the water.

'You must know it's a sheep, Danny . . .' but he wasn't listening. His face was white and his eyes glittered. Completely nutty . . . mad as a snake . . . absolutely bonkers.

'Get it for me, Tyke.'

'What?'

'Get it for me. I want it.'

'You gotter be joking.'

'You get it for me, Tyke.'

'Get stuffed.'

'Please.'

I looked at the dirty, scummy water. This leat always got choked up, yet in the centre the current ran fast and fierce. Danny gazed at the bones as if they were the Crown Jewels.

'My Mum will wallop me if I get mucky again. She said so.'

'I want them bones.'

'Get 'em, then.'

'It's too steep for me.'

'Then it's too steep for me, too!'

'But you're clever. You can do anything.'

'Gee t'anks. For nothing.'

'If I take it to school I'll get some house points.'

'I thought you wanted to be famous. You won't get on the telly with sheep's teeth and house points. Make up your mind.'

'If it's a murdered man's skellinton, then I'll go on the telly and be famous, and if it's a sheep's I'll get some house points.'

He was starting to talk faster and faster and suddenly I thought maybe he'd gone completely bonkers, and I'd

better humour him, so I said what about some chips because I'm starving and I could fix him up with some fossils to take to school instead.

He wasn't listening.

'Get them bones for me, Tyke.'

'I don't want to . . .' and then I stopped. You can't get through to Danny when he's got an idea in his head, for there's only room for one at a time. I studied the water down below. The bottom was covered with broken bricks over which lay tins, bits of metal, sticks and wire, and the bones veiled in their green slime drifting and weaving in the current. It looked pretty deep. I wasn't likely to get drowned here – not like the river – but it looked cold and unfriendly. I thought of me Mum, and I looked at Danny still gazing at the bones and talking. Holding on to a tree root I lowered myself into the mucky, muddy, slimy water. It didn't seem worth taking my shoes and socks off as my trousers would get soaked anyway. Anyway I'd got my doom feeling by now. My doom feeling is when I know I'm slap bang in the middle of something that will lead to trouble, but I can't stop doing it all the same. I could hear my Gran saying:

'You might as well be hung for a sheep as a lamb.'

She used to say a lot of things like that.

Danny danced about on the edge of the bank.

'That's it, Tyke. You've nearly got 'em.'

There was a slithering noise, and an enormous splash. A piece of weed hit me on the nose and I was wet all over. Crumble had arrived to help. She lifted her nose in the air and started to swim, back legs kicking hard. She flurried all the water and I lost the bones. I couldn't see a thing.

'You stupid fool of a dog, get out,' I yelled. She swam

round and round me, nose in the air. The water was icy even through shoes, socks and trousers. I reached into the mud and found the bones.

'It's the teethy ones I want,' Danny jumped up and down.

'It stinks!'

It was slimily, horribly soft to the touch as well, a yellow jawbone with long teeth. I moved to the bank to hand it up to Danny. Crumble tried to follow this delightful pong and, getting to the bank, snapped at the teeth, then fell back into the water again.

'And the rest,' Danny roared, hopping, by now.

I got the rest. They felt really horrible. They smelt worse.

Danny cradled them in his arms, making little humming noises.

'I got a bag,' he said, bringing one out of his pocket. He put the bones in it and gathered it to his chest. The bag went soggy. Crumble and I started to climb the bank. Danny went over the wall.

'Hey! Gimme a hand!'

He managed to remember me for a moment and stretched out a mitt, but the bank was so churned up with all his leaping about that he suddenly slipped, and fell flat on his back, bones clasped to his chest.

Down I crashed on to the slimy stones in that stinking leat. Crumble joined me, licking my face as I tried to get to my feet. Danny Price sat on the bank, laughing like a drain.

Wild with fury, I travelled up that bank at a thousand miles per hour, dragging Crumble by her collar.

'I'm gonna exterminate you, and bury you with your rotten ole bones!'

# KATHERINE PATERSON

FROM *Bridge to Terabithia*

He was awake, jerked suddenly into consciousness in the black stillness of the house. He sat up, stiff and shivering, although he was fully dressed from his windbreaker down to his sneakers. He could hear the breathing of the little girls in the next bed, strangely loud and uneven in the quiet. Some dream must have awakened him, but he could not remember it. He could only remember the mood of dread it had brought with it. Through the curtainless window he could see the lopsided moon with hundreds of stars dancing in bright attendance.

It came into his mind that someone had told him that Leslie was dead. But he knew now that that had been part of the dreadful dream. Leslie could not die any more than he himself could die. But the words turned over uneasily in his mind like leaves stirred up by a cold wind. If he got up now and went down to the old Perkins place and knocked on the door, Leslie would come to open it, P.T. jumping at her heels like a star around the moon. It was a beautiful night. Perhaps they could run over the hill and across the fields to the stream and swing themselves into Terabithia.

They had never been there in the dark. But there was enough moon for them to find their way into the castle, and he could tell her about his day in Washington. And apologize. It had been so dumb of him not to ask if

Leslie could go, too. He and Leslie and Miss Edmunds could have had a wonderful day — different, of course, from the day he and Miss Edmunds had had, but still good, still perfect. Miss Edmunds and Leslie liked each other a lot. It would have been fun to have Leslie along. *I'm really sorry, Leslie.* He took off his jacket and sneakers, and crawled under the covers. *I was dumb not to think of asking.*

*S'OK,* Leslie would say. *I've been to Washington thousands of times.*

*Did you ever see the buffalo hunt?*

Somehow it was the one thing in all Washington that Leslie had never seen, and so he could tell her about it, describing the tiny beasts hurtling to destruction.

His stomach felt suddenly cold. It had something to do with the buffalo, with falling, with death. With the reason he had not remembered to ask if Leslie could go with them to Washington today.

*You know something weird?*

*What?* Leslie asked.

*I was scared to come to Terabithia this morning.*

The coldness threatened to spread up from his stomach. He turned over and lay on it. Perhaps it would be better not to think about Leslie right now. He could go to see her the first thing in the morning and explain everything. He could explain it better in the daytime when he had shaken off the effects of his unremembered nightmare.

He put his mind to remembering the day in Washington, working on details of pictures and statues, dredging up the sound of Miss Edmunds's voice, recalling his own exact words and her exact answers. Occasionally into the corner of his mind's vision would come a sensation of falling, but he pushed it away from the view of another picture or the sound of another conversation. Tomorrow he must share it all with Leslie.

The next thing he was aware of was the sun streaming through the window. The little girls' bed was only rumpled covers, and there was movement and quiet talking from the kitchen.

Lord! Poor Miss Bessie. He'd forgotten all about her last night, and now it must be late. He felt for his sneakers and shoved his feet over the heels without tying the laces.

His mother looked up quickly from the stove at the sound of him. Her face was set for a question, but she just nodded her head at him.

The coldness began to come back. 'I forgot Miss Bessie.'

'Your daddy's milking her.'

'I forgot last night, too.'

She kept nodding her head. 'Your daddy did it for you.' But it wasn't an accusation. 'You feel like some breakfast?'

Maybe that was why his stomach felt so odd. He hadn't had anything to eat since the ice-cream Miss Edmunds had bought them at Millsburg on the way home. Brenda and Ellie stared up at him from the table. The little girls turned from their cartoon show at the TV to look at him and then turned quickly back.

He sat down on the bench. His mother put a plateful of pancakes in front of him. He couldn't remember the last time she had made pancakes. He doused them with syrup and began to eat. They tasted marvellous.

'You don't even care. Do you?' Brenda was watching him from across the table.

He looked at her puzzled, his mouth full.

'If Jimmy Dicks died, I wouldn't be able to eat a bite.'

The coldness curled up inside of him and flopped over.

'Will you shut your mouth, Brenda Aarons?' His mother sprang forward, the pancake turner held threateningly high.

'Well, Momma, he's just sitting there eating pancakes like nothing happened. I'd be crying my eyes out.'

Ellie was looking first at Mrs Aarons and then at Brenda. 'Boys ain't supposed to cry at times like this. Are they, Momma?'

'Well, it don't seem right for him to be sitting there eating like a brood sow.'

'I'm telling you, Brenda, if you don't shut your mouth . . .'

He could hear them talking but they were farther away than the memory of the dream. He ate and he chewed and he swallowed, and when his mother put three more pancakes on his plate, he ate them, too.

His father came in with the milk. He poured it carefully into the empty cider jugs and put them into the refrigerator. Then he washed his hands at the sink and came to the table. As he passed Jess, he put his hand lightly on the boy's shoulder. He wasn't angry about the milking.

Jess was only dimly aware that his parents were looking at each other and then at him. Mrs Aarons gave Brenda a hard look and gave Mr Aarons a look which was to say that Brenda was to be kept quiet, but Jess was only thinking of how good the pancakes had been and hoping his mother would put down some more in front of him. He knew somehow that he shouldn't ask for more, but he was disappointed that she didn't give him any. He thought, then, that he should get up and leave the table, but he wasn't sure where he was supposed to go or what he was supposed to do.

'Your mother and I thought we ought to go down to the neighbours and pay respects.' His father cleared his throat. 'I think it would be fitting for you to come, too.' He stopped again. 'Seeing's you was the one that really knowed the little girl.'

Jess tried to understand what his father was saying to him, but he felt stupid. 'What little girl?' He mumbled it, knowing it was the wrong thing to ask. Ellie and Brenda both gasped.

His father leaned down the table and put his big hand on top of Jess's hand. He gave his wife a quick, troubled look. But she just stood there, her eyes full of pain, saying nothing.

'Your friend Leslie is dead, Jesse. You need to understand that.'

# MICHELLE MAGORIAN

FROM *Goodnight Mr Tom*

Mrs Black was to have all the local children and non-Catholic evacuees from five years old to eight.

Willie watched Mrs Hartridge approach him and Zach. Zach told her his age, which was nine, and spelt out his name, apologizing for it at the same time. She smiled. Willie handed her his label and said nothing. Her long flaxen hair was coiled up in a thick plait at the top of her head. Willie gazed with pleasure at her soft, pink-cheeked face then suddenly his heart fell.

She leaned over to Zach and said, 'Now, Zacharias.'

'You can call me Zach if it's too much of a mouthful.'

'I think I can manage, thank you. Now tell me, what were you doing at your last school? You can read and write, can't you?'

At this juncture, Willie's ears filled up. Zach's chattering was only a faint rumbling echo in the distance. He felt her hand on his shoulder.

'Now, William,' she said. 'How about you? Can you read and write?'

He remained silent. He didn't dare look at the others. What would they think of him?

'What did you say, William?'

'No,' he answered, and he picked at one of the nails on his fingers and stared at the floorboards wishing he could disappear into them.

'Oh, I'm sorry about that, William. I would have liked

you in my class. You'll have to go and sit with Mrs Black's class,' and she pointed to the little ones seated on the floor. Willie looked up in anguish and quickly down again.

The burning inside his ears seemed to spread into his jaw. He rose as if in a daze, found a space on the floor and sat down. He clasped his hands tightly together and bowed his head. He felt utterly humiliated.

Mrs Hartridge's class were dismissed. They were to have school in the afternoons and wouldn't be starting until Friday.

Willie was left with Mrs Black and she and the remaining children filed over to the school. There were two girls even older than him who also couldn't read, but it didn't make him feel any better. One of them ignored everyone including Mrs Black and just filed her nails and stared out of the window.

Tom was weeding the graveyard when Willie returned. He watched his dejected figure walk past him into the cottage and, after allowing a few minutes to elapse, followed him in and discovered him sitting at the table in the living room, his bag of apples and sandwich lying untouched.

'I could just do with a cuppa,' he said brightly. 'You too, William?'

Willie gave a nod.

He pushed a mug of tea towards him. 'How was it then?'

Willie scraped the toes of his boots together.

'Bad, was it?'

Willie nodded.

'Best tell me then.'

He raised his head. It was difficult to look at Tom

without his lips trembling.

'I'm with the babies.'

'Oh, and whose class is Zacharias in then?'

'Mrs Hartridge's.'

'Why ent you? You're near enuff the same age, ent you?'

'Yeh, but he can read.' He paused. 'And write.'

'And the ones that can't are with Mrs Black, that it?'

'Yeh.'

'I see.'

Tom stood up and looked out at the freshly weeded graveyard.

'Mrs Black'll teach you to read. Did you learn anythin' today?'

'Gas drill,' he mumbled.

'What's that?'

'Gas drill,' he repeated, only louder. 'We did gas-mask drill.'

He blew the top of his tea and sipped it.

'There ain't even enuff pencils.'

Tom had seen some of the roughnecks that gentle old Mrs Black would have to deal with. Most of her time, he reckoned, would be taken up trying to keep discipline.

'We'll begin this evenin',' he said sharply. 'That do?'

'Wot?'

'Learnin' to read and write. I'll teach you to write yer own name fer a beginnin'.'

Willie's eyes stung as the ground moved in a gentle haze beneath him. He beamed. 'Aw, mister,' was all he could manage to say.

Tom was surprised to find a lump in his own throat.

'Go and have a run with Sammy,' he growled huskily. 'I'll get supper.'

Sammy, who had sensed Willie's misery and had until now remained motionless, began to bark and run after his tail.

'Go on with you, boy,' said Tom.

Willie rose and clattered down the hallway. He ran through the gate, down the lane and across to the dirt track faster and faster, leaping and jumping. He wanted to yell for joy but when he tried he couldn't get any sound out. He felt annoyed at first but then he realized that he was running far better than he had been the previous day and that he wasn't even trying. It takes time and practice, that's what Mister Tom had said.

After supper had been cleared Tom put a piece of paper and a pencil in front of him. On the paper were several straight lines and in between each pair was a series of dots.

'Now, William,' said Tom. 'You jest join up the dots from the top downwards and when you done that, yous'll have written yer name. Now jest takes yer own time.'

Willie held the pencil nervously and then pressed it hard on to the paper. The lead snapped. Tom sharpened it again.

'Easy now,' he said, handing him back the pencil. 'You got plenty of time.'

Willie stared frantically at the paper.

'I can't,' he said, 'I can't.'

Tom looked sharply at him. Willie was frightened. His face had turned quite pale and beads of perspiration had broken out across his forehead.

'I won't beat you, if that's what's bothering you. Come on, let's have a go,' he added reassuringly. 'I'll sit beside you and tell you how yer doin'.'

Willie placed the lead on to the paper and slowly

followed the dots down and up, down and up, making the letter W.

He sat back and looked at it.

'It's bad, ain't it? Ain't it, Mister Tom?'

Tom peered at it. He was surprised.

'No,' he said with honesty. 'No, it ent,' and Willie knew by the certainty in his voice that he was telling the truth.

'Ain't it?' he queried.

'No,' he repeated. 'It certainly ent. You carry on. You'se doin' fine.'

Willie returned to the dots and apart from the occasional wobble he wrote 'William' in a remarkably smooth hand.

'That's good,' said Tom.

'Is it?'

'Do it again.'

Willie carried on following the dots between the lines and then stopped.

'Mister Tom,' he said. 'I can look at my name and draw it. Is writin' like drawin'?'

'I don't think so. Show me what you mean.'

Willie found a clean unlined space, looked at what he'd done, drew two straight lines and wrote William in between them.

'Those lines are almost straight,' gasped Tom. 'Where you learn to do that?'

'Nowhere,' said Willie. 'I jest looked at 'em and done it.'

Tom was speechless for a moment. When he had re-covered, he picked up a pencil and ruler, drew two straight lines, wrote 'Beech' in between them and handed the pencil to Willie.

Willie drew the two lines again and, while carefully scrutinizing the new word, copied it.

'That's very good,' remarked Tom.

'Is it?'

'Don't you know?'

He shook his head.

'You've jest written yer name, boy.'

'Have I?' and he stared down at the letters. He couldn't understand why those shapes were his name. Tom took his hand and made him point to the letters, going from left to right, sounding out each one. Willie joined in the second time round.

'Good,' said Tom. He was about to suggest that he had a break when Willie pointed to the letters and sounded them out on his own. He became stuck at the double ee sound.

'Wot was that one agin, Mister Tom?'

'ee.'

'B . . . ee . . .'

'Wot's that?'

'ch.'

He started again and succeeded in sounding all the letters through.

'You picked that up very quick,' said Tom. 'Very quick.'

'It's copyin', though, ain't it?'

'Yes, I suppose so.'

'Mister Tom,' said Willie after some thought, 'ain't that bad?'

'Copyin'?'

'Yeh.'

'Not when yer learnin',' said Tom, 'only if yer bein' tested, like.'

'Oh,' he said, 'I thought it were bad.'

There was a knock on the front door. Sam started barking.

'Now who can that be?' said Tom.

'Mister Tom?' said Willie. 'Does that mean that, if I copy, I won't go to hell?'

'Hell!!' said Tom in amazement as he strode out of the room. 'Don't be daft, boy. Whatever put such a thought in yer head.'

Willie felt enormously relieved and returned to his writing. He was interrupted by voices in the hallway. He turned, and George and the twins walked in.

'Before you ses anythin',' said Carrie as Willie stood up, crimson, 'we've jest come to tell you that we're miserable about you not being in our class and that we still wants you to come round with us like.'

'Yes,' interjected Ginnie.

'And,' said George, 'yer not to feel bad about not bein' able to read and that. Anyway, it ent all that good when you can. You jest gits given more lessons.'

Carrie, at this juncture, gave him a poke.

'What we wanted to tell you,' she continued, 'was that we'se goin' up the woods on Saturdee and we was wonderin' if you'd come with us like.'

Willie opened his mouth to speak but was interrupted by another loud knock. Tom was hardly out into the hallway when in burst Zach.

'Will,' he said breathlessly and stopped in midstream. 'I say, what's going on here? Is this a party?'

Tom closed the door and was about to speak when a further rally of knocks was hammered on it and Charlie Ruddles, the warden, strode angrily in.

'The front door wuz open, Mr Oakley, and I saw a definite chink of light from where I wuz situated.'

'Oh, and where would that be, Mr Ruddles?' asked Tom, a little perturbed at so many dramatic entrances in one evening. 'Would that be from lying on the hall floor with yer nose under the door?'

The twins at this point turned hurriedly away and bit their lips. Charlie stood back aghast.

'I won't go into the legalities, Mr Oakley. There were a definite chink. Don't you know there's a war on!' and with that he slammed the door and everyone except for Willie, who was feeling somewhat stunned, erupted into gales of laughter.

# VIVIEN ALCOCK

FROM *The Sylvia Game*

The Sylvia Game. It sounded harmless: not like a game that would nearly cause the death of one boy and lead to the banishment of the other. Two small boys in a large, lonely house, inventing an imaginary companion; choosing from the long line of portraits in the gallery, Sylvia Mallerton, the girl who had drowned in the lake when she was only twelve.

'She was always wet,' said Kevin, 'that had to be part of it. "Excuse me, Sylvia," we'd say, "you've gone and got a poor little goldfish tangled up in your hair." We was only kids,' he added, catching sight of Emily's face, 'you couldn't expect us to cry over her. It was just a game.'

They'd tell her off for dripping water all over the polished floors, pretend to pluck weeds from her invisible skirts, and frogs from her ears. Any mud or mess they brought into the house, they'd blame on her.

'Sylvia did it! It wasn't us! It was Sylvia!' they'd claim, pointing to an empty chair, until the grown-ups got thoroughly sick of it.

Lady Mallerton wanted them to stop playing the game; thought it was morbid. But Kevin's mother, down in the servants' hall, said it was only natural. Boys would be boys, and anyway, it was that Nanny, filling their heads with her stories.

For nearly three years, the imaginary girl presided

over their games. Sometimes as their older sister, sometimes as a princess, she'd sit, wringing the water from
her wet, white skirts; and issuing imperious commands.
Or so Oliver said.

'The things she'd have us do!' said Kevin, 'Dangerous!
I tell you straight, I wouldn't do them now, not if you
paid me! See these scars —' he rolled back his sleeve to
show her the thin white lines on his brown arm, 'got
those falling through the conservatory roof. And that
'un,' he showed her the palm of his hand, 'that's when
we tried to kidnap old Farley's peacock. Got him in the
old tennis net – peck! He fair skewered my hand! Then
there was the time I had to tie red ribbons on the horns
of Blair's bull . . .'

'Didn't Oliver do anything?' asked Emily indignantly.
'Why did it have to be you all the time?'

'Oh, he took his turn, fair enough. Only I couldn't
never think up anything fancy like that. Only ordinary
things, like climbing trees or scrumping apples. He was
the one with ideas.'

'And you were the mug who carried them out.'

'It was a dare, see? If you didn't do what she said,
she'd come and get you in the night. She used to creep
out of her picture frame when the house was asleep, and
go down to the lake to lie among the water-lilies. But if
you refused a dare, she'd come back and tap on your
window – like this!' He knocked softly three times on
the wall beside him, 'So's you'd know she was coming
for you. Then, next minute, she'd be there, leaning over
the bed, all white and staring. She'd spill dirty water
over you, and toads and dead fish. She'd bind you up
tight with weeds so you couldn't move, and stuff your
mouth with mud so you couldn't scream . . . The times I

lay in my bed, with the sheets up to my eyes, listening to a branch on the window, tap . . . tap . . . tap.'

'The little beast!'

But he shook his head. He had forgotten his anger; his face showed nothing but old affection and amusement. He was a good friend to have, thought Emily. She could never forgive anyone who'd spoken of her like that! Never!

'It was only the game,' he said tolerantly. 'Funny thing,' went on Kevin, 'he frightened himself most. He come to believe it. Many a night he'd wake up screaming – "She's coming for me! She's coming for me!" Annie said it made her blood run cold to hear him.'

'Annie?'

'Annie Larkin, the upstairs maid. I slept in the servants' wing, see, so I never heard him myself. Fair curdled her blood, she said. Poor old Oliver. Mum always said they'd drive him mad between them. That old witch with her tales, and Lady Mallerton fussing over him every time he sneezed, and Sir Robert trying to make a man of him.'

He paused for a moment, gazing into the fire; then said, 'D'you think you can *make* things happen? Just by saying them, by thinking them hard enough – like you sort of created them?'

'No,' said Emily. But she remembered Tim had been afraid you could – claimed that their father had told him so.

'That's what I said when he asked me. No, I said, that's silly. But – he always said as how she was awaiting him. Down in the lake. She damn near got him in the end.'

The last time they played the Sylvia Game was in the

summer holidays. When he was eight, Oliver had gone away to his prep school, and Kevin to the local Primary. Before that, they had both been taught at Mallerton House by a Miss Tott, who'd come in the mornings. Kevin's mother had not been happy about this, thinking it would be harder for Kevin later, joining the Primary as a new boy when all the other kids had been together for years, but she'd been talked round.

'Don't go thinking you and Master Oliver can be proper friends,' she'd warned Kevin, 'you're useful to them now he's got nobody else. But once he goes off to his posh school, he'll make friends with his own kind, and then it'll be – "Clean my shoes, Kevin!" or "Oil my cricket bat!" or "You fetch the balls while I play tennis with little Lord What's-it." He'll drop you, son. He'll not mean to, but that's the way the world goes. The more shame on us all for it!'

Kevin had not believed her.

'And it wasn't like that,' he said. Then, catching Emily's eye, he flushed a deep painful red, remembering, as she did, Oliver's cruel, careless words. 'No, it wasn't, not then!' he said defiantly. 'He was pleased to see me. He was jumping with joy to be back at Mallerton!'

Oliver had not said much about his new school. Kevin had got the impression he was unhappy there. Certainly he was delighted to be back home again. They had spent the long, dusty summer days together, and it was just as it had always been, except that they had not played their old game. Not until the last day, when Oliver had suddenly said he wanted to say goodbye to Sylvia.

'We'll take the boat out to the lilies,' he'd said, 'that's where she'll be, lying at the bottom with the fish swimming in and out of her eyes.'

Kevin had been unwilling. He had grown out of the game; it was kid's stuff. Besides it always landed him in trouble. He pointed out that Oliver was wearing his new trousers and Nanny would skin him if he got them wet and muddy. But it was no good. Oliver had his way. He always did.

It was Kevin who had rowed out to the water-lilies, he who had handed the oars to Oliver, telling him to keep the boat steady; — and Oliver who had jerked the boat, so that Kevin had fallen in.

'He was laughing. He done it on purpose, a'course. He stood up in the boat, holding the oars and calling out, "Look behind you, Kevin! She's coming for you!" So I grabbed hold of the oar and pulled him in too. I didn't see why I should be the only one to get wet. But — but he got caught in the weeds! It must've been just the weeds, mustn't it? I thought I'd never get him free, thought we'd both drown! It was like something — someone — was holding him down. But I got him in the end. I won!'

It was a doubtful victory. Oliver had been ill for weeks. The water had got on his chest and he'd nearly died. Kevin and his mother had been asked to leave.

# RACHEL ANDERSON

FROM *The Poacher's Son*

There was a sick heavy feeling in my stomach when I heard the sound of that mournful bell tolling out across the fields. It was like a death sentence. I couldn't face the bread and dripping Ma had set out for breakfast. But with Pa home, there was no chance to feign illness.

Slowly, reluctantly, I took up my dinner and my two pence for Mr Pooley, my penny for the slate and my halfpenny for the pencil, and set out with Alice and Humphrey. It seemed madness to spend good money paying for me to go where I didn't want to be. I kicked at the new grass springing up in the lane. I walked slower and slower. The school bell seemed to clang faster and faster.

Alice waited for me to catch up and then pulled my arm. 'Please keep up, Arthur! We'll be late. You know Mr Pooley hates us being late.'

It was against Governor's rules to be late. Lateness was marked against your name in the black book, and the Governors saw it. The rector was a Governor. So was his lordship, though he didn't go to Governors' meetings. He was always busy.

'You go on, Alice. I'll catch up,' I said and stopped altogether. Four rooks circled overhead and then moved lazily towards the thicket behind our cottage. They seemed to beckon me.

'*No! Please*, Arthur, You know you won't,' Alice
begged.

I didn't want to disappoint her. I didn't want my
name entered in the black book. But still less did I want
to suffer a whole dragging day's boredom, a whole seven
hours of frustration and humiliation in that stuffy over-
crowded hall, sitting on the bench with tiny children half
my size, always being shown up for the dunce.

A soft wind ruffled the wheat seedlings in the field,
and white spring clouds drifted swiftly across the sky so
that the dark landscape was broken with sudden streaks
of brightness.

'Why must I?'

'You know perfectly well why!' said Alice sharply.
She sounded for a moment like our Ma. 'Because it's the
law.'

There hadn't been a law when my Pa was a boy. He
had been free to leave school when he was twelve.

'And so you can learn to *read*.'

For six years, Mr Pooley had been trying. Alice was
still trying. But there was no reason why, after all this
time, someone should suddenly be able to teach me now.

'You know I don't need to. I'm going to be a keeper
when they let me leave. Pa didn't read.'

Why should I still have to waste my days in school?
Mr Wilkins's son had already been apprenticed to a
keeper on a nearby estate. Why couldn't I?

Alice finally gave up persuading me. I watched her
hurry on down the lane, leaping and skipping over the
campion. As the death-knell stopped, I saw her take
Humphrey's hand and they ran helter-skelter towards the
village. I knew that I could trust her. She would make
some excuse.

'He's sick today, sir. He's needed home helping with the heavy work. Dad won't have the twopence to spare this week, sir. He's got no boots, sir. He's gone tatering, sir.'

They were all excuses made by other children, less fortunate than ourselves.

I skirted the edge of the wheatfield and saw a partridge hen followed by four of her young, bobbing between the green stalks. Then up to Pit Bottom wood behind our cottage. All the country around here had to be explored and discovered so that I could know every branch, every distorted limb, every hollow and grassy path so that I could hold them as my own, just as I had possessed Great Wood.

As I entered the wood, I broke through a new web spun between two bushes. It was so fine I could not see it and it was only as I felt the invisible stickiness stroke against my cheeks and saw the blowflies dangling in mid-air, that I realized I had destroyed the spider's food source. I climbed a young oak on the edge of the wood, settled myself comfortably into the curved arm of the tree to listen, to watch, and to become part of the life of the wood. A woodpigeon, startled by my arrival, settled down again on the branch immediately above to preen. So long as I stayed still, there was little chance that he would see me. A pigeon, once perched, rarely looks straight down.

From that height, I could see right across the fields as far as the village, where the low blueish shapes of the dwellings and the church and the school stood out against the brown and green of the fields.

I wondered if perhaps Humphrey was standing in for me, to call out for me when the register was taken. He had done so before now, answering to both his name and mine so that my absences – as recorded in the black book – did not seem quite as many as really they were. With nearly forty children in his care, from little 'uns of barely five years, up to big boys of going on fourteen, Mr Pooley was often confused.

Humphrey was three years younger than me, but I was small for my age and we both had the same bright hair and red cheeks. Many people took us for the same person, so long as they didn't see us together.

I looked away from the village and back up into the wood. Already Humphrey could read and write better than I could. He had passed his Standard 3 last year. Perhaps he would end up with brains as good as Alice, and then, like her, he might become a teacher. If that happened, I should certainly be proud of him, but it wouldn't make me envy him.

With my catapult, I shot a crow for sport. I picked up the corpse and fastened it to a fence, alongside six dead weasels whose shrivelled skins flapped in the breeze like grey washing.

I watched a kestrel hover, sizing up a creature in the rough grass below. It plummeted like a dropped stone, caught nothing and within moments, was up again, quivering in the same spot, as though that piece of sky was visibly marked. It waited and swooped four times before it finally caught its prey and made off to the privacy of the woods.

All day, sounds of school drifted up from the village. At intervals, I heard the shouts of children released into the yard, the slam of a door, a distant wavering of a handbell, then silence. At school, children had to do everything by the bell, whether or not they were ready.

Here, time did not rule my day. When I was hungry, I dropped down from the tree, like the kestrel to the ground, and found a place to eat. Our dokey on school-days was always the same. Two pieces of bread spread thickly with dripping. It tasted rich and salty and, though not as filling as a proper hot meal, the pork taste reminded you of the supper you had had the night before, and more important of the hot meal you were going to get in the evening.

The poor prisoners in school had to eat their dokey sitting at their desks. I ate mine in the comfort of an old hayrick. If they were thirsty, they had to ask permission to go out to the pump.

I lay down on the grass and drank from the stream. I trailed my hands amongst the weeds, I tried to catch water-snails on a blade of grass. I smelled the sweet smell of crushed watercress that grew all along the bank.

I didn't like its sharp mustardy taste, but Ma and Pa did, so I gathered a big armful to give to them. Then I remembered, and threw it back into the stream and watched it drift away downstream like a green swan's nest. To take it back would show where I had spent the day.

It had been a good day, as were all days spent in the woods. I was cheerful and confident as I made my way back across the fields to meet up with Alice and Humphrey on their way home from school.

Pit Bottom was isolated, I did not have to be as careful to keep myself hidden as I used to be round Keeper's Lodge. Without even checking to see if the lane was deserted, I slithered down through a gap in the black-thorn and tumbled on to the track.

I could not have chosen my moment worse. The lane was not deserted.

I thought for a moment, I hoped, that the dark figure, scruffy and mottled-black like a starling, might have his back towards me and be striding *away* down the lane. But I could see his eyes, dark and beady, swivelling. And he was coming directly towards me, the Bible under his arm. My heart stopped beating as I hesitated, wasting precious seconds. I would run for it, make a clean getaway before he should see who I was. But unlike the partridge, I would never get across the open wheatfield, unseen. I scrambled back up the bank, and under the hedge, but not quickly enough. He had seen me. He ran, on his thin black legs like a bird. He caught up with me, grabbed my ankle, and hauled me backwards out through the blackthorn twigs.

'In trying to hide, you make your truancy all too obvious. Name? Your name, boy?'

I seemed to have lost my voice. I trembled. I shuffled uneasily. My hands were scratched. I tried to will myself away. I tried to pull up my shoulders, stand tall so that I might seem to be older, a farmboy returning from work. The rector was never fooled. He had the dark shiny eyes of a starling that swivelled slyly and saw everything. He would tell a boy's age even from a distance.

'Your name. What is your name?'

Why did the rector insist on hearing my name? He knew well enough who I was, or certainly ought to. Perhaps he enjoyed the power he gained by constantly asking one's name. Or perhaps the inhabitants of his parish really *did* look to him exactly the same, one totally indistinguishable from the next, just like the sheep of the fold that he constantly told us we were supposed to be.

His long strong fingers clutched hold of my shoulders like yellow claws, and without warning he shook me backwards and forwards, again and again.

The world in front of my eyes was quite dizzy from the shaking. The rector banged me on the side of the head with his Bible, first one side, then the other.

'Betts, sir.'

'Ah! So you can speak now? I met a boy called Betts in school today.'

'My brother Humphrey, sir. He is coming up the lane now, sir.'

'So there are two boys by the name of Betts?'

'There are three, sir.'

'And does the third Betts also truant?'

'No, sir. Pa says that he won't ever be able to go to school, sir.'

'And why not, may I ask? Does your father not know that according to the law he is obliged to send his sons regularly to school, or risk imprisonment of up to twenty-one days? Does he not know that schooling has been provided so that children may have a little learning, and become less dull than they mostly are?'

'Yes, sir.'

'Yes, sir? What do you mean by Yes, sir? Does your father wilfully keep your brother away from school?'

'My brother Jonas was born an idiot, sir.'

For once I felt grateful to Jonas. By talking about Jonas, the rector would forget about my misdeeds.

'Jonas Betts, aha yes. Unfortunate creature.' The rector rolled his eyes to the sky. 'May the Lord have mercy on him.'

Of course the rector knew who I was, who Jonas was. He had refused to baptize Jonas, saying that a cretin had no soul and therefore no need of baptism. Ma had cried. Pa became so angry that in the end the rector had been forced to baptize Jonas, out of fear that Pa would knock him down.

'Betts, how old are you?'

'Nearly fourteen, sir,' I said, with a lowered voice, while pulling up my shoulders and standing tall.

'You are a liar, Betts.'

'Yes, sir.'

'Your father is a liar too. Evil runs in the blood. Game-keepers tend, by nature of their work, towards cunning. You may tell him that if he does nothing to punish you for your deceit and truancy, I shall be forced to see to it myself.' I had once seen the rector punish a boy for blasphemy. I did not want to be punished by him.

'Remember, Betts, the eyes of the Lord are in every place. He can see even into your very heart.'

He finally released me, and made off on his black legs towards old Widow Craske's hovel.

# MARGARET MAHY

'I'm being haunted and I don't know why!' Barney
burst out. 'It's been going on for two days now.'
And he told her about the boy in blue velvet meeting
him on the way home from school and about the picture
of the same boy in the old scrapbook. As he told his
story he could feel his fear edging around him, but it was
eased away by Tabitha's presence and by her sharp interest. He felt lighter and freer, almost ordinary again.

'Hey! Wow!' breathed Tabitha at last. 'That's completely weird. Are you sure you're not making it up?'

'You made me tell you and now you don't believe
me,' Barney said indignantly. 'Look – I wouldn't make
up something I hate so much, would I?'

'You *did* faint,' Tabitha pondered. 'That's a sort of
proof. You weren't pretending about *that*. What did the
ghost say? "Barnaby's dead! I'm going to be so lonely."'

'Very lonely,' corrected Barney. 'And that's what's
written in the scrapbook.'

'I like so lonely better,' complained Tabitha. 'If I were
a ghost, that's what I'd say: "sssooooooooo lonely" –
like that. But listen – there's something *you* don't know.
While they were all saying goodbye and worrying about
the tea stain on the carpet, I sneaked a quick look at that
old scrapbook and I found the page with that picture on
it because I wanted to read exactly what it had written.'
Tabitha paused.

'Did you read it?' Barney asked, to hurry her up.

'Well, it wasn't there. There was the picture all right – that was real – but there wasn't any writing, no smudges, no ink, no anything.' She looked at Barney enviously.

'Gosh, I wish it were happening to me,' she cried. 'It's wasted on you. You're scared of it. And here's me long-ing for life to be mysterious, and it just goes on day after day being all dull and ordinary. I have to *force* it to be interesting.'

'I'd let you have my ghost, if I could,' Barney answered. 'I don't want it. I want things to stay still for a bit and just be ordinary. I don't get bored.'

'Well, I must go and think about this,' Tabitha said. 'If you have bad dreams you can come and get into bed with me. Don't just lie there suffering.' She went to the door, suddenly came back, gave him a clumsy hug and kissed him on the ear and then hurried out shutting the door after her.

Barney looked after her in surprise, thinking how dif-ferent family kisses were from one another. Tabitha had hugged and kissed him as if she had run out of words and had been practising with some new way of talking to him. Then he began to think about the possibility of having bad dreams, which he had not thought of before. With frightening memories behind him, and dreams wait-ing on ahead, he felt as if he were besieged and sighed heavily into his pillow. After Claire had come in and read him a story, kissed him goodnight and turned the light out, he lay in the darkness trying not to think either backwards or forwards. Instead he closed his eyes and tried to make sleep come quickly. It wasn't his usual drowsy drifting but a watchful sentry-duty sort of wait-ing. A dream might come and refuse to give the password. Then he could drive it away. The darkness behind his eyelids was streaked with lights like dim, slow fireworks going off, and it was impossible to feel sleepy. A face flashed into his mind and was gone again, but he knew the face well. It was the face in a photograph of his mother Dove, which stood on the dressing-table in Troy's room. Barney wondered if it was Dove who was haunting him, perhaps angry because he had grown so fond of Claire. However he could not really believe she would mind. She looked too cheerful for that. And anyway, because of the message, he was certain that he was being haunted because Great-Uncle Barnaby had died. Something was being required of him, but he could not think what it might be.

'It's no use bothering about it,' he told himself sternly and saw his own words float by, lighting up his shut-eyed darkness with letters of fire.

'Think different!' he commanded his anxious mind. 'Different!' he said aloud, to hear his own determination. It was very convincing and he opened his eyes to clear his head by staring into the real outside darkness. The rockets and the fiery letters vanished. 'A circus!' he commanded, and shut his eyes again. No circus came into his head, but something nearly as good, for he found himself remembering a Punch and Judy show he had once seen.

Pink and white curtains flew open and Punch squeaked and waved a stick. Barney made himself remember Judy, the baby, a crocodile and a policeman. His memories began to run out and he was still not asleep. But somehow he could not stop watching the Punch and Judy show. The tiny curtains swept closed and then opened again on another scene – not on a puppet play but on a real place, one that Barney had never seen before. This was not something from his own mind, but something that someone was deliberately showing him. Barney was being haunted again.

It seemed to be not night but early morning between the pink and white curtains. There were hills and dark trees and a road winding towards him. Along the road a solitary figure moved at a steady, dogged pace. He could hear footsteps like the tick of a clock, the beat of a heart, but the face was shadowy and hard to see. Barney could not tell whether the person was a man or a woman, but something about its shoulders and its way of walking reminded him of a shorter, angrier version of Great-Uncle Guy. It stopped and stared out between the curtains.

'So there you are,' it said. It was a pleasant, light, husky voice and seemed to come from inside Barney's head and not from outside in his bedroom. It was a man's voice and one he was sure he had not heard before. 'I'm on my way, you see. We belong together – you and I.'

Barney still could not see the face that belonged to that rustling voice.

'I belong here,' he whispered back. 'This is where my family is – Dad and Claire and Troy and Tabitha. I belong here.'

'You may think you do,' the voice replied, 'but you'll find that, in the end, there's no place in a family for people like us. It is a discovery we all make. You are taking longer to realize it than I did, that's all.'

Barney tried to open his eyes, but they would not open. He was not asleep, but the treacherous lids stayed shut, obeying someone else's wishes.

'You obviously don't realize just what you are yet,'

the voice said doubtfully. 'You are a Scholar magician, don't you understand?'

'I'm a boy,' Barney said stubbornly. 'Just a boy.'

'*I* know,' the voice went on. 'I can feel you there. I can see you. You're like a line of crimson across the world's rainbow. You're the strongest of us all.'

'Who are you?' hissed Barney wildly.

'I'm coming,' the voice said, not answering his question, perhaps not even hearing it. 'I could be there now, this minute, but I'll travel slowly so that you'll have time to get used to the idea of me. You'll get my messages. I'll share my journey with you.'

The figure thrust a hand towards him, not threateningly, but as if it wanted to show him something it held. However, the hand was empty. Barney saw long fingers and a palm lined like a map of some unknown continent. Then the fingers branched like twigs, put out green leaves and blossomed pink and white. From between them flew little scarlet birds, no bigger than bumblebees. The pink and white curtains closed and Barney was free to open his eyes again.

He was frightened, but only in a very tired way. If he got up and scrambled into bed with Tabitha she would ask him questions and talk all night. What he really wanted was to tell Claire and hear her voice, warm and cool at the same time, reassure him that there was nothing to worry about, as she went off to do something about it. But he dared not bother her. He knew that when mothers were expecting babies they should have simple, happy lives and not be alarmed with ideas that their children were haunted or perhaps mad. And though his father was closer and kinder than he had been before he married Claire (in those days he had always seemed to be going to work or coming home from it) he was still somebody Barney was not sure about ... a jolly man who might turn out to be not very interested in his children in the long run. As it happened, Barney had only a few minutes to think about this, for suddenly he knew that sleep had crept up on him and taken him by surprise.

'I must be getting used to ghosts,' he thought. 'It shows you that you can get used to anything,' and a moment later he sank thankfully into a kind of darkness without any dreams to trouble him.

# JANE GARDAM

FROM *Kit*

The weather was so wonderful that after six days of cutting and baling the hay, it was dry and sweet as lavender bags and The Kit's father said, 'There's miracles about. I've never known a year like it. We can elevate tomorrow.'

Elevating is lifting the hay blocks up into the stone barns for winter. Rich farmers – most farmers – have electric, caterpillarish machines for this and it is easy; but poor farmers have to toss the blocks up with a fork from a pick-up below. It is very hard work and gets harder as you get nearer the end, because the smaller the pile gets in the farm-yard, the higher you have to toss it up. The Kit's father took over the hardest work right up to the finish, but, when it was nearly all done, The Kit and her mother who had been catching and stacking, which is very hard, too, looked out of the high barn door above his head with sore eyes and sneezing noses and aching arms and pitiable faces.

'What's this then?' said he.

'We're done. We can't finish. We've got to stop stacking,' said The Kit's mother.

'Stand aside then,' he said, and he tossed up the last bales. 'Come on. Down the ladder and I'll up and finish them.'

They came down the ladder and up went he, and in the dark of the barn he heaved and jigsawed the last big, heavy bales of hay into place until all was tidy and safe, and the barn was full.

Then he took a step back to look at how beautiful it all was and fell out of the high barn door in to the farm-yard far below and broke his leg!

You never heard such a noise except perhaps from Geoffrey the bull when he'd been shut up in the hull too long in fine weather. The Kit's father was a big strong man and when he fell on anything it was usually the thing he fell on that broke, not he. But farm-yards don't break, and if this one had not still had a good layer of hay on it, more of The Kit's father than just his leg would have broken, and he wouldn't have been able to roar at all.

The Kit's mother rushed to the telephone while The Kit hugged Lisa tight, and chickens, sheep-dogs, calves and Geoffrey clamoured for their supper in vain.

Soon from far away, The Kit could see the ambulance coming and then ambulance men walked firmly across the yard with a stretcher.

'Take away that stretcher,' roared The Kit's father, 'I'm not leaving this farm.'

'You can't stay lying there in the hay,' said the ambulance men. 'You'll have broken something. You'll have to be X-rayed.'

'X-ray me here,' commanded The Kit's father with rolling, Geoffrey-like eyes, his beard twitching with rage and pain. The ambulance men talked together and went away, and soon another van was to be seen winding its way up the dale, with the Doctor's car ahead of it.

The Doctor took no notice at all of The Kit's father's roars – simply directed the X-ray men to help him into

the house with him. Then, after the X-ray men had taken the photographs to the van to develop, and a lot of telephoning had gone on, and The Kit's father had said about a hundred times that he would not leave the farm, the Doctor said, 'Very well – but if you stay here you'll not be able to move. Maybe not for six weeks. You'll have to be put in *traction*.'

'Tied in my bed?'

'Yes.'

'But where I can keep my eye on things?'

'We can really manage on our own –' said The Kit's mother.

'WHERE I CAN KEEP AN EYE ON THINGS?' roared The Kit's father.

'If you must,' said the Doctor, 'though I'm glad the telephone is half-way up the stairs, where you won't be able to get at it.'

'Put me in traction then,' he said, shutting his eyes and pointing his beard at the ceiling.

Then The Kit and Lisa and their mother went for a walk by the beck, far out of the way, and Lisa laughed the whole time and their mother cried and The Kit thought that this was being a very long day.

# DICK KING-SMITH

FROM *The Sheep-Pig*

Fly ran left up the slope as the sheep began to bunch above her. Once behind them, she addressed them in her usual way, that is to say sharply.

'Move, fools!' she snapped. 'Down the hill. If you know which way "down" is,' but to her surprise they did not obey. Instead they turned to face her, and some even stamped, and shook their heads at her, while a great chorus of bleating began.

To Fly sheep-talk was just so much rubbish, to which she had never paid any attention, but Babe, listening below, could hear clearly what was being said, and although the principal cry was the usual one, there were other voices saying other things. The contrast between the politeness with which they had been treated by yesterday's rescuer and the everlasting rudeness to which they were subjected by this or any wolf brought mutinous thoughts into woolly heads, and words of defiance rang out.

'You got no manners! . . . Why can't you ask nicely? . . . Treat us like muck, you do!' they cried, and one hoarse voice which the pig recognized called loudly, 'We don't want you, wolf! We want Babe!' whereupon they all took it up.

'We want Babe!' they bleated. 'Babe! Babe! Ba-a-a-a-a-be!'

Those behind pushed at those in front, so that they

actually edged a pace or two nearer the dog.

For a moment it seemed to Babe that Fly was not going to be able to move them, that she would lose this particular battle of wills; but he had not reckoned with her years of experience. Suddenly, quick as a flash, she drove in on them with a growl and with a twisting leap sprang for the nose of the foremost animal; Babe heard the clack of her teeth as the ewe fell over backwards in fright, a fright which immediately ran through all. Defiant no longer, the flock poured down the hill, Fly snapping furiously at their heels, and surged wildly through the gateway.

'No manners! No manners! No ma-a-a-a-a-nners!' they cried, but an air of panic ran through them as they realized how rebellious they had been. How the wolf would punish them! They ran helter-skelter into the middle of the paddock, and wheeled as one to look back, ears pricked, eyes wide with fear. They puffed and blew, and Ma's hacking cough rang out. But to their surprise they saw that the wolf had dropped by the gateway, and that after a moment the pig came trotting out to one side of them.

Though Farmer Hogget could not know what had caused the near-revolt of the flock, he saw clearly that for some reason they had given Fly a hard time, and that she was angry. It was not like her to gallop sheep in that pell-mell fashion.

'Steady!' he said curtly as she harried the rear-guard, and then 'Down!' and 'Stay!' and shut the gate. Shepherding suited Farmer Hogget – there was no waste of words in it.

In the corner of the home paddock nearest to the farm

buildings was a smallish fenced yard divided into a number of pens and runways. Here the sheep would be brought at shearing-time or to pick out fat lambs for market or to be treated for various troubles. Farmer Hogget had heard the old ewe cough; he thought he would catch her up and give her another drench. He turned to give an order to Fly lying flat and still behind him, and there, lying flat and still beside her, was the pig.

'Stay, Fly!' said Hogget. And, just for fun, 'Come, Pig!'

Immediately Babe ran forward and sat at the farmer's right, his front trotters placed neatly together, his big ears cocked for the next command.

Strange thoughts began to stir in Farmer Hogget's mind, and unconsciously he crossed his fingers.

He took a deep breath, and, holding it . . . 'Away to me, Pig!' he said softly.

Without a moment's hesitation Babe began the long outrun to the right.

Quite what Farmer Hogget had expected to happen, he could never afterwards clearly remember. What he had not expected was that the pig would run round to the rear of the flock, and turn to face it and him, and lie down instantly without a word of further command spoken, just as a well-trained dog would have done. Admittedly, with his jerky little rocking-horse canter he took twice as long to get there as Fly would have, but still, there he was, in the right place, ready and waiting. Admittedly, the sheep had turned to face the pig and were making a great deal of noise, but then Farmer Hogget did not know, and Fly would not listen to, what they were saying. He called the dog to heel, and began to walk with his long loping stride to the collecting-pen in

the corner. Out in the middle of the paddock there was a positive babble of talk.

'Good morning!' said Babe. 'I do hope I find you all well, and not too distressed by yesterday's experience?' and immediately it seemed that every sheep had something to say to him.

'Bless his heart!' they cried, and, 'Dear little soul!' and, 'Hullo, Babe!' and, 'Nice to see you again!' and then there was a rasping cough and the sound of Ma's hoarse tones.

'What's up then, young un?' she croaked. 'What be you doing here instead of that wolf?'

Although Babe wanted, literally, to keep on the right side of the sheep, his loyalty to his foster-mother made him say in a rather hurt voice, 'She's not a wolf. She's a sheep-dog.'

'Oh all right then,' said Ma, 'sheep-dog, if you must have it. What dost want, then?'

Babe looked at the army of long sad faces.

'I want to be a sheep-pig,' he said.

'Ha ha!' bleated a big lamb standing next to Ma. 'Ha ha ha-a-a-a-a!'

'Bide quiet!' said Ma sharply, swinging her head to give the lamb a thumping butt in the side. 'That ain't nothing to laugh at.'

Raising her voice, she addressed the flock.

'Listen to me, all you ewes,' she said, 'and lambs too. This young chap was kind to me, like I told you, when I were poorly. And I told him, if he was to ask me to go somewhere or do something, politely, like he would, why, I'd be only too delighted. We ain't stupid, I told him, all we do want is to be treated right, and we'm as bright as the next beast, we are.'

'We are!' chorused the flock. 'We are! We are! We a-a-a-a-a-are!'

'Right then,' said Ma. 'What shall us do, Babe?'

Babe looked across towards Farmer Hogget, who had opened the gate of the collecting-pen and now stood leaning on his crook, Fly at his feet. The pen was in the left bottom corner of the paddock, and so Babe expected, and at that moment got, the command 'Come by, Pig!' to send him left and so behind the sheep and thus turn them down towards the corner.

He cleared his throat. 'If I might ask a great favour of you,' he said hurriedly, 'could you all please be kind enough to walk down to the gate where the farmer is standing, and to go through it? Take your time, please, there's absolutely no rush.'

A look of pure contentment passed over the faces of the flock, and with one accord they turned and walked across the paddock, Babe a few paces in their rear.

Sedately they walked, and steadily, over to the corner, through the gate, into the pen, and then stood quietly waiting. No one broke ranks or tried to slip away, no one pushed or shoved, there was no noise or fuss. From the oldest to the youngest, they went in like lambs.

Then at last a gentle murmur broke out as everyone in different ways quietly expressed their pleasure.

'Babe!' said Fly to the pig. 'That was quite beautifully done, dear!'

'Thank you so much!' said Babe to the sheep. 'You did that so nicely!'

'Ta!' said the sheep. 'Ta! Ta! Ta-a-a-a-a-a! 'Tis a pleasure to work for such a little gennulman!' And Ma added, 'You'll make a wunnerful sheep-pig, young un, or my name's not Ma-a-a-a-a-a.'

As for Farmer Hogget, he heard none of this, so wrapped up was he in his own thoughts. He's as good as a dog, he told himself excitedly, he's better than a dog, than any dog! I wonder . . .!

'Good Pig,' he said.

Then he uncrossed his fingers and closed the gate.

# K. M. PEYTON

FROM '*Who Sir? Me Sir?*'

The cattle-truck moved down the concrete road across the industrial estate and came to a halt beside the knot of boys outside the refrigerator warehouse. Hoomey thought it was like one of those old war films with a bomber coming in to land along a bleak runway and all the ground-crew waiting to know the worst. With the gaunt warehouse and the high vista of derelict open space all round him, he sat on an oil drum, chewing gum. No old bomber pilot, making a forced landing with no wheels, on a load of unused bombs, could possibly have felt as bad as he did at the moment. Jazz and Gary and Bean stood silently beside him. Mr O'Malley, of the Parents' Association, having arrived to see what they had got for their money, stood with the rest of the interested parties, Mr Sylvester and Mrs Bean and Mr and Mrs Singh and quite a lot of the Sports Committee.

Mr Bean got down from the cab, grinning happily.

'Here we are an' all. Quite a reception committee, eh? Just what the doctor ordered! We got plenty to do, turning this lot into stables, an' all. Have a look at the horses first, shall we? Don't get too excited, I'm warning you! The money we got to spend – well, that's the way it is. Give 'em three months on a load of good grub and you won't know 'em.'

The eager parents advanced to undo the ramp.

Hoomey stood up, trying to look nonchalant. His knees felt funny – there really was something wrong with them, he thought, that clicking noise and the way they felt weak. If he were to go to the doctor and ask about it he might find out –

'Mind yer backs! Mind yer backs!'

An extremely large horse was towing Mr Bean down the ramp. It slithered on to the road, looked round for the nearest tuft of grass and made straight for it, pulling Mr Bean after it. Hoomey happened to be standing on the grass, thinking he was well out of it, saw the horse's great gobbling mouth advancing towards his ankles and leapt back, swallowing his chewing-gum. Speechless, he felt the rope halter pressed into his hand.

' 'E's taken a fancy to you, John mate. Let's make 'im yours, eh? Chose you like, didn't he? That's a boy.'

'*Christ!*' Gary said, staring.

The horse was devouring every clump of grass, thistles, docks, dandelions, sorrel and bindweed that its large upper lip quested upon, clearing the area like a council mower. It was brown, as far as Hoomey could see, and its ribs stuck out like his own, and its great projecting hip-bones were on a level with his head, sticking out like girders as if to hold the gaunt body together. Its legs were knobbled and scarred like old trees, and had some bleeding fresh cuts on them. Its head was aquiline, eyes bloodshot and wary. Hoomey stood paralysed, clutching the rope. The horse, moving to juicier thistles, lifted a great chipped hoof large as a soup-plate and put it down beside Hoomey's plimsoll. Hoomey leapt.

'It could break all your foot like that. It's bloody dangerous,' he whispered. 'Oh, jeez, I don't want it!'

'Yeah, well, you got it, didn't you?' Jazz said. 'Whacko for you. I hope mine's prettier.'

'Circus mare,' Mr Bean grinned. 'Just the thing for you, lad. Make a right pair, you will. Feed 'er up, get a gold lamé turban and you could be back in the ring with 'er no time at all.'

Jazz scowled. Mr Bean's mate was bringing out an extraordinary white horse covered in black spots. It wasn't as large as Hoomey's, but was as thin, and without its companion's extraordinary capacity for ground-clearing. It sniffed at the ground and stood, dejected, motionless. Jazz took its halter. A faint recollection of his great-grandfather's photograph on the quivering, shining, warrior pony came into his mind.

'You don't see one like that every day!' Mr Bean said cheerfully. 'What do you think?'

'Just as well, if you ask me.'

Nutty, unnoticed, had joined the group on Midnight, and sat surveying the new horseflesh without enthusiasm. Her Midnight, gleaming, keen, delicately mothering his bit with impatience at being asked to stand still, under-lined the contrast in quality. She knew it, and said, with the quick tact of the born captain, 'Well, it's what you make of them. Midnight was a pretty tatty beast when we bought him. You can't expect them to be anything *yet*, straight from – well –' Better not underline their intended destination before being deflected by Uncle Knacker.

Gary and Bean were looking understandably nervous by now, their eyes fixed hypnotically on the ramp of the horse-box. Even Mr Bean looked slightly apprehensive.

'Might be a bit of trouble. Keep clear. Bit nervous, this one. Bin in bad 'ands. Needs a bit of lovin', you could say.'

There was a lot of crashing from inside the box, which rocked sympathetically. A shout and a lot of bad language.

'Mind yerselves then!'

A horse came down the ramp in one bound, as if on wings, hit the concrete in a shower of sparks. It wheeled round, took in the scene with dark, terrified eyes, and stood trembling. It was covered in sweat, and was more presentable than the others in looks, but far less so in demeanour. Both Gary and Bean took a step backwards. Even the parents looked worried this time – probably thinking of legal liabilities, Hoomey thought. He felt fanatically encouraged that this wasn't to be his horse. Mrs Bean stepped forward and said, 'You're not giving that to our David.' Her voice was full of authority, and Mr Bean hesitated.

'Gary, it's only frightened because of the journey. It's the best by miles. Take it.' Nutty slipped off Midnight's back, gave the reins to her uncle and went forward and took the creature's halter. She stroked its neck, led it away from the interested crowd and over to the grass. It went in a series of bounds, its eyes showing white, flecks of foam scattering from its lips.

'Poor sweetie,' Nutty said gently.

'Not you. She means the horse,' Bean said to Gary.

Gary was as frightened as the horse. Hoomey thought he could easily start frothing at the mouth, the way his colour had drained. Himself, he felt better and better. His horse was quite normal compared with the other two, only large and hungry, quite acceptable characteristics. He was keeping his feet well out of the way, following where his horse ate. He thought he would soon be out of sight.

'I'll hold it for you,' Nutty said to Gary. 'Don't worry. It'll settle. It's just upset.'

She was the only one encouraged by this choice of Uncle Knacker's, recognizing the touch of class she desired. It was the only horse so far which was the right size and the right shape – or perhaps it was only the spots that detracted from Jazz's mount. You couldn't really see the shape of the spots. But this one . . .

'It'll be nice when it's calmed down. You're lucky.'

'I want to live.'

'I thought you liked trouble?' Nutty spoke with some asperity, not encouraged by the marked lack of enthusiasm her team was displaying. God help her, as if there weren't problems enough . . .' The last horse, Bean's own, stood half-way down the ramp, surveying his reception committee with benign, sleepy eyes. He would move no further, his front hooves clamped down hard, his underlip drooping, his tail clamped in. He was a very large, skinny, washed-out chestnut. Nutty, picturing in her mind the agility required of the cross-country performer, ground her teeth with frustration. Sam Sylvester, she thought, you've something to answer for! She glowered at him, but he was chatting up Mrs O'Malley, looking perfectly at ease. It wasn't possible, she thought! Hoomey was being towed along over the field by an animal that was scarcely recognizable as a horse, so thin and sway-backed as it was. Some figures were coming up from the road to meet him, a girl and a couple of boys. Frowning dreadfully, Nutty struggled with her reluctant sight to recognize the faintly familiar figures . . . yes, her sister Gloria and – no, it couldn't be? – yes, it was! – Sebastian Smith and Antony Royd. Spying. The rats! She'd give Gloria a piece of her mind when she got home! Come to laugh, no doubt, and what a splendid opportunity they were being presented with! Grinning as they approached – as well they might – pretending they were just passing by, brimming with glee, big muscular athletic boys. She had seen them on their expensive horses, swooping across country, confident in the saddle. *Beasts!*

The parents had all departed into the warehouse with Uncle Knacker to 'knock up a few loose-boxes'. How and what with, Nutty could not imagine, but that wasn't her department. Morale was her department. She got back on Midnight, in order to look down on Sebastian and Antony, and squared her shoulders. Gary's nervous mare stayed at her side and Gary, perhaps inspired by her example, straightened up and changed his expression from scared to belligerent, which made him look remarkably like his brother Nails. Their adversaries approached, having given Hoomey a hand, geeing his horse up from behind with some hearty arm-waving.

'These your nags then?' Sebastian asked. 'Better keep that one away from the others' – he nodded towards Jazz's spotted beast – 'in case they all catch it.'

Nutty said icily, 'Not *everyone* can afford made horses that do it without any effort on the part of the rider, like yours. My uncle, with his vast professional knowledge of the saleyard, has managed to find four horses which, although in bad condition – and therefore within our price range – are what *Horse and Hound* calls proven performers. The spotted mare came from Billy Smart's and jumps a flaming hoop suspended at five feet, the chestnut in the horsebox is an ex-hunter who once belonged to the Duke of Beaufort, this one I'm holding has been placed twice round Badminton, and Hoomey's –'

She paused for inspiration and Seb said, 'Won the Grand National in nineteen thirty-two.'

'No, the Cheltenham Gold Cup in sixty-nine, as a matter of fact.' She needled him with such venom from behind her thick lenses that Seb was visibly squashed.

'You're joking?'

'You don't think we'd get just any old horses, do you, for such inexperienced riders? The horses all know the game all right, so we're half-way there, aren't we? Just a matter of getting them fit again, no trouble there. We're not *stupid*, Sebastian, you know. Merely lacking in opportunity.'

She spoke with such hauteur and conviction that even Hoomey wondered whether she was telling lies or the truth. Was his old Bones really a Gold Cup winner? He thought only footballers won Gold Cups. Was old Bones the equine equivalent of Manchester United then, fallen on hard times? Footballers grew old and fell on hard times, so perhaps it was the same for horses. But what had she said about badminton? He couldn't see a horse playing badminton. No way did that fit.

'Badminton isn't –' he started.

'Three-day eventing – what Princess Anne does – did –' Nutty snapped at him. 'This mare went clear round the cross-country. Just a matter of getting her fit again, like I said.'

Seb and Antony were looking at the horses dubiously, trying to see past glories and failing.

'Anyway, what are you doing up here?' Nutty pushed her advantage. 'Don't tell me you were just passing by? Come to have a nose by any chance? Gloria tell you?'

'We came to see your eyelashes, Deirdre,' Antony said in a soft, taunting voice. Nutty let out a genuine snort of rage, nudged Midnight with her heels and rode Antony into a large patch of thistles, towing the Badminton mare with her.

'Clear off! You're trespassing – you too, Gloria, you cow! You wait till I tell Mum!'

They were unequal to her belligerence and departed, giggling.

'Is all that true?' Hoomey asked, when they were out of earshot.

'Well, why not? You can't prove it isn't, can you? Horses like this, they were good once. It's true enough, isn't it?'

Her eyes flashed on him, silencing criticism.

'It's up to you,' she said. 'They're going to laugh on the other side of their faces before they're through.'

It was beginning to dawn on Hoomey that horses like this – surely? – were going to need quite a lot of attention, feeding, brushing and all that stuff. He supposed the Parents' Association would make a rota of some sort, to come up and do it. They were obviously keen, for the sound of activity from inside the refrigerator warehouse was impressive. Mr Bean had bales of straw in the truck which were being unloaded, and hay and sacks of food, and buckets. The parents were scurrying about like ants. Nutty rode into the warehouse to see if it was ready, and Hoomey followed her, towing Bones, who was ready to go wherever the food sacks were going.

Along one wall of the warehouse, four loose-boxes had been partitioned off by old refrigerators pushed together, which made very satisfactory walls. Mr Bean was opening out bales of straw making deep beds. Mr O'Malley brought the hay, and Sam was filling buckets of water.

'Bring 'em in, lad,' Mr Bean said to Hoomey. ''E'll think 'e's in paradise.'

The parents stood round proudly as, one by one, the horses were led into their new home. Even Bean's reluctant character, inevitably christened Whizzo, came at the rattle of a food bucket. They nosed at their deep straw, sampled the hay, straddled out their legs and peed, then settled their noses into the food buckets, which Mr Bean and Nutty between them had prepared. The evening light came through the skylights high overhead, glossing the scurfy backs, the sores, the scabby manes, and a soft echo came back from the walls of the vast, bare concrete building of animal content, feeding. Hoomey, for a moment, felt a strange satisfaction at making his old Bones happy. Even the parents had stopped chattering, watching with communal pride the appreciation of their efforts by the reprieved animals. Pleased, they trailed outside, disappeared down the concrete road. Mr Bean started up his lorry, his mate got in, they waved and drove away. The four boys were left with Nutty. It was nearly dark.

'That's it then?' Hoomey said hopefully.

'For tonight,' Nutty said. 'In the morning they'll need feeding again, and mucking out.'

'Who's going to do that?'

'You, of course.'

The boys stared at her.

'They're yours aren't they? Not everyone's so lucky, being given a horse. I'll meet you up here at seven, show you what to do.'

'Seven?'

They rolled their eyes, staggered by the news.

'You mean we've got to look after them? We've got to do it? As well as ride them?'

'Who else, dimwit?'

'But –'

Nutty got back on Midnight, swung round and glared at them.

'*I* get up at six every morning to do Midnight. *And* ride him. And in the evening again, feed and muck out. *I* do it, and *I'm* only a girl. So you jolly well be here at seven, else there'll be real trouble.'

And she turned away, Midnight's shoes striking sparks in the darkness, and set off at a fast trot in the direction of Sam Sylvester's semi-detached in Acacia Avenue.

# CYNTHIA VOIGT

FROM *Homecoming*

Sammy asked if he could ride his bike and Dicey gave him permission. Maybeth went into the house to help their grandmother clear up. James and Dicey worked out plans for mending the biggest holes in the side of the barn.

'Whadda you think, Dicey,' James finally asked. 'Are we going to stay?'

'I think so,' Dicey answered. 'I think we've shown her we can be useful. And not too much trouble. I think she likes Sammy – maybe because he's named after her son – '

'Our uncle. Did you think of that?'

'And I'm pretty sure we'll be OK here. All of us.'

'What about schools?'

'We can ride our bikes downtown and find out. Tomorrow. You want to?'

'Tomorrow's Sunday.'

'Then the next day.'

'That's Labour Day.'

'Then Tuesday or next week. Why are you quarrelling James? Don't you want to stay?'

'I guess so. I like it, and all those books. Do you think our grandfather was smart? Do you think he went to college or just read? What do you think he was like?'

'I don't know anything about him except what she said. Would it be OK with you if we stayed?'

'Sure. It's a good place. But Dicey, why did all of her children leave her? She's not so bad.'

'Do you think there's something we don't know? Do you think it's dangerous for us?' Dicey asked him.

'Do you like her?' James asked.

Dicey considered this. 'You know? I could. I mean, she's so odd and prickly. She fights us, or anyway I feel like I'm fighting her and she's fighting back, as if we both know what's going on but neither of us is saying anything. It's fun.'

'You're crazy,' James said.

'Maybe. But she's a good enemy – you know? In that way. Cousin Eunice wasn't.' Dicey thought some more. 'So she might make a good friend,' Dicey said finally.

'You are crazy,' James said. He looked at her. 'But you might be right. You're smart too, Dicey, do you ever think about that?' Dicey hadn't. It didn't seem very important to her, not the way it was to James.

Sammy had ridden out of sight, beyond the long driveway. He wasn't back in an hour and he wasn't back in two hours. The rain clouds blew away, leaving room for a bright red sunset, where fiery lights burned behind the clouds that gathered around the lowering sun.

They had cold ham for supper, and Sammy hadn't returned when they sat down. Dicey was worried. She didn't dare say anything though. They sat down in a troubled silence.

When she heard Sammy's feet on the steps of the porch, Dicey's appetite revived. He burst in the door to the kitchen, his cheeks red, his eyes sparkling.

'Wash your hands,' Dicey said. She could see him and he was fine, he was safe and back again. Relief dissolved into anger then. She looked at her grandmother.

'When you've done that, go to your room,' their grand-mother said.

Sammy turned. 'But I'm hungry.'

'That'll help you remember. Did you tell your sister where you were going?' Sammy's jaw went out. He wasn't going to answer, not to tell a lie.

'Did he tell you?' Dicey shook her head. 'Did he have your permission?'

'Sort of,' Dicey said.

'Sort of?' their grandmother said in a sharp, sarcastic voice. 'Sort of? How do you sort of give permission to disappear for hours at a time? What do you say? "OK, Sammy, go sort of run wild and sort of let people worry?" Are you stupid, girl?'

Dicey chewed her lip. Why did every adult send kids away from the table? Maybe because nobody sent *them* to bed hungry. Maybe they'd forgotten what hungry was. But it wasn't right. Dicey knew what hungry was, and so did Sammy.

'It's not Dicey's fault,' Sammy said. 'It's my fault. Don't yell at Dicey.'

'I will yell at whom I please,' his grandmother answered him. 'I have told you to go to your room.'

'No,' Dicey said quietly.

'Dicey!' James whispered.

'It's not right, James,' Dicey said. 'It's not right to send him to bed hungry. I can't let that happen, and I was wrong when I let Cousin Eunice do it. Sit down and eat, Sammy,' Dicey said.

Then she turned to try to explain to her grandmother. Her grandmother's eyes flashed. Her face was stiff and pale. Her lips were hard together.

'You,' Dicey said. She wanted to call her by name, but she had no name to call her. 'You don't understand, not what it is to be hungry. It doesn't serve any purpose to punish Sammy that way.'

Her grandmother's fury burned behind her immobile face. Her hand clenched the handle of the fork.

Dicey was frightened, with a fear that swelled up deep within her. This fear had two heads, and Dicey was caught between them: she was afraid to speak and lose what they had gained of a place for themselves in this house; she was afraid to keep silent and lose what she felt was right for Sammy, for her family. This was more difficult danger than any she had faced before. It wasn't the kind of danger you could run away from, or fight back at. Dicey wasn't even sure she wanted to fight. She just knew she had to stand by her brother and her family.

'Whose house is this?' their grandmother said. 'Whose food? Whose table?'

'You're right,' Dicey said. 'It's not our house, that's what you said from the beginning. But we're not your family, you meant that too, didn't you.'

Her grandmother stared at her.

'Sit down and eat,' Dicey said to Sammy. James and Maybeth were staring at her. Everybody was staring at her. 'But you're not to ride the bike again for two days.'

'Aw, Dicey,' Sammy said. He slipped into his chair and cut his meat.

'I mean it. No matter what. Will you obey?'

Sammy nodded.

'You have to say when you're going off,' Dicey said. She ignored her grandmother, who was sitting at the head of the table in a silence of furious anger.

Sammy nodded again. 'I know. I will, I'm sorry, Dicey,' he said, with a weak smile. Then he turned to his grandmother. 'I'm sorry to you, too. I didn't mean to make trouble. But it's my fault, not Dicey's.'

'You're a child,' his grandmother answered.

'So is Dicey,' Sammy said.

'I will not have this talking back!' their grandmother snapped.

'But it's not talking back,' James said. His voice was high and frightened. 'It's explaining. We're trying to get at the truth.' His grandmother stared at him before she answered, as if he had said something she didn't understand.

'You are in my home,' their grandmother said. She looked around the table at the four pairs of hazel eyes, none as dark as hers. And none, except Dicey's, as angry as hers. 'My home, not yours,' their grandmother said.

We might as well have it out now as any other time, Dicey said to herself. She felt as if she had been running away from this for days, and she had only the last of her strength left. She had to turn and fight now. She took a deep, shivering breath.

'Are you expecting us to stay then?' she demanded. Her voice sounded thin and hard.

Her grandmother's mouth worked, and she looked surprised, as if she hadn't understood what it was they were fighting about this time. Her mouth formed words, but no sound came out. Finally she spoke:

'No.'

The word ballooned out and filled all the air of the kitchen. Dicey didn't even try to argue. She just nodded her head and ate her supper in silence and helped with the dishes, and when the little children went up to bed she went with them. The *No* filled the whole air of the house. Every time she breathed in she breathed in that *No*. Dicey wasn't even frightened any more. She was simply defeated. She fell asleep suddenly and without any thought.

# BEVERLY CLEARY

Ramona could feel her heart pounding as she finally climbed the steps to the hospital. Visitors, some carrying flowers and others looking careworn, walked towards the lifts. Nurses hurried, a doctor was paged over the loudspeaker. Ramona could scarcely bear her own excitement. The rising of the lift made her stomach feel as if it had stayed behind on the first floor. When the lift stopped, Mr Quimby led the way down the hall.

'Excuse me,' called a nurse.

Surprised, the family stopped and turned.

'Children under twelve are not allowed to visit the maternity ward,' said the nurse. 'Little girl, you will have to go down and wait in the lobby.'

'Why is that?' asked Mr Quimby.

'Children under twelve might have contagious diseases,' explained the nurse. 'We have to protect the babies.'

'I'm sorry, Ramona,' said Mr Quimby. 'I didn't know. I am afraid you will have to do as the nurse says.'

'Does she mean I'm *germy*?' Ramona was humiliated. 'I took a shower this morning and washed my hands at the Whopperburger so I would be extra clean.'

'Sometimes children are coming down with something and don't know it,' explained Mr Quimby. 'Now, be a big girl and go downstairs and wait for us.'

Ramona's eyes filled with tears of disappointment, but

she found some pleasure in riding in the lift alone. By the time she reached the lobby, she felt worse. The nurse called her a little girl. Her father called her a big girl. What was she? A germy girl.

Ramona sat gingerly on the edge of a couch. If she leaned back, she might get germs on it, or it might get germs on her. She swallowed hard. Was her throat a little bit sore? She thought maybe it was, way down in the back. She put her hand to her forehead the way her mother did when she thought Ramona might have a fever. Her forehead was warm, maybe too warm.

As Ramona waited, she began to itch the way she itched when she had chickenpox. Her head itched, her back itched, her legs itched. Ramona scratched. A woman sat down on the couch, looked at Ramona, got up and moved to another couch.

Ramona felt worse. She itched more and scratched harder. She swallowed often to see how her sore throat was coming along. She peeked down the neck of her blouse to see if she might have a rash and was surprised that she did not. She sniffed from time to time to see if she had a runny nose.

Now Ramona was angry. It would serve everybody right if she came down with some horrible disease, right there in their old hospital. That would show everybody how germfree that place was. Ramona squirmed and gave that hard-to-reach place between her shoulder blades a good hard scratch. Then she scratched her head with both hands. People stopped to stare.

A man in a white coat, with a stethoscope hanging out of his pocket, came hurrying through the lobby, glanced at Ramona, stopped, and took a good look at her. 'How do you feel?' he asked.

'Awful,' she admitted. 'A nurse said I was too germy to go see my mother and new sister, but I think I caught some disease right here.'

'I see,' said the doctor. 'Open your mouth and say "ah".'

Ramona *ahhed* until she gagged.

'Mh-hm,' murmured the doctor. He looked so serious Ramona was alarmed. Then he pulled out his stethoscope and listened to her front and back, thumping as he did so. What was he hearing? Was there something wrong with her insides? Why didn't her father come?

The doctor nodded as if his worst suspicions had been confirmed. 'Just as I thought,' he said, pulling out his prescription pad.

Medicine, ugh. Ramona's twitching stopped. Her nose and throat felt fine. 'I feel much better,' she assured the doctor as she eyed that prescription pad with distrust.

'An acute case of siblingitis. Not at all unusual around here, but it shouldn't last long.' He tore off the prescription he had written, instructed Ramona to give it to the father, and hurried on down the hall.

Ramona could not remember the name of her illness. She tried to read the doctor's scribbly cursive writing, but she could not. She could only read neat cursive, the sort her teacher wrote on the blackboard.

Itching again, she was still staring at the slip of paper when Mr Quimby and Beezus stepped out of the lift. 'Roberta is so tiny.' Beezus was radiant with joy. 'And she is perfectly darling. She has a little round nose and — oh, when you see her, you'll love her.'

'I'm sick,' Ramona tried to sound pitiful. 'I've got something awful. A doctor said so.'

Beezus paid no attention. 'And Roberta has brown hair —'

Mr Quimby interrupted. 'What's this all about, Ramona?'

'A doctor said I have something, some kind of *itis*, and I have to have this right away.' She handed her father her prescription and scratched one shoulder. 'If I don't, I might get sicker.'

Mr Quimby read the scribbly cursive, and then he did a strange thing. He lifted Ramona and gave her a big hug and a kiss, right there in the lobby. The itching stopped. Ramona felt much better. 'You have acute sib-lingitis,' explained her father, '*itis* means inflammation.'

Ramona already knew the meaning of sibling. Since her father had studied to be a teacher, brothers and sisters had become siblings to him.

'He understood you were worried and angry because you weren't allowed to see your new sibling, and pre-scribed attention,' explained Mr Quimby. 'Now let's all go buy ice-cream cones before I fall asleep standing up.'

# GERALDINE KAYE

FROM *Comfort Herself*

Comfort settled on a wooden box behind the stall
and gazed across Akwapawa market. At last she
had got herself to the market there where she wanted to
be, just as she had got herself into Ghana. The shrill
tumult rang in her ears. There was a concrete floor and
high above her head a corrugated iron roof supported on
green-painted pillars mottled with rust. There were dozens
of stalls under the roof and outside its protection there
were women sitting with baskets as far as the eye could
see. Hundreds of women who simply laid their goods
out on the ground, oranges, yams, cassava, tomatoes and
lettuces grown on their own farms, cloth, soap and plastic
combs bought to trade.

Everything was round, round woven baskets like cottage loaves, round head-scarves circled the heads of
married women, round fruit in round piles, round bumps
of babies tied to their mothers' backs. The market women
themselves were round too as they settled like plump
pears on the ground beside their goods, *bottom power* as it
was called, the power of the market mammies. Even the
patterns on their cloths were round, Ata's had round
yellow leaves on a black ground, Abla's at the next stall
had scarlet vines with round dark-blue fruits, balloons
floated on Comfort's.

The hubbub bounced against the roof and echoed
back, morning greetings, babies crying, lorries revving,

the shout of book-men and the cries of the market women calling to possible customers, their voices falling with a lower price as the customer walked away showing a real or feigned lack of interest.

'And who is this then?' Abla shouted above the din and her smile flashed white. She had a baby sleeping on her back and two small children playing on the ground beside her.

'Comfort, child of my brother, Mante,' Ata said but her eyes were anxious as she settled Bolo on a bed of cloth under the stall. Bolo was feverish. The fetish priest had given medicine but the child seemed no better.

'Ah, Comfort who comes from England,' Abla said. 'No wonder she stares like an owl caught in the daylight. The stranger has big eyes but does not see what is happening.' Comfort smiled gently to herself. She was surely no stranger who was allowed to come to Akwapawa market to watch Grandmother's lorry as well as learn to trade in cloth.

'I have brought the medicine,' Abla said handing a bottle of spinach-green liquid to Ata. 'My son, Dublo, had a fever and bad leg just the same as Bolo and now he is well, Onyame be praised. Dublo hold out your leg.' There was a grey scar patch where the sore had healed. Many of the children round the market had such grey scars.

'How much do I owe you?' Ata said pouring a large dose into a cup for Bolo.

'Pay me when the child is well,' Abla said with a shrug. Most of the stalls sold the same goods, competing with each other but the competition stayed friendly. Trading was only part of market life and the market women were almost a family in themselves, a friendly society helping each other in time of trouble, a force to be reckoned with.

'Come and buy my cloth, fine-fine cloth,' Ata called as the market filled and the sun rose high in the sky. Her eyes searched the passing faces for likely customers. 'Fine cloth. Very cheap price.'

'What is the *right* price for cloth?' Comfort asked, trying to follow Ata's movements and do exactly as she did. The price called seemed to vary with every customer.

'Aye-aye, you will soon learn how it is,' Ata said. 'The price depends how a person looks, whether he or she is well-dressed and prosperous, a cheerful face will pay a better price.'

'I see,' said Comfort not quite sure that she did.

'But you have to be very careful,' Ata explained. 'We market mammies of Ghana are very powerful people according to the government. They blame us when the price rises. Now prices are fixed by law, everyone must sell at the fixed price but there is always a dash as well and the dash is not fixed.'

'But . . .' said Comfort still not sure she understood. It sounded like a trick.

'People do not always want to buy at first,' Ata explained. 'You have to hook them like fish in the river, persuade them how cheap the cloth is, you will soon learn how it is done. Look after the stall while I see when the clinic opens.'

'But I . . .' Comfort began but Ata was already making her way across the crowded market and in Ghana people did not care for too many questions. For a moment Comfort watched her aunt and then she smiled down at Bolo, his eyes shone very bright under the stall.

'Very nice cloth,' Comfort muttered and a woman passing in a blue print frock turned her head and glanced curiously. 'Come and buy my very nice cloth.'

'Louder,' whispered Bolo. 'You sound like a small frog croaking in a dry pond.'

'Come buy my cloth. Very fine cloth,' Comfort called and this time several heads turned and at the next stall Abla laughed.

'Aye-aye, Comfort has found her voice,' she said, suckling her baby now but continuing to call to customers. 'The green fruit ripens fast.'

And Comfort had found her voice. 'Come buy my cloth. This is a very fine cloth,' she chanted like the others and soon she was making up new calls too, partly to entertain Bolo. 'Buy this cloth and you will look as gay as a pineapple.' A small snicker of laughter came from under the stall. In Grandmother's compound Comfort had to be so careful what she said and the freedom of the market was very exciting. Here you had to push and shout and grab to survive.

'You call like an oriole bird already,' Bolo muttered as she leant down and gave him a drink from the bottle of orange. His forehead seemed very hot and there was a sour smell about him, white clay was smeared round a deep cut on his leg. Comfort took Grandmother's amulet from her neck and put it round Bolo's. It was all she could do. Hadn't it kept her safe and well, perhaps it would help him. There was a note of desperation in her voice as she called now. Nobody seemed to realize how sick Bolo was. A woman stopped and fingered a cloth patterned with orange, brown and black diamond-shapes like a snake skin.

'How much?' she asked.

'Well, two hundred cedis,' Comfort said snatching the first price which came into her head. It was a high price she knew but the woman looked both prosperous and cheerful. 'Just to you this cloth is two hundred cedis.'

'Two hundred cedis is far too high,' said the woman sharply. 'You will land yourself in prison charging such prices. If I report you to the people's court you will be certainly fined and quite right too.'

'To you it's fifty cedis, I made a mistake,' Comfort said hastily, her stomach turning to a hard cold lump. How she hated it when people got angry. Everything changed when people got angry. 'It is a fine-fine cloth and will suit you well. See how it brings out the brightness of your eyes and the snake smoothness of your skin.'

'What?' said the woman loudly. 'Are you telling me that I am like a snake? You have too much to say for yourself. The fixed price for a cloth like this is thirty cedis.' She turned away.

'Thirty cedis then,' Comfort called after her. 'You can have the cloth for thirty cedis.'

'Now we are getting somewhere,' the woman said coming back. She was smiling now, she seemed quite pleased with the bargain. Comfort did not know whether to be proud of her first sale or not as she wrapped the cloth in a piece of brown paper and the woman walked away.

'I have sold the snake-pattern cloth,' Comfort said when Ata returned. 'For thirty cedis, the fixed price.'

'And did you get the dash too, what was the dash?' Ata asked her eyes lack-lustre.

'No dash, I forgot,' Comfort said.

'Aye-aye, you must learn our ways quick-quick or you

will make beggars of us all,' Ata said but she was half-abstracted as she gazed down at Bolo who had fallen asleep. The clinic would be open later, she would take Bolo over then but already dozens of children were waiting. 'Didn't I tell you that each cloth has a fixed price because the government says so but you must ask for a dash as well?'

'Sorry,' said Comfort very cast down. She was half-Ghanaian but sometimes she wondered if she would ever get things right. 'Sorry.'

In the afternoon Ata carried Bolo to the clinic on her back like a cloth baby and when she brought him back his leg had been covered with white bandage and he had been given pills. Ata tipped the pills, white and gritty, into her palm and sniffed them doubtfully. Nobody had told her what kinds of pills they were, she only knew they were expensive. Already her eyes were glazed with sadness. Every day children got sick and went back to their sky-families, she accepted such an outcome fatalistically since too much hope and struggle would only cause further pain. It was the will of Onyame.

# JILL PATON WALSH

FROM *Gaffer Samson's Luck*

He woke in the moonlight, suddenly knowing what to do. 'I'll do that when you've done it,' he had said to Terry. And Terry had done it; the rules didn't say you had to succeed, only that you mustn't funk it. So now it was up to James. Earlier in the day he had been terrified of the weir; now he knew there were worse things, and he had a choice. His father often said, talking about climbing and fell-walking, that people got into trouble because they rushed at things, and didn't take time to think. So James took time to think. He sat in the pool of moonlight on the attic floor, and thought about the weir. He thought of the rush of water, knee-deep, or deeper, the slack chain, the slimy sill beneath. Then he got his climbing boots out of the cupboard. The row of heavy studs on the soles glinted in the cold silver light.

Now. It would have to be now. Tomorrow the flood might have gone down a bit, the fierceness of the weir abated. But if he did it the same day, the same night, there could be no arguing about it. James looked out of the window. The world was dim, but clear. Shadow spires stood into a faint sky. A bright full moon was shining in a cloudless night, littered with brilliant stars. Just the same, he would need a torch. He crept about barefoot, finding his clothes. He had to retrieve his jeans from the airing cupboard, where his mother had put them to dry. He took a boot in each hand, and crept down the stairs.

His bike was still propped on the fence beside the lock; he would have to walk. He tiptoed across the gravel, for fear the crunch would wake someone. In the street he sat on the kerb beneath a lamp-post, and put on his boots, and laced them up. Then he set off for the trailer park.

Angey woke easily; one or two taps on the pane, and there she was, yawning, and dressed. Now he came to think of it, she looked as if she slept in her clothes.

'You don't have to,' she said, at once.

'Yes, I do,' he said. 'But I need someone to see me, or they'll never believe us. Can you get someone?'

She nodded. 'I'll get my trainers, and I'll be right with you,' she said.

They went to Tracy's house first. Angey thought Tracy slept downstairs, but they woke an angry dog before they woke her. Next they tried Ted. James thought wistfully of Scarf, but Scarf was kept in hospital, Angey said. She threw a light handful of grit at Ted's window, and in a while he put his head out. 'Coming,' he said when he saw them, but seemed to take hours. James got desperate, waiting for him.

'I can't wait, Angey,' he said. 'I've just got to go and do it. Bring anyone you can, OK?'

The road through the village, under the tall trees was dark. The lamp-posts were still on, but the limited dim pools of light they made failed to meet each other. James had no idea what time it was, he hadn't brought his watch. No point in wrecking a good watch. He picked his way by torchlight between the pools of lamplight. His boots rang and clattered on the road. And he felt like a thief going by; anyone who saw him would stop

him. At last he crossed the bridge, thudding over the
planks, and came into the open, gleaming meadow.
Threads of silver, broken shards of moon lay in the
ghostly grass. He marched on regardless through the
pools on the path, to the bank. He did not look at the
lock, he couldn't afford to. Hearing the solid roar of the
river through it was bad enough. As he crossed the first
weir he couldn't help looking where the water ran as
hard as ever, leaping and shouting to the distant and
disinterested stars. And then he trudged through the
bushes, and was there.

The river gave off a steely glint as it curved over the
slope. Were the chains hanging just above the water
instead of just into it? James dared not consider now, or
stop to think. Instead he turned his back on the river,
and lowered himself into the water, going in very deliberately on the riverward side of the chain.

He had expected more depth; it came up to his knees,
no more. He had not expected the weight and force of its
thrust. It was so cold his skin burned intensely, he felt
the violent flushing of his body all over, but he was
hanging on to the first post. He felt for the sill, the
concrete edge below the water, and carefully hooked the
first row of studs on his boots over the lip. He picked up
the chain, lifted it over his shoulders, and leaned back
into it, pushing against the thrust of the water. Then he
began very slowly, holding himself rigid and leaning
backwards with all his might to slide sideways.

As long as he kept leaning against the weight of the
water, as long as he didn't let it push him forward, and
topple him over the chain, he would be all right. The
warm flush of his skin ebbed away leaving him trembling
and gasping from cold. Somehow he had eased himself

along the first length of chain. As he moved towards the middle it got harder, and he leaned back so far he was looking straight up at the icy stars. He got to the second post. Then he found he couldn't move; he was clinging on to it frantically, terrified of going on, and terrified of going back while his mind replayed to him the sight of Terry being plucked off the chain and flung away. 'But you can't stay,' he told himself. 'You'll get tired, and get washed off, so *move!*' Slowly he unclenched the grip of his right hand, and transferred it to the next length of chain.

He was right in the middle of the weir now, hanging on to the central chain, and fighting for his balance. The water was immense, ruthless. It pushed him forward, and he fought with all the thrust in his frozen limbs to keep himself leaning away from the water-slide, to keep his boots locked over the sill, while the water roared round his knees, and tried to tear his feet from under him. He slid his boots along the sill; he reached the next post. Above the sound of the water, faintly, something reached him; bird-like sounds, voices, calling. He had no mind to spare for that. Somewhere between the third and fourth posts he lost his footing; the sill was crumbling and rough, and he couldn't slide his boots along it. For a moment he teetered, closed his eyes, and gave up. His body flinched all over at the thought of the drubbing and knocking it would take, being dashed down into the pool; and then somehow he had recovered his posture, and was leaning outwards in the loop of chain again. And the force of the water was lessening now with every step he took. He was reaching the lee of the other shore.

The water sped past this length, and turned sideways moments later as though it did not know at first that it was free to go over. Even so, James, suddenly aching and mortally tired, hardly managed the last few steps to the bank. And there he hung on, leaning on the last post, and barely able to drag his soaking body out of the water, and roll himself on to the bank.

Dimly he heard shouting. His name, being called. He looked back across the shining terrifying moon-silvered stretch of water. Like a solitary glow-worm the torch was dancing. Someone had found it lying on the bank, and was waving it. The shadows in the willows on the other side, moved, and called his name. Lots of shadows. Angey had brought the whole village mob out to watch him.

# JANNI HOWKER

FROM *The Nature of the Beast*

I've a slow-burning temper, the long-fused kind, Dad says, but with him and Chunder it's light the blue touch-paper and retire. Chunder's the worst. He can swat a wasp with his tongue if he's that way out.

Dad says I get that slow burning from my mam. He says it's the only thing I inherited from her, and it's dangerous and he wishes I hadn't. You see, they only set a long fuse to light a real explosion — like a case of dynamite. The sort of explosion that blows your right leg to Preston and your left leg to Wigan Pier. Or, as in Mam's case, left me on Long Moor Lane, and blew her to Canada.

The blue touch-paper brigade seem more scary at first. A lot of sparks and cracks, belts and swearing, but it's quickly passed over and usually there's no harm done.

Mind you, my great-great-grandad, Snowy Coward, was a blue touch-paper man, and got hisself hanged for it. He was a horse-dealer and he married this gypsy woman called Queenie who was in the same line of trade. They had rows and a baby who was my great-grandad (or, to put it another way, Chunder's Dad), then her real husband, another gypsy man, turns up. And Snowy, being a Coward, chucks him out of the window and he lands on his head, dead. Snowy was hanged at Lancaster Castle. The baby was brought up by neighbours and I expect Queenie went back to the gypsies.

I'm not sure.

Dad and Chunder don't really like me talking about this – having a streak of gypsy blood. But you can see it, especially in my dad. He's got black curly hair, and blue eyes that go black when he loses his rag, but just before he goes mad, his eyes go sort of milky, calm and milky. I expect that's what Snowy Coward's eyes were like when he chucked that gypsy feller out of the window.

People say that I'm the spitting image of my dad and a chip off the old block.

While I'm on about family history, I'd better tell you about my mam. I'd have to tell you sometime, so it may as well be now.

My mam and dad weren't married when they had me. They were going to be, then three weeks before the service my mam looks in my cot, and says, 'I'm not going to marry you, Ned Coward.'

'Why not?' says Dad.

'Me name's Anne. If I married you my name would be A. Coward.'

'That's not a reason,' says Dad. 'You've got to marry us, Annie. That's my lad. It is my lad, isn't it?'

'Oh yes,' says Mam. 'He's yours all right. And I was a coward to think of marrying you just because of him.'

'Me name may be Coward, but there's never been a Coward run away from his kin!'

'That may be,' says Mam. 'But I'm not a Coward. I'm off. You want him, you keep him.'

And she left the house and never came back. Not once. Never. Three weeks later she was in Canada. And a year after that she got married to some bloke. I don't know where she lives. I don't think about her often. But what I've told you is the exact words she spoke, just as

Dad told them to me. He was that surprised he didn't have a chance to lose his temper, though he's made up for it since.

Anyway, that's why I was brought up by Dad and Chunder on Long Moor Lane, although they lived in separate rented houses. Sometimes I stayed at Number 3 – which was Chunder's house right on the edge of the moor, and last but one house in Haverston. And sometimes I stayed at Number 17, with Dad, until I was eight and old enough to fend for myself. I've lived with Dad ever since.

Well, anyway, to get back to January. The next morning there were some sparks flying round our kitchen. (There usually are sparks if Dad and Chunder spend more than a couple of hours together, which is why they decided to live in separate houses in the first place, to stop themselves falling out every five minutes.) Chunder had spent the night on the sofa. His clothes were all crumpled and his chin was covered with white bristles, and there was a smell on the room of fag ends, stale beer, leather and sweat. It was the smell of Chunder's house and he had brought it with him.

Dad was cursing Chunder for letting the fire go out. It gets very cold in our house in January, even with the fire in. And it was a thin grey morning. The rain was blowing against the window and it was so dark that we had the light on in the kitchen. The cloud was that low and thick over the valley that you couldn't see the rest of Haverston, not even the chimney of Stone Cross Mill.

'Isn't that flaming kettle boiled yet?' yelled Dad, when I came down.

'Nearly,' I said, and went and put it on. I stayed over

by the gas cooker because it was the warmest place, and to keep out of the way of them fighting.

'You could have just put a shovel of coal on before you went to sleep!' says Dad, and he's angrily raking and rattling and poking at the fire, getting soot and clinker all over the rug. 'You feckless old bugger!'

'Feckless! I'll give thee flaming feckless!' Chunder shouts back, yanking at a knot in his shoe-lace. 'Baah! I don't know why I bother wi' thee and tha brat. I shoulda washed me hands of thee! Tha's that self-righteous tha'd sleep in thee Sunday boots!'

'And yer that sodding idle you'd sooner sleep int' grate than set yer loafing carcass in a bed!'

'It'd be a damn sight warmer if I did! It's a cold welcome in a cold house is all I ever get from thee, Ned Coward. I'd be warmer in me flaming grave!'

This went on. I made a pot of tea and got the bacon out of the cupboard. This was normal with Dad and Chunder. Cowards can fight Cowards, but there's closed ranks and thief-thick blue bloody murder if an outsider says owt against them.

At least, I thought it was normal, until suddenly Chunder looks out into the dark rainy morning and stops silent in the middle of what he's yelling. Then he says, terrible quiet, 'Ned? Ned? I can't see t'chimney . . .'

I could have told him that, but Dad goes quiet as well. 'Neither can I,' he says, and he goes over and puts his hand on Chunder's shoulder. 'But it's still standing yet . . .'

It's so quiet I daren't even light a match to set the frying-pan on, for fear of the loudness of the noise.

'It's only the rain,' I say at last, because I'm getting a strange silky feeling in my guts. The silence. The sound of the rain. And them staring out of the window like that. 'It's only a cloud over the valley,' I say.

'It's a blacker bloody cloud than you've mind of,' says Dad, quietly.

Chunder nodded. Looking at them, I got the feeling that the weight of my dad's hand on Chunder's shoulder was making my grandad stoop, and then I looked at my dad's back, and it was as if an even heavier invisible hand was pressing down on his shoulders, making him hunched and bowed. That silky feeling in my belly got worse. I forgot about the bacon and went and stood next to my dad – for a very long time, it seemed.

It's strange now, looking back. I can see a picture in my mind of all the windows of the terraced houses on Long Moor Lane on the dark morning, with the moor behind. And at the yellow squares of glass, people are standing. All silent. Whole families. Standing and gazing down at the valley, with their breath steaming up the cold glass, looking for Stone Cross Mill chimney in that smoky cloud, and for the first time in their lives, fearing that it wouldn't be there.

I didn't know what I was looking at. Only that I was peering into the valley as if my life depended on it.

Then Dad straightened his back.

Chunder said, 'What time's Jim Dalton called that meeting for?'

(Jim Dalton is my mate's – Mick Dalton's – dad. He was the shop steward.)

'Eleven. In the car park.'

'Eleven,' repeated Chunder. He went over to the table and poured himself a mug of tea, and he looked for a long time at the teapot. 'I'll not go, Ned,' he said, after a while, 'I'm too old to hear that noise.'

'What about your vote?' said Dad, without looking round.

'Vote?' says Chunder. 'Me vote won't make a tinker's cuss of difference.' And he drank his tea all the way to the leaves without remembering that he'd forgotten to put sugar in. That gave me a shock. Chunder drinking tea without sugar, and not even noticing! He's a sweet tooth, has Chunder.

'What's to do, Dad?' I said.

'Get to school!' said Dad.


Mick said, 'Well, are we bunking off or what?'

He was scratching something into the green paint of the bus shelter. Above it, someone had scratched MOOR MODS ROOL OK – which is stupid, because there's no such thing as real Mods round here any more. I expect they just liked the sound of it.

'Looks like we are,' I said, because the bus had gone. Then I said, 'What's happening?'

'That's just what I asked!' said Mick, making his eyes all dramatic and exasperated like Oggy. (Oggy – Mr Oglethorpe – is our form master. He also teaches us history and English since Mrs Clegg went off to have a baby.)

I crouched down on my heels, wedged in the corner of the bus shelter. It smelled a bit like Chunder's house down there. All the slush and snow had gone. All the cleanness and coldness of the winter had gone. Today, everything was grey and chilly and bleak. 'No, I mean . . . is it a strike your old feller's calling?'

'No,' said Mick. 'Didn't your dad say?'

'No.'

'Oh . . .' There was a bit of silence.

'WELL?'

'They're closing Stone Cross. Making the work-force repugnant.'

'Repugnant?'

'Redundant – repugnant. It was me dad's joke – sort of joke. He wants them to accept the terms.'

'Closing Stone Cross!' I couldn't believe it. Then I saw what he was scratching into the paint.

Stone Cross
R.I.P

and the date.

'And your dad says yes!'

Mick shrugged. 'It's done. There's nowt to say yes or no about, except the settlements.'

'They'll kill him,' I said to myself.

'That's what I said,' said Mick. His voice went odd, whiny and scratchy. He was my best mate, but at that moment I thought I hated him, because he looked frightened, and because his dad was meant to be the union and had let them close Stone Cross.

Then the next moment it was me that was afraid. A sort of blue rippling fear in my belly. Stone Cross chimney was like a church spire in West Haverston. It was like seeing a church spire demolished by lightning; and Chunder and Dad, they were like the congregation standing with their shoulders hunched, waiting for the mortar and bricks to land on them. A hundred tons of bricks on each shoulder, enough to crush every bone in their chests.

For a moment even thinking about it was like spitting splintered bones.

'Don't be daft! They'd not close Stone Cross! Not sudden. Not like that!'

No answer.

'Chunder's worked there since he was thirteen! He's only got two more years to do. Cowards don't go on the dole, Dad says. Cowards don't go on the dole!'

'Do you know what my dad says?' hissed Mick, suddenly fierce. 'Do you?'

I shook my head.

Mick was still scratching the paint with the stone. Not writing, but scratching. Screek-screek-screek. 'He says he's been fighting a losing battle. He says he's spent eight years trying to wake up Stone Cross shop-floor. Now they've got what they had coming to them – and serves them bloody well right!'

'I don't get it,' I said. It was that cold and wet in the bus shelter I began to shiver. Haverston. Our town. Stone Cross chimney. And a thin bitter wind off the moor. The last bus gone. I looked at Mick.

'He says he's been warning them for two years it was coming, but they'd not believe him. He says they think Stone Cross is holy untouchable blooming sanctuary. He says he's seen more pigs fly than pickets from Haverston.'

'There must have been a lot of talking in your house this morning,' I said.

'This morning!' Mick made a noise in his mouth. 'They talked all night!'

'Come on,' I said. 'Let's go up the allotments. We can sit in Chunder's shed.'

So that's where we went, threading our way through the scruffy old corrugated iron and the tatty planks and bits of Formica, and last year's dead leaves, until we came to Chunder's patch, which is the last one and the biggest because it's next to the moor. Every year Chunder digs a bit further into the moor, moves his fence a few feet further up the slope. Puts more hens on. The C.E.C. Reclamation Scheme, he calls it. (C.E.C. stands for Charles Ernest Coward.)

Chunder's shed is all made of old doors, all painted red, and the numbers are still on them, and he's painted the numbers very neatly in yellow. The hen-house is made of doors as well and painted just the same. It always reminds me of dodgems and fair-grounds for some reason, and I think it might be something to do with the gypsy in Chunder that he paints things like that. Even the handles of shovels and forks and that are painted. He collects the doors from skips and demolitions and there's always a few stacked by the shed, ready to be turned into something or other.

It's dark in the shed, and smells of soil and tar and fag ends and chicken feed.

We sat on some sacks and left the door open so we could watch the rain and so we could watch the daft way the hens kept scurrying out of their coop and nipping back in again, shaking their bum-feathers with annoyance at getting wet. We might have laughed at that if we'd been in a different mood. Instead, we just crouched there, smoking. I'd found a packet with eight fags in, that Chunder must have left last time he was up, and I still had the matches in my pocket from forgetting to set the bacon on. And because the day was so wet and grey, the smoke hung in the shed in coils and layers.

I crouched on my heels, cupping the fag in my hand and watching the blue smoke snake and ribbon between my fingers. It stains your fingers if you hold a fag like that, but I just wanted to watch the smoke, and not think about anything, until my eyes and my thinking were full of these cool blue coils of smoke and I'd almost forgotten that Mick was there.

Then he said, 'What will your dad do?'

'Kill the buggers,' I said, without thinking. And then I thought of Snowy Coward, and my heart gave this one cold jerk. But that was daft, really daft.

Dad would do what Chunder was already doing – get drunk, swear, shout, fall into bed with his clothes on and I'd have to undress him and cover him with a blanket so as he didn't catch cold. And the next morning he'd be in a worse temper because he'd have a thick head, and I'd keep out of his way. And the morning after that, we'd manage.

# PATRICIA MacLACHLAN

FROM *Sarah, Plain and Tall*

The rain came and passed, but strange clouds hung in the north-west, low and black and green. And the air grew still.

In the morning, Sarah dressed in a pair of overalls and went to the barn to have an argument with Papa. She took apples for Old Bess and Jack.

'Women don't wear overalls,' said Caleb, running along behind her like one of Sarah's chickens.

'This woman does,' said Sarah crisply.

Papa stood by the fence.

'I want to learn how to ride a horse,' Sarah told him. 'And then I want to learn how to drive the wagon. By myself.'

Jack leaned over and nipped at Sarah's overalls. She fed him an apple. Caleb and I stood behind Sarah.

'I can ride a horse, I know,' said Sarah. 'I rode once when I was twelve. I will ride Jack.' Jack was Sarah's favourite.

Papa shook his head. 'Not Jack,' he said. 'Jack is sly.'

'I am sly, too,' said Sarah stubbornly.

Papa smiled, 'Ayuh,' he said, nodding. 'But not Jack.'

'Yes, Jack!' Sarah's voice was very loud.

'I can teach you how to drive a wagon. I have already taught you how to plough.'

'And then I can go to town. By myself.'

'Say no, Papa,' Caleb whispered beside me.

'That's a fair thing, Sarah,' said Papa. 'We'll practise.'

A soft rumble of thunder sounded. Papa looked up at the clouds.

'Today? Can we begin today?' asked Sarah.

'Tomorrow is best,' said Papa, looking worried. 'I have to fix the house roof. A portion of it is loose. And there's a storm coming.'

'We,' said Sarah.

'What?' Papa turned.

'*We* will fix the roof,' said Sarah. 'I've done it before. I know about roofs. I am a good carpenter. Remember, I told you?'

There was thunder again, and Papa went to get the ladder.

'Are you fast?' he asked Sarah.

'I am fast and I am good,' said Sarah. And they climbed the ladder to the roof, Sarah with wisps of hair around her face, her mouth full of nails, overalls like Papa's. Overalls that *were* Papa's.

Caleb and I went inside to close the windows. We could hear the steady sound of hammers pounding the roof overhead.

'Why does she want to go to town by herself?' asked Caleb. 'To leave us?'

I shook my head, weary with Caleb's questions. Tears gathered at the corners of my eyes. But there was no time to cry, for suddenly Papa called out.

'Caleb! Anna!'

We ran outside and saw a huge cloud, horribly black, moving towards us over the north fields. Papa slid down the roof, helping Sarah after him.

'A squall!' he yelled to us. He held up his arms and Sarah jumped off the porch roof.

'Get the horses inside,' he ordered Caleb. 'Get the sheep, Anna. And the cows. The barn is safest.'

The grasses flattened. There was a hiss of wind, a sudden pungent smell. Our faces looked yellow in the strange light. Caleb and I jumped over the fence and found the animals huddled by the barn. I counted the sheep to make sure they were all there, and herded them into a large stall. A few raindrops came, gentle at first, then stronger and louder, so that Caleb and I covered our ears and stared at each other without speaking. Caleb looked frightened and I tried to smile at him. Sarah carried a sack into the barn, her hair wet and streaming down her neck, Papa came behind, Lottie and Nick with him, their ears flat against their heads.

'Wait!' cried Sarah. 'My chickens!'

'No, Sarah!' Papa called after her. But Sarah had already run from the barn into a sheet of rain. My father followed her. The sheep nosed open their stall door and milled around the barn, bleating. Nick crept under my arm, and a lamb, Mattie with the black face, stood close to me, trembling. There was a soft paw on my lap, then a grey body. Seal. And then, as the thunder pounded and the wind rose and there was the terrible crackling of lightning close by, Sarah and Papa stood in the barn doorway, wet to the skin. Papa carried Sarah's chickens. Sarah came with an armful of summer roses.

Sarah's chickens were not afraid, and they settled like small red bundles in the hay. Papa closed the door at last, shutting out some of the sounds of the storm. The barn was eerie and half lighted, like dusk without a lantern. Papa spread blankets around our shoulders and Sarah unpacked a bag of cheese and bread and jam. At the very bottom of the bag were Sarah's shells.

Caleb got up and went to the small barn window.

'What colour is the sea when it storms?' he asked Sarah.

'Blue,' said Sarah, brushing her wet hair back with her fingers. 'And grey and green.'

Caleb nodded and smiled.

'Look,' he said to her. 'Look what is missing from your drawing.'

Sarah went to stand between Caleb and Papa by the window. She looked a long time without speaking. Finally, she touched Papa's shoulder.

'We have squalls in Maine, too,' she said. 'Just like this. It will be all right, Jacob.'

Papa said nothing. But he put his arm around her, and leaned over to rest his chin in her hair. I closed my eyes, suddenly remembering Mama and Papa standing that way, Mama smaller than Sarah, her hair fair against Papa's shoulder. When I opened my eyes again, it was Sarah standing there. Caleb looked at me and smiled and smiled until he could smile no more.

We slept in the hay all night, waking when the wind was wild, sleeping again when it was quiet. And at dawn there was the sudden sound of hail, like stones tossed against the barn. We stared out of the window, watching the ice marbles bounce on the ground. And when it was over we opened the barn door and walked out into the early-morning light. The hail crunched and melted beneath our feet. It was white and gleaming for as far as we looked, like sun on glass. Like the sea.

# JAN MARK

FROM *Trouble Half-Way*

'But when are we going to stop?' Amy asked.
     'Hungry?'

'No, but you were going to ring Mum.'

'Plenty of time for that.'

'Suppose she rings us?'

'She can't – no phone in this lorry. We're a bit old-fashioned.'

Amy could not tell whether he were being sarcastic or not.

'But if she rings home –'

'She'll think you're at school and I'm shopping. She won't be worried, if that's what you're worried about. *You* stop worrying. There's a place along here that I usually pull in at on this run. Not much further. I'll ring from there.'

Amy was not altogether looking forward to the first stop. It would be a transport café, she guessed, and she had wild ideas about what transport cafés were like: greasy vinyl floors, dirty Formica tables awash with slops and floating swollen fag-ends, thick chipped mugs of fierce brown tea, oily platefuls of sausages and chips and baked beans, tomato sauce bottles with gory crusts round the necks, the dark air solid with cigarette smoke and made hideous by juke-boxes and space invaders, while through the fume and gloom and the steam from the coffee machine, moved Neanderthal lorry drivers and sinister ladies with dyed blonde hair and nylon overalls. There would be enamel signs on the fascia and damp noisome toilets round the back. The transport café stood in a gritty car park where oil swilled in dingy rainbows over rain-filled puddles, and bare scrubby thorn bushes rattled dolefully in the wind. Discarded Coke cans clanked in the overflowing waste bins and wallowed sluggishly in the flooded pot-holes, while white spectral scraps of paper cartwheeled lethargically over the tussocks of bleak winter grass in the dismal field beyond the hedge that stretched on and on to the treeless horizon.

'Out you get,' Richard said. Amy blinked, woke up and refocused on the road. It had gone. Richard had stopped the lorry in a layby and in front of them was not the rolling tarmac that she had last seen but a weeping willow tree, just coming into leaf, and hanging over a garden wall. On the far side of the road were some nice-looking semi-detached houses. Amy thought that someone might object to the smelly presence of the lorry in these surroundings.

'Why have we stopped here?'

'You'd like a drink, wouldn't you?' He flicked the switch on the tachograph. 'There's a phone in the café, too.'

Amy looked all round. 'Where's the café?'

Richard was already out of the cab. The door clouted itself shut and Amy found herself marooned until he came round and opened her door.

'Out you get,' he said again. He was so far below her, looking up.

'How?' said Amy.

'Jump. You're the gymnast.' There was no alternative unless she scrambled down backward as she had come up, over the hub. She jumped, and Richard caught her.

'Steady on. You don't have to do a double back somersault here to finish off with, you know.'

Amy thought that it was foolhardy of him to make jokes about gymnastics, under the circumstances.

'But where's the café?'

'Just back here. I did point it out, but you were dreaming.'

'I wasn't.' She had not been dreaming. She had been having a nightmare. 'I was counting cat's-eyes.'

Richard turned into the porch of a red brick building beyond the far end of the layby. The porch, running the length of it, was also floored with red brick and there were brick pillars to support the tiled roof. It looked like a superior kind of health centre but a sign in the window, in front of the delicate white net curtains, said TEA, COFFEE, SOFT DRINKS AND LIGHT REFRESHMENTS SERVED ALL DAY.

'We can't go in here, can we?'

'Whyever not?' Richard said.

'But . . . the lorry . . .'

'We aren't taking the lorry in,' Richard said. 'It'll be quite safe in the layby.'

'But don't they mind?'

'Why should they? We're quite clean. We're going to pay for our coffee. We shan't put our feet on the table and strike matches on the wall. I'm not going to throw food about, are you?' He opened the door and Amy followed him in.

It was warm and quiet inside. Wooden tables and chairs stood on a green tiled floor. Music, very polite music, swelled gently from a loudspeaker on a shelf among house plants and trickled down through the trailing leaves. There was no Formica, no space invaders, no crushed cigarette ends bloating in spilled tea. It was a lot nicer, in fact, than Sally's Pantry, up on the estate, where Mum sometimes took Amy and Helen for a drink on Saturdays, while they were shopping.

'Coffee?' Richard said.

'Yes, please.'

He went to the counter, which was not rigged with hissing coffee machines like a scaled-down oil refinery, and was kept by a respectable little woman who looked like Gran, and came back with two cups, in saucers. The crockery was made of white glass with a pattern round the rims, the same as in Sally's Pantry. There were biscuits, too.

Richard sat down and hung his donkey jacket tidily on the back of his chair.

'Does that tacky thing know we're in here?' Amy said.

'Tachograph. It knows we've stopped.'

'How?'

'I told it. I have to alter the mode switch if I'm taking a break or unloading. Then I have to put it back to "Driving Mode" when I start again.'

'Why?'

'So it knows whether I'm moving or not. We aren't allowed to drive for more than four hours without a break.'

'Suppose you can't find anywhere to stop?'

'That happens more often than you might think. The real limit's eight hours a day. You head for a lorry park in, say, Newbury, and find that the rules have been changed. Big sign up: NO LORRIES. Same with the transport cafés – they close down suddenly. You think you're coming to one and when you get there you find it isn't there any more.'

'What happens if you can't stop, then?'

'I'm breaking the law.'

'Even if you can't help it?'

'As soon as I go over the eight hours I'm breaking the law, and if I'm parked in the wrong place I'm breaking the law.'

'Can't you fiddle it?'

'The tachograph? No – that's why it's there. We call it the spy in the cab.'

'Why d'you have it, then?'

'It's the law again,' Richard said. 'For safety. A driver who stays on the road too long might fall asleep at the wheel. Think what a mess that might make – in a Scammell, for instance.'

Amy had no idea what a Scammell might be but she took his point. 'Oh, it saves lives.'

'You sound like a Government Health Warning,' Richard said. 'I dunno; the sort of people who used to break the law go on breaking it anyway.' He shrugged himself back into his donkey jacket. 'Fit?'

'Fit what?' Amy said, thinking he meant the jacket.

'Are you fit – fit to move?'

'Oh, yes.'

'Want the loo? It's over there, with the little lady on the door.'

'I wonder what they have in Scotland?' Amy said.

'Eh?'

'Well, you can only tell she's a lady by her skirt. I wonder what they do in Scotland, with kilts. Do the little men have skirts, too, on the gents? How can they tell which is which?'

'Strike a light,' Richard said, ungratefully. 'You made a joke.'

*

Steep walls rose on either side of the road.

'Are we going under ground?' Amy said. 'It's like the Dartford Tunnel.'

'Dartford Tunnel goes under the Thames. We went over it.'

'I *know*. But it looks like this.'

They came out into daylight again.

'It's part of the M4 extension into Wales.'

'Are we on the M4?'

'M40 – or we shall be in a little while. On your right, the Hoover factory. Coming shortly, Northolt.'

'I've just remembered,' Amy said, 'you didn't phone Mum.'

'Oh God, so I didn't,' Richard said.

'You didn't do it on purpose.'

'I know I didn't.'

'I mean,' Amy persisted, unforgivingly, 'you didn't do it by accident. You didn't *not* phone by accident.'

Amy, too intent on making her accusation, had forgotten to take into account what Richard would say when she had made it. He did not look at her because they were being overtaken by a tanker loaded with noxious chemicals.

'What do you take me for?' Richard said.

Amy mumbled and counted cat's-eyes.

'I forgot. I'll ring from High Wycombe, I promise.'

They drove on in silence, or at least as near to silence as they could get in the thrumming cabin. It suddenly occurred to Amy that she was sitting on top of the engine. It was down there, directly underneath her.

'What happens if it blows up?'

'*What?*'

'Suppose the engine blows up?'

'Not very likely. What makes you think it might?'

'Well . . . if it did, we're right on top of it.'

'Not quite,' Richard said. 'Move a couple of inches to the left − all right, five centimetres − and you should be OK. I was driving a van once and I picked up a hitch-hiker when one of the piston heads blew. It frightened the life out of him because the connecting rod broke and went on revolving. It just kept clouting the inside of the engine − you never heard such a row. Mind you, if the piston hadn't stopped where it did it would very likely have carried on up, straight through the hitch-hiker and the Luton, before continuing skywards.'

Amy thought that Richard sounded rather too poetic, given the subject. 'What happened?'

'Nothing. But if it *hadn't* stopped where it did and he'd been sitting where you're sitting now . . .'

Amy shifted hurriedly.

'Whyn't you warn me?'

'You didn't ask. Anyway, it's not likely to happen again.'

'It might.'

'You could say that about anything. A USAF Hercules might come down on the box just as we pass the runway.'

'What runway?'

'I told you, Northolt. We're just coming to it.'

'Is it an airport?'

'An airfield. They still call it an aerodrome, I think. Over on the right.'

They were travelling downhill now, maintaining speed, sucking up the road beneath them. Amy, looking in the left-hand mirror that stuck out like a lug on the far side of the door, was surprised to find the road still there, spinning away behind the rear wheels.

'This place always bothers me,' Richard said.

'What does?'

'Northolt. Look at the lamp-posts.'

'They're just lamp-posts.'

'Yes, they are *now* – but keep looking. Notice anything?'

'Oh.' The lamp-posts, on either side of the dual carriage-way, and in the central reservation, had suddenly become very much shorter, as if someone had been past with a very large mallet and driven them further into the ground.

'Why are they so much smaller?'

'You ain't seen nothing yet,' Richard said, 'Now look.'

'Why are they like that?' The shorter lamp standards had given place to very short lamp standards, so close to the ground that they looked like fencing posts.

Richard grinned. 'I wasn't joking when I said a Hercules might land on the roof. See those lights over the hedge? That's the end of the runway. The planes take off over the road.'

'What – as low as the street lamps?'

'Not quite,' Richard said, 'but low enough. That's what bothers me. Those lamps are lower than the top of the box.'

'You mean, a plane might hit us?' Amy found that while she was watching the stunted lamp-posts slide by she had drawn her head right into her shoulders.

'Not this time – unless it's badly off course,' Richard said, cheerfully. 'We're clear of the runway now.'

The lamp-posts were back to normal height. Amy unfolded herself. 'Does Mum know about that?'

'The lamp-posts? Of course she does.'

'Doesn't she worry?'

'Not about them, in particular, but she worries. Of course she does.'

'Don't you mind?'

'*I* worry about *her*.'

'Why? She's at home.'

'Accidents can happen at home,' Richard said. 'I don't know till I get back of a Friday whether you three are all right, do I? I do plenty of worrying, never you mind.'

They came to a roundabout. The box of maps began its travels up and down the ledge again.

'You never fixed that down when we stopped,' Richard said.

'You never phoned Mum.'

'Yes . . . well . . . this is Uxbridge Hill. See that water at the bottom?'

'The river?'

'The Grand Union Canal — over we go. We're in Buckinghamshire now. That's the last of London.'

'*London?*'

'London Borough of Hillingdon.'

'But it was all fields.'

'Still London.'

Amy looked in the mirror again and watched the last of London vanish over the hill-top behind them.

'Did I ever tell you,' Richard was saying, cruelly, 'about that time I brought down the high voltage cable in Wales . . .?'

# JAN NEEDLE

FROM *A Game of Soldiers*

The soldier did not know what made him take the headphones off. By luck or instinct, he pressed the switch to stop, and eased the curved plastic forward over his head. Instantly he heard the other sounds, the outside sounds.

This time there was no mistake. This time it was not sheep. This time it was people.

Surprising himself by his lack of panic, the soldier stuffed the cassette player into his pocket and began to move. Although it cost him much in agony, he began to put himself into position. His position of defence. This time, nothing could catch him unawares.

Michael led the way into the outer building, walking half-crouched, his back to the wall, his knife arm stretched in front of him. Sarah and Thomas followed on, half mockingly, but half joining in the game. They did not giggle, they did not speak.

Slowly, like something from a film, Michael crept up to the door. He gestured to the others to keep well in, then looked through. He stopped, listening and watching.

There was nothing but the wind to hear. And on the shelter floor, nothing new. Planks, stone tiles, rocks, sheep droppings. Except . . . there was a piece of cloth opposite him, a sort of blueish-grey in the sunlight. It could be new, it could be old. He could not, truly, remember.

Michael walked confidently through the doorway and waved the others in. Sarah spotted the cloth immediately.

But before she could speak, or move towards it, the soldier, behind them, hardly able to support the weight of his rifle, sick – put pressure on the trigger.

As the rifle jerked and blasted in his hand, he let out a cry of horror.

Which the chidren did not hear.

For many moments, the children were deafened by the noise of the shot. They did not hear the soldier's cry, nor did they hear the rock and concrete that clattered to the ground as the bullet struck into the stonework above their heads. They knew the shot had been fired from behind them, and they froze.

Before they turned, at last, Michael and Sarah looked at each other, with wide eyes. Thomas's were closed, screwed tightly, as were his fists. But as the others turned, so did he. As he opened his eyes, he began to make a sound.

It was a high, whining noise, a jerky squeaking, and it was quite nerve-racking. Sarah and Michael, wound up like wire strings, could hardly bear it, it was so unhuman. Whatever little courage they had left was being drained by it.

The soldier was still covering them with his rifle; they were under guard. But both of them could see that he was ill. He was propped crookedly against the wall, beside the doorway, almost as if he were broken in the middle, as if at any moment he might fold up like a deckchair, and collapse. His face, behind a growth of stubble, was grey and yellowish-white, twisted with pain. The eyes were not full-open.

And he was young. Despite the greyness of his skin, despite the stubble, despite the gun, he was young. Sarah, for some reason, was deeply shocked by this. He was not much older than she was, or Michael. A matter of a few years. He was a *boy*.

Almost as if he was responding to Thomas's awful whine, the soldier moved his gun. It wavered, wandered even farther away from them. He was staring, staring, staring. The rifle shook.

It was too much for Michael. He hissed at Thomas, violently: 'Shut it, Thomas! For God's sake stop that row.'

At Michael's voice, the rifle twitched up towards them, as if jerked. Thomas sprang at Sarah, and hid his face in her anorak. She stiffly put her arm round him.

'There there,' she said. 'There there. Don't shoot, please, don't shoot. Please don't shoot.'

Thomas, unable to bear the thought of dying with his eyes hidden, pulled his head clear.

'He's going to kill us,' he said. His voice began to rise. 'He's going to shoot us!'

'Shut it,' snapped Michael. 'Thomas! Shut it!'

The rifle wavered, but Thomas was still. Sarah said carefully: 'Please don't shoot us, Mister. We're only harmless children. Please.'

The eyes of the soldier, not fully open, moved and settled on her face. They seemed brown, and drenched in agony. They moved away, and Sarah followed their direction. She understood.

'Michael,' she whispered. 'God, you *fool*. Michael!'

She gestured, still with care. Michaél saw the knife, in his own hand, as if it were in someone else's. As if it were a bomb. He was standing in a commando stance, threatening. He swallowed.

'It's a toy,' Sarah told the soldier. 'Do you understand? It's a toy.'

Humbly, Michael allowed her to take the knife. She closed it carefully, without a click, and gave it back to him. Michael slipped it into his pocket, and stood upright. Not like a commando, anything but that. Like a child. The rifle barrel, as if in response, wavered slowly downwards, towards the earth.

'I want my Mum,' said Thomas, low and whiny. 'Sarah, make him let us go. *Make* him.'

Michael whispered: 'I'm going to make a dash! I'm going to –'

'No!'

The rifle twitched once more. Sarah, the muscles in her face aching, smiled.

'We don't want to hurt you, sir,' she said, slowly. 'We're just kids playing. We don't want to hurt you. Do . . . you . . . understand?'

Perhaps the soldier tried to smile. His face changed, then he groaned. The rifle barrel drooped until it almost touched the ground.

'Not hurt,' he said. It was a croak, hardly audible. 'Am cold. Am food.'

He said something else, in a language they did not know. His eyes closed, and the muzzle rested on the soil.

Michael, staring at him fascinated, whispered to Sarah: 'He's useless! We could rush him! We could get that gun and kill him! I –'

He broke off as the brown eyes opened. Sarah whispered: 'Shut up, Michael. You'll get *us* killed. *Please* shut up.'

The soldier blinked. He spoke to them in his own language, saw their blank faces.

'Am hungry,' he finished up.

Sarah, waiting for a polite moment or two, said: 'Can we go, sir? Please. We'd better go now, honestly. Will you let us go?'

After a moment, the soldier moved his shoulders. His face tensed in pain. His eyes closed, then opened.

'No tell soldier,' he whispered. 'Please. Am hurt. No tell soldier.'

Thomas Wyatt suddenly jumped away sideways from Sarah and shouted.

'My Dad'll do you in, mate! You dirty rapist! My Dad'll bring his –'

Impossible to tell which of the three of them was more shocked. The soldier waved his gun, wildly. Sarah became rooted to the ground – and Michael sprang. He seized Thomas by the shoulder and clamped his other hand over his mouth.

'Shut up!' he shouted. Then there was only the wind, and Michael's panting. Slowly the soldier lowered the gun to the earth. He could hardly keep his eyes upon them.

'Friend,' he said. It was almost a breath, only. 'Am friend.'

After fifteen seconds, Sarah took Thomas by the arm. She started to guide him past the soldier.

'Out,' she said softly. 'Go on, Tom, get out. Slowly. Slowly. Out.'

When they were almost in the inner doorway, the soldier opened his eyes. All three of them turned to stone.

His face changed. Maybe he tried to smile. They could barely hear his voice.

'Am friend. Please. No tell the soldier.'

They watched him intently until his eyes drooped closed. Then they left. By the time they reached the outer doorway, they were running as if the devil himself were after them . . .

# BERLIE DOHERTY

FROM *Granny was a Buffer Girl*

Today was a special day for Dorothy. It was Saturday, February 26th, 1931. Dorothy was seventeen today. It was also the day of the cutlers' ball, when her firm was to hold its annual dance at the Cutlers' Hall in town. This year everyone who worked for the firm had been invited.

'It'll be a right birthday treat for you, Dolly!' Louie had said. Her big awkward husband, Gilbert, had gladly given her leave to go without him, and she was grateful for that. She was going to find it hard enough to coax Dorothy to go, and to enjoy herself when she got there, without dragging Gilbert along too.

Dorothy had been cold with excitement all day. It was the first time she'd been to a dance of any sort. It was the first time she'd celebrated a birthday.

'Come on, Dolly, let's get you fettled!' Louie called up to her, and Dorothy ran downstairs to wash the muck of work off her hands and her face, and out of her long thick hair. She and Louie scrubbed each other down, and then Louie sat her in the hearth while she crimped her hair for her. They chattered away, full of it all, holding the curling tongs in the heat of the coals till they glowed, and then wrapping Dorothy's hair quickly round them.

'Hold it still,' Louie ordered. 'Don't wriggle or the lines will come out all wobbly.'

'You'll ruin that girl's hair,' Mrs Beatty warned. She

was pressing their frocks. She held the iron near her face to feel it heat. Her spittle fizzed on it. 'It'll drop out before she's twenty-one, you'll see.'

'I don't care if it does drop out before she's twenty-one.' Louie's laugh was the sort that cracked inside your ear-hole. She could break bones in half with her voice. 'So long as it's all right for tonight, that's all.'

Mrs Beatty draped the hot dresses over the chair-back and settled down for a rest. She nagged on comfortably. 'When I was a girl it didn't do for young ladies to show their hair at all, never mind cook it.' But when old Mrs Beatty had been Dorothy's age the year had been 1876, and the world of young ladies then was a foreign land to them. 'I've seen more changes in my life-time than you're ever likely to see in yours, or would want to see, neither. Things have got wicked.' She purred into her cocoa and nodded off, missing the fun of seeing Dorothy put on her lisle stockings and the blue satin dress with red posies that she'd helped her to make.

The little ones crowded round for a good look at their sisters before they set off, and their clamour woke Mrs Beatty up again briefly. She had come to keep an eye on them while their widowed father was on night-shift at the steelworks, and to take advantage of a fire that she herself couldn't afford.

'You look bonny enough,' she murmured, and was asleep again before the girls had time to put on their powder. They slipped out into the street and ran arm in arm across the cobbles to where their friends were waiting for them at the tram stop.

The Cutlers' Hall was in Church Street, near the middle of town. Lights blazed from all its windows. Even from the street outside, with all its bustle of trams and traffic, you could hear the strains of the orchestra, and the babble of voices and laughter. Dorothy, shy, held on to her sister's arm as they went up the steps to the entrance hall. She gazed round at the black and green walls that gleamed like marble, the crystal chandeliers, the glowing polish of the woodwork; at the height of the pillars and the decorated ceiling, and at the broad sweep of the grand staircase that she was going to have to climb up if she was ever going to get near the ballroom. A woman in a pale green taffeta dress rustled down from the top flight on the arm of a young man and stood poised on the landing. She turned to smile at another group who were coming down to her, and the huge mirror behind her held her poised like one of the paintings round the walls. Her hair was permed in rows like the deep waves of the sea, in the newest fashion, and real jewels flashed at her throat.

'That's boss's wife,' Louie whispered. 'And that's boss's son, Mr Edward. In't he a peach!' She laughed loudly, in the shrieking way she had, and the party on the stairs turned their heads slightly towards them, and away again, and Dorothy blushed – not at her sister's coarseness, but because Mr Edward, son of the owner of one of the most famous cutlery firms in the world, had caught her eye and was staring coolly at her.

And she felt his eyes on her all evening, especially when she found herself laughing for joy at the dancing and singing to herself the tunes that she had only heard before in the singing at work. The little orchestra now filled them out with harmonies: 'Danny Boy', 'I'll Take You Home Again, Kathleen', 'Roses are Blooming in Picardy' . . .

'I say,' whispered a voice in her ear. 'Did you know you're the prettiest girl here?'

'Am I?' She daren't turn her face to look at Mr Edward, even though his breath was warm on her cheek.

'You've eyes the colour of bluebells.'

She smiled at a plate of cakes on the buffet table.

'I'd like to ask you for the next dance,' he went on. 'And I shan't take no for an answer.'

She looked round for her friends, but they'd all gone off somewhere; smoking, or blotting their glowing cheeks with powder. Mr Edward put his hand on her shoulder and steered her out to the centre of the floor and she stood rigid with mortification while they waited for the music to start. She knew how to dance all right. Louie had seen to that, giving her lessons in the kitchen under the dripping clothes-rack while old Mrs Beatty hummed the tunes and tapped out the rhythm with her steel-tipped stick, and all her little brothers and sisters sat in their night-gowns on the kitchen bench to watch. She knew every dance there was to know, and was as light and lively on her feet as her mother had been. And Mr Edward could dance too. Now she knew that everyone's eyes were on her, and she didn't care. She wanted all the girls to notice her triumph. At the end of the dance his arms still held her and what's more his eyes held her too; and even though the music had stopped and all the other dancers were moving back to their seats she wanted that moment to hold her there for ever.

But, 'Edward! Edward!' his mother hissed at him, in a voice that was a shade too harsh for the smooth face under the permanent waves, and Mr Edward's firm grasp wilted.

'Wait for me after the ball,' he whispered. 'Will you?' Not looking at her but at his mother. 'Say you will.' And, 'I'll drive you home.'

'I'll drive you home!' Never had a motor car been in
Dorothy's street! At the end of the dance, when she was
queuing with her sister for her coat and easing her feet
out of her shoes, she told Louie that even though the last
tram had gone she wouldn't be walking home with her.

'Mr Edward's taking me in his car,' she whispered.

'Don't be mad!' said Louie. 'Him, bring you home!
Down Attercliffe, with me dad waiting to strap him for
his cheek. Forget it, Dorothy. He's having you on.'

So arm in arm the sisters and their friends scuttled
down from the scented ballroom and limped their blis-
tered way home through the dark streets to Attercliffe.

But Dorothy couldn't forget Mr Edward that easily.
That night she dreamt about him, and all next day too,
when she was busy with the cooking and the housework,
and she held a picture of herself with him, a still, coloured
image like a painting, but with music in the background,

and it showed him with his face bent down towards her at the end of the dance, and her with her face held up to his. When Albert Bradley from over the road lingered, as he always did, till Dorothy's father had gone to work, and knocked on her door for his morning kiss before racing down the street to clock on at the steelworks, he met with a fullness of lips that he'd never come across before.

'Why, Dolly, tha's coming on!' he said, stepping back for air, and Dorothy opened her eyes, shocked to think that Albert's blotched and bristly face should have put her in mind of Mr Edward.

'Get away with you, Albert Bradley,' she said, and he did, haring up the street to beat Dorothy's dad to the works gates, and grinning all day long at Dorothy's new magic.

Louie's strange husband, Gilbert, left for work at the same time, and she came round to Dorothy's house to help her to get the little ones up. Then they got ready for work together. They had to protect themselves from the gritty dust of the buffing wheel. They took newspapers from the pile that the neighbours brought round for them at the end of every week and tied sheets of them round each other – chest, arms, stomach, legs, till there was no clothing left to be seen except for the newly washed and daisy-white calico head-squares that they tied round their crimped hair. They collected their sandwiches, and left Mrs Beatty her penny for taking the little ones to school and back; and set off, rustling, for their tram, gathering their friends on the way. The girls chattered and shrieked and gossiped as the tram swayed down to town, and Dorothy gazed out at the houses with sunlight as pale as sand on their windows and thought of the rich gleam of chandeliers, and felt the warmth of Mr Edward's breath on her cheeks.

Much later that morning Mr Edward arrived at work. He'd had a bad weekend, dreaming about Dorothy. He was quite determined to find her again. All the people who had been to the ball had been employed by his father, so he knew that she would be in the building somewhere. He wouldn't let her slip away from him again, in her shyness.

In between inspecting the neat rows of boxed cutlery and candlesticks and meat plates that were lined up for export, he roamed from office to office and from floor to floor, anxious to get a glimpse of her; and Dorothy, standing all day long over her buffing wheel while clouds of black dust settled over her newspaper arms and body and her calico head-square, kept casting glances over her shoulder, sensing with every nerve that he was somewhere in the building and that he was looking for her. But it never occurred to him to look among the buffer girls, even though the sickly metal-and-hot dust smell of their work lay heavy in every room, and the whirr of their machinery wound interminably through the day, and the lusty singing of the girls at their work chimed in every corner. If he had climbed up to the top floor of his father's building he would have seen the long buffing shop hot and bright with sunlight pouring through the roof windows, and the forty girls standing in their row putting the gleam on all those articles he inspected. They would be holding their faces away from the sand-dust that the wheel sprayed back at them, and from time to time they'd dash with their mugs to the tap in the corner and swill their mouths out, or they'd stretch back their

shoulders to ease the ache, or flex the muscles of their
feet.

'I'll take you home again, Kathleen' they'd be singing,
or 'My old man, said follow the van, and don't dilly
dally on the way . . .' All day long they'd be singing, and
from time to time the little one with eyes like bluebells in
her blackened face would look over her shoulder for
someone.

But at last it was clocking-off time. The machine stopped.
The girls put out their pieces of holloware to be counted,
and those with husbands' meals to cook and shopping to
do on Attercliffe Common urged the ones who wanted
to chat and dawdle to hurry up. They crowded out of
the building together; newspaper arms and legs, faces,
hands, calico head-squares, all as black as soot.

Dorothy clattered out behind the others, listening to
their jokes and laughter and wrapped up still in her
warm thoughts of the dance; and saw Mr Edward by the
steps, dapper as a new sixpence and holding a posy of
violets.

'For me!' she breathed.

His eyes flashed up and up the steps as the workers
streamed out. Dorothy broke away from her sister to run
to him but Louie pulled her back.

'Don't,' she warned. 'He's never waiting for you.'

'He *is*,' said Dorothy, breaking free.

'Not *you*!' Louie's voice wailed.

Dorothy ran right up to Mr Edward, her newspapers
flapping away from her arms. He had moved away as the
top floor workers came down, and was about to give up
his vigil.

'Mr Edward!'

He half turned, knowing the voice, and went back towards the steps. He had to push past the grimy blue-eyed girl on the pavement, and she brushed her dust off his coat in annoyance. The buffer girls yelled at Dorothy to hurry or they'd miss the tram; and, as she ran past him again, he realized that the girl he was looking for had vanished like the music and the lights and all the scents and laughter of the dance. He dropped the violets in the gutter and strode back to his car, and Louie, coming to hook Dorothy's arm in her own, bent down and picked them up for her kitchen table.

# JENNY NIMMO

FROM *Snow Spider*

He waited until his grandmother had settled herself in the armchair and sipped her tea before he knelt beside her and took out the matchbox. He wanted her undivided attention for his revelation. Even so he was unprepared for the ecstatic gasp that accompanied Nain's first glimpse of the spider, when he gently withdrew the lid. The tiny creature crawled on to his hand, glowing in the dark room, and Nain's eyes sparkled like a child's. 'How did it come?' Her whisper was harsh with excitement.

'In the snow,' Gwyn replied. 'I thought it was a snowflake. It was the brooch, I think. I gave it to the wind, like you said, and this . . . came back!'

'So,' Nain murmured triumphantly, 'you are a magician then, Gwydion Gwyn, as I thought. See what you have made!'

'But did I make it, Nain? I believe it has come from somewhere else. Some far, far place . . . I don't know, beyond the world, I think.'

'Then you called it, you brought it here, Gwydion Gwyn. Did you call?'

'I did but . . .' Gwyn hesitated, 'I called into the snow, the names you said: Math, Lord of Gwynedd, Gwydion and Gilfaethwy. Those were the only words.'

'They were the right words, boy. You called to your ancestors. The magicians heard your voice and took the brooch to where it had to go, and now you have the spider!' Nain took the spider from Gwyn and placed it on her arm. Then she got up and began to dance through the shadowy wilderness of her room. The tiny glowing creature moved slowly up her purple sleeve, until it came to her shoulder, and there it rested, shining like a star beneath her wild black curls.

Gwyn watched and felt that it was Nain who was the magician and he the enchanted one.

Suddenly his grandmother swooped back and, taking the spider from her hair, put it gently into his hands. 'Arianwen,' she said. 'White silver! Call her Arianwen; she must have a name!'

'And what now?' asked Gwyn. 'What becomes of Arianwen? Should I tell about her? Take her to a museum?'

'Never! Never! Never!' said Nain fiercely. 'They wouldn't understand. She has come from another world to bring you closer to the thing you want.'

'I want to see my sister,' said Gwyn. 'I want things the way they were before she went.'

Nain looked at Gwyn through half-closed eyes. 'It's just the beginning, Gwydion Gwyn, you'll see. You'll be alone, mind. You cannot tell. A magician can have his heart's desire if he truly wishes it, but he will always be alone.' She propelled her grandson gently but firmly towards the door. 'Go home now or they'll come looking, and never tell a soul!'


The farmhouse was empty when Gwyn reached home. Mr Griffiths could be heard drilling in his workshop. Mrs Griffiths had popped out to see a neighbour, leaving a note for her son on the kitchen table,

## 'SOUP ON THE STOVE.
## STOKE IT UP IF IT'S COLD'

'The soup or the stove?' Gwyn muttered to himself. He opened the stove door, but the red embers looked so warm and comforting he was reluctant to cover them with fresh coal. He turned off the light and knelt beside the fire, holding out his hands to the warmth.

He must have put the matchbox down somewhere and he must have left it open, because he suddenly became aware that Arianwen was climbing up the back of the armchair. When she reached the top she swung down to the arm, leaving a silver thread behind her. Up she went to the top, and then down, her silk glistening in the firelight. Now the spider was swinging and spinning back and forth across the chair so fast that Gwyn could only see a spark, shooting over an ever-widening sheet of silver.

'A cobweb!' he breathed.

And yet it was not a cobweb. There was someone there. Someone was sitting where the cobweb should have been. A girl with long pale hair and smiling eyes: Bethan, sitting just as she used to sit, with her legs tucked under her, one hand resting on the arm of the chair, the other supporting her chin as she gazed into the fire. And still Arianwen spun, tracing the girl's face, her fingers and her hair, until every feature became so clear Gwyn felt he could have touched the girl.

The tiny spider entwined the silk on one last corner and then ceased her feverish activity. She waited, just above the girl's head, allowing Gwyn to contemplate her creation without interruption.

Was the girl an illusion? An image on a silver screen?

No, she was more than that. Gwyn could see the im-presson her elbow made on the arm of the chair, the fibres in her skirt, the lines on her slim, pale hand.

Only Bethan had ever sat thus. Only Bethan had gazed into the fire in such a way. But his sister was dark, her cheeks were rosy, her skin tanned golden by the wind. This girl was fragile and so silver-pale she might have been made of gossamer.

'Bethan?' Gwyn whispered, and he stretched out his hand towards the girl.

A ripple spread across the shining image, as water moves when a stone pierces the surface, but Gwyn did not notice a cool draught entering the kitchen as the door began to open.

'Bethan?' he said again.

The figure shivered violently as the door swung wider, and then the light went on. The girl in the cobweb hovered momentarily and gradually began to fragment and to fade until Gwyn was left staring into an empty chair. His hands dropped to his side.

'Gwyn! What are you doing, love? What are you staring at?' His mother came round the chair and looked down at him, frowning anxiously.

Gwyn found that speech was not within his power, part of his strength seemed to have evaporated with the girl.

'Who were you talking to? Why were you sitting in the dark?' Concern caused Mrs Griffiths to speak sharply.

Her son swallowed but failed to utter a sound. He stared up at her helplessly.

'Stop it, Gwyn! Stop looking at me like that! Get up! Say something!' His mother shook his shoulders and pulled him to his feet.

He stumbled over to the table and sat down, trying desperately to drag himself away from the image in the cobweb. The girl had smiled at him before she vanished, and he knew that she was real.

# GERALDINE McCAUGHREAN

FROM *A Little Lower Than the Angels*

Hell was a wooden arch with a cloth tunnel behind it and a simple catch holding shut the green eye. It smoked because there was a length of tarry rope nailed up behind the gullet which Lucie set alight before going on stage. God reached Heaven by climbing a ladder behind the wooden scenery. His world was peopled by half a dozen ragged individuals who had followed an assortment of callings, from seasonal shearing to thatching, cowherding to churchyard sexton. Mischief or discontent, a hard master or some family tragedy that made home hateful to them had shuffled together these jacks and knaves. All they had in common – Hob and Jack, Lucie and Garvey, John and Simon, Adam of Wendle, and the youth who played Eve – was a knowledge of the words of the Mysteries, some or all. Their affection for the plays varied. Some were there because, well, elsewhere they would starve. Some would have starved rather than give up the playing. The music was played by two musicians, Rolande and Ydrys, sitting cross-legged under the cart with a hurdy-gurdy, a reed-pipe, a drum and a shawm, all hidden from sight by a straw bale. On a windy day, guy ropes were needed to hold the flat scenery upright.

Gabriel quickly discovered why a replacement was needed for the angel. They left behind the pot-bellied shearer who had played him previously. They left him slumped in a drunken stupor against the church wall. Lucie forced a penny into his soft, sleeping palm, dumped his shearing tools in his lap, and pulled his cap down over his face in the hope that nobody would recognize him for one of the players.

In the next town the Abbot politely told them they were not wanted. The craftsmen of the local Guilds had been performing a play on the Feast of Corpus Christi for eighty years. No outsiders could do it better, and the city's working men and women were too busy to waste another day in idleness.

'In the west, the Guildsmen threw stones,' said Izzie. 'When once we've been to a place, we're liked. You liked us.'

She had a bald, stark way of speaking, never looking Gabriel in the eye but staring over his shoulder with a slight frown creasing her curd-yellow forehead. Before Gabriel acted for the first time, she spent hours brushing his hair and fluffing it out with a hazel twig into a frizzy golden cloud, quite indifferent to his squeaks and ouches. It was as if she were arranging flowers or carding wool. It was just one of her many tasks.

She made his costume, cutting down a white linen shirt and fitting it tight up round the neck. Nobody asked her to make it. She made all the costumes. It was one of her jobs. Her father left things with her for mending, like a sheep leaves its wool on a fence, in passing. She always had some piece of sewing stuck in her belt while she cooked. (Preparing meals for the players was another of her jobs.) She washed down the horses if they started to look or smell disreputable. So she washed down Gabriel on the day he first played an angel.

*

The ladder trembled as soon as he put one bare foot on it. He stood there, one foot up, one foot down, and watched the top of the ladder bounce against the rickety scenery. He was mesmerized.

'Is that ladder nervous again?' said a quiet voice behind him. 'You'd think it would have stopped shaking by now. But no. Every time a new player sets foot on it, it starts to shake. Pay it no heed.' And a green-gloved hand reached over his shoulder to hold the ladder firm. Gabriel turned and looked straight into Lucie's green-stained face glistening with grease; a leather forked tongue was clenched between his teeth, and his black hair was slicked down with water in front of the green knitted hood. Gabriel went up the ladder two rungs at a time, and stood sweating behind his cloud. All he could hear was his heart beating. Perhaps the audience had picked up their stools and gone home. He was not sorry.

After Izzie finished playing her recorder, it was her job to loosen off the ropes and allow the scenery clouds to flop forwards on their hinges, revealing God and all His angels . . . God and His angel. The cloud in front of Gabriel flopped down. He bent his knees, hoping to stay hidden.

'Aaaah!' A long, sentimental gust of female sighs burst from the audience. They were all faces – just a mass of white ovals, like a dish of eggs. Viewed from so high up, their bodies were foreshortened and hidden by the faces in front. They looked so eager, so willing to be pleased. Gabriel put his flat trumpet to his lips and pretended to blow – and, underneath the cart, a shawm blew a nasal fanfare: the timing was so good that it startled even Gabriel. Perhaps the small wooden area with its pulleys and flaps and tricks and traps and splinters and rags was magic, after all.

He saw the tree rise up off the stage and did not see the rope and pulleys that raised it. He began to know how God had felt, looking down on Creation on the seventh day, resting from making the World. It was all very good.

They were three towns away from the Mason. Gabriel had broken his apprentice's bond and no one had hanged him or flogged him or thrown him into prison. In fact the players did not seem to think it was important. They shared their food with him. They gave him a *linen* shirt to wear! And they never mentioned his girlish features or his brush of hair or the fact that he was so small and puny for his age. All they wanted was for him to sit still as a stone – to be a piece of scenery, a decoration like one of the stone angels he had watched the Mason carve, up in the roofs of churches. It was easy.

'Don't pick your nose.'

'Don't scratch.'

'Don't yawn.'

'Don't fidget.'

'Don't go to sleep.'

It was so simple, however hard Izzie tried to make it sound difficult with all her 'don'ts'. Perhaps she did not realize how easy it was to sit perfectly still while you studied the faces one by one of the people in the audience, imagining their names, learned the words of the speaking players, and then – best of all! – played the Wishing Game. He saved up the Wishing Game till last, and then he let his imagination loose.

One day the players would drive through countryside that looked dimly familiar. They would set up the stage among buildings he felt he somehow knew. The audience would gather, one particular yeoman turning aside, out

of curiosity, to see these strange outsiders everyone was talking about. The yeoman's wife would tussle for a good place to set down her stool. The chatter would die away. The music would start. Then, seeing the hinged clouds fold down to reveal God and all His angels, the wife would look once and look again and stand up and point and clutch her apron to her mouth . . . And the people round about would tug at her and shout, 'Sit down, Missus!' But she would refuse and say, 'But it's *Gabriel*. It's my Gabriel! Father! Look up yonder. It's our Gabriel and he's an *angel*!'

He would not wave when his mother spotted him. He would just smile and dip his head a little, and she would have to wait until the very end to be reunited with him. They would see how still he could sit!

Why shouldn't it happen? More extraordinary things had happened! One month ago, each new day had lain in wait to ambush Gabriel: he had woken up cringing. Now he was fed and clothed just for sitting still, and crowds looked at him and sighed – 'Aaaah!' There was nothing to be afraid of, except perhaps Lucie. (No one who looked so evil could be quite safe.) But Garvey had a big, round, jolly face. Gabriel could shelter in God's good grace.

Such a weight of worry and terror and contempt had been lifted off his shoulders that he sometimes thought, when the end-music started up beneath the wagon and the audience began to toss like a field of corn, that he could spread his arms, if he wanted, and soar off his ledge, above their heads and round the church tower. As free as a bird. By the time he reached the bottom of the ladder, he was almost laughing out loud with happiness.

# RUTH THOMAS

FROM *The Runaways*

'What you doing here then?' he asked Julia.
'Hiding, of course, what's it look like?'
'Well you can't stay in the street.'
'Why not?'
'Don't you know *nothing*?' said Nathan, contemptuously. 'They come out looking for you after Assembly. Mrs Peters – the Welfare Assistant – comes out in her car, and she goes all round the streets looking. We got to hide properly.'
'Where?'
'I know a place.' Again, Nathan half regretted what he had said. 'You got to promise not to tell, though.'
'A secret?'
'Yeah – it's a secret place. You got to promise not to tell.'
Julia gaped at him. She had never been asked to share a secret before, and she was enormously flattered that someone was asking her now – even if it *was* only horrible Nathan Browne, whom nobody liked either.
'I promise,' she said, trying to sound casual.
'Come on then, Rat-bag.'
Dumbly, Julia followed; round the corner, and into the next street. A derelict house, the garden full of weeds, and the windows long since smashed and splintered, defaced the otherwise neatly kept terrace. A train rumbled past, somewhere behind the row of houses. 'It's here,'

said Nathan. 'In here.'

Julia was disappointed. 'That's not a secret place,' she objected. 'Everyone knows *that* house is empty.'

'Nobody knows I go there though,' said Nathan. 'It's *my* secret den. Wait a minute, what you doing?' Julia had made to take a step through the weeds, but Nathan stopped her. 'We got to make sure nobody sees us going in.'

He made a great performance of making sure. First, he paraded nonchalantly backwards and forwards, looking everywhere but at the house. There was a woman with a shopping basket at the end of the road, but too far away to count. Then the windows of the nearby houses had to be studied. 'See if anybody's looking out,' Nathan instructed Julia. He spoke in a conspiratorial whisper, and

Julia began to enjoy herself very much. 'Nobody's look-ing,' she assured him, entering into the spirit of it.

'Right – now!' Nathan hissed, making a dive for the half-open door of the empty house. Julia followed. The two children stood together in the fusty passage way, smelling of damp and rotting wood. The small black boy with the glowering face and the poor eyesight, and the gawky white girl with a stoop. They looked at one an-other warily, mistrustfully. Then without a word, Nathan plunged deeper into the recesses of his secret den, Julia creeping at his heels.

They sat on bare boards, hardly warmer than outside, but dry at least. Another train went past, louder now, shaking the building with vibrations.

'If you really want to know,' said Nathan, 'it probably isn't just *my* den. It's probably a pirate's den as well.' His head was so full of *Treasure Island* just at the moment that he dreamed of pirates all the time.

'Don't be silly,' said Julia. 'Pirates are by the sea. There ain't no seaside here.'

'There's the river,' said Nathan, unwilling to relinquish his dream.

'What river?'

'You know, where the Houses of Parliament is.'

'Oh, *that* river.'

Julia had been to Westminster Pier once, last summer or perhaps the summer before. But it had taken so long to get there by public transport that she hardly connected the River Thames with her own home area. It was actually about four miles away.

'Come on, come on, come on,' said Nathan suddenly, in a different voice. For a moment, Julia thought he was talking to her. He had gone mad, perhaps. Then she saw the round eyes, gleaming in the dim light, as a shaggy black cat crept out of the shadows and into the children's view.

'Come on, come on, come on, I got something for you.' Out of his pocket, Nathan produced a torn plastic bag, and out of the bag some scraps of food – a piece of bacon, some cheese, a lump of gristly meat saved from last night's supper. He held out the bacon, and the cat stepped warily forward, but would not take the food from his hand. It stood two paces away, its gaze intent, quivering with longing. Half one ear was missing, and the nearest eye totally closed.

'He's really wild, this one,' Nathan explained. 'He don't trust no one.'

He placed the bacon on the floorboards and shuffled back a few feet. The cat sprang to the food as if it had not had a square meal for months, as indeed it probably had not.

'I call this one Sooty,' said Nathan. 'There's another one somewhere. Tiger, Tiger, come on Tiger!'

A second cat appeared, in no better condition than the first, but not nearly so scared. This one came right up to Nathan, mewed a greeting and took the lump of meat from his hand. Nathan divided the cheese between the two cats and, fed, the one with the ginger stripes allowed him to stroke its head. Its purrs echoed through the empty room.

'Took me weeks to tame him, but I eventually done it,' said Nathan proudly.

'Wish I had a cat,' said Julia. 'Would he let me touch him?'

'Shouldn't think so,' said Nathan. 'You could try. Mind he don't scratch!'

Julia stretched her hand out hesitantly. The cat eyed her with suspicion, but submitted to her caress. Nathan regarded her with the faint beginnings of respect, but he was none too pleased. 'Definitely peculiar,' he muttered. 'He's only supposed to like me.'

The children lapsed into silence for a while.

'Why you bunking off then?' said Nathan, suddenly.

'None of your business,' said Julia. 'Anyway, Nathan, *you're* in trouble. You got to go to Mr Barlowe, Mrs Henrey said.'

'She'll forget,' said Nathan, not worried.

Another long pause.

'What's this place got to do with pirates?' asked Julia, who had been thinking about it. 'Why d'you think pirates come here?'

He didn't *really* think they did. He just thought it would be nice if they did. It was an exciting idea that he could pretend to believe in when he was alone.

'I find things,' he said, mysteriously. 'I found a pipe one time, and a old shoe.' Indeed, piles of similar rubbish were littered all over the room, in between the cobwebs.

'Probably a tramp,' said Julia.

Probably she was right, but much more interesting to think it was pirates. 'I found a paper once with some funny marks on it. Most likely a message in code.'

Julia thought for a long moment. 'Don't pirates bury treasure?' she asked at last. 'Perhaps they've buried some treasure here.'

'Nah – they always bury it on a island, with a cross on the map to show where it is.'

'Don't they never bury it in a house? Shall we look and see? Shall we, Nathan?'

'Nah,' he said.

'Why not? We *might* find something. Where would they put it if they did?'

How stupid she was! She didn't understand it was a game, she thought it was real.

'Where do you think they'd put it, Nathan?'

'Under the floorboards, I suppose,' said Nathan reluctantly. It was silly to think the pirates were real, but of course, things that were buried in houses were always under the floorboards. Everyone knew *that*.

Half-heartedly, Nathan tried to prise up a board in the corner of the room which looked loose.

Julia frowned. 'Not there,' she said.

'Why not?'

'It's all thick dirt. Nobody's moved that lately.'

Nathan looked at Julia sharply. She couldn't be that stupid after all. 'Let's go in the other rooms,' he suggested.

They wandered through the house, peering carefully. It *was* only a game, of course – but on the other hand, you never knew . . .

'There!' said Julia.

Nathan saw immediately what she meant. A piece of floorboard with fresh scratches on it, and the dirt scraped over to cover up the scratches. The board was quite loose, it came up easily in Nathan's hands. The hole revealed was empty. 'There's nothing there,' he said, disappointed but hardly surprised.

Julia lay full length on the dirty floor and thrust her arm into the space beyond where the piece of board had been pulled up.

'I got something,' she exclaimed, excitedly.

'What is it?'

'I dunno. Here it is.' She withdrew her arm, and in

her hand was a large brown envelope. The envelope was stiff and new, and hardly dirty at all. Julia was quite dizzy with triumph. Without speaking, she lifted the flap off the envelope and tipped its contents on to the floor. *Money!* Lots of real paper money, all in twenty pound notes. The two children stared at what they had found.

'Look at that,' Nathan breathed, his eyes round with incredulity. 'Just look at that!'

'You was right, Nathan,' Julia whispered in awe. 'It *was* pirates.'

Nathan shook his head. He was still struggling to grasp the reality of what had happened. This stupendous discovery that in one moment had put all the previous highlights of his life in the shade. 'It ain't pirates though,' he said. 'It ain't pirates.'

'But we found the money they buried.'

'It's the wrong sort of money for pirates,' said Nathan. 'Pirates' money is all gold coins. This is ordinary money.'

'Who put it there then?'

'I dunno. Robbers I suppose.'

'Where they get it from?'

'How should I know? Burglared a house most likely.'

'What did they put it under the floor for?'

'So the police won't find it in *their* house of course!' What was the matter with her – stupid thing? Didn't she ever watch telly?

'We found it, didn't we, Nathan! We found all that money! I can't believe we really found all that money, can you? How much is it?'

'I dunno. Hundreds of pounds anyway. Thousands, probably.'

'Thousands of pounds! How did the robbers get in here, Nathan? Suppose somebody saw them coming in?'

'You don't know nothing, man,' said Nathan, irritably. 'They come in the back of course, over the railway. It's perfect. I bet lots of these houses been burglared like that.'

The children's eyes, and their thoughts, went back to the money, lying between them, spilled over the dusty floor. Over the quivering excitement of having found it, an unspoken question hovered. Nathan prodded the money with his foot. Julia chewed the end of her pigtail.

'Nathan,' said Julia at last, 'is it *our* money?'

'Course. We found it, didn't we!'

'Do you think we ought to take it to the police?'

'I ain't taking my half to the police. You can do what you like with your half.'

'Oh.'

'What you going to do then, with your half?'

'Keep it, I suppose,' said Julia. 'Same as you.'

'Shall we share it out then?'

'Half for you and half for me?'

'Suppose that's fair. You found it, but it's my secret place.'

'Yeah, all right, that's fair.'

Dividing the money was easy. They dealt the notes like a pack of cards, and there were sixty-five each.

'We're rich now, aren't we!' said Julia. 'I can't believe I'm rich.'

'We mustn't tell nobody though.'

'Course not.'

'What you going to spend yours on, Julia?'

'I dunno yet.' Actually she was beginning to have an idea, but the idea was a private thing at this stage.

Nathan's plans were also private. He was thinking in terms of saving his half until he was grown up, and then buying a house. There would surely be enough money for that; there might even be some left over. He would put his notes in a very safe place meanwhile. And that thought raised another question.

'Julia – where we going to keep our money?'

Julia considered. 'Couldn't we keep it here? In another part of the house?'

'No, we couldn't! That's one thing we certainly couldn't do!'

'Why not?'

'Think, stupid! The one that put it here is going to come back for it, isn't he.'

'So. He won't find it in the place, it'll be gone. We could hide it again, so he won't know where to look.'

'But he might find *us*. He might come back any time and find us. Or somebody might see us going in, and tell.'

'Oh yeah – then he'd take it away from us again.'

'Then he'd *kill* us, probably.'

'Really? Really kill us?' Julia's pale eyes were round with horror and fright. 'When's he coming back, Nathan? Is he coming back now?'

'I dunno, do I?'

'Perhaps he's coming right this minute. Perhaps he's coming over the railway line now. Let's go, Nathan, before he comes to kill us.'

'Wait a minute, we got to think first.' But Julia's fear was infectious, and Nathan was already feeling uneasy and jumpy. 'All right, we'll go. Put your money safe first though. You can have the envelope. Have you got a pocket?'

The plastic mac had no pocket, neither had the cotton dress beneath it. 'Turn round, Nathan, don't look,' said

Julia, primly. She stuffed the envelope with the money in it inside her knickers, where it felt scratchy but reassuring, against her skin.

# DIANA WYNNE JONES

FROM *The Lives of Christopher Chant*

The largest thing among the clutter was a fat arm-chair. Dr Pawson was sitting in it, not moving a muscle except for a quiver from his vast purple jowls. He was probably too fat to move. He was vastly, hugely, grossly fat. His belly was like a small mountain with a checked waistcoat stretched over it. His hands reminded Christopher of some purple bananas he had seen in Series Five. His face was stretched, and purple too, and out of it glared two merciless watery eyes.

'How do you do, sir?' Christopher said, since Papa trusted him to be polite.

'No, *no!*' shouted Dr Pawson. 'This is an examination, not a social call. What's your problem – Chant your name is, isn't it? State your problem, Chant.'

'I can't do magic, sir,' Christopher said.

'So can't a lot of people. Some are born that way,' Dr Pawson bawled. 'Do better than that, Chant. Show me. Don't do some magic and let me see.'

Christopher hesitated, out of bewilderment mostly.

'Go on, boy!' howled Dr Pawson. 'Don't do it!'

'I can't not do something I can't do,' Christopher said, thoroughly harassed.

'Of course, you can!' yelled Dr Pawson 'That's the essence of magic. Get on with it. Mirror on the table beside you. Levitate it and be quick about it!'

If Dr Pawson hoped to startle Christopher into

succeeding, he failed. Christopher stumbled to the table, looked into the elegant silver-framed mirror that was lying there, and went through the words and gestures he had learnt at school. Nothing at all happened.

'Hm,' said Dr Pawson. 'Don't do it again.'

Christopher realized he was supposed to try once more. He tried, with shaking hands and voice, and exasperated misery growing inside him. This was hopeless! He hated Papa for dragging him off to be terrorized by this appalling fat man. He wanted to cry, and he had to remind himself, just as if he were his own Governess, that he was far too big for that. And, as before, the mirror simply lay where it was.

'Um,' said Dr Pawson. 'Turn round, Chant. No, *right* round, boy, slowly, so that I can see all of you. Stop!'

Christopher stopped and stood, and waited. Dr Pawson shut his watery eyes and lowered his purple chins. Christopher suspected he had gone to sleep. There was utter silence in the room except for clocks ticking among the clutter. Two clocks were the kind with all the works showing, one was a grandfather and one was a mighty marble timepiece that looked as if it had come off someone's grave. Christopher nearly jumped out of his skin when Dr Pawson suddenly barked at him like the clap of doom.

'EMPTY YOUR POCKETS, CHANT!'

Eh? thought Christopher. But he did not dare disobey. He began hurriedly unloading the pockets of his Norfolk jacket: Uncle Ralph's sixpence which he always kept, a shilling of his own, a greyish handkerchief, a note from Oneir about algebra, and then he was down to shaming things like string and rubber bands and furry toffees. He hesitated.

'All of it!' yelled Dr Pawson. 'Out of every single pocket. Put it all down on the table.'

Christopher went on unloading: a chewed rubber, a bit of pencil, peas for Fenning's pea-shooter, a silver three-penny bit he had not known about, a cough drop, fluff, more fluff, string, a marble, an old pen nib, more rubber bands, more fluff, more string. And that was it.

Dr Pawson's eyes glared over him. 'No, that's *not* all! What else have you got on you? Tie-pin. Get rid of that too.'

Reluctantly Christopher unpinned the nice silver tie-pin Aunt Alice had given him for Christmas. And Dr Pawson's eyes continued to glare at him.

'Ah!' Dr Pawson said. 'And that stupid thing you have on your teeth. That's got to go too. Get it out of your mouth and put it on the table. What the devil's it *for* anyway?'

'To stop my teeth growing crooked,' Christopher said rather huffily. Much as he hated the toothbrace, he hated even more being criticized about it.

'What's wrong with crooked teeth?' howled Dr Pawson, and he bared his own teeth. Christopher rather started back from the sight. Dr Pawson's teeth were brown, and they lay higgledy-piggledy in all directions, like a fence trampled by cows. While Christopher was blinking at them, Dr Pawson bellowed, 'Now do that levitation spell again!'

Christopher ground his teeth – which felt quite straight by contrast and very smooth without the brace – and turned to the mirror again. Once more he looked into it, once more said the words, and once more raised his arms aloft. And as his arms went up he felt something come loose with them – come loose with a vengeance.

Everything in the room went upwards except Christopher, the mirror, the tie-pin, the toothbrace and the money. These slid to the floor as the table surged upwards, but were collected by the carpet which came billowing up after it. Christopher hastily stepped off the carpet and stood watching everything soar around him – all the clocks, several tables, chairs, rugs, pictures, vases, ornaments and Dr Pawson too. He and his armchair both went up, majestically, like a balloon, and bumped against the ceiling. The ceiling bellied upwards and the chandelier plastered itself sideways against it. From above came crashing, shrieks, and an immense airy grinding. Christopher could feel that the roof of the house had come off and was on its way to the sky, pursued by the attics. It was an incredible feeling.

'STOP THAT!' Dr Pawson roared.

Christopher guiltily took his arms down.

Instantly everything began raining back to the ground again. The tables plunged, the carpets sank, vases, pictures and clocks crashed to the floor all round. Dr Pawson's armchair plummeted with the rest, followed by pieces of the chandelier, but Dr Pawson himself floated down smoothly, having clearly done some prudent magic of his own. Up above, the roof came down thunderously. Christopher could hear tiles falling and chimneys crashing as well as smashings and howls from upstairs. The upper floors seemed now to be trying to get through to the ground. The walls of the room buckled and oozed plaster, while the windows bent and fell to pieces. It was about five minutes before the slidings and smashings died away, and the dust settled even more slowly. Dr Pawson sat among the wreckage and the blowing dust and stared at Christopher. Christopher stared back, very much wanting to laugh.

A little old lady suddenly materialized in the armchair opposite Dr Pawson's. She was wearing a white night-gown and a lacy cap over her white hair. She smiled at Christopher in a steely way. 'So it was you, child,' she said to Christopher. 'Mary-Ellen is in hysterics. Don't *ever* do that again, or I'll put a Visitation on you. I'm still famed for my Visitations, you know.' Having said this, she was gone as suddenly as she had come.

'My old mother,' said Dr Pawson. 'She's normally bed-ridden, but as you can see, she's very strongly moved. As is almost everything else.' He sat and stared at Christopher a while longer, and Christopher went on struggling not to laugh. 'Silver,' Dr Pawson said at last.

'Silver?' asked Christopher.

'Silver,' said Dr Pawson. 'Silver's the thing that's stopping you, Chant. Don't ask me why at the moment. Maybe we'll never get to the bottom of it, but there's no question about the facts. If you want to work magic, you'll have to give up money except for coppers and sovereigns, throw away that tie-pin and get rid of that stupid brace.'

Christopher thought about Papa, about school, about cricket, in a flood of anger and frustration which gave him courage to say, 'But I don't think I do want to work magic, sir.'

'Yes you do, Chant,' said Dr Pawson. 'For at least the next month.' And while Christopher was wondering how to contradict him without being too rude, Dr Pawson gave out another vast bellow. 'YOU HAVE TO PUT EVERYTHING BACK, CHANT!'

And this is just what Christopher had to do. For the rest of the morning he went round the house, up to every floor and then outside into the garden, while Dr

Pawson trundled beside him in his armchair and showed him how to cast holding-spells to stop the house falling down. Dr Pawson never seemed to leave that armchair. In all the time Christopher spent with him, he never saw Dr Pawson walk. Around midday, Dr Pawson sent his chair gliding into the kitchen, where a cook-maid was sitting dolefully in the midst of smashed butter crocks, spilt milk, bits of basin and dented saucepans, and dabbing at her eyes with her apron.

'Not hurt in here are you?' Dr Pawson barked. 'I put a holder on first thing to make sure the range didn't burst and set the house on fire – that sort of thing. That held, didn't it? Water pipes secure?'

'Yes sir,' gulped the cook-maid. 'But lunch is ruined, sir.'

'We'll have to have a scratch lunch for once,' said Dr Pawson. His chair swung round to face Christopher. 'By this evening,' he said, 'this kitchen is going to be mended. Not holding-spells. Everything as new. I'll show you how. Can't have the kitchen out of action. It's the most important place in the house.'

'I'm sure it is, sir,' Christopher said, eyeing Dr Pawson's mountain of a stomach.

Dr Pawson glared at him. 'I can dine in college,' he said, 'but my mother needs her nourishment.'

For the rest of that day Christopher mended the kitchen, putting crockery back together, recapturing spilt milk and cooking sherry, taking dents out of pans, and sealing a dangerous split at the back of the range. While he did, Dr Pawson sat in his armchair warming himself by the range fire and barking things like, 'Now put the eggs together, Chant. You'll need the spell to raise them first, then the dirt-dispeller you used on the milk. *Then* you can start the mending-spell.' While Christopher laboured, the cook-maid, who was obviously even more frightened of Dr Pawson than Christopher was, edged round him trying to bake a cake and prepare the roast for supper.

One way and another, Christopher probably learnt more practical magic that day than he had in two and a half terms at school. By the evening he was exhausted. Dr Pawson barked, 'You can go back to your father for now. Be here at nine tomorrow prompt. There's still the rest of the house to see to.'

'Oh Lord!' Christopher groaned, too weary to be polite. 'Can't someone help me at all? I've learnt my lesson.'

'What gave you the idea there was only one lesson to learn?' bawled Dr Pawson.

# ANNE FINE

FROM *Goggle-Eyes*

I know a storm warning when I hear one. On Thursday I was determined to make sure that there'd be nothing in the bad manners line that she could pin on me. When he rang the doorbell I made as if I simply hadn't heard, so it was Jude who reached the door to let him in, while I stood in the shadow at the bottom of the stairs.

He stepped inside. He was Mum's height, a little tubby, and he had silvery hair. His suit was nowhere near as smart as any of Simon's. There again, he wasn't a posh banker, though he did have the most enormous box of chocolates tucked under one arm.

He shifted the chocolates, and shook hands.

'Judith,' he said. 'Right?'

She nodded. I sidled out of the shadow.

'And Kitty.'

He smiled, and kept his hand stuck out for a moment, but I pretended that I hadn't noticed it. And after one of those infinitesimal little pauses of his, he handed the huge box of chocolates to Jude.

They were those rich, dark, expensive, chocolate-coated cream mints. I've had a passion for them all my life. The box was three layers deep at the very least. I saw Jude's eyes widen to saucers.

'Are these for Mum?' she asked.

'No. They're for you.'

He could have meant either *you*, or *you two*. It wasn't

clear. As he spoke, he was looking at Jude, but he did glance at me briefly. It was terribly clever. It meant that when I didn't pile straight in with Jude, thanking him lavishly, he wasn't in the slightest embarrassed. He didn't have to be, you see. He might not have meant to include me at all.

'I'll tell Mum.'

Jude rushed upstairs, clutching her booty to her chest, and Gerald Faulkner and I were left alone in the hall. I thought I'd discomfit him with my silence, but no, not at all. He simply swivelled away as though he wanted to inspect the pictures on the wall, and peered closely at a photo of me as a toddler.

'What a face!' he said admiringly. (I wasn't quite sure what he meant by that.) 'It looks as if it might be you.'

Really cunning, right? He doesn't actually *ask* if it's me, and then he can't look silly if I don't answer.

Just then Floss padded in through the front door, and started rubbing up against his trouser legs as if she'd known and loved him all her life. He stopped to pet her. 'Puss, puss, puss.' I thought now he'd be bound to try and get me to speak. It's hard to fondle someone else's cat in front of them, and not ask its name. But Gerald Faulkner's made of sterner stuff than that.

'Up you come, Buster,' he said, scooping Floss up in his arms. 'Who's a *nice* Kitty?'

I wasn't quite sure what he meant by that, either. I was still trying to work it out (and Floss was still purring shamelessly) when Jude came thundering downstairs.

'Mum says to help yourself to a drink, and she'll be down in a minute.'

'Right-ho.'

He tipped the enraptured Floss into Jude's arms, and

ambled past me with a nod. I realized that he must have been in our house at least once before. How else would he know which door led into the kitchen? Jude padded after him like a pet dog, and I was forced to lean back against the door frame so I didn't look ridiculous, standing there doggedly staring the other way.

He stood at one end of the cabinets and opened the first two doors, looked in, then closed them. He moved along and did the same again, and again. I said nothing, just leaned against the door frame and watched. But Jude caught on before he'd gone very much further.

'Do you want glasses? They're in here.'

And she rushed about, finding him the only sharp knife, and a lemon, and groping about on the floor for a couple of ice-cubes that slithered off the table. The two of them kept up a steady chat about nothing at all – how quickly bottled drinks lose their fizz, how long it takes for water to freeze in an ice tray. I was astonished. Jude's not a talker, on the whole. It's like the business of the telephone. She can go hours without bothering. But here she was, burbling away merrily to this perfect stranger.

He only spoke to me directly once. He'd just pushed my school bag further along the table to keep it safe from a small puddle of melted ice. The bag was open and my books were showing – not just *France Aujourd'hui* and *Modern Mathematics*, but also the things I'm reading on the bus and at bedtime: *A Thousand Worst Jokes* and that thriller *Coma*, about a hospital where the anaesthesia goes haywire.

He tapped the jacket of *Coma* with his knuckle.

'Is this a book about punctuation?' he asked me. 'Because, if it is, the author can't spell.'

I couldn't resist.

'A pity the other book isn't *A Thousand and One Worst Jokes*,' I snapped. 'You could have offered them yours.'

There. I had spoken to him. I had done my bit. So I turned on my heel and walked out of the kitchen.

Mum was half-way down the stairs, wearing a frilly blouse and smart velvet trousers. I glowered at her and, misunderstanding, she said:

'Listen, I'm really sorry about missing the meeting tonight.'

'Missing the meeting?'

This was him. He had sneaked up behind me with the tray. On it four glasses fizzed, tinkling with ice, and I could smell the tang of lemons.

Mum took the glass he offered her, and smiled at him.

'Kitty and I always go together on Thursdays,' she explained. 'She's a bit cross because, now I'm not coming, she'll have to take the bus.'

I *hate* it when people just assume they know the reasons for everything. I don't mind taking the bus. I never have. I like Mum to come because our car ride together to the meeting is about the only time – the *only* time – I'm sure I've got her on my own. That's one of the worst things about Dad moving away to Berwick upon Tweed. Jude and I hardly ever get to be alone with him or with Mum. We're either both with the one or we're both with the other. And they can't split themselves in two, so one of us can have a private chat down the back garden while the other is pouring out her heart on the sofa.

I was about to say 'I am *not cross*' when Gerald Faulkner touched my elbow with his, proffering his tray.

'Here,' he said, nodding at the closest glass. 'That one's yours.'

Without thinking, I lifted the drink off the tray. I could have kicked myself. In spite of all the effort he'd put into making them, I had intended to refuse mine. But at least I could still refuse to say thank you. Unfortunately, just as Mum opened her mouth to prompt me, he waved his hand as if to cut off all the profuse and gracious thanks on which he was sure I was going to embark any second, and said, as if I were *eighteen*, or something:

'I didn't put any alcohol in yours because I didn't know if you liked the taste.'

That threw Mum. She doesn't like anyone even to suggest within ten miles of my hearing that, one day, I might be old enough to go to a pub without being sent home to bed by the landlord. For someone to imply, even if only out of tact and politeness, that I might be on the verge of growing out of fizzy lemonade, well, that was more than she could handle. Changing the subject as fast as she could, she plucked at the frilly blouse and the velvet trousers, and asked us both:

'Are these all right?'

'Yes,' I said. 'They're all right.' (I was still mad.)

She turned to him.

'Gerald?'

He put his head on one side. 'They're lovely,' he said. 'Absolutely smashing. You look tremendous. But won't you spoil me a little? Wear the blue suit with those tiny wooden toggle fasteners, the black diamond stockings and the shiny bow shoes.'

I stared. I absolutely *stared*. Was he some wardrobe pervert, or something? Dad lived with her for years, and he could no more have described any of her clothes like that than flown up in the air. In fact, I don't think Dad even noticed what Mum wore. Obviously if she came down the stairs all tarted up to go out somewhere special, he'd say, 'Oh, you look very nice.' But ask her to go back up and change into something he liked even better? You have to be *joking*.

And her? Blush and shrug, and turn round to trot obediently back upstairs to change, holding her glass high? Was this my mum?

# INDEX OF AUTHORS

# Biographical Notes

RICHARD ADAMS was born in Berkshire. Until 1974 he worked in the Civil Service and rose to Assistant Secretary in the Department of the Environment. *Watership Down* (1972) and his two other novels involving animals, *Shardik* (1974) and *The Plague Dogs* (1977), were written both for children and adults.

JOAN AIKEN was born in 1924 in Sussex, daughter of American poet Conrad Aiken. She has written suspense fiction for adults, but writes mainly for children at various age levels. Titles include *The Wolves of Willoughby Chase* (1962), *A Necklace of Raindrops* (1968) and *Tales of Arabel's Raven* (1974).

VIVIEN ALCOCK was born in 1924 in Sussex. She is married to fellow children's writer Leon Garfield. Among her novels for children are *The Sylvia Game* (1982) and *The Monster Garden* (1988).

RACHEL ANDERSON was born in 1943 in Surrey. She is a freelance writer and broadcaster. Among her books for children are *The Poacher's Son* (1982) and *The Fruitcake Bus* (1988).

BERNARD ASHLEY was born in 1935 in London. Since 1957 he has taught in junior schools and is currently a headteacher. His novels include *The Trouble with Donovan Croft* (1974) and *Dodgem* (1981).

GILLIAN AVERY was born in 1926 in Surrey. She has edited, as well as written, many books for children. Her novels include *The Warden's Niece* (1957) and *A Likely Lad* (1971).

J. M. (JAMES MATTHEW) BARRIE (1860–1937) was born in Kirriemuir, Scotland. Of his many plays for adults, *The Admirable Crichton* (1914) has remained successful. But his most famous creation is *Peter Pan*. The stage version was first produced in 1904 and later became the story *Peter and Wendy* (1911).

NINA BAWDEN was born in 1925 in London. She writes novels for children and for adults. Among her children's books are *Carrie's War* (1973), *The Peppermint Pig* (1975) and *The Outside Child* (1989).

B. B. (1905–1990) is the pen-name of D. J. (Denys James) Watkins-Pitchford, born in Northamptonshire. From 1930 to 1947 he taught art at Rugby School and illustrated his books under his real name. *The Little Grey Men* (1942) won the Carnegie Medal. Other books include *Brendon Chase* (1944) and *The Wizard of Boland* (1959).

JUDY BLUME was born in 1938 in New Jersey. She writes novels for teenagers that are notable for their frankness. Her books include *Tales of a Fourth Grade Nothing* (1972) and *Tiger Eyes* (1981).

LUCY M. BOSTON (1892–1990) was born in Lancashire. She began to write in her sixties. *The Children of Green Knowe* (1954) was the first in the Green Knowe series, of which *A Stranger at Green Knowe* (1961) won the Carnegie Medal.

FRANCES HODGSON BURNETT (1849–1924) was born in Manchester. She emigrated to the United States in 1865, where she became a popular novelist. She is now best known for her three books for children: *Little Lord Fauntleroy* (1886), *A Little Princess* (1905) and *The Secret Garden* (1911).

BETSY BYARS was born in 1928 in North Carolina. Among her many books are *The Summer of Swans* (1970), which won the Newbery Medal, *The Eighteenth Emergency* (1973) and *The Burning Questions of Bingo Brown* (1988).

JOHN CHRISTOPHER is one of the pen-names of Christopher Samuel Youd, born in 1922 in Lancashire. He writes science fiction for adults and for children. *The Tripods Trilogy* (1980), which begins with *The White Mountains* (1967), became a popular television serial.

PAULINE CLARKE was born in 1921 in Nottinghamshire. She also writes under the pseudonym Helen Clare. *The Twelve and the Genii* (1962) won the Carnegie Medal.

BEVERLY CLEARY was born in 1916 in Oregon. She is best known for her books about the children of Klicktat Street, Portland, a setting introduced in her first book *Henry Huggins* (1950). Subsequent titles in the series include *Beezus and Ramona* (1955) and *Ramona Forever* (1984).

SUSAN COOPER was born in 1935 in Buckinghamshire. Since 1963 she has lived in the United States. Her sequence of five fantasy novels, under the overall title *The Dark is Rising*, was published between 1965 and 1977, and *Greenwitch* (1974) is the third in the series. *The Grey King* (1975) won the Newbery Medal.

HELEN CRESSWELL was born in 1934 in Nottinghamshire. She has written prolifically for children, including her four-part saga of the Bagthorpe family, which opens with *Ordinary Jack* (1977). Among her other books are *The Night-Watchmen* (1969) and *Moondial* (1988), which was written simultaneously for television.

RICHMAL CROMPTON (1890–1969) was born in Lancashire. She taught Classics until 1924 when she contracted polio. A writer for both adults and children, she is famed for the William books which, beginning with *Just William* (1922), comprise thirty-eight titles in all.

ROALD DAHL (1916–1990) was born in Glamorgan, Wales, of Norwegian parents. He is best known for his highly successful books for children, including *Charlie and the Chocolate Factory* (1967), *The BFG* (1982), *The Witches* (1983) and *Matilda* (1989).

MARJORIE DARKE was born in 1929 in Birmingham. She began to write fiction for children in her forties and the first of her historical novels, *Ride the Iron Horse*, appeared in 1973. Subsequent books include *The First of Midnight* (1977).

PETER DICKINSON was born in 1927 in Zambia. He was Assistant Editor of *Punch* magazine from 1952 to 1969. Two of his children's novels, *Tulku* (1979) and *City of Gold* (1980), have won Carnegie Medals, and other titles include *The Devil's Children* (1970).

BERLIE DOHERTY was born in 1943 in Liverpool. Her writing for children includes plays for stage and radio as well as fiction. *Granny was a Buffer Girl* (1986) won the Carnegie Medal.

ANNE FINE was born in 1947 in Leicester. Humour features strongly in her children's novels, which include *The Stone Menagerie* (1980) and *The Granny Project* (1983). *Goggle-Eyes* (1990) won the Carnegie Medal.

JANE GARDAM was born in 1928 in Yorkshire. She writes fiction for children and adults. Several of her novels, such as *A Long Way from Verona* (1971) and *Bilgewater* (1976) explore adult themes, and other titles include *Kit* (1983).

LEON GARFIELD was born in 1921 in Brighton. He is a prolific writer of historical adventure stories, largely set in the eighteenth century. These include *Jack Holborn* (1964), *Smith* (1976) and The Apprentices series (1976–78).

ALAN GARNER was born in 1934 in Cheshire. He writes for children in several media, including radio and television. His books include *Elidor* (1965), *The Owl Service* (1967) which won a Carnegie Medal, and *The Stone Book* (1976).

EVE GARNETT was born in Worcestershire. She was an artist as well as a writer and illustrated her own books. *The Family from One End Street* (1937) won the Carnegie Medal. Its sequel, *Further Adventures of the Family from One End Street*, appeared in 1956. She died in 1990.

KENNETH GRAHAME (1859–1932) was born in Edinburgh, but from the age of five, when his mother died, he grew up in Berkshire. He became an official of the Bank of England. Early titles include *The Golden Age* (1895) and *Dream Days* (1898) but it is *The Wind in the Willows* (1908) that has become a classic.

RUSSELL HOBAN was born in 1925 in Pennsylvania. Since 1969 he has lived in London. He has written a number of picture books, including *How Tom Beat Captain Najork and His Hired Sportsmen* (1974) and *The Dancing Tigers* (1979). *The Mouse and His Child* was published in 1967.

JANNI HOWKER was born in 1957 in Cyprus. She was educated, and now lives, in the north of England. Her first book *Badger on the Barge and Other Stories* appeared in 1984, followed by *Nature of the Beast* (1985) and *Isaac Campion* (1986).

TED HUGHES was born in 1930 in Yorkshire. He became Poet Laureate in 1984. His writing for children includes the verse-collection *Season Songs* (1975) and the stories of *How the*

*Whale Became* (1963), *The Iron Man* (1968) and *Tales of the Early World* (1988).

DIANA WYNNE JONES was born in 1934 in London. She writes humorous fantasy fiction for children and teenagers and has published more than twenty novels in the genre. They include *Charmed Life* (1977), *Witch Week* (1982) and *The Lives of Christopher Chant* (1988).

GERALDINE KAYE was born in 1925 in Watford. She has worked in Malaysia and her fiction for children draws on her knowledge of Asian and African cultures. Among her many publications are *The Day after Yesterday* (1981) and *Comfort Herself* (1984).

GENE KEMP was born in 1926 in Staffordshire. She worked as a teacher from 1963 to 1979, when she became a full-time writer for children. *The Turbulent Term of Tyke Tiler* (1977) won the Carnegie Medal. Other publications are *The Clock Tower Ghost* (1981) and for teenagers, *Juniper: A Mystery* (1986).

CLIVE KING was born in 1924 in Surrey. He worked abroad for many years for the British Council and his fiction for children reflects his nomadic life. Among his stories are *The Town That Went South* (1959), *Stig of the Dump* (1963) and *Ninny's Boat* (1980).

DICK KING-SMITH was born in 1922 in Gloucestershire. He was a farmer and later a primary school teacher before he began to write for children. His stories include *The Sheep-Pig* (1983), *Noah's Brother* (1986), *The Water Horse* (1990) and many titles for early readers, including *E.S.P.* (1987).

RUDYARD KIPLING (1865–1936) was born in Bombay of English parents. From 1899 he lived most of his life in England as a full-time writer, receiving the Nobel Prize for Literature in 1907. His classic books for children are

*The Jungle Book* (1894), *Kim* (1901) and the *Just So Stories* (1902).

E. L. (ELAINE LOBL) KONIGSBURG was born in 1930 in New York City. She won the Newbery Medal for *From the Mixed-Up Files of Mrs Basil E. Frankweiler* (1967) and its runner-up was *Jennifer, Hecate, Macbeth, William McKinley, and Me, Elizabeth* (1967).

ROBERT LEESON was born in 1928 in Cheshire. From 1956 to 1984 he worked for the *Morning Star* and became its literary and children's editor. His stories for children, ranging from social realism to science fiction, include the teenage novel *It's My Life* (1980) and *The Third Class Genie* (1975).

C. S. (CLIVE STAPLES) LEWIS (1898–1963) was born in Belfast. He was a distinguished literary scholar and taught at Oxford until 1954, when he became Professor of Medieval and Renaissance Literature at Cambridge. For children he wrote his sequence of seven fantasy novels, *The Chronicles of Narnia* (1950–1956), of which the first is *The Lion, the Witch and the Wardrobe*.

JOAN LINGARD was born in 1932 in Edinburgh. She published adult novels before turning to children's fiction. Several of her stories are set in present-day Belfast, including *The Twelfth Day of July* (1970). *The Clearance* (1974) begins a series of novels set in Edinburgh, which were dramatized for television as *Maggie*.

PENELOPE LIVELY was born in 1933 in Cairo. She came to England in 1945 to attend boarding-school and subsequently settled here. Her novels for children include *The Ghost of Thomas Kempe* (1973) and *The House at Norham Gardens* (1974). She also writes fiction for adults and *Moon Tiger* (1987) won the Booker Prize.

GERALDINE McCAUGHREAN was born in London. She has worked in children's publishing and has made several adaptations of classic stories for children, including *The Canterbury Tales* (1984). Her first novel, *A Little Lower Than the Angels*, was published in 1987 and her second, *A Pack of Lies* (1988), won the Carnegie Medal.

PATRICIA MacLAUGHLIN was born in 1938 in Wyoming. She lives in Massachusetts and has taught English and Creative Writing courses. Her stories for children include *Sarah, Plain and Tall* (1985) and *The Facts and Fictions of Minna Pratt* (1988).

MICHELLE MAGORIAN was born in 1947 in Portsmouth. She trained as an actress and at the Marcel Marceau School of Mime in Paris. She has worked in theatre, television and film. Her two novels for children are *Goodnight, Mister Tom* (1981) and *Back Home* (1984), both involving wartime evacuees from London.

MARGARET MAHY was born in 1936 in New Zealand, where she has worked as a librarian since 1958. Her numerous picture-book stories include *The Boy with Two Shadows* (1971). Among her longer stories for children are *The Haunting* (1982) and *Memory* (1987).

JAN MARK was born in 1943 in Welwyn Garden City, London. From 1965 to 1971 she worked as a teacher. Her first novel *Thunder and Lightnings* (1976) won the Carnegie Medal, as did *Handles* (1983). *Trouble Half-Way* was published in 1985.

JOHN MASEFIELD (1878–1967) was born in Herefordshire. At fifteen he went to sea and it was *Salt-Water Ballads* (1902) that established him as a writer. He became Poet Laureate in 1930. He also wrote fantasy fiction, including two classics for children, *The Midnight Folk* (1927) and its sequel *The Box of Delights* (1935).

WILLIAM MAYNE was born in 1928 in Hull. He is a full-time writer for children and has published close to one hundred books. They include *A Swarm in May* (1955), *A Grass Rope* (1957), which won the Carnegie Medal, and a sequence of stories set in Australia, *Salt River Times* (1980).

A. A. (ALAN ALEXANDER) MILNE (1882–1956) was born in London. He was a successful dramatist. But it is the books written for his son, Christopher Robin, that have become classics: *Winnie-the-Pooh* (1926), *The House at Pooh Corner* (1928), and, in verse, *When We Were Very Young* (1924) and *Now We Are Six* (1927).

JAN NEEDLE was born in 1943 in Hampshire. During the 1960s he was a reporter and worked for the *Daily Herald* and the *Sun*. He has also written for television. His fiction for children includes *A Fine Boy for Killing* (1979) and *A Game of Soldiers* (1985).

E. (EDITH) NESBIT (1858–1924) was born in London. Her father died in 1861 and thereafter she had a nomadic childhood. She was a founding member of the Fabian Society and she wrote fiction and poetry for adults. But she is best remembered for her children's stories such as *The Story of the Treasure Seekers* (1899) and *The Railway Children* (1906).

JENNY NIMMO was born in 1944 in Berkshire. She worked for the BBC from 1964 to 1975, when she became a full-time writer. The landscape and legends of Wales, where she lives, feature in her stories for children, which include *Snow Spider* (1982) and *The Red Secret* (1989).

MARY NORTON was born in 1903 in London. She lived in Portugal and then in New York, where her first book *The Magic Bed-Knob* (1943) was published. In *The Borrowers*

(1952), which won the Carnegie Medal, she created a race of tiny people who have reappeared in several sequels, the last being *The Borrowers Avenged* (1982).

KATHERINE PATERSON was born in 1932 in China. In 1940 she moved with her family to the United States. She worked as a missionary in Japan from 1957 to 1961. She has twice been awarded the Newbery Medal, for *Bridge to Terabithia* (1977) and *Jacob Have I Loved* (1980).

JILL PATON WALSH was born in 1937 in London. She began to write after she gave up her work as an English teacher in 1962. She has published several historical novels, including *The Emperor's Winding Sheet* (1974) and other titles include *A Parcel of Patterns* (1983) and *Gaffer Samson's Luck* (1984).

PHILIPPA PEARCE was born in 1920 in Cambridgeshire. She worked for BBC Schools Radio and in children's publishing before becoming a full-time writer in 1959. *Tom's Midnight Garden* (1958) won the Carnegie Medal. Other notable books are *A Dog So Small* (1962) and *The Way to Sattin Shore* (1983).

K. M. PEYTON is the pen-name of Kathleen Wendy Peyton, born in 1929 in Birmingham. She collaborated on adventure stories with her husband for *Boy Scout Magazine*, but later began writing novels for teenagers. She won the Carnegie Medal for *The Edge of a Cloud* (1969), the second part of the Flambards series. Other titles include *A Pattern of Roses* (1972) and *'Who, Sir? Me, Sir?'* (1983).

SYLVIA SHERRY was born in Newcastle upon Tyne. From 1960 to 1964 she lived in Singapore, the setting for her first novel *Street of the Small Night Market* (1966). She is best known for her three books set in Liverpool: *A Pair of Jesus-Boots* (1969), *A Pair of Desert-Wellies* (1985) and *Rocky the Ratman* (1988).

IVAN SOUTHALL was born in 1921 in Victoria, Australia. During the 1950s he wrote escapist adventure stories but, with *Hill's End* (1962), began to portray children realistically under extreme circumstances. Other titles include *Ash Road* (1965) and *Josh* (1971), which won the Carnegie Medal.

NOEL STREATFEILD (1895–1986) was born in Sussex. She was an actress during the 1920s but then turned to writing adult fiction. Her first book for children, *Ballet Shoes* (1936), initiated a vogue for career novels. Her other books include *The Circus is Coming* (1938), which won the Carnegie Medal.

ROSEMARY SUTCLIFF was born in 1920 in Surrey. Early in childhood she became confined to a wheelchair and at school was regarded as almost illiterate. Among her many historical novels are *Simon* (1953), *The Eagle of the Ninth* (1954) and *The Lantern Bearers* (1959), which won the Carnegie Medal.

RUTH THOMAS was born in Somerset. She worked for many years as a primary school teacher in London. In 1984 she took early retirement and subsequently began to write children's fiction. *The Runaways* (1987) was her first book. Several more novels have followed, including *The Class That Went Wild* (1989).

J. R. R. (JOHN RONALD REUEL) TOLKIEN (1892–1973) was born in South Africa and came to England when he was three. From 1925 to 1959 he was a Professor in the field of Anglo-Saxon at Oxford. During the 1960s *The Hobbit* (1937) and its epic sequel *The Lord of the Rings* (1954, 1955) achieved world-wide fame.

P. L. (PAMELA LYNDON) TRAVERS was born in 1906 in Queensland, Australia. She came to England at seventeen and worked on the stage and as a journalist. *Mary Poppins*

(1934) was the first of several collections of stories featuring the magical nanny.

GEOFFREY TREASE was born in 1909 in Nottingham. He worked with slum children in the East End of London, was a teacher and a journalist. His books include *Bows Against the Barons* (1934), *No Boats on Bannermere* (1949) and his influential survey of children's fiction, *Tales Out of School* (1949, 1964).

HENRY TREECE (1911–1966) was born in Staffordshire. He was an English teacher from 1946 until his death. An influential poet before turning to historical fiction in the 1950s, he published twenty-five novels for younger readers. They include *The Viking's Dawn* (1955) and *The Children's Crusade* (1958).

CYNTHIA VOIGT was born in 1942 in Boston, Massachusetts. Since 1965 she has taught English at high school in Maryland. *Homecoming* (1981) was her first book and begins the saga of the Tillerman family. The second in the series, *Dicey's Song* (1982), won the Newbery Medal.

ROBERT WESTALL was born in 1929 in Northumberland. He worked as an art teacher from 1958 to 1985. His first book, *The Machine Gunners* (1975), received the Carnegie Medal, as did *The Scarecrows* (1981).

E. B. (ELWYN BROOKS) WHITE (1899–1985) was born in New York. He was a humorous essayist well known for his contributions to *The New Yorker*. He published three books for children: *Stuart Little* (1945), *Charlotte's Web* (1952) and *The Trumpet of the Swan* (1970).

T. H. (TERENCE HANBURY) WHITE (1906–1964) was born in Bombay of English parents. *The Sword in the Stone* (1938) begins his four-part retelling of the Arthurian legends, completed as *The Once and Future King* (1958). It was not intended primarily for children, unlike his other enduring book *Mistress Masham's Repose* (1946).

Laura Ingalls Wilder (1867–1957) was born in Wisconsin into a pioneer family. In her sixties she began to recount her memories of childhood in the Little House books. The series comprises nine titles including *Little House in the Big Woods* (1932), *The Little House on the Prairie* (1935) and *The Long Winter* (1940).

# ACKNOWLEDGEMENTS

The editor and publishers gratefully acknowledge the following for permission to reproduce copyright material in this anthology in the form of extracts taken from the following books:

*Watership Down* copyright © Richard Adams, 1972 (Rex Collings Ltd); *Tales of Arabel's Raven* copyright © Joan Aiken, 1974 (BBC Books) reprinted by permission of A. M. Heath & Co. Ltd; *The Sylvia Game* copyright © Vivien Alcock, 1982 (Methuen Children's Books); *The Poacher's Son* copyright © Rachel Anderson, 1982 (Oxford University Press); *The Trouble with Donovan Croft* copyright © Bernard Ashley, 1974 (Oxford University Press); *A Likely Lad* copyright © Gillian Avery, 1971 (The Bodley Head); *The Peppermint Pig* copyright © Nina Bawden, 1975 (Victor Gollancz Ltd); *The Little Grey Men* copyright © B. B., 1942 (Methuen Children's Books); *Tales of a Fourth Grade Nothing* copyright © Judy Blume, 1972 (The Bodley Head); *The Children of Green Knowe* copyright © Lucy M. Boston, 1954 (Faber and Faber Ltd); *The Eighteenth Emergency* copyright © Betsy Byars, 1973 (The Bodley Head and Viking Penguin Inc.); *The White Mountains* copyright © John Christopher, 1967 (Hamish Hamilton Children's Books); *The Twelve and the Genii* copyright © Pauline Clarke, 1962 (The Bodley Head); *Ramona Forever* copyright © Beverly Cleary, 1984 (William Morrow & Co.) published in the UK by Walker Books Limited; *Greenwitch* copyright © Susan Cooper, 1974 (Jonathan Cape Ltd); *The Night-Watchmen* copyright © Helen Cresswell, 1969 (Faber and Faber Ltd); *Just William* copyright © Richmal Crompton, 1922 (Pan Macmillan Children's Books); *Charlie and*

(Viking Kestrel); *A Box of Delights* copyright © John Masefield, 1935 (Heinemann Young Books), reprinted by permission of the Society of Authors as the literary representative of the Estate of John Masefield; *A Swarm in May* copyright © William Mayne, 1955 (John Goodchild Publishers); *Winnie-the-Pooh* copyright © A. A. Milne, 1926 (Methuen Children's Books and E. P. Dutton); *A Game of Soldiers* copyright © Jan Needle, 1985 (André Deutsch Ltd); *Snow Spider* copyright © Jenny Nimmo, 1986 (Methuen Children's Books); *The Borrowers* copyright © Mary Norton, 1952 (J. M. Dent & Sons Ltd); *Bridge to Terabithia* copyright © Katherine Paterson, 1977 (Victor Gollancz Ltd and Harper & Row Publishers Inc.); *Gaffer Samson's Luck* copyright © Jill Paton Walsh, 1984 (Viking Kestrel, 1985); *Tom's Midnight Garden* copyright © Philippa Pearce, 1958 (Oxford University Press); *'Who Sir? Me Sir?'* copyright © K. M. Peyton, 1983 (Oxford University Press); *A Pair of Jesus-Boots* copyright © Sylvia Sherry, 1969 (Jonathan Cape Ltd); *Ash Road* copyright © Ivan Southall, 1965 (Angus & Robertson Publishers Australia); *Ballet Shoes* copyright © Noel Streatfeild, 1936 (J. M. Dent & Sons Ltd); *The Eagle of the Ninth* copyright © Rosemary Sutcliff, 1954 (Oxford University Press); *The Runaways* copyright © Ruth Thomas, 1987 (Hutchinson Children's Books); *The Hobbit* copyright © J. R. R. Tolkien, 1937 (Allen and Unwin Ltd); *Mary Poppins* copyright © P. L. Travers, 1934 (HarperCollins Publishers Ltd); *Bows Against the Barons* copyright © Geoffrey Trease, 1934 (Hodder & Stoughton Ltd); *The Viking's Dawn* copyright © the Estate of Henry Treece, 1955 (The Bodley Head); *Homecoming* copyright © Cynthia Voigt, 1983 (HarperCollins Publishers Ltd); *The Machine Gunners* copyright © Robert Westall, 1975 (Macmillan Children's Books, London); *Charlotte's Web* copyright © E. B. White, 1952 (Hamish Hamilton Children's Books and Harper & Row Publishers Inc.); *The Sword in the Stone* copyright © T. H. White, 1938 (HarperCollins Publishers Ltd); *Little House in the Big Woods* copyright © Laura Ingalls Wilder, 1932 (Methuen Children's Books).